Jerry Baker America's No. 1 DIY Expert

VINEGAR MAGIC

1,574 Healthy Secrets, Strategies, and Solutions to Live Your Best Life!

jerrybaker.com

Other Jerry Baker Books:

Goof Proof Your Life!
Jerry Baker's Vital Vinegar Cookbook "Cures"
Jerry Baker's Live Rich, Spend Smart, and Enjoy Your Retirement
Jerry Baker's Vinegar: The King of All Cures!
Jerry Baker's Fix It Fast and Make It Last
Jerry Baker's Solve It with Vinegar!
America's Best Practical Problem Solvers
Jerry Baker's Can the Clutter
Grandma Putt's Old-Time Vinegar, Garlic, and 101 More Problem Solvers
Jerry Baker's Supermarket Super Products

Jerry Baker's Supermarket Super Gardens
Jerry Baker's Bug Off!
Jerry Baker's Terrific Garden Tonics!
Jerry Baker's Backyard Problem Solver
Jerry Baker's Green Grass Magic
Jerry Baker's Great Green Book of Garden Secrets
Jerry Baker's Old-Time Gardening Wisdom

Jerry Baker's Backyard Birdscaping Bonanza
Jerry Baker's Backyard Bird Feeding Bonanza
Jerry Baker's Year-Round Bloomers
Jerry Baker's Flower Garden Problem Solver

Jerry Baker's Grow Younger, Live Longer
Healing Remedies Hiding in Your Kitchen
Jerry Baker's Cure Your Lethal Lifestyle
Jerry Baker's Top 25 Homemade Healers
Healing Fixers Mixers & Elixirs
Jerry Baker's Supermarket Super Remedies
Jerry Baker's The New Healing Foods
Jerry Baker's Anti-Pain Plan
Jerry Baker's Oddball Ointments and Powerful Potions
Jerry Baker's Giant Book of Kitchen Counter Cures

To order any of the above, or for more information on Jerry Baker's amazing home, health, and garden tips, tricks, and tonics, please write to:

Jerry Baker, P.O. Box 1001, Wixom, MI 48393

Or, visit Jerry Baker online at:

jerrybaker.com

Jerry Baker America's No. 1 DIY Expert

VINEGAR MAGIC

jerrybaker.com

Published by American Master Products, Inc.

Executive Editor: Kim Adam Gasior
Writer: Vicki Webster
Design and Layout: Alison McKenna
Copy Editor: Nanette Bendyna
Production Assistant: Emily Ehr
Indexer: Nan Badgett

Publisher's Cataloging-in-Publication Data
provided by Five Rainbows Cataloging Services
Names: Baker, Jerry, author.
Title: Vinegar Magic: 1,574 healthy secrets, strategies, and solutions to live your
    best life! / Jerry Baker.
Description: Wixom, MI : American Master Products, 2021. | Includes index.
Identifiers: ISBN 978-0-922433-34-6 (hardcover)
Subjects: LCSH: Vinegar. | Cooking (Vinegar) | Formulas, recipes, etc. | Cookbooks. |
    Older people--Health and hygiene. | Aging--Nutritional aspects. | BISAC: COOKING /
    Specific Ingredients / General. | HEALTH & FITNESS / Diet & Nutrition / General. |
    SELF-HELP / Aging.
Classification: LCC TX819.V5 B35 2020 (print) | DDC 641.6/2--dc23.

Printed in the United States of America
2 4 6 8 7 5 3 hardcover

TABLE OF CONTENTS

INTRODUCTION

It's no secret that in recent years, vinegar—one of the oldest substances on the planet—has risen to new heights of superstardom in natural health, beauty, and home upkeep circles. But here's something you might not realize: As you move through your life, this multi-talented marvel becomes even more valuable as you age because it can be a major ally in holding back the hands of time. The good news is you don't have to wait for any aging milestone to start reaping big benefits from this book. In these pages, you'll find a treasure trove of tips, tricks, tonics, and timely techniques that'll help you put this youth-enhancing powerhouse and some of its key allies to work at any age. For example, you'll learn how to:

- **Relieve aches, pains, and minor ailments** that strike more frequently as time goes by—without the adverse side effects of prescription and OTC medications (Chapters 1 through 3).

- **Safeguard, or even improve,** your physical, mental, *and* emotional health as the years march onward (Chapter 4).

- **Make your hair, nails, and skin "lie" about your age** with simple DIY treatments that can also actually help to improve your long-term health (Chapters 5 and 6).

- **Clean out, spruce up, and organize every room** in your home along with using easy, budget-friendly tweaks to help you age in place safely and comfortably (Chapters 7 through 10).

- **Keep your outdoor scene** and everything in it (including cars and other vehicles) in tip-top shape and make simple alterations, when necessary, to suit your changing needs (Chapters 11 through 13).

- **Travel about in safety and comfort**—while saving money—whether you're trotting the globe, road-trippin' across the USA, or not-so-roughing it in a nearby campground (Chapter 14).

- **Have fun with and provide TLC** for your kids and grandkids, elderly loved ones, and pets (Chapters 15 through 17).

- **Create handmade gifts** for family and friends, treasures for your home, and maybe even turn your favorite craft into a second-prime career (Chapter 18).

Leading the charge in this exciting adventure is an all-star cast of 160 tonic recipes that put the prodigious power of vinegar to work in every facet of your life. Just to whet your DIY appetite, the ***Exceptional Elderberry Elixir*** on page 24 not only helps relieve the symptoms of a cold, flu, and bronchitis, but it also strengthens your immune system so you can battle the "bugs" better the next time around. The ***Crackerjack Carpet Cleaner*** on page 166 will make shampooing your carpets a lot cheaper than if you hired a pro to do the job; plus, it's perfectly harmless to the tiniest toddler or most curious canine. The ***Say It with Roses Bath Vinegar*** on page 350 is an antioxidant, skin-softening marvel that makes an ideal gift for any occasion. And on page 314, you'll find a tonic that's just what the doctor ordered to help you relax after a non-stop day of caring for elderly loved ones: ***A Calming Caregiver Cocktail.***

And that's just for starters! In every chapter, you'll find fabulous features like **Anti-Aging Matters** Q&As, which address pressing concerns about things such as taking in a new pet (page 328), launching a new career (page 235), and even "armoring up" against dangerous insects in a new retirement community (page 50). Also, you'll find answers to straight-from-the-hip questions like, "Is it true that papaya is a perfect superfood for more mature adults?" (page 74).

Help Wanted? directs you to professionals who specialize in meeting the particular needs of aging adults. This is your go-to source for expert aid if, for example, you're looking for the best ways to make your home safer and more comfortable to live in as  you head into your golden years (page 134). In some cases, though, you'll learn why you might not want any help for a particular task if you're aiming to stay sleek, spry, and youthful for as long as possible (page 148).

The **Early Bird Specials** focus in on fabulous discounts and deals that can come your way once you've reached a certain age. These range from  discounts on youth-enhancing, farm-fresh produce at your local farmers' market (page 36) to possibly free hair- styling at upscale salons (page 84). You'll also learn about a gold mine of travel benefits you can start tapping into as soon as you've turned 40 (page 272), and a nationwide consortium of neighborhood support systems that can help you stay independent for the long haul (page 164).

Safe & Sound lives up to its moniker with spot-on strategies that'll help make your surroundings safer and more secure no matter what age, but especially as you grow older and less steady on your feet. For example, you'll discover an easy maneuver that'll help reduce your "collection" of bumps and bruises (page 18). This feature also alerts you to simple safety precautions that can avert far more serious trouble, like an annual automotive chore  that you may not think is necessary, but it could actually help save your life (page 246).

Labor Saver

Last, but not least, the trifecta of the **Time, Labor, and Money Saver** boxes delivers exactly what the names imply: tips, tricks, and helpful hints on how to perform prodigious feats more quickly, more easily, and for less of your hard-earned cash than you might otherwise fork out. For example, you'll discover the ultimate no-muss, no-fuss, and no-mix healing power for arthritis pain (page 8) and the quickest, surest way to calm down

Money Saver

your pup during a stressful situation (page 319). I'll share the least labor-intensive anti-aging tonic you could ever hope to find (page 37), along with an ultra-easy, and mighty tasty, way to reduce the incidence and intensity of hot flashes and night sweats (page 71). On the frugality front, there's a toning, nourishing facial treatment, tailor-made for mature skin, that'll cost

Time Saver

you next to nothing (page 113), and a very simple way to extend the life of your deck or porch for a whopping $0.00! (page 234).

In short, *Vinegar Magic* is your one-stop "shop" for plenty of super solutions, power-packed potions, and cutting-edge tricks that'll help you look, act, and feel years—maybe even decades—younger than your birth certificate says you are. So without further ado, let's get this show on the road, and let the fun begin!

As you'll soon see, holding back the hands of time doesn't get any easier, or more enjoyable, than this!

CHAPTER 1

ACHES & PAINS

Unexpected pain strikes us throughout life, beginning in the delivery room with that first slap on the fanny. Unfortunately, though, the older we get, the more minor aches and pains tend to befall us. The good news is that the right down-home remedy can work better than the expensive prescription or over-the-counter medicines. One of the most effective pain relievers of all is vinegar. Alone, or in combination with other healthy, easy-to-come-by ingredients, it can help ease your discomfort and put you back in action fast.

Here's an example: If you've ever had too many cocktails, there's no worse feeling than the throbbing pain of a hangover. The fix: Mix 2 tablespoons of apple cider vinegar in 8 ounces of water, and drink up. Repeat that process twice during the day, and you should soon be back in the land of the living. ACV helps balance your pH levels while replenishing the iron, potassium, calcium, magnesium, and sodium that the overload of alcohol has drained from your system.

That's just for starters! Read on for a boatload of other ways in which vinegar and its partners can help provide soothing relief for the minor aches and pains of aging.

The comfort-giving teamwork of vinegar may also help the debilitating pain that often accompanies chronic fatigue syndrome (CFS). To get you back on your feet, mix 3 tablespoons of apple cider vinegar (ACV) with 1 cup of pure, raw honey, and take 2 tablespoons of the mix as needed.

ALL-PURPOSE HEADACHE RELIEVER

This remarkable remedy works like magic on any type of headache, including those brought on by sinus congestion and migraine attacks. But, attention, ladies! This recipe is especially effective for soothing the tension headaches that tend to occur during the lead-up to menopause (a.k.a. perimenopause), when your hormones seem to go on a continuous roller-coaster ride.

1 tbsp. of apple cider vinegar	**Juice of 1/2 lemon**
1 tbsp. of honey	**8–10 oz. of lukewarm water**

Mix the vinegar, honey, and lemon juice in a glass of water, and drink up. Repeat up to twice a day until your pain has packed off.

Taters trounce head pain. As wacko as it sounds, this root-cellar remedy has been curing headaches for well over a century—and it still works wonders today. All you need to do is soak three or four thin, peeled potato slices in vinegar (either white or ACV) until they're saturated, but still firm enough to handle. Then tie a bandanna around your head, and tuck the slices into it at your temples and forehead. Leave it on for a few hours. When you take it off, the spuds will be hot and dry, and your head should be cool and ache-free!

And the winner is... Across the board, natural health pros give peppermint essential oil top marks for topical relief of tension and stress-induced headaches. It works through its long-lasting cooling effect on your skin, while it can also help to inhibit muscle contractions and stimulate blood flow in your forehead. The fix: Mix 3 drops of peppermint essential oil per tablespoon of either jojoba oil or coconut oil, and rub the mixture into wherever you need relief.

HELP WANTED? When using hormone replacement therapy, before or after menopause, if you are suffering recurring tension headaches, there's a good chance the meds are causing the problem. So see your doctor. He or she may lower your dose, take you off the meds altogether, or switch you to a different type.

Rosemary rides to the rescue. This common culinary herb doesn't just make your food more flavorful. It also helps stimulate your nervous system and improve your circulation, which should make short work of a headache. To start the action, first make a strong cup of rosemary tea. While it's steeping, fill a foot basin with water that's as hot as you can handle without burning. Pour in the tea, followed by 2 tablespoons of apple cider vinegar. Soak your feet for 20 minutes or so. As your body's circulatory system kicks into high gear, the blood in your head will be drawn to your feet, taking your pain along with it!

Halt high-tech headaches. One very common cause of headaches as well as neck and shoulder pain is staring at the screens of electronic devices for hours on end. The good news is, this is one pain trigger that can become easy to dodge as you age. How so? Think about it: Maybe you've left a job that demanded full-time computer use. Or perhaps your children are grown, and you no longer need to be on constant alert for their "Come get me!" phone calls. The bottom line is that the more hours you can or choose to shed from your connected status, the less likely you are to be plagued by these painful screen-induced headaches.

Stay hydrated. Another prime cause of head pain, especially in the summer, is dehydration—and it happens a whole lot more as we age. The tricky thing is that you may not even be aware of your thirst until it's too late. So ideally on regular days, but especially when the temperature starts to rise, make sure you guzzle plenty of H_2O throughout the day. Your head will be happy, and your improved health will thank you!

Time Saver

The scent of lavender is renowned for its ability to relax jangled nerves and help lull you to sleep at night. But that same gentle aroma can also provide fast-acting headache relief—even from the excruciating pain of a migraine attack. Just taking deep whiffs of either fresh or dried lavender will raise your comfort level. But for even quicker results, open a bottle of lavender essential oil and start sniffing.

ROLL AWAY EARACHE BLEND

Older adults who wear hearing aids are especially susceptible to painful ear infections. This powerful potion helps promote healing from the outside in.

1 tsp. of apple cider vinegar   **5 drops of lavender essential oil**

1 tsp. of castor oil   **5 drops of tea tree essential oil**

Combine all the ingredients in a glass roller-ball bottle (available from essential oil retailers). Pop the ball into place, screw on the lid, and shake well. Roll the blend onto your skin, focusing on the area behind your ear canal and down toward your neck. Rub the mixture in with your fingers, working downward to facilitate proper drainage. Store the remainder in a cool, dark place for up to six months. **Note:** *Never put essential oils of any kind inside your ear.*

Let garlic go at it. Thanks to its potent antimicrobial and pain-relieving powers, garlic is one of most powerful natural remedies to take down ear infections. To use its healing power, peel three to four fresh cloves, and boil them in a cup or so of water until they're soft. This will typically only take five to seven minutes. Then using the back side of a spoon, crush the soft cloves and mix in a sprinkle of salt. Wrap the mixture in a piece of cheesecloth or clean muslin, and hold the little package against your affected ear. It shouldn't take long for you to start feeling incredible relief and for your ear to feel better than ever!

SAFE & SOUND In most cases, ear infections will clear up on their own within a few days when using simple home treatments. If they last longer than that, see a doctor. The exception is if fluid is emerging from your ear canal. In that case, don't try *any* DIY remedies! Instead, get medical help ASAP! The discharge could indicate that your eardrum has ruptured, or that you have a serious ear infection.

Holy cow—what a remedy! Make that holy basil (*Ocimum tenuiflorum*). To put its pain-relieving power to work, crush four fresh holy basil leaves, and mix them with a tablespoon of coconut oil or olive oil. Warm the mixture gently in a pan or on low heat in the microwave. Then soak a cotton ball in the oil and wipe it around the outside and the visible inside of your stricken ear (not in the ear canal!). Repeat twice a day, and you should soon be pain-free.

Never use any DIY remedy on a child under two years of age; see a doctor instead.

Preventive tips for hearing-aid users. In addition to giving your device as much down-time as possible, mix equal parts of white vinegar and rubbing alcohol in a glass bottle with a dropper top. Then, once a week or so, place 2 drops of the solution into each ear. It'll help keep your ear canal dry, thereby discouraging the growth of bad bacteria. **Note:** *This also helps prevent that annoying and painful condition called swimmer's ear. Just put 2 drops in each ear after you've taken a dip in a body of non-chlorinated water.*

Keep hearing aids clean and germ-free. Here's how: Always wash your hands thoroughly before removing your hearing aid. Wipe it all over with a clean, dry tissue, then go over all the surfaces with a non-alcohol-based disinfectant towelette. Or, use a spray disinfectant on a soft, clean cloth. Never clean a hearing aid with any product that contains alcohol because it will damage the surface. Instead, ask your audiologist to recommend a cleaner that's best for your particular device.

Labor 👍 Saver

Hearing aids encourage ear infections because they trap moisture inside the ear canal, providing a prime home for bacteria, which multiply in a moist environment. To spare yourself the hassle and the pain of battling frequent afflictions, simply remove your hearing aid as often as you can and leave it out for as long as possible. This will give your inner ear a chance to dry out before bacteria can grow.

TIME-TESTED TOOTHACHE TOSSER

This remedy is about as simple as it gets, but it's relieved agonizing pain for generations of toothache victims.

2 tbsp. of apple cider vinegar   **1/2 cup of warm water**
1 tbsp. of salt

Combine the ingredients in a glass and stir to mix thoroughly. Then swish the mixture around in your mouth, concentrating (of course) on the area surrounding the afflicted tooth. Repeat as needed until you can get to the dentist's office for a permanent fix. **Note:** *Vinegar of any kind will erode tooth enamel. So after you've used it as a mouthwash or gargle, either alone or as part of a mixture, rinse your mouth thoroughly with clear water.*

Extreme pain calls for a five-star chart topper. This ultra-simple routine wins rave reviews for its ability to soothe even the most sensitive teeth, including those that are broken or infected. Just mix equal parts of salt and pepper with a few drops of water to form a paste. Apply it to the affected tooth down to the gum line, and let it sit for about five minutes. Then rinse with lukewarm water. You'll be amazed at the pain-free results!

EARLY BIRD SPECIALS

Of all the perks available to the 50-plus set, few are more useful, or more financially advantageous, than the ability to join an organization that offers discounted dental insurance, among numerous other benefits. The most widely known group is AARP, but it's far from the only game in town. And depending on your situation and priorities, it may not be the best fit for you. So before you join or pay your next annual membership fee, do some comparison shopping. A search for "alternatives to AARP" will bring up plenty of options, including, to name just a few, the Association of Mature American Citizens (AMAC), American Seniors Association (ASA), and The Seniors Coalition (TSC).

Mighty mouthwash for healthy teeth and gums. This winner will not only ease any toothache, gum pain, or mouth sores that you may have, but it can also help prevent future problems. To make it, combine 1 cup of distilled water, 1 teaspoon of pink Himalayan salt, and 1 teaspoon of calcium magnesium citrate powder (available at most pharmacies and health-food stores) in a glass bottle. Then add 10 drops of cinnamon essential oil, cap the bottle tightly, and shake vigorously. Use it twice a day, after brushing your teeth (shaking before each use to make sure the oil stays blended).

The fine print on mouthwash.

So what makes the DIY mouthwash (above) so great? Well, Himalayan salt is rich in minerals that inhibit the growth of bacteria, reduce gum inflammation, and speed the healing of cuts and sores, while calcium magnesium citrate helps remineralize your teeth. Last but far from least, out of all essential oils, cinnamon ranks number one in antimicrobial potency against bacteria that cause both tooth decay and gum disease, which are common among older adults.

Take direct action. When you're hurting too much to fuss with a mixture of any kind, saturate a cotton ball or a piece of paper towel in vinegar—either white or ACV. Put it on the sore chopper, and bite down. Almost instantly, the pain will vanish, but only temporarily. For long-term relief, see your dentist.

Money Saver

Having a regular oral care routine is incredibly important as you get older. If you're using a top-quality, natural toothpaste, you're likely spending almost five dollars for a tiny tube. You can make a similar toothpaste for well under a dollar, and it's still great for your health. Start by combining 2/3 cup of baking soda and 1 teaspoon of finely ground sea salt or Himalayan salt in a bowl. Mix in 10 to 15 drops of your favorite essential oil, until you get the flavor intensity you like. Then add distilled water to form a toothpaste-like consistency. Store the mixture in a lidded container, and scoop or spread the paste onto your brush to use it.

JUMPIN' JOINT JUICE

Vitamin C is renowned for its ability to prevent or reverse free radical damage in cartilage that leads to arthritis and other inflammatory conditions. This C-filled beverage can help ease joint pain and support overall good joint health.

Juice of 1 grapefruit (about 1 cup)	**1 tbsp. of magnesium**
Juice of 1 lemon (about 2 tbsp.)	**citrate powder**
Juice of 1 orange (about 1/3 cup)	**2 cups of water**
2 tbsp. of apple cider vinegar	**Honey to taste (optional)**

Mix the juices, vinegar, magnesium citrate, and water in a container that has a tight-fitting lid. Taste, and add honey if desired. Drink a glass of the mixture each morning with breakfast. Store the leftovers, tightly covered, in the refrigerator, where they'll keep for up to two weeks.

Put the gloves on. If arthritis has settled in your hands, stretch gloves could be just what the doctor ordered. The tightness may help reduce the swelling in your fingers, and the warmth generated by the hand coverings can actually help soothe the discomfort in your joints.

Time Saver

There are plenty of DIY bath blends that can ease arthritis discomfort, but the ultimate in no-muss, no-fuss, no-mix healing power may be right in your yard. What is it? Roses. What's more, the petals' joint-soothing power increases as the flowers fade, so you can make your "medicine" from blooms that you'd otherwise toss in the compost bin. Just pull the petals from three or four over-the-hill flowers, toss them into your bathwater, and settle in for a good soak. (Don't forget to cover the tub's drain with cheesecloth first!) **Note:** *Make sure the roses you use have not been treated with chemical pesticides or fertilizers.*

Live better electrically. If you're of a certain age, you might recognize that tagline from old TV commercials. In this case, though, it relates to the pain in your joints, rather than the comfort and upkeep of your home. Take a tip from hunters, fishermen, and folks who work outdoors in cold weather: Deliver soothing warmth to your ailin' appendages by wearing battery-powered thermal gloves and/or socks. Put them on when you go to bed at night or during the day whenever the coverings won't interfere with the business at hand (or foot). Either way, electric wearables can make staying pain-free easier.

Pectin packs pain relief.

It may be best known for its role in making jams and jellies, but pectin is a water-soluble carbohydrate that's found in virtually all plants. It helps bind the cells together and firms up ripening fruit. In your aging body, it can help lubricate the tissue in your joints and make them more elastic. When you team up pectin's loosening power with the inflammation-fighting properties of grape juice, you've got a tasty beverage that's a champion at helping you move more easily, with a lot less pain. Your game plan: Once or twice a day, drink an 8-ounce glass of pure, organic grape juice with 1 tablespoon of liquid pectin mixed into it. Within a week or two, you should start to see your pain subside and your mobility improve. You'll feel like a brand-new you!

Q: Lately, I've been making it a point to get more exercise because I've heard it could help relieve the pain in my joints. It's working, too! My joints move as though they've grown years younger. But now my muscles are stiff much of the time, even though I'm not doing anything really strenuous—just walking our dog more, easing back into golf, and my husband and I have joined a ballroom dance group. What's going on, and what can I do about it?

A: Most likely, lactic acid has built up in your muscles. It can happen to anyone, but it's especially common when you suddenly increase your daily activity level. Simply adding more vinegar to your diet can help break down the acid crystals so your body can eliminate them at a faster pace.

ANTI-AGING MATTERS

CHEERY CHERRY GOUT CHASER

Contrary to folklore, gout is not limited to old men who eat too much rich food. Rather, this excruciating form of arthritis can strike anyone whose body can't eliminate uric acid effectively. It most commonly sets in between the ages of 40 and 60, with women becoming more vulnerable after menopause. There is no cure for gout, but there are ways to help minimize the misery. One of the most effective, and tastiest, is this tonic.

2 tbsp. of apple cider vinegar	**8 oz. of water**
2 tbsp. of black cherry concentrate	**Honey to taste (optional)**

Mix the vinegar and black cherry concentrate in a glass of water. Add honey to taste if you like. Drink a glass each morning after breakfast until you are no longer entertaining what founding-father Ben Franklin (himself a sufferer) used to call "Madam Gout."

Help for gout-plagued feet. Of all the body parts gout could strike, the most common is the big toe. Why? No one seems to know for sure. But if the uric acid in your system has settled there or anywhere else in your tootsies, this simple soak is for you. Mix 2 cups of apple cider vinegar and 1/2 cup of Epsom salts in a foot basin filled with hot water. Then sit back in a cozy chair, insert your stricken feet in the basin, and relax until the water gets cold. Repeat the routine once a week or so until your symptoms have sailed off into the sunset.

SAFE & SOUND Whenever a topical remedy calls for hot water (for example, "Help for gout-plagued feet," above), make absolutely certain the solution is comfortable to the touch and not burning hot. I know that may seem like a no-brainer, but many people are in such a hurry to ease their pain that they forget to test the water temperature before plunging in—often winding up with nasty burns that are far worse than the problem they set out to solve.

Nettles nix nasty joint pain. Yes, those same weeds that deliver major discomfort when their sharp prickles come in contact with your skin. Inside those menacing leaves are compounds that decrease inflammation and neutralize uric acid before it crystallizes. That double-dip wizardry can bring major relief from both osteoarthritis and gout pain.

The best way to use nettles is to mix 2 teaspoons of dried nettles* per cup of just-boiled water. Cover and steep for 10 minutes. Then strain out the solids, and stir in honey to taste if you like. For more anti-inflammatory action, add a spoonful of cinnamon. Drink a cup once or twice a day, and your joints should soon be singing a happier tune.
Available wherever bulk dried herbs are sold.

> Dark chocolate, with 85% cocoa, can help reduce painful inflammation as effectively as OTC pain relievers.

Get ginger and bid gout goodbye. Uric acid crystals are sitting ducks for the anti-inflammatory power of fresh ginger. Depending on the severity of your gout, simply incorporating the pungent root into your cooking could solve the problem. For backup action, mix a tablespoon or so of freshly grated ginger with enough water to make a paste, and spread it onto the affected area (use more ginger if needed for complete coverage). Leave it on for 30 minutes, then rinse it off with lukewarm water. Repeat every day or two until your pain subsides.

Labor Saver

To relieve the agony of gout, no potion is better than this one. Mix 6 drops of frankincense essential oil per tablespoon of jojoba oil in a dark blue or brown glass bottle. Then two or three times a day, massage the blend into your ailing joint(s). Frankincense works to dissolve uric acid crystals and helps ease other forms of arthritis. Jojoba's resemblance to your skin's own sebum helps it deliver any essential oils straight to the internal problem. Plus, it promotes skin suppleness and helps boost cell rejuvenation—making it a great choice for mature or aging skin.

EASE YOUR ACHIN' BACK SOAK

Almost everyone suffers a debilitating backache at some point, but the problem most commonly strikes people between the ages of 40 and 60. Whether you've hurt your back on the golf course, slipping on the ice, or just going about your daily chores, this simple formula can help soothe your aching back fast.

1/3 cup of baking soda   **1/3 cup of sea salt**

1/3 cup of dry mustard powder   **1 cup of apple cider vinegar**

Mix the baking soda, mustard, and salt in a container. Dump the mixture into a tub of hot (not burning hot!) water, then pour in the vinegar and swish the water around with your hand. Settle in and soak for 20 to 30 minutes. You should feel the pain drain away as your tight muscles loosen up. Repeat every day or two, until your back is back in action.

On a tangy note... Turmeric, which helps give Indian food its distinctive kick, also helps relieve pain and reduce inflammation. You can use it in one of two ways. For healing from the inside, mix 1 teaspoon of turmeric powder in 1 cup of milk, warm it up over low heat, and sip it slowly. If you prefer an external treatment, mix equal amounts of freshly grated turmeric, lemon juice, and salt. Rub the paste onto your aching muscles, leave it on for 30 minutes, then rinse it off with warm water. Whichever you choose, do it twice a day until your pain is gone.

EARLY BIRD SPECIALS

One of the most effective pain relievers of all is a body of water, whether you choose to swim, perform aquatic exercises, or simply walk through a pool. Many swim and health clubs, as well as most YMCAs, offer discounted memberships to seniors. Plus, if you're on Medicare, you're eligible for the SilverSneakers® program, which gives you free membership at more than 16,000 gyms and other facilities across the country—including many with swimming pools. To learn more on that score, check out www.silversneakers.com.

Enlist a pain-relieving dream team. A gentle massage with the help of garlic-infused coconut oil can provide blessed relief from a backache, or any other muscle pain, and also reduce swelling. To make your supply, heat 1/4 cup of extra virgin coconut oil until it's hot, but not boiling. Toss 8 to 10 peeled garlic cloves into the pan, and leave them, stirring occasionally, until they turn dark brown. Discard the garlic, and let the oil cool to a comfortably warm temperature. Then massage it into the painful areas using small circular motions.

Vinegar and clay keep sprains away. There are few injuries that are more debilitating, or that can take longer to heal, than a sprained ankle. To make matters worse, the older you get and perhaps become less steady on your feet, the easier it becomes to twist the wrong way and suffer the consequences. Well, it just so happens that one of the most effective remedies of all is as old as the hills. Just mix bentonite clay (available online and in health-food stores) with enough white vinegar to form a paste and heat it up in a pan. Spread a thick layer of the mixture on the injured area, cover it with plastic wrap, and then toddle off to bed. Come morning, the pain should be gone, or at least be greatly diminished. If any further discomfort lingers, repeat the procedure until you're fit as a fiddle again.

All-purpose muscle reliever. Whether your body aches come from long hours on the golf course or a rousing game of Frisbee with your grandchildren, this simple formula will help save the day. Mix 1 tablespoon of petroleum jelly with 6 or 7 drops of peppermint essential oil in a bowl, and set it in a basin of warm water for about 3 minutes. While you wait, put a towel in warm water to soak. When the 3 minutes are up, wring out the towel, dip it right into the jelly/oil mixture, and then massage your sore muscles.

Money Saver

Eliminate back pain that comes with aging for free—just go for a walk! At the first sign of discomfort, step outside for an easygoing stroll. That alone may be enough to stop trouble in its tracks. Even if more intense pain has set in, walking slowly and gently will help speed its exit. Try to walk as much as you can in the course of your daily routine. This small change will help you feel younger, get in better shape, and feel great.

SWIFT RELIEF FOR SORE LEGS

When too much time on your feet leaves your leg muscles so sore and strained you can hardly stand up, whip up this cool and spicy combo. It'll get you back on your feet fast!

1 cup of apple cider vinegar

6 drops of clove essential oil

6 drops of peppermint essential oil

6 drops of wintergreen essential oil

2 soft, clean cotton cloths (one for each leg), dampened with water

Warm the vinegar over low heat. Whisk in the oils, one at a time. Divide the emulsion equally between two containers, and soak a cloth in each one. Sit in a comfortable chair, with your feet propped up, and wrap a compress around each leg. Then lean back and relax for 20 minutes or so. After that, and a restful night's sleep, you should feel like your old, or make that young, self again.

Pack some portable cramp relievers. Here's a way to stop those muscle cramps you get on the golf course or tennis court or maybe even when you're out shopping, while making good use of the extra little mustard packets that come with your lunchtime sandwiches. Keep a supply of the handy condiment envelopes in your golf bag, gym bag, or even in your purse. Then, whenever you feel a cramp coming on, open a package, swallow the contents, and chase it with water. Repeat this process every two minutes or so until the painful twinges stop. Even though some things don't seem to come as easy now as they did when you were younger, that doesn't mean you should have to suffer through the pain. This hack will definitely help you get back on track, swinging like a pro on the course or on the court.

HELP WANTED? If you are taking medications that lower cholesterol, and you have been experiencing any unexplained aches, pains, or cramps in your muscles, call your doctor immediately. That discomfort could indicate a rare, but life-threatening side effect in which muscle tissue, including heart muscle, is being destroyed.

Scram, cramps—now! No matter how painful muscle cramps may be, they eventually relax on their own. If you get one that wants to linger, treat it to this routine: Mix equal parts of vinegar and water in a saucepan, heat until comfortably hot, and soak a small towel in the solution. Wring it out and hold it against the painful area for five minutes. Then replace it with a towel that's been soaked in cold water, and leave that one on for one minute or so. If the cramp still lingers, repeat the cycle two more times—always ending with the cold treatment. That should do the trick!

Before you use any topical remedy for the first time, test it on a small area to make sure it doesn't irritate your skin.

A hot tip for sore arms. Maybe too much time at the computer has left you with aching arms or shoulders, or an outbreak of carpal tunnel syndrome (CTS)? If so, this DIY ointment can help. Just add about 3 or 4 drops of hot-pepper sauce to 2 teaspoons of olive oil, multiplying the ingredients as needed. Massage the mixture into the affected area three or four times a day. Not only will you start to feel your pain quickly fade away, but while the mixture goes to work, take a break and cut your keyboard time down as much as you possibly can.

Labor Saver

We've all been there, especially in our older years: You're sound asleep when, out of nowhere, a leg cramp jolts you wide awake. Well, don't just lie there in agony. Instead, hobble into the kitchen, pour an 8-ounce glass of tonic water, and drink it down. The quinine in the mixer should be enough to uncramp your muscles in a flash. If you don't care for the taste of plain tonic, jazz it up with a squirt of orange juice, a wedge of lime—or maybe even a shot of gin!

BYE-BYE BURSITIS BEVERAGE

Bursitis goes by a number of monikers, including housemaid's knee, tennis elbow, and weaver's bottom. But whatever you choose to call it, it's a royal pain in the you-know-what and, like many other physical woes, it tends to occur more frequently as we age. This topical tonic works from the inside to reduce the inflammation in your bursae and strengthen your joints. Plus, it helps ramp up your immune system so your whole body reaps the benefits.

1/2 cup of apple cider vinegar   **1 tsp. of cayenne pepper**

2 tbsp. of honey   **12 oz. of water**

One hour before breakfast, mix the vinegar, honey, pepper, and water in a glass, and drink 'er down. Repeat each morning until your joints seem to be moving freely and effortlessly again.

Put vinegar to work on the outside. In the Bye-Bye Bursitis Beverage (above), vinegar can help reduce pain in two ways: by restoring your body's proper alkalinity level, and also by delivering a quartet of minerals—calcium, magnesium, phosphorus, and potassium—that help reduce inflammation. Luckily, ACV can perform those same feats when used externally. First, mix 1 teaspoon of honey in 1/2 cup of vinegar. Next, saturate a washcloth with the mixture, and hold it against the stricken area for 15 minutes. Repeat as needed several times throughout the day.

ANTI-AGING MATTERS

Q: I'm well into my 60s and I'm watching friends my age go through agony with bursitis. Are there ways to avoid it?

A: Sure! First, avoid sustained pressure on your joints. For example, don't sit on hard chairs or rest your elbows on hard surfaces for long periods. When you spend time on your knees in your garden, use knee cushions. And if you do a job that requires repetitive movements, take breaks. It also helps to exercise the muscles around joints that tend to get bursitis, the most common being the shoulders, elbows, and hips.

Give the joint some garlic! It helps vanquish any inflammatory process that comes with age, like bursitis. Just peel and mash several cloves, and fold them up inside a square of cheesecloth. (To prevent skin irritation, fold the cloth over six to eight times.) Then lay the pouch over the affected joint, and top it with a hot-water bottle or hot-water compress. Repeat the process twice a day, leaving the topper in place for 10 to 15 minutes. The pungent vapors will directly penetrate into the joint and help douse the flames.

Jelly jumps to the rescue. One of the most effective ways to take down bursitis pain is also one of the easiest. Just mix 4 to 6 parts of petroleum jelly with 1 part cayenne pepper, and spread the mix over the area of pain. Your beleaguered bursa should feel a whole lot better in no time!

Tendinitis relief: It's a wrap. Like bursitis, tendinitis can affect anyone of any age, but it most often hits people over 40 and tends to occur more frequently as we age. When inflammation erupts in your tendons, turn to this hot and cold vinegar treatment. Just heat a mixture of half white vinegar and half water in a pan. In a separate container, mix equal parts of white vinegar and cold water. Soak a soft, clean towel in each mixture. Then alternatively apply the wraps to the painful area, leaving each one on the spot for about 10 minutes or so.

Hooray for helichrysum! Many natural health pros give helichrysum essential oil high marks for its ability to relieve pain in both tendons and joints, while relaxing the surrounding tissue. To use it, simply mix 3 drops of the oil per tablespoon of olive oil or coconut oil, and massage the mixture into your skin.

Time Saver

For fast, hands-on relief of aches and pains anywhere in your body, fill a new, clean rubber glove with a half-and-half mixture of rubbing alcohol and water, and put it in the freezer. Then the next time a bruise, muscle strain, or other injury demands cold treatment, pull the glove out. Since alcohol doesn't freeze, you'll have a cold, but pliable, hand to drape over the trouble spot.

BRUISE-BANISHING POULTICE

The dynamic duo of sage and vinegar is tops for easing the discomfort of bruises and promoting fast healing.

1 cup of fresh, whole sage leaves   **Cheesecloth or gauze**

2 cups of white or apple cider vinegar

Gently bruise the leaves with a rolling pin, put them in a pan, and pour in just enough vinegar to cover them. Simmer for five minutes on low heat. Don't let it boil! Using tongs, remove the hot leaves, and place them in the center of the cheesecloth or gauze. Fold the sides in to form a packet that's just big enough to cover your bruise. When the poultice cools to a tolerable temperature, apply it to the site. Cover it with a towel, and leave it in place for 60 minutes. The swelling in the bruised area should be history.

Give bruises the blues. Healing bruises doesn't get any easier or more pleasant than this: Simply eating 1/2 cup of blueberries each day will not only speed the healing of current bruises, but also strengthen your blood vessels. This will make your blood vessels better able to fend off future, and possibly much more serious, damage. The secret lies in the fruits' rich supply of bioflavonoids, which are essential for repairing blood vessels. **Note:** *This very same vessel-strengthening prowess can also help reduce the swelling of varicose veins.*

SAFE & SOUND
If you or other folks in your household keep bumping into things and winding up with bruises, there may be a simple solution to the problem: Cast a cold eye on the furniture layout in each room and weed out any pieces that you don't like or don't use. Then rearrange the keepers to allow as much space as possible for free and easy movement in the room, especially for elderly adults, toddler grandchildren, or anyone who might be a little, shall we say, "unsteady" on their feet.

Lose the blues with parsley. Simply chill a handful of fresh sprigs, crush them, apply them to the bruise, and cover the site with a bandage. Within 24 hours, your colorful bruise will start to fade away.

Make varicose veins vamoose. It's not just women who suffer from these painful, bulging blood vessels. Men can get them too, and in both sexes the risk increases with age. Apple cider vinegar can help solve the problem. Twice a day, after breakfast, and just before bedding down at night, take 2 teaspoons of ACV in 1 tablespoon of water. It will help reduce edema, strengthen your blood vessels, and rev up your circulation.

More vinegar help for veins. As often as you can, soak a thin cloth or bandage in apple cider vinegar, and affix it to the affected area. Used alone, or in combination with the oral remedy above (see "Make varicose veins vamoose"), it will help hasten the departure of your unsightly blue "road map."

Hurt less with … magnesium! And the best source of it is Epsom salts. In addition to improving your blood circulation, lowering your stress levels, and relieving aches and pains, this powerful soak can help alleviate arthritis, bruises, gout, and so much more. Three times a week, pour 2 cups of Epsom salts into a tub of warm water, and soak for 12 to 20 minutes. If you like, add 1/2 cup of your favorite bath oil. Just don't use soap of any kind because it'll interfere with the action of the salts.

Money Saver

The closest thing you'll ever find to a magical, pain-fighting, and anti-aging elixir is clear, fresh water. Getting an adequate supply of H_2O is essential for flushing toxins out of your body, fighting inflammation, and keeping your joints well lubricated. It can even help prevent gout attacks and lessen the severity of arthritis. Best of all, the fluid that flows from your own taps is every bit as healthy, if not more so, than the bottled stuff. And don't even think of forking out cash for fancy "enhanced" waters. The amounts of nutrients, electrolytes, or antioxidants they contain are generally very minuscule.

Your Vim & Vinegar Dream Team

In cooking, any dish is only as good as the ingredients you put into it, and the same goes for DIY health and beauty formulas. To keep your body in tip-top shape as you age, look for the following when using any ingredient that goes into your mouth or onto your body:

APPLE CIDER VINEGAR. The best is the raw, organic, unfiltered kind (available at health-food stores and in the health-food sections of most supermarkets). You'll know it by its cloudy consistency, with strand-like sediment at the bottom of the bottle. The so-called "mother" contains the enzymes and friendly bacteria that give ACV its all-around healing power. Make your own supply using the instructions in Chapter 2 (page 21).

DISTILLED WHITE VINEGAR. Look for a version that is labeled "food-safe" and has an acidity level of 5 percent. Beware of "horticultural" and "cleaning" vinegars, which are much more acidic and in many cases are petroleum derivatives made from 99 percent acetic acid (not grain).

HONEY. Use a pure, unprocessed, preferably organic version. The common commercial brands undergo a heating and filtering process that destroys the health-giving enzymes and nutrients. Find the good stuff in health-food stores, the natural-food sections of supermarkets, and at farmers' markets.

HERBS AND SPICES. Buy these in bulk from local herb shops or reputable online specialty sites. Supermarket brands can be vastly overpriced and far from fresh. They've also been treated to destroy bacteria and lengthen shelf life, which also destroys their health-giving properties.

ESSENTIAL OILS. They're highly concentrated and, for skin use, should be diluted in a cream, lotion, or carrier oil. The optimum dilution rate varies for each oil, so follow the instructions in the recipe. Always insist on 100 percent pure, therapeutic-grade oils from a reputable specialist.

CARRIER OILS. These are typically cold-pressed vegetable or fruit oils that "carry" essential oils into your body. Popular choices include sweet almond, coconut, jojoba, and sunflower oils. Buy them where you get essential oils.

CHAPTER 2

INTERNAL AILMENTS

Internal maladies have three things in common with the aches and pains covered in Chapter 1. First, while they can strike at any time, the chance of suffering a body-system malfunction increases as we age. Second, on a brighter note, there are plenty of steps you can take on your own right now to help prevent or alleviate everything from the common cold to much more serious issues later. Third, as you might guess, many of those DIY tactics involve the use of what else—VINEGAR!

Another upside to this whole process is while advancing in age may pose a heightened risk of various physical troubles, it generally also hands you more leisure time. That, in turn, gives you the chance and provides an opportunity to create your own medicine chest in a bottle—in the form of apple cider vinegar. It's fun, it's easy, and it'll give you the satisfaction of saying, "I made it myself!"

Here's how to do it: Peel and dice 12 apples (organic if possible). Put them (cores and all) into a deep glass bowl, then add 1 package of baker's yeast and a quart of distilled water. Cover with cheesecloth, secure with a rubber band, and set in a warm place for up to four months or until the natural sugars are converted to alcohol. You'll know it's done when it tastes like hard cider. Strain out the apples, pour the liquid into a clean container, and return to a warm place, uncovered, for another four months. Then pour the vinegar into a jar with a tight-fitting lid. Store at room temperature, and use in any of the tips, tricks, and tonics in this book.

AT-THE-READY CONGESTION FIGHTER

This sweet-and-sour syrup is specifically formulated to help fight upper respiratory infections. And boy, does it ever pack a punch!

1 part dried rosemary   **Apple cider vinegar to taste**

1 part dried sage   **Honey to taste**

Fill a 1-pint glass jar one-quarter of the way with rosemary and sage, and fill the remainder with vinegar and honey. A half-and-half blend works best, but you can vary the proportions to suit your taste. Cap the jar tightly, shake it well, and set it in a cool, dark place for two weeks, shaking it a few times a week. Then strain the syrup into a clean jar, and store it at room temperature for up to a year. Take it by the spoonful, as needed, for sore throats, coughs, nasal congestion, or other respiratory symptoms. **Note:** *This remedy should not be used by pregnant or nursing women.*

Stop it, doggone it! Does it seem that whenever you come down with a coughing kind of cold, it seems to linger longer than it did in your younger days? If so, you're not alone. Colds that want to settle in for long haul go hand in hand with aging. That's why, for generations, legions of older and wiser folks have sworn by this simple formula for getting rid of any seemingly unstoppable coughs: Mix 1 tablespoon each of unsalted butter, sugar, and apple cider vinegar in a nonreactive pan. Heat the mixture over low heat, stirring continuously, until the butter has melted. Then pour the potion into a mug, and drink it while it's still warm. That trick should halt your hacking in a hurry!

Most colds clear up in about a week. If yours lasts longer than that, or it's getting worse rather than better, see a doctor immediately. Also, seek medical help if your temperature is over 101°F, you notice shortness of breath, feel any pain in your chest, develop an earache or a headache that painkillers won't budge, or start coughing up green- or yellow-colored phlegm.

When your funny bone isn't tickled—but your throat is...

This is the Rx to reach for. It's just what the doctor ordered for defeating a super-annoying cough that doesn't stop. Whenever the irritation occurs, drink a glass of water with 2 teaspoons each of apple cider vinegar and honey mixed into it. It's also a good idea to keep a glass of the mixture by your bed so you can sip it as the need arises throughout the night.

Stronger medicine for a cough. If you have a high heat tolerance, or you're simply ready for some desperate measures, it's time to haul out the big guns. Mix 1/2 cup of apple cider vinegar, 1/2 cup of water, 4 teaspoons of honey, and 1 teaspoon of cayenne pepper in a glass jar. Take a tablespoon of the mixture each time your cough erupts, and another tablespoon at bedtime.

Keep the side effects in mind.

Just about any internal medication under the sun, natural or otherwise, affects your system in ways that go beyond its intended purpose. And the At-the-Ready Congestion Fighter (at left) is no exception on that score. Only in this case, two of the active ingredients—namely rosemary and sage—deliver side effects that can provide mighty big benefits to cold sufferers who have reached a certain age. In fact, natural health pros rank these herbs among the best of the bunch for aging adults. Why? That's because both rosemary and sage help keep your brain healthy and youthful by stimulating cognition, memory, and concentration. So don't wait until a cold strikes to enjoy these delicious and versatile superstars. Make these incredible ingredients a regular part of your everyday diet to boost your health.

Time Saver

We've all been there at least a few times: A nagging cough latches on and just won't quit, even at night when you and everyone else within hearing distance needs to be sleeping. Well, here's a quick and real ultra-simple solution: Sprinkle apple cider vinegar on a cloth, and lay it on top of your pillow (with the moistened part to one side of your head, of course!). As you breathe in the vapor, it'll quiet your cough and give you and yours a health-giving forty winks.

EXCEPTIONAL ELDERBERRY ELIXIR

This formula helps strengthen your immune system so that you're better able to stay happy and healthy as you age.

1 1/2 cups of dried elderberries	1–1 1/2 cups of honey
2 cinnamon sticks	2/3 cup of apple cider vinegar
3 cups of water	Juice of 2 lemons
1–2 tbsp. of freshly grated ginger	

Put the berries, cinnamon, and water in a pan and bring to a boil. Reduce the heat and simmer until the water is reduced by one-third to one-half (30 to 40 minutes). Add the ginger in the last 15 minutes. Let the mixture cool, remove the cinnamon, and strain into a glass jar. Stir in the honey, vinegar, and lemon juice. Store it, tightly lidded, in the fridge for up to a week. The standard dose is 1 tablespoon for adults and 1/2 to 1 teaspoon for children, taken three times a day.

Ah, there's the rub! Simply inhaling eucalyptus essential oil can break up congestion, boost your immune system, and help energize your mind and body. But what if you're so clogged up that breathing becomes a struggle? Here's what: Once or twice a day, mix 3 drops of eucalyptus oil with 1/2 teaspoon of a carrier oil, and massage it into your chest and/or the bottoms of your feet. The clearing essence will seep through your system, and you should be breathing easy again. Avocado oil makes an especially good carrier for this purpose because it's one of the most effective at delivering the benefits of essential oils deep into the skin. It's also one of the most beneficial carrier oils for mature and aging skin.

SAFE & SOUND It's a fact—the older you get, the less vigorously your immune system responds to any illness. So while your body is busy battling a cold or flu virus, another infection can slip in under the wires. The solution is to choose remedies that not only ease your symptoms, but also help boost your immunity.

Soak rather than rub. Another simple way to rake in the anti-aging benefits of eucalyptus oil is to use it in a bath. Just mix 2 or 3 drops of the oil with 8 or 12 drops of Solubol dispersant (available from essential oil suppliers), pour the mixture into a tub of warm water, and swish it around with your hand. Then ease into the tub and relax for 20 to 30 minutes. While your nasal passages clear up and your immunity is growing stronger, any tension and anxiety will be flowing right out of your body. So when you emerge from the tub, you'll be primed for sound sleep and that's another must for a stronger immune system and a younger you!

> Even if you've always been allergy-free, sensitivities from pollen and dust to foods and medications can stage a midlife sneak attack.

Clove oil cuts the mustard. When it comes to soothing upper respiratory woes while helping to shore up your immunity, clove essential oil can't be beat. It's one of the most potent antioxidant substances on earth, and its antiviral, anti-inflammatory, and antibacterial properties make it ideal for taking the edge off a sore throat. For that reason, this DIY gargle makes a valuable addition to your cold— and flu-fighting kit. Just mix 2 drops of clove oil with 1 teaspoon of sea salt, stir the mixture into a glass of warm water, and gargle in your usual way. Repeat as needed throughout the day, and before long, you should be ready to warble again.

Labor Saver

Here's a simple congestion reliever with highly effective immunity-boosting properties: Just pour 1 cup of apple cider vinegar into a heat-proof bowl, followed by 1 cup of boiling water. Then lean over the bowl, put a towel over your head to focus the steam, and breathe in the vapor. Just keep enough distance between your face and the hot liquid so that you don't burn yourself! **Note:** *If you don't have apple cider vinegar, use the distilled white kind. It won't jolt your immune system, but it can still help clear out your nasal passages.*

HIP-HIP-HOORAY ALLERGY TONIC

Whether you're a late-onset allergy sufferer, or pollen has plagued you since childhood, this tonic will have you welcoming spring with open arms and open nasal passages!

1/2 cup of dried elderberries   **Apple cider vinegar**

1/2 cup of dried nettles   **Locally produced honey**

1/2 cup of rose hips (fresh or dried)

Add the elderberries, nettles, and rose hips to a 1-quart glass jar. Pour apple cider vinegar in until it reaches three-quarters to the top, and fill the remainder with honey. Close the lid, and shake the jar vigorously. Set in a cool, dark place for 30 days, shaking once a week. Strain the mixture through cheesecloth into a clean jar and store at room temperature. The blend will retain its full strength for up to a year. About a month ahead of allergy season, take 1 teaspoon three times a day to beat the sneeze.

At the ready anti-allergy juice. Besides helping relieve a runny nose and weepy eyes, this bracing beverage is chock-full of antioxidants and other nutrients that'll rev up your whole internal system. To make it, just mix 3 parts carrot juice, 1 part beet juice, and 1 part cucumber juice in a glass pitcher. Store the mix, tightly covered, in the refrigerator, and drink two or three 8-ounce glasses each day.

ANTI-AGING MATTERS

Q: Suddenly, at age 55, I've developed pollen allergies. I hear that consuming local honey will help relieve my symptoms. Does this really work? And why does knowing where the honey comes from make a difference?

A: The theory is that by ingesting pollen from local plants that may trigger symptoms, you can build up your resistance and lessen the severity of your reaction. And, yes, it does seem to work for many people. You may not feel 100 percent better, but you might feel a lot more comfortable.

Crack out the crackers. Looking for a no-muss, no-fuss way to relieve allergy symptoms? Well, look no further! About 30 days before the time that watery-eye season arrives, start eating crackers spread with locally produced honey. As few as two or three of these delectable morsels a day may help your immune system lessen your misery significantly.

Is it asthma, or...? Asthma does not pose any more health risks for seniors than it does for anyone else. For folks over 60, the symptoms of asthma—wheezing, coughing, shortness of breath, and chest tightness—can mimic and complicate those of other serious conditions, like emphysema, bronchitis, and heart disease. You can rule out those copycats if your symptoms occur after you are exposed to a substance that irritates, inflames, and narrows air passages. For older adults, chemicals and strong odors in general are some prime asthma triggers. Common culprits can include paint, tobacco, perfume, room deodorizers, hair spray, and cleaning products.

Look to lobelia. In natural health circles, and among many conventional doctors, lobelia (*Lobelia inflata*) is the star of stars for easing the acute symptoms of asthma and other respiratory disorders. To use it for a mild asthma attack that does not demand medical attention, mix 3 parts lobelia tincture with 1 part capsicum (a.k.a. cayenne pepper) tincture. At the start of an attack, take 20 drops of the mixture in a glass of water. Repeat every 30 minutes for up to four doses. If that doesn't fix the problem, call your doctor immediately!

Money Saver

One free way to help stave off both allergy and asthma problems is simply to guzzle a steady supply of water. When your body is dehydrated, as it can be without your knowing it (especially if you're in an older age bracket), your system ups its production of histamines. These are organic nitrous compounds that help regulate your immune response. When too many of them are circulating, you feel congested, have difficulty breathing, and have other allergic reactions triggered by your body's response to the presence of foreign substances.

NAUSEA-NIXING TEA

Anything from an unwise choice of snacks to a wild roller coaster ride with a grandchild can bring on a bout of nausea. But regardless of what caused it, this taste-tempting tea can help tame the turbulence in your tummy.

1 tbsp. of fennel seeds

1 cinnamon stick, broken

2 cups of boiling water

1 tbsp. of apple cider vinegar

Honey to taste

Put the fennel and cinnamon in a teapot or other heat-proof container, and pour the water over them. Cover and steep for 5 to 10 minutes. Let the tea cool slightly, then stir in the vinegar and honey, and sip the brew slowly. You should be feeling better in no time at all.

An old-time tummy tamer. Here's another remedy that your mama or your grandma might have given you way back when. To make it, mix 1/2 cup of fresh-squeezed orange juice, 2 tablespoons of clear corn syrup, and a pinch of salt in 1/2 cup of water. Store the mixture in a covered jar in the refrigerator. Take 1 tablespoon every half hour or so until your queasiness has flown the coop.

EARLY BIRD SPECIALS

If you suffer frequent bouts of nausea, and your doctor has ruled out any physical ailments, the cause could be stress or maybe a bad case of the retirement blahs. If that's the issue, the remedy could be as simple as putting a little more variety and fun in your life. And your senior status gives you plenty of low- or even no-cost remedies, ranging from discount vacation packages where you could develop a fun new pastime (bird-watching, anyone?) to adult-ed classes at your local senior center or community college. So don't just sit there—jump into an activity you've always wanted to try, or one that you drifted away from when you were busy working and raising a family. You've got nothing to lose but the butterflies in your stomach!

Mind your meds. For folks in the 60-plus set, medication is a common cause of nausea. It could be that you're sensitive to a particular drug you're taking. Or a combination of products might be interacting to irritate your stomach, your brain, or both. What's more, even if you've been taking a certain medication for years, there is a chance that you simply don't tolerate it as well as you did in your younger days. So if you have persistent nausea or queasiness, and you're taking one or more drugs on a routine basis, see your doctor. Changing the dose or switching to a different Rx might solve the problem lickety-split.

Leave it to the leaves. Avocado leaves, that is. No matter what has your stomach bouncing around like a roller coaster ride, give this magical mixer a try. It comes highly recommended by an old pal of mine who's used it for years. Simply steep 1 tablespoon of dried avocado leaves (available online) in 1 cup of boiling water for 10 to 15 minutes. Strain out the leaves, add a drizzle of honey, and sip the drink slowly. You should be back in action fast!

Turn back the clock. When you were a child, what did your mom give you for an upset stomach? Ginger ale? Coke? Maybe cinnamon toast? Well, if one of those remedies worked then, there's a good chance it'll work just as well now. Plus, it'll give you the added benefit of feeling comforted and reassured.

Time Saver

Nausea remedies don't come much faster than this one: Stir 1 teaspoon of apple cider vinegar into 1 cup of water and sip it slowly. Flavor it up with honey to taste. Repeat every few hours or as needed, until the butterflies land.

Soothe your stomach from the outside. When you don't feel like putting anything into your mouth, use this trick: Mix 3 drops of peppermint essential oil in 1 teaspoon of carrier oil, multiplying the measurements as needed. (Either apricot, avocado, or camellia oil will work especially well.) Rub the mixture over your abdominal area. Then sit back in a cozy chair, put your feet up, and sit a spell. All by itself, that should end your queasiness. But if possible, choose a spot outdoors, or at least by a window overlooking a pleasant view—that's an all-but-guaranteed way to speed up the feel-better process.

OIL-YOUR-INNER-PLUMBING CHEWS

Even teenagers can suffer from constipation, but as we grow older, we become more vulnerable to it. These yummy gummy treats give you an effective way to get your internal workings back in action.

Silicone candy molds
1 cup of coconut oil, melted
1/4 cup of orange juice
3 tbsp. of honey

1 tbsp. of apple cider vinegar
1 tsp. of slippery elm powder
    (available from herb suppliers)
1/2 tsp. of sea salt

Put the molds in the freezer for 10 minutes. Blend all the ingredients in a blender or food processor. Pour the mixture into the chilled molds, and freeze until each chew can be removed in one piece. Store them in an airtight glass jar in the refrigerator for up to seven days, and use them once or twice a day until things are moving again. The adult dose is four chews; for a child, it's two.

Try a classic bedtime story. You may have forgotten this old-time remedy, but it works just as well as ever. To refresh your memory, you simply mix 1/2 cup of applesauce with four to six chopped prunes and 1 tablespoon of bran. Eat the concoction before you go to bed, and chase it down with a tall glass of water. By morning, things should be moving smoothly once again!

Labor Saver

Here's a remedy for constipation that I learned from a pal of mine who happens to be a Sioux Indian—and one of the older members of his tribe. He said it goes way back in tribal medicinal lore. What is it? Eat fresh strawberries. That's all there is to it. It works because the soluble fiber in the berries eases the passage of waste through your colon. You couldn't ask for an easier, more pleasant or more delicious way to end your misery.

Lose the laxatives. Just like your immune system, your gut naturally works a little more slowly as the years pile up. So if you're not moving your bowels every single day, don't panic and resort to gulping laxatives in an effort to solve the "problem." If you do, it's a good bet that you'll wind up with the opposite issue, namely diarrhea, and possibly more serious conditions to boot.

Vinegar stops the runs. Correction: It acts as an antiseptic to your digestive tract, thereby allowing the elimination process to proceed in a more comfortable manner. I say this because diarrhea is your body's natural attempt to rid itself of something that's irritating your digestive tract. Here's a way to make the process go easier: Six times a day, before and between meals, drink a glass of water with 1 teaspoon of apple cider vinegar mixed into it. If the problem hasn't resolved itself within 48 hours, or you have other symptoms, like blood in your stool, constant pain, or just a fever, see your doctor immediately to rule out any more serious health conditions.

Replace those electrolytes.

Diarrhea or vomiting can whisk electrolytes right from your body. After middle age, it's crucial to replace these anti-aging elements. This simple elixir will put them back in no time. To make it, mix the juice of 1 lemon, 1 tablespoon of honey, and 1/2 teaspoon of sea salt or Himalayan salt in 1 quart of water. Drink 2 cups of the mixture every hour until you're in tip-top shape again.

Q: Why is it that the older we get, the more frequently we're troubled by constipation?

A: One reason is that many older folks lose interest in food, which leads to a lack of dietary fiber. The solution is to maintain a healthy diet—even if that means asking friends to nag you about it. Lack of physical activity can also cause trouble. So keep moving as much as you possibly can! Certain medications and supplements, including calcium and iron, could lead to constipation. Talk to your doctor about any supplements and prescription meds that you're taking. And whenever possible, use natural remedies rather than OTC drugs.

ANTI-AGING MATTERS

HEROIC HEARTBURN HELPER

Obviously, heartburn has nothing to do with your heart. It occurs when stomach acid backs up into your esophagus. Just like constipation, heartburn can afflict folks of any age but, yet again, it tends to occur more frequently as we get older. This fruity beverage is a delicious way to relieve that blasted burning sensation without the nasty side effects that OTC remedies can deliver.

1/2 banana, sliced

1/2 cup of raspberries (fresh or frozen; red, black, or mixed)

1/3 cup of apple chunks

1/4 cup of crushed ice

1 tbsp. of apple cider vinegar

Combine the ingredients in a blender until they're liquefied. Pour the mixture into a tall glass, and drink to cooler internal conditions!

Wait before you sleep. For many older adults it's easy to fall into the trap of eating a late dinner, then heading to bed. While that works for some folks, it causes major heartburn in others. If you're among the latter crowd, eat early so that you can wait two to three hours before you lie down. The delay will give your system time to digest the vittles so you won't be awakened by the process in the middle of the night.

Sleep on a slant. If you're prone to heartburn at night, one simple way to get relief is to elevate the head of your bed 6 to 8 inches. Many furniture and online stores offer special bed risers that will do that job. Or simply prop the frame's legs up on blocks. But don't just put more pillows under your head. All that will do is fold your body sharply in the middle, causing even more acid to back up into your esophagus.

Most often, heartburn is simply a price you pay for eating the wrong thing at the wrong time. But if you feel heartburn pain during physical activities, like climbing the stairs or shifting storage boxes around, see your doctor ASAP. For folks past the middle-age mark, this can sometimes indicate a hidden heart problem.

Please pass the acid. The real cause of conditions like acid reflux and heartburn is not too much stomach acid but rather too little. One study showed that more than half the population age 60 and older has low stomach acidity. This condition is responsible for incomplete digestion that causes some indigestion, and can also cause nutritional deficiencies. So instead of loading up on antacids, get to the root of the problem. Before each meal, drink a glass of water with 2 teaspoons of apple cider vinegar mixed into it.

> Chewing a piece of sugar-free gum for 30 minutes after a meal increases saliva flow and washes away trouble-causing excess acid.

It's not just for bunnies. Chamomile tea was just what Mama Rabbit ordered for curing Peter's ailing tummy. It's also a first-class way to relieve indigestion. Just drink 1 cup of chamomile tea after meals until you feel better. If you have a chronically sensitive digestive system and no underlying health issues, make a post-meal cup part of your routine. **Note:** *If you're on blood-thinning drugs, consult with your doctor before consuming chamomile; it contains coumarin, which reacts with blood thinners.*

Sauerkraut relieves heartburn. Why? Well, cabbage contains glutamine, an amino acid that appears to promote healing in the digestive tract. If you suffer from frequent heartburn, eating sauerkraut a few times a week may prevent future problems. Plus, if you're over 60 and, therefore, at a greater risk for anemia, the lactic acid in sauerkraut promotes iron absorption.

Money Saver

You could spend megabucks on OTC heartburn relievers, but you can spare yourself that cash outlay, and the potentially aging side effects of the meds, by heeding some advice that your mother probably gave you every day: Slow down and chew your food thoroughly. This increases your saliva production and enhances your digestive process—thereby preventing, or at least greatly lessening, heartburn and acid indigestion.

LIVEN-UP-YOUR-LIVER LIBATION

If your memory is a little hazy lately, don't automatically blame the problem on your advancing age. It could be that your liver (your designated filtering organ) has simply absorbed too many of the toxins that are all around us. If that's the case, then the detoxing combo of cranberry juice and apple cider vinegar in this refreshing cocktail can help clear the crud out of your system, and the fog out of your brain.

1/2 cup of 100% cranberry juice　　　**1 cup of water**

1 tbsp. of apple cider vinegar　　　**Lime juice to taste**

Mix the cranberry juice, vinegar, and water in a glass. Sweeten it with lime juice as desired, and drink to happy memories! Don't hesitate to have another whenever you feel the need. Unlike many popular detox routines, this one delivers no negative side effects at all.

Enjoy some toxin-tossin' tea. Brain fog isn't the only toxin-triggered condition that can be falsely attributed to your advancing years (see the "Help Wanted?" box, below). Fortunately, there are plenty of easy ways you can reduce the harmful effects of all that unsavory stuff. One of them is to brew a cup of green tea, then stir in a tablespoon of apple cider vinegar, add honey to taste, and sip away. The rich load of antioxidants in the tea joins forces with the vinegar's supply of pectin and minerals to give your liver function a healthy boost.

HELP WANTED?

When you're taking in too many toxins—whether they're coming from your surroundings, your food, or both—your body can show symptoms that mimic those of many age-related annoyances. But these same discomforts can be signs of a disease in its early stages. So if you're experiencing pains in muscles or joints, constant fatigue or sluggishness, mood swings, or recurring headaches, see your doctor before you launch any DIY detox efforts.

Take a deep breath. And then another and another... Breathing deeply on a regular basis is one of the simplest and most effective ways of all to get toxins out of your system and help keep them out. And, unlike many trendy detox regimens, this habit is not only perfectly safe for even the oldest and most fragile golden-agers, but it also has incredible health benefits. For example, it keeps your air passages clear, which in turn helps prevent asthma attacks and alleviate allergy symptoms. Plus, it can even lower your stress levels—and that's a major step toward healing or avoiding physical and mental woes of just about any kind.

Fine-tune your technique.

As we grow older and become less physically active, our breathing naturally tends to grow more shallow. Practicing this simple yoga exercise is an effective way to acquire the habit of taking in your full supply of health- and youth-enhancing air. Start by sitting in a comfortable chair, and put one hand on either side of your lower rib cage, with your fingers touching lightly. Breathe in through your nose, letting the air fill your lower lungs, and then the lower part of your chest. Focus on making your ribs expand sideways as your lungs fill. (You should feel your fingers draw apart as your chest expands.) Then inhale gently for about 10 seconds—you should feel no strain in your stomach or chest muscles. Exhale as slowly as you can, for about 10 seconds or longer, if possible—again through your nose. You can perform this routine as often as you like throughout the day. In no time at all, you should start to find that you can automatically breathe more deeply, and feel and act younger as a result.

Time Saver

Scads of elaborate diets are touted for their ability to "miraculously" detox your system. Don't fall for them! Not only are they potentially dangerous (especially for older adults), but they're also time-consuming to follow. Furthermore, you don't even need 'em. Simply adding more of three foods to your diet will safely and gently speed up your body's natural detox processes. The heroic triad is berries, citrus fruits, and leafy green vegetables— organic versions, please!

CHOLESTEROL-SUBTRACTION SOLUTION

If your LDL (bad) cholesterol numbers are higher than you'd like—as they are for a great many folks in the 50-plus age bracket—give this tonic a try. It's proven successful for many of your contemporaries. Plus, it's easier to follow than a low-cholesterol diet and has none of the side effects of prescription drugs like Lipitor® and its generic buddies.

2 cups of 100% grape juice　　**1/4 cup of apple cider vinegar**
1 cup of 100% apple juice

Mix all the ingredients in a glass container that has a tight-fitting lid. Store the mixture in the refrigerator, and drink between 1/2 cup and 1 cup before your largest meal each day.

Take the pressure off. If you're among the millions of seniors who are taking prescription meds to lower your blood pressure, you know that they can deliver a lot of nasty side effects. The good news is there are safe, natural remedies that can get your numbers down without collateral damage, like this tasty beverage. Mix 2 tablespoons each of apple cider vinegar and lemon juice, 1 teaspoon of honey, and 1/4 teaspoon of cinnamon in 12 ounces of warm water. Enjoy a healthy glass each day. Along with a few simple lifestyle changes and a healthy diet, this new routine could get your BP score down to its proper level. **Note:** *Talk to your doctor before using this or any other DIY remedy—and don't even think of quitting your medications without conferring first with the doc!*

EARLY BIRD SPECIALS

There's nothing better for your heart and your overall health than fresh and locally grown organic fruits and vegetables. And you might be able to fill your plate for less money, thanks to discount coupons provided through the Senior Farmers' Market Nutrition Program (SFMNP). Exact dollar figures, along with age and income requirements, vary from state to state. So to learn the details for your home ground, search for "SFMNP state agencies."

Alliums alleviate high blood pressure. Garlic and its kissin' cousins, onions, are two of Mother Nature's most powerful blood pressure controllers. In fact, consuming as little as half an ounce of raw garlic per week has been proven to reduce hypertension. A half ounce equals roughly six cloves, so I guess you could say that a clove a day helps keep the cardiologist away!

As for onions . . . The recommended dose is 2 to 3 tablespoons of onion oil or juice, or about 2 ounces of fresh onion (either cooked or raw) per day. They can help to significantly lower moderately high blood pressure.

Make magic with magnesium. Studies have shown that most people are deficient in this essential mineral—which just happens to be essential for keeping both cholesterol levels and blood pressure numbers where they should be. However, magnesium supplements can be dangerous, especially for aging adults. The simple and safe solution: an Epsom salts bath. The salt is absorbed through your skin to benefit not only your cardiovascular system but also every part of your body. The basic Rx for maximum benefit: Three times a week, pour 2 cups of Epsom salts into a tub of warm water, and soak for about 20 minutes or so.

Maximize your magnesium experience. To make your Epsom salts bath even more relaxing, add 3 drops of lavender essential oil mixed with 12 drops of Solubol dispersant. Lavender in any form is a guaranteed stress buster, and this alone has been proven to be a major factor in reducing both blood pressure and LDL cholesterol levels. But that's not all! Lavender is widely lauded as one of the most therapeutic oils of all for mature, elderly, or sensitive skin.

Labor Saver

There are plenty of heart-healthy, anti-aging tonic recipes out there, but you'll never find an easier version than this one: Just mix 1 or 2 tablespoons of red wine vinegar in a glass of still or sparkling water, and drink up. Enjoy a daily dose, or use it as a substitute on those days when you don't want to fuss with a more elaborate formula.

YEAST RELIEF BATH

As women age, they become more prone to vaginal yeast infections. That's because fluctuating hormone levels brought on by menopause can trigger an overgrowth of the *Candida albicans* fungus that causes the condition. This blend helps bid the foul fungi "Bye-Bye".

1 cup of apple cider vinegar	**1 tbsp. of fresh tarragon**
1 tbsp. of fresh mint	**1 1/2 tsp. of fennel seeds**
1 tbsp. of fresh rosemary	**1 cup of water**

Mix all of the ingredients in a pan, and heat gently to just the boiling point. Remove the pan from the heat, let the mixture cool, and strain out the solids. Pour the liquid into a warm bath, and soak for 15 to 20 minutes. Repeat as needed until you feel soothing relief.

Use a yeast-demolishing cleanse. Here's an easy-does-it remedy that uses the solo power of (you guessed it!) vinegar to end your pain and itchiness: Just mix 2 tablespoons of apple cider vinegar in 2 quarts of warm water. Then twice a day, dip cotton balls or cotton pads in the solution, and gently swab your whole vaginal area. Repeat the process until your symptoms have vanished.

Cushion the cure with coconut oil. If you find that straight vinegar stings the affected area—which it might depending on the intensity of the infection—use this creamier formula: Make the vinegar-water solution as described above. Then three times a day, mix 2 tablespoons of the dilution with 1 tablespoon of extra virgin coconut oil, and gently apply it to the affected areas.

Do not douche with any substance to prevent a yeast infection or any other problem. If you do, it's likely to alter the vagina's normal pH and also disrupt the balance of good and bad bacteria. The result could be severe discomfort, a highly unpleasant odor, or both. Furthermore, douching can cause vaginal dryness.

Drink to a yeast-free system. To speed up the healing process, whether you use a bath, a douche, or both, add a vinegar beverage to your arsenal. Two or three times a day, drink a glass of water or a cup of herbal tea (any variety) with 1 ½ to 2 teaspoons of apple cider vinegar mixed in. Once the condition has cleared up, drinking a cup a day can help prevent a recurrence—without the risks of douching.

How dry it shouldn't be. Vaginal dryness will most often strike women in their post-menopausal years, when their estrogen levels run low and their natural lubricants stop flowing. Doctors often prescribe hormone replacement therapy to reverse the condition, but that can deliver a lot of highly unpleasant side effects. So before you go that route, try some safe DIY remedies. One of the best is extra virgin olive oil. Rubbing it directly into your vagina will not only lubricate the tissue, but will also supply a good dose of anti-aging vitamin E.

> Prevent yeast infections by eating 1/2 cup of yogurt daily containing live *Lactobacillus acidophilus.*

Perform a hormone-balancing act. Natural health pros advise that eating the right foods can help prevent vaginal dryness. In particular, you want to pack in plenty of foods that are rich in estrogen, as well as in vitamin A and omega-3 fatty acids. These just happen to be anti-aging superstars, including sweet potatoes, avocados, flaxseeds, and fresh-water fish. Aside from fighting free radicals, they keep your skin healthy and looking young, while supporting strong vaginal walls.

Money Saver

One way to prevent vaginal dryness is frequent rolls in the hay with your hubby. Regular sexual intercourse keeps your vaginal tissues toned and healthy, which in turn keeps their lubrication flowing. Also, sex is a renowned stress reliever and vaginal dryness is yet another condition that can frequently be brought on or worsened by stress.

REACH FOR THE FOUNTAIN OF YOUTH

It's as close as your kitchen sink, or maybe the water fountain at work. We've discussed ways that good old H_2O can help you stay young longer, but here are more ways the elixir of life can contribute to your anti-aging efforts:

COMBATS FATIGUE. Water helps your body perform the enzymatic activities that contribute to better sleep, the maintenance of bodily systems, and the production of enough energy to get you through the day.

REDUCES HIGH BLOOD PRESSURE. When your body is fully hydrated, your blood consists of roughly 92% water. This consistency keeps the blood moving freely through your veins and arteries, thereby helping to prevent high blood pressure and other cardiovascular problems.

LOWERS CHOLESTEROL. Your cells need a certain amount of cholesterol to function properly. If your body isn't getting enough water, it produces more of the Big C just to keep your systems running smoothly.

PREVENTS DIGESTIVE DISORDERS. Getting an adequate supply of water can eliminate or reduce the incidence and severity of acid reflux, bloating, gas, gastritis, irritable bowel syndrome, and ulcers.

REDUCES OR ELIMINATES BLADDER AND KIDNEY INFECTIONS. Water helps to flush out bad bacteria, other toxins, and waste material that otherwise would linger in these organs.

RELIEVES STIFFNESS AND HELPS JOINT AND CARTILAGE REPAIR. Most of the padding in your cartilage consists of water. If you don't drink enough of it, your joints take a beating, and you feel stiff. Proper hydration also leads to faster joint recovery after exercise or injuries.

MAINTAINS—OR HELPS YOU REACH—A HEALTHY WEIGHT. When your cells run low on water, they can't create the energy you need to function, so they send an "I'm hungry!" signal to your brain. So you eat more than you need to and, most likely, pay the price in extra pounds.

SLOWS THE AGING PROCESS. If you're dehydrated, every cell, organ, and system in your body has to work harder, which makes you age faster. But drinking plenty of H_2O keeps you feeling, looking, and acting younger longer.

CHAPTER 3

EXTERNAL WOES

Older adults are susceptible to the same scrapes, stings, and skin rashes as younger folks are, but there are a couple of differences. First, as we age, we tend to become less steady on our feet, and our vision becomes less acute. That makes it easier, for example, to take a tumble, hit the wrong target with a kitchen knife, or try to wave a fly away—only to discover too late that it was a bee. Second, many of those remedies that once worked fine may now irritate our more sensitive skin. This chapter is packed with healers that are strong enough to relieve the condition at hand without causing any collateral damage of their own. And many of them actually help nourish your skin!

One fine example is an herbal vinegar tincture, which you can apply directly to a blister or other external affliction. Or mix a drop or two into a cup of hot or warm water to make a nice herbal tea, which you can then drink, pour into bathwater, or, as noted, apply to your skin.

To make a tincture, fill a glass jar loosely with dried or chopped fresh herbs (see "Anti-Aging Herbal Superstars" on page 60). Cover them completely with apple cider vinegar, and then cap the jar tightly. Leave it in a warm, dark place for at least four to six weeks, shaking the container occasionally. Then strain the liquid into some sterilized bottles, label them, and store them in a cool, dark place. The tincture will retain its full potency for about a year.

PACK-OFF PLANTAR PASTE

Plantar warts are harmless from a health standpoint, but they can be as painful as the dickens because the pressure of walking makes them grow inward and press on the nerves in your feet. Enter this amazingly effective good-riddance formula.

1 tsp. of bentonite clay (available at natural-food stores and online)

1/2 tsp. of apple cider vinegar

2 drops of frankincense essential oil

2 drops of oregano essential oil

Mix all of the ingredients to form a thick paste, adjusting the clay or vinegar amounts as needed to achieve the right consistency. At bedtime, spread the mixture onto each wart and cover it with a snug bandage. The next morning, remove the covering, and wipe the paste and (hopefully) the wart away. Repeat the process for another night or two if necessary.

Make a double play. Or maybe a triple play. If you've got painful plantar warts and your feet are tired, achy—or both—this footbath is just what the doctor ordered for all-around relief. Simply fill a foot basin or similar-size tub with hot water, and mix in 1/4 cup each of sea salt and apple cider vinegar. Soak your sore dogs for 15 to 20 minutes, then use a pumice stone and soap to slough off the warts. Rinse with clear water, dry your feet, and rub on a rich skin cream.

SAFE & SOUND

Both plantar and "regular" warts are caused by the human papillomavirus (HPV). Keeping your immune system strong can help you dodge that bullet. But with plantar warts, your best defense is to always wear sandals or flip-flops when using a steam room, sauna, or public shower, or when you're walking around swimming pools, locker rooms, and other places where people are going barefoot. And don't pick at any wart! Not only will this spread the virus, but the original bump could grow back even bigger and nastier.

Here's a dandy idea! Have you found that the more life experience you gather, the more you appreciate the simple, down-home remedies your grandma swore by? I know I do! Well, if you have warts growing anywhere on your body and dandelions growing in your yard, you've got a golden chance to try one of those time-tested healers. Just pluck one of the yellow posies, squeeze the sap from the stem, and apply it to the unsightly growth. Perform this routine three times a day until the wart has vanished.

Polish it off. As kooky as this may sound, clear nail polish can remove warts. Here's the drill: Before you go to bed, gently wash and dry the wart. Paint it with the polish, let it dry, and then cover it with a bandage. Leave it on through the next day. That night, remove the bandage and apply another coat of polish right over the existing one. Let it dry, and put on a new bandage. Repeat the procedure every night until the wart has separated from your skin. It might flake off in sections or layers, or it may fall off all at once. The timing of the departure varies. The process could take anywhere from a few days to a few weeks, depending on the severity of the condition.

Can the calluses. If you use a cane, walker, or even crutches, then you're well acquainted with the calluses that develop in the palms of your hands from all the constant pressure and rubbing. To remove those painful, annoying bumps, simply mix 1 tablespoon of mashed avocado with 1 to 2 tablespoons of cornmeal to form a paste. Take the mixture in the palm of one hand, and rub both "paws" together, working the gritty stuff into the calluses and around your fingers. Repeat once or twice a week, and before you know it, your skin will be soft and smooth again.

Time Saver

Warts on your hands can be especially bothersome. Not only do you have to look at the unsightly things all the time, but as you go about your daily routine, you run the constant risk of breaking them open and spreading the virus. Well, here's a no-extra-time-needed solution to the problem: Once or twice a day, simply use castor oil instead of your regular hand cream. You'll get rid of the warts and soften your skin at the same time!

BYE-BYE BOIL PASTE

These painful, pus-filled bumps form under your skin when bacteria infect and inflame one or more hair follicles. This is one of the best boil remedies for adults because it combines the healing powers of vinegar and turmeric with the soothing, skin-nourishing properties of milk.

1 tsp. of apple cider vinegar   **1 tsp. of whole milk**
1 tsp. of turmeric

Mix all of the ingredients to form a paste, adding a little more of the liquid or powder as needed to get the right consistency. Gently apply the mixture to the boil, being careful not to break it—and whatever you do, don't squeeze it! Either action could spread the infection. Let the paste dry thoroughly, then rinse with lukewarm water, and pat dry. Repeat three or four times a day until you've banished the blasted bump.

Beat boils from the inside. Vinegar can go beyond healing your boils from the outside. It can also work internally to kill the bacteria that caused the painful problem in the first place. Here's just what the doctor ordered for that purpose: At least twice a day, drink a cup of hot water with 1 tablespoon of apple cider vinegar and 1 tablespoon of honey mixed into it. Meanwhile, be sure to drink plenty of water throughout the day to help flush the nasty germs out of your system. Also, until your body has become a boil-free zone, steer clear of any chocolate and soda pop, whether it's diet or otherwise. Both substances seem to worsen the infection.

If you have a cluster of boils that form a connected area of infection (a.k.a. a carbuncle), see your doctor. Also dial your doc if an individual boil appears on your face, worsens quickly or is extremely painful, is also accompanied by a fever, has not healed after two weeks of DIY treatment, or goes away but recurs in the same spot.

Taters trounce boils. Believe it or not, the common spud can draw out skin infections of all kinds—including the bacteria that cause boils. Just cut two squares of gauze that are big enough to cover your boil and the surrounding skin. Then wash and grate a firm, raw potato, and cover one piece of the gauze with some shavings. Top them off with the second piece of gauze, put the "sandwich" over your boil, and tape it in place. Keep the poultice on all day. At bedtime, remove it, wash the site gently, and apply a fresh version. Come morning, the boil could actually be gone. If it isn't, continue the routine until your skin is clear again.

> Factors like chronic diseases, nutritional deficiencies, and a weakened immune system increase the risk for boils in older adults.

Give cold sores the cold shoulder.

Between 50 and 80 percent of all adults in the US are infected with the herpes simplex virus (HSV-1) that causes cold sores (a.k.a. fever blisters). It can remain dormant in your system for years before any problem appears. In fact, first-time flare-ups occur most often in people over the age of 50. But there is an easy way to dry up the painful blisters and help keep them from spreading: Just dampen a cotton ball with apple cider vinegar, and hold it against the sore for three or four minutes. Then rinse the area with luke-warm water. Repeat the process once or twice a day until the sore is no more. **Note:** *If you develop eye symptoms of any kind during a cold sore outbreak, call your doctor immediately. Infections caused by the herpes simplex virus can lead to permanent vision loss if they're not treated promptly.*

Labor Saver

One of the most effective ways to heal cold sores is also one of the easiest: Simply dab them with aloe vera gel several times a day. You can use gel fresh from a plant or a high-quality commercial version. Either way, the potent compounds will not only dry up the blisters, but also heal any resulting skin lesions and help prevent future outbreaks by keeping HSV-1 under control.

ALL-PURPOSE POISON-PLANT SPRAY

Poison ivy, oak, and sumac can be especially irritating for aging skin. Beyond that, as your eyesight declines in youthful sharpness, it becomes much easier to brush up against—or even grab hold of—the vexatious vegetation without knowing it. When that happens, this powerful, but gentle formula will relieve the pain and itch lickety-split.

1/4 cup of aloe vera gel	**3 drops of peppermint essential oil**
1 tbsp. of apple cider vinegar	**3 drops of tea tree oil**
3 drops of lavender essential oil	**1/4 cup of distilled water**

Combine all of the ingredients in a 4-ounce mist-spray bottle, shake thoroughly, and spritz the affected skin. Repeat as needed, shaking the bottle again before each use. Store it at room temperature or in the refrigerator for even cooler comfort.

Dish up relief. If you're close to home when poison ivy "bites," you're in luck because one of the most effective remedies of all will be close at hand. Just beat a fast path to the kitchen, and wash your stricken skin with dishwashing liquid and water. The grease-cutting ingredients in the detergent will break down the urushiol, the oil in the plant that causes the trouble. As you'd expect, an extra-strength brand like Palmolive® Oxy™ works best, but whatever kind you have on hand will jump-start the healing process or—if you've acted in time—stop trouble in its tracks. If a rash does develop, wash the area once or twice a day with this kitchen standby until it clears up.

SAFE & SOUND When you're treating poison ivy, on yourself or anyone else, do not touch the area with your bare hands. Instead, wear disposable latex gloves, and throw them away immediately after you've applied any creams or lotions. Also (again wearing gloves), remove any clothes that may have come in contact with the plants. It's safest to discard these too, but if you can't, wash them several times (alone!) in hot water and dishwashing liquid.

Spray on a coat of armor. If you're headed for the great outdoors on a camping trip with your grandchildren or maybe to a vacation cabin in the woods, be sure to take along a can of spray antiperspirant that contains aluminum chlorhydrate. Then, before you venture into any spot that's likely to harbor poison ivy or its ilk, spritz all areas of exposed skin. The aluminum will deactivate the urushiol, and you should emerge unscathed from any encounters with the vile vegetation.

When it's too late for prevention... Wash the affected skin with soap and water, then spray on the antiperspirant. The sooner you act, the better, but even when oozing blisters have appeared, you'll feel immediate relief and your skin will start to heal. **Note:** *Simple deodorants will not work for this purpose because they lack the magic bullet. Arrid*™ *Extra Dry is one favorite among campers, but any spray antiperspirant that lists aluminum chlorhydrate as a key ingredient will do the job just fine.*

What's good for digestive troubles... is also a great comfort giver for poison ivy and other skin rashes. To be more specific, the alkaline properties in stomach meds like Pepto Bismol® and milk of magnesia can cool your inflamed skin and help control the itching. Simply soak a cotton ball or pad in the liquid, and smooth it over the affected skin.

Money Saver

If a poison ivy affliction extends over just a small area, here's a quick and free way to save the day: Lay strips of banana peel, inner side down, over the irritated spots. Chemicals in the peel will stop the itching, and the rash will begin to heal almost immediately.

Cool it! No rash is fun, but there's no worse kind than one that's itchy and burning. For quick relief, mix 1/3 cup of vinegar (either white or apple cider) with 1 cup of water, and pop the container into the freezer. Leave it there until the mixture is good and cold, but not frozen solid. Then soak a soft cloth in the blend, and hold it against your stricken skin. Boy, will that feel good!

BYE-BYE SUNBURN BLEND

As your skin grows more fragile, it becomes easier and faster for Ol' Sol to do a number on you. Whether the "attack" occurred when you were playing golf, gliding along in a boat, or doing lifeguard duty at your grandchildren's backyard wading pool, this DIY ointment can save the day. And it works just as well on any other kind of minor burn.

1/3 cup of aloe vera gel **1 tsp. of white or apple cider vinegar**
1 tsp. of lavender essential oil **Contents of 2 vitamin E capsules**

Mix all the ingredients together, and gently massage the mixture onto the affected areas. Leave it on for 15 minutes or so, then wash it off with cool water. Store any leftovers in a covered glass container in the refrigerator for future use. It'll last for up to a year.

Keep summertime skin relief on ice. There's almost no end to the warm-weather woes that can be especially irritating to aging skin. That's why it pays to keep a stash of these multitasking soothers on hand. To make them, fill a plastic squeeze bottle with 6 ounces of aloe vera gel and add 20 drops of lavender essential oil. Put the cap on the bottle, and shake thoroughly. Squirt the mixture into the compartments of a silicone ice cube tray, and use the flat edge of a knife to level the surface of each one. Then pop the tray into the freezer. When the cubes are frozen, transfer them into a plastic freezer container. You can use them as needed to treat poison ivy, insect bites or stings, or minor scratches and scrapes.

When you're having fun in the sun, skin mishaps could be the least of your worries. Older adults can be especially prone to potentially fatal heatstroke. So get medical attention immediately if you experience any of these symptoms: racing heart, rapid breathing, dizziness, altered behavior, nausea, vomiting, a throbbing headache, a body temperature of 102°F or higher, or unusually hot, dry skin.

Everything's coming up roses. Depending on the location and extent of your painful sunburn, you have two ways to rally flower power to the cause of healing. If the burn is on your face or confined to a small section of skin elsewhere, dilute 1 part rose-infused vinegar with 7 to 10 parts cool water. Then soak a soft cotton cloth in the mixture, wring out the excess moisture, and apply it as a compress every couple of hours, or as needed for relief, throughout the day. For a burn that covers a larger part of your body, add a cup or two of the infused vinegar to a tub of tepid water, and settle in for 20 to 30 minutes. Either way, you should feel blessed relief more quickly than you might think possible! **Note:** *Coming up on page 81, you'll find the easy DIY recipe for infused vinegars of all kinds.*

Yay for yogurt! This dietary superstar has won kudos in natural health and beauty circles far and wide. But its benefits go far beyond its edible nutrients. For example, fresh from the fridge, plain yogurt will help heal your sunburn—or any other minor burn—while cooling, nourishing, and moisturizing your skin at the same time. (Just make sure you use the real deal with active cultures!) To put it to work, just spread the yogurt over the affected area(s), let it sit for 15 to 20 minutes, then rinse it off with cool water. Repeat as often as you like throughout the day.

Labor Saver

One of the easiest ways to treat minor burns is to wrap them in cloths or bandages that you've saturated with white vinegar. Not only will it help quicken the healing process, but it will also prevent infection. In fact, hospitals throughout the world use this treatment even for severe burns because (are you ready for this?) the acetic acid in vinegar has been proven to kill more than 24 different forms of bacteria that are known to cause infections. WOW! Just remember that DIY measures should be used only on minor first-degree burns you get from a brief encounter with a barbecue grill, hot pan, or steam iron. For any burn that's more serious than that, or if it's on your face, get medical help ASAP!

YELLOW JACKET RELIEF COMPRESS

Unlike their milder-mannered honeybee cousins, yellow jackets are mean, short-tempered, and highly protective of their nests. What's more, also unlike bees, which sting once and then die, these villains can shove their smooth weapons into you again and again—and given half a chance, they will. When they do, this cooling compress can relieve the heat, burning, and itching.

1/4 cup of white vinegar

2 drops of eucalyptus essential oil

2 drops of lavender essential oil

1/4 cup of cold water

Mix all the ingredients together in a bowl. Depending on the number and location of the stings, dip either a cotton ball or a soft, clean cotton cloth into the solution, and press it firmly onto the afflicted site(s). Repeat as needed until the discomfort subsides.

Plan on plantain. If you still think of plantain as nothing but a pesky weed, think again. It's actually a medicinal powerhouse that pulls out toxins from bug bites and stings, soothes sunburn, and clears up skin issues like eczema and dandruff. But that's not all! Thanks to its big supply of an anti-inflammatory phytochemical called allantoin, plantain also kills germs, speeds wound healing, and stimulates growth for new skin cells. One of the best ways to use it on bites and stings is to saturate a cotton ball with a plantain-vinegar tincture and apply it to the "crime" scene.

ANTI-AGING MATTERS

Q: In our retirement community, fire ants seem to be *everywhere*! I know their stings can be dangerous for older folks. Is there a DIY remedy I can make and keep on hand?

A: Of course! Put 25 uncoated aspirins in a bottle of 91% rubbing alcohol, and shake well. Let it sit for a few hours, shaking occasionally until the aspirins dissolve. Shake again before each use, and wipe the solution generously onto the bites using a cotton pad. Then to play it safe, if you get more than a few bites, hightail it to the closest ER or urgent care clinic!

How sweet it is! Sweet basil is renowned for its internal healing powers. But it's also a heavy hitter when it comes to treating stings and bites from mosquitoes and other multi-legged marauders. Simply crush some fresh leaves and rub them on the bitten area. Repeat as needed until the swelling and pain diminish.

Milk this one for all it's worth. This bite remedy is as old as the hills, but potent and gentle enough to use on extra-fragile elderly skin. Just mix equal parts of whole milk and water, then apply the mixture to your skin using a cotton ball. Let it sit for a couple of minutes, then wash with warm soapy water and pat dry. Repeat as needed. Only whole milk will work. It's the fat and protein that reduce inflammation, help prevent infection, and speed overall healing.

To quickly reduce the swelling, heat, and pain of any bug bite or sting, simply rub a little coconut oil onto the site.

Gotta love that lavender! Here's another senior-friendly fixer for stings and bites: Mix about 22 drops of lavender essential oil per tablespoon of sweet almond oil in a dark blue or amber glass bottle. When you rub the blend onto a bite or sting, you'll feel instant relief and your skin will get a little anti-aging kick to boot.

Ice is nice. When you need a fast first response for any kind of bite or sting, reach into the freezer and grab some ice. Then rub it back and forth over the stricken spot. It will immediately reduce the pain and itching while your body's natural immune response gets to work to reduce the inflammation and swelling.

Time Saver

When a bee plants its stinger in your unsuspecting skin, there's no time to waste. You need to get the buzzer's weapon out pronto. And here's a quick and easy way to do it: Just grab a bar of soap and rub it over the area. The "needle" should slide right out.

DISINFECTING WOUND WASH

Dermatologists and surgeons tell us that one of the best wound disinfectants is also one of the oldest—white vinegar. Here's a way to put it and a few key partners to work on your later-life "owies."

- **2 cups of distilled water**
- **1 tbsp. of white vinegar**
- **1–2 tsp. of extra virgin coconut oil**
- **3–5 drops of lavender essential oil**
- **3–5 drops of tea tree essential oil**
- **1–3 cups of warm water**

Mix the distilled water and vinegar in a bowl and saturate a cotton ball or pad in the solution. Wipe away any dirt and debris, moving from the center of the wound outward. Next, mix the oils in the warm water, and wipe the wound again. Let it dry, then apply a natural antiseptic, and cover it with a nonstick bandage.

Don't touch the peroxide! Contrary to what you probably learned in your younger days, you should never clean a cut with hydrogen peroxide—or rubbing alcohol either. We now know that both of these classic cleansers can actually damage healthy tissue surrounding the wound and delay the healing process. Also, don't think of applying a topical medication like iodine, Mercurochrome, or Merthiolate to fight germs. These and other ultra-strong antibiotics can interfere with your body's natural healing mechanisms. The older you get, it's crucial to use DIY remedies that strengthen your inner workings while relieving your discomfort.

EARLY BIRD SPECIALS

If the last first-aid class you took was longer ago than you care to remember, it might be time to take a refresher course. Many local fire departments, Red Cross chapters, and community colleges offer free or low-cost training in CPR and basic first aid—including courses that are specifically geared toward the needs of older adults. To find classes near you, just do a search for "first-aid classes [name of your town]." Or to simply brush up on your skills and learn about the latest supplies and recommended techniques, check out www.firstaidforfree.com.

Keep it covered. Another first-aid "truism" that's been debunked is the idea that you should keep a cut dry and let air get to it so that a scab can form. Research now shows that wounds that are kept moist and scab-free heal more efficiently, and are less likely to leave scars, than those that are kept dry.

Keep it clean. Every few days, clean the wound with a mild saline solution (2 teaspoons of salt per quart of boiling water, cooled to room temperature) or a rinse made from 1 part calendula vinegar tincture to 10 parts water.

Call on some timely teamwork. Honey and aloe vera gel have well-earned reputations as healing and senior-friendly superstars. And their territory includes cuts, scrapes, and scratches of all kinds. Just blend equal parts of the duo and spread the mixture across the cleaned wound. Refrigerate the leftovers in a lidded glass jar so you'll always have it close at hand.

Cranberries can do what!?
Heal cuts, that's what. It's just another old-time kitchen-counter cure that's well worth tucking into your mental first-aid manual—and your freezer. All you need to do is blend or chop 1/4 cup or so of cranberries (either fresh or frozen), apply the mash to the cut, and cover it with a bandage. Change the dressing every few hours until the wound has healed. To make sure that healing help is always close at hand, simply keep a stash of crushed cranberries in your freezer.

Money Saver

Attention, tea drinkers! Studies have shown that tannins and other substances in tea leaves accelerate the wound-healing process. So when you gash yourself, simply apply a moist tea bag to the wound. Either a black or green version will work just fine.

Avocados get an A+ for wound care. And they can be especially convenient when you cut yourself while you're slicing an avocado for guacamole or use in a salad. Just break off a little piece of the flesh and apply it to the cut. The fruit has antibiotic properties that will get right to work on healing the wound. Plus, the soft, mellow pulp will help ease the pain.

RING-OFF RINGWORM TONIC

Ringworm is caused by three different types of fungi. They tend to attack elderly folks and those with weaker immune systems more often and with greater severity. And here's the clincher: These foul fungi have become resistant to many antifungal medications. For that reason, your best treatment options may be down-home remedies like this one.

1 tbsp. of fresh-squeezed lemon juice	1/2 tsp. of cinnamon
1 tsp. of apple cider vinegar	Lukewarm water
1 tsp. of honey	

Mix the lemon juice, vinegar, honey, and cinnamon in a glass of lukewarm water, and drink it first thing each morning for as long as the symptoms persist. This will help clear up your current miseries, and ramp up your body's immune defenses against any future ringworm outbreaks, as well as eczema, acne, and other skin disorders.

Ring(worm) around the head. If on your scalp, ringworm can be downright agonizing. This two-step routine can make short work of the sores. First, soak a gauze pad in a solution made from 1 teaspoon of salt dissolved in 2 cups of distilled water, and put that on your (or the victim's) head for about half an hour. The next day, repeat the process using a gauze pad soaked in a solution made from 1 part white vinegar mixed with 4 parts distilled water. Alternate these compresses—salt one day, vinegar the next. In a week or so, the foul fungi should be gone.

SAFE & SOUND
Ringworm is contagious, so the older you are and the weaker your immune system is, the more likely you are to pick up the fungus. It is spread not only by direct contact with anyone who has an active outbreak, but also through unwashed clothing and surfaces in showers, swimming-pool decks, saunas, and similar damp environments. Bottom line: Keep your feet covered in moist public areas, and be careful what you touch!

Rub-a-dub-dub—relief's in the tub. When ringworm has broken out on places other than your scalp, soak for 20 to 30 minutes each day in a warm bath laced with a tablespoon or two of extra virgin coconut oil. It contains caprylic acid, which is a strong antifungal agent, but it's gentle enough for daily use on aging skin. Within just a few days, you should start to see favorable results. **Note:** *Both sea salt and vinegar can also deal a death blow to ringworm fungi, but they're too drying to use as bath ingredients every day.*

Ax athlete's foot. Contrary to the name, you don't need to be a gung-ho athlete, or even a casual walker with your grandchildren, to suffer from the nasty fungus (*Tinea pedis*) that seems to cause so much misery. As in the case of many ills, this one can take a direct aim at seniors, who tend to have more weakened immune systems, suffer from diabetes, or routinely use antibiotics. The good news is that all foul fungi hate acids, which makes this ultra-simple soak one of the best remedies of all. Simply fill a basin with equal parts of vinegar and warm water, soak your tootsies for 10 minutes, then dry the areas between your toes. Repeat the process once a day, until your foot woes have been booted out. **Note:** *If you have even mild diabetes, don't soak your feet in anything without your doctor's okay!*

Time Saver

To treat isolated ringworm lesions on your body, simply apply extra virgin coconut oil or aloe vera gel to the spots three or four times a day. Both healers are deadly to the ringworm and nourishing to delicate aging skin (or any other kind, for that matter!).

Bid a spicy farewell to athlete's foot. Twice a day, add 2 tablespoons of fresh, chopped ginger to 1 cup of boiling water, and simmer for 20 minutes. Strain, let the tea cool to a comfortable temperature, and wipe it onto your freshly washed feet. The ginger will demolish the fungus and give your tootsies an aroma that'll remind you of old-fashioned gingerbread cookies, just like the ones your mama—or maybe your grandma—used to bake. **Note:** *As in the case of a foot soak, if you have diabetes, check with your doctor before using this remedy.*

BATH-TIME BLEND FOR PSORIASIS & ECZEMA

Both psoriasis and eczema are more prevalent in older adults than in their younger peers. Also, like other topical ailments, they cause greater discomfort as your skin becomes more sensitive. If either condition covers a large part of your body, you'll love this formula.

1 tsp. of Solubol dispersant*	**1 cup of bentonite clay**
1/4 tsp. of frankincense essential oil	**1/2 cup of apple cider vinegar**

Mix the Solubol and frankincense in a small bowl, and set it aside. Fill your bathtub with (comfortably) hot water, and pour in the clay. Add the vinegar, followed by the Solubol-oil mixture, and swirl the water around to disperse all the ingredients. Then settle in and soak for 20 to 30 minutes. Repeat as needed to ease the pain and itching.
Available from essential oils suppliers.

Tailor the treatment to the real estate. When a mild psoriasis or eczema outbreak occurs in one or two isolated spots, mix bentonite clay with enough apple cider vinegar to make a paste. Apply it to the lesions, leave it on for 20 to 30 minutes, then wash it off. Repeat as needed until you feel relief. **Note:** *This remedy also makes quick work of minor burns, cuts, and insect bites.*

Money Saver

When psoriasis breaks out on your scalp, you could use a commercial product to heal the irritation. But why spend your retirement cash on that stuff when apple cider vinegar can do the job for pennies? A few times a week, put some vinegar on your head, let it dry, then rinse it off. If your scalp is bleeding or cracked, use extra virgin coconut oil instead. You'll need to rinse a little more thoroughly, but it won't burn your opened skin, as vinegar would.

A mouthful of help for your head. If you suffer from an itchy or irritated scalp as a result of eczema or dermatitis, antiseptic mouthwash can deliver quick relief. Just massage a tablespoon or so of it into your scalp, then rinse it off thoroughly with clear water. You'll have a soothed scalp instantly!

Cucumber juice conquers eczema. To ditch the painful itch, dab some juice onto your skin once or twice a day using a cotton pad. No need to rinse. To make cucumber juice, wash and peel a couple of cukes, chop 'em up, and puree the pieces in a blender with a cup or so of water. Strain out the pulp, and store the liquid in a covered container in the refrigerator.

Feel your oats. An oatmeal bath is exactly what the dermatologist ordered for any skin condition under the sun, including eczema, psoriasis, shingles, poison-plant rashes, insect bites, and wind- and sunburn. You can buy colloidal oatmeal that is especially formulated to dissolve in bathwater so it won't clog up the pipes as it flows down the drain. But if you don't have any on hand, simply stuff a cotton drawstring bag or a panty hose leg with a cup or two of uncooked oatmeal. Toss it in the tub as you run cool to lukewarm water, then settle in and relax for 15 to 20 minutes. To intensify this feel-good power, let yourself air-dry when you're finished, if possible. **Note:** *Do not use hot water in this or any other skin-soothing bath. It'll dry out your birthday suit and make your affliction even worse!*

Q: Is it true that following a particular diet can lessen the effects of psoriasis?

A: No. There is no confirmed connection between specific foods and the severity, frequency, or duration of flare-ups for people of any age. While food can play a role in psoriasis, sensitivities are a highly individual matter. What sets off major eruptions in one person may pose no trouble at all for another. Your best bet: Keep track of what you eat, and if you find that something bothers you, don't eat it again. If you must avoid particular foods that are major sources of key nutrients (for example, iron-rich red meat, which can cause flare-ups), ask your doctor about supplements.

ANTI-AGING MATTERS

TRIPLE-THREAT SHINGLES RELIEF BLEND

If you had chicken pox as a kid, your body still harbors the herpes zoster virus that caused it, and it could come back to haunt you in the form of shingles, if it hasn't already. Either way, this versatile formula can provide much-needed relief from the agonizing blisters.

1 tsp. of Solubol dispersant

10 drops of lavender essential oil

7 drops of peppermint essential oil

5 drops of clove essential oil

1 cup of apple cider vinegar

Mix the Solubol and oils, then combine the mixture with the vinegar. For immediate use, pour the entire amount into a warm bath and soak for 20 to 40 minutes. Store the formula in a dark blue or amber glass bottle, and then spray or dab it onto your skin as needed. Multiply the ingredients as desired—the potion will keep for at least a year.

Clean 'em up. Few skin disorders are more painful than shingles blisters, except infected shingles blisters. To keep that nightmare at bay, wash the affected areas twice a day with soap and water. Resist the urge to cover the trouble spots with bandages; that'll lengthen the healing period. Then just hang in there. The rash generally runs its course in three weeks or so.

Hang loose. Shingles blisters can be so sensitive that the pressure from even moderately heavy clothing can be all but unbearable. So do your skin a favor: Make it a habit to wear light, loose-fitting clothing, even if that means cranking up the thermostat higher than you normally would.

HELP WANTED?

If you're over 50, there's a good chance that nerve damage caused by the shingles virus will cause lingering pain called postherpetic neuralgia. So at the first sign of blisters, see your doctor immediately. You may need help for the pain. Also, certain drugs can shorten the duration of attacks, if you start them within 24 hours after the blisters appear.

Hit high C with rose hips. And stay hydrated, too! When you're battling shingles, it's important to keep your body well hydrated and maintain a steady intake of vitamin C to strengthen your immune system. This delicious tea can help on both counts. To make it, add 3 to 4 tablespoons of dried rose hips (available from herb suppliers) to 1 quart of boiling water. Let it steep for at least 15 minutes, then strain the liquid into a fresh container. Drink the brew throughout the day, either cold or reheated.

Fight fire with fire. As unlikely as this may sound, capsaicin, the chemical that gives hot peppers their firepower, also blocks pain signals. And that makes cayenne pepper a crucial part of your anti-shingles arsenal. It is one key ingredient in many OTC ointments, and a snap to make your own supply. Start by mixing 1 teaspoon of cayenne pepper into 1/4 cup of skin cream or lotion. Then gently dab it onto the skin around the blisters. Don't put it on the blisters. The purpose is not to heal them, but rather to ease your overall pain. It'll do a great job on that score!

> Simply bathing or shampooing with pine tar soap can greatly relieve the discomfort of psoriasis and eczema.

Don't spread the "wealth." Shingles blisters can cause chicken pox in folks who haven't had it. So don't let anyone near the blisters, and if you touch them, wash your hands thoroughly with hot, soapy water. For good measure, wear disposable latex gloves when you apply any topical treatment.

Labor Saver

Two of the easiest shingles soothers of all are as close as your pantry. What are they? Baking soda and cornstarch. Grab whichever one is within easiest reach, and pour some into a bowl. Mix your staple of choice with enough water to make a paste, and apply it to the blisters. Wait 10 to 15 minutes, then gently rinse the mixture off. Repeat this process several times a day, as needed, to relieve the pain and itching.

ANTI-AGING HERBAL SUPERSTARS

For centuries, savvy folks have been relying on herbs to cure their illnesses, and enhance their overall health and good looks. Some of these ancient plants contain rich loads of compounds that can particularly benefit older adults. An easy way to keep this plant power at your beck and call is to use herbs in vinegar tinctures or infused vinegars (more on that score in Chapter 5). Here's a rundown of some of the key players on the senior circuit:

CHAMOMILE reduces pain and inflammation in the digestive tract and relaxes both the body and nerves.

GARLIC kills bacteria, clears lung congestion, lowers blood sugar, lowers high cholesterol levels, boosts circulation, and acts as an antihistamine.

GINGER can help lower blood pressure, fights inflammation, and is especially effective at reducing arthritis pain.

LAVENDER enhances the quality of sleep; relieves stress, anxiety, and depression; and improves mental clarity and focus.

MARJORAM and **OREGANO** relieve aching joints and muscles.

PARSLEY aids digestion, controls blood pressure, keeps your immune system strong, helps maintain strong bones, relaxes stiff muscles, and eases joint pain.

PEPPERMINT energizes mind and body and safely relieves upset stomachs.

ROSEMARY stimulates memory, cognition, and concentration; boosts energy; and helps lift your spirits.

SAGE restores vitality and strength and (research suggests) can alleviate early symptoms of Alzheimer's disease.

ST. JOHN'S WORT promotes sound sleep and helps relieve mild depression and anxiety as effectively as many drugs—without nasty side effects.

THYME detoxifies the liver, boosts the immune system, and fights fatigue.

Caution: *If you're on medication of any kind (even aspirin); you suffer from high blood pressure, diabetes, or any other chronic condition; or you're pregnant or think that you might be pregnant, check with your doctor before you dose yourself with these or any other herbs.*

CHAPTER 4

GREAT HEALTH

In earlier chapters, we focused on conquering specific physical woes that can befall older adults. Now, we're going to zero in on ways you can help safeguard your overall health as the years go by. You may even be able to improve the picture because chances are you have the opportunity to get your full forty winks each night, prepare healthier meals, or simply de-stress by slowing down enough to smell the roses.

As usual, vinegar marches at the front of this anti-aging parade. And one of the most versatile health givers of all is hot-pepper vinegar. It can help you lose or maintain weight; reduce inflammation; and fend off heart disease, diabetes, and other chronic conditions. There are no precise dosages. Simply add it to your menu in any way you like. But never take it straight, because it can give your mouth and tongue a nasty burn. To find your comfort level, shake a drop or two of the fiery fluid onto a forkful of food.

Wash 12 to 15 hot peppers (any kind you fancy) and pierce them with a needle. Pack them with two sprigs of fresh parsley into a sterilized 8- to 10-ounce glass bottle or jar. Fill the container with enough white wine vinegar to cover the contents completely, and cover it with a tight-fitting lid. Let it steep for seven days at room temperature. Then refrigerate and use it to your heart's (and tummy's) content. Whenever you use some of your spicy condiment, replace it with enough fresh vinegar to completely cover the peppers and parsley. It should keep for up to four months.

DEEP SLEEP TINCTURE

One key to staying healthy and vibrant well into your golden years is to get your full share of high-quality sleep. If that's getting harder to do as you grow older, then this blend can help.

3 tbsp. of dried catnip

3 tbsp. of dried passionflower

3 tbsp. of dried skullcap

3 tbsp. of dried valerian root

Apple cider vinegar

Combine the herbs in a 16-ounce glass jar to within about 1 inch of the top, then pour in enough vinegar to cover the contents. Attach the lid, and shake the jar. Set it in a cool, dark place for four to six weeks, shaking it occasionally. Strain the tincture into 4-ounce dark blue or amber dropper-top bottles (available from many essential oil suppliers), and store them in a cool, dark place. The potion will retain full potency for about a year.

Dosing your Deep Sleep Tincture. If you have trouble falling asleep at night, take 2 or 3 dropperfuls about an hour before you plan to hit the hay. If you're still rarin' to go at bedtime, take another dropperful or two. Either put the tincture directly on your tongue, or mix it with a small glass of water—the smaller, the better to avoid middle-of-the-night bathroom visits! If you tend to wake up during the night, keep the bottle on your bedside table so you can give yourself a quick booster "shot." You'll be back in dreamland before you know it!

SAFE & SOUND

Too much sleep can be as harmful to your health as too little. If you're getting more than seven to nine hours a night—the amount needed by the average adult, including seniors—see your doctor to determine the cause of the problem. It could just be a side effect of a medication you're taking, or it may indicate an underlying health condition. Although, maybe you're simply bored and need to put more "oomph" into your daily routine!

Reach for a sleepy-time bath blend. Nothing whispers "Shhh—time for bed" like a soak in this formula. Not only will it relax you all over, but it also softens and soothes aging skin. To make it, mix 1/4 cup each of baking soda and Epsom salts in a container. Pour the blend into the tub as warm water flows from the tap. Add 1 to 2 cups of lavender-infused vinegar, and swirl the water around to disperse. Settle in and soak for 15 minutes or so. Then rinse off, pat dry, rub in a moisturizing body cream, and toddle off to bed. You'll sleep like a baby!

> Studies show that lack of sleep increases cravings for junk food and alters your metabolism in ways that contribute to weight gain.

Good food does bad things at bedtime. Some of the healthiest things you can put in your mouth can disrupt your sleep at night, especially as you get older. For example, celery, ginger, and parsley are natural diuretics, which can translate into middle-of-the-night bathroom runs. Citrus fruits and juices increase your stomach's acidity, and that could jolt you awake with heartburn pain. The same goes for any spicy, greasy, or fried foods. So avoid all of these wake-up triggers for several hours before bedtime.

Snack wisely and sleep well. Melatonin supplements are a popular sleep aid, but seniors beware: It can interact with hundreds of drugs, including blood thinners and diabetes meds. So instead, eat a bedtime snack of raspberries or tart cherries. These all-around, anti-aging superstars also happen to be two of the very few natural sources of melatonin.

Time Saver

This maneuver takes only seconds, but it can give a big boost to your sleep quality: On laundry day, put some dried lavender into a small, zippered pillowcase or tightly closed cheesecloth bag, and toss it into the dryer with your bed linens. They'll emerge with a delicate aroma that should keep you cuttin' Zzz's all night long.

BERRY-BANANA WEIGHT-LOSS BLAST

Any vinegar-enhanced drink can help you shed unwanted pounds. But the older you get, the more important it becomes to include ingredients that not only help you slim down, but also help you dodge conditions that can haunt you as the years go by. This one not only serves up heaping helpings of anti-aging antioxidants but also ramps up your energy and mental clarity.

2 medium bananas, peeled and frozen

1 cup of blueberries

1 cup of hulled strawberries*

1 tbsp. of apple cider vinegar

2 cups of water

1 cup of ice

Put all the ingredients in a blender and whirl 'em on high speed until they're thoroughly combined and frothy. Toss back half of the mixture, and refrigerate the rest for later, or share it with a fellow weight-losing warrior and drink a toast to your vanishing baggage! *Fresh or frozen*

Grab an apple. Better yet, make it two. Over the years, study after study has shown that eating one or two of Eve's favorite fruits every day increases your body's production of both brown fat and skeletal muscle—in the process, ramping up your calorie-burning power and helping to stabilize your blood sugar levels. The secret to success here is to keep the peels intact. That's because the key active ingredient is ursolic acid, a compound that's abundant in apple skins.

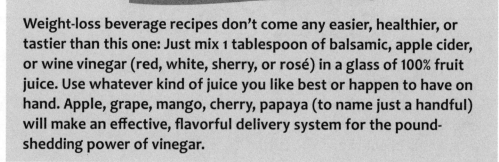

Labor Saver

Weight-loss beverage recipes don't come any easier, healthier, or tastier than this one: Just mix 1 tablespoon of balsamic, apple cider, or wine vinegar (red, white, sherry, or rosé) in a glass of 100% fruit juice. Use whatever kind of juice you like best or happen to have on hand. Apple, grape, mango, cherry, papaya (to name just a handful) will make an effective, flavorful delivery system for the pound-shedding power of vinegar.

Chill out and earn some brownie points. Brown adipose tissue (a.k.a. brown fat) is metabolically active "good" fat that burns calories, maintains your body temperature, and may play a role in preventing diabetes and obesity. We're all born with it, but it tends to become inactive, and can even be lost, as we age. And that can result in, or contribute to, a stubborn middle-age "fat attack." The good news is that activating your brown fat can actually help you shed pounds or maintain a healthy weight as the years go by. The most effective way to ramp up the action is simply to spend at least two hours a day at a slightly less-than-comfortable temperature. Even when you're just a tad chilly, your tissues activate brown fat as a way to generate heat, which burns calories in the process.

Let vinegar help boost your brown fat supply. While apple skins are a major source of ursolic acid, it's also found in cranberries, holy basil (*Ocimum sanctum*), thyme, oregano, peppermint, and lavender. These edibles all make delicious and anti-aging ingredients in everyday cooking, but they're also great to use for infusing in vinegar. So make a batch, or a bunch of batches, following the easy process on page 81. Then use the finished product as more fuel for your calorie-burning fire.

Some like it hot. If you're one of those folks hankering to lose weight or maintain your slim and youthful figure, this tip is for you: Simply consuming hot-pepper vinegar helps your efforts in a big way. For one thing, it ramps up your metabolic rate, so you burn calories more quickly. Plus, 1/5 ounce of the stuff can burn at least 76 more calories than it contains!

Q: Now that I'm 50, I'm developing belly fat, which I know can be dangerous. Can balsamic vinegar help get rid of it?

A: Yep! It activates genes that cause your body to distribute fat more evenly, rather than storing it at your waist. But that's not the only feat balsamic vinegar can perform. Thanks to the Trebbiano and Lambrusco grapes that it's made from, it's packed with compounds that reduce triglyceride and total cholesterol levels, fight cancer, strengthen immunity, and destroy the free radicals that cause premature aging and hardening of the arteries. A good amount to take is 5 teaspoons a day, which has been found to increase insulin sensitivity in diabetics.

ANTI-AGING MATTERS

BERRY FINE MOCKTAIL MIXER

Many folks who are trying to drink less find that it's not so much the booze they miss. Rather, it's the idea of cocktails. Enter the vinegar shrub to fill the void.

1 1/2 cups of raspberries   **3/4 cup of balsamic vinegar**
1 1/2 cups of white sugar (or to taste)   **3/4 cup of red wine vinegar**

Put the berries in a bowl, add the sugar, and mix to coat the fruit. Cover, and let it sit at room temperature for an hour. Mash up the berries, cover, and wait until most of the juices have been released (about one hour). Mash the fruit again, and let it sit, covered, at room temperature for 24 hours. Stir in the vinegar, cover again, and then wait another seven days, stirring daily. Strain the mixture into a sterilized glass bottle, cap it tightly, and store it in the refrigerator for up to three weeks.

Mocktail mixology 101. Here's one example of a booze-free beverage that would be right at home at the fanciest cocktail party in town: Put three Key limes (quartered) and eight fresh mint leaves in a cocktail shaker, and muddle them. Add 1 ounce of raspberry shrub and ice, and shake well. Strain into a tall ice-filled glass, and top with ginger ale. Or for a simpler refresher, stir an ounce or so of shrub into sparkling water, lemonade, or ginger ale to cool you down on even the hottest day.

HELP WANTED? It's never easy to conquer a serious drinking problem, and the older you get, the harder it becomes. That's why Alcoholics Anonymous has launched a whole new division dedicated to seniors and has published a brochure titled A.A. for the Older Alcoholic—Never Too Late. It profiles eight folks who kicked the habit around the age of 60 or older. You can read the large-print pdf version on the A.A. website at www.aa.org/assets/en_US/p-22_AAfortheOlderAA.pdf.

To kick the smoking habit, wake up and smell the pepper.
To be specific, inhale the aroma of black pepper (*Piper nigrum*) essential oil. Extensive studies on longtime smokers who were trying to quit have found it to be the closest thing there is to a magic bullet. And the older you are when you launch your boot-the-butts campaign, the more ammunition you need to have in your arsenal. To use it, you can either sniff the oil directly from its bottle, put a few drops on a tissue or cotton ball and smell that, or put the oil in a diffuser and send the vapors wafting through your home. Your cigarette-craving gremlins won't stand a chance!

Pepper has heroic side effects, too. One reason that so many wannabe quitters go right back to smoking is the load of all the nasty collateral damage that nearly always comes with the effort to give up the habit. Well, it turns out that in addition to dampening your desire to light up, inhaling black pepper oil can alleviate common withdrawal symptoms such as anxiety, depression, hostility, impatience, reduced heart rate, inability to concentrate and, yes, even weight gain.

Discover the power of positive addiction. It's a fact that all long-standing habits become harder to kick as the years go by. What's more, mental health pros tell us that for folks with obsessive personalities, it's essentially impossible to shed one fixation without latching on to another. If that description seems to fit you, it could be a blessing in disguise because it gives you a chance to replace your unwanted compulsion with a healthy pastime that can add sparkle to your golden years. So go ahead and plunge into a new hobby, return to one you abandoned long ago, or go back to school and study a subject that fascinates you—the possibilities are virtually endless!

Time Saver

Here's one of the best anti-aging time savers around: Pour black pepper essential oil, or any other type, into a special kind of oil-diffusing pendant necklace (available from many essential oil retailers). Then wear it as you go about your daily routine. You'll get a steady flow of the health-giving vapors without even lifting a finger.

A GINGER-PEACHY STRESS BUSTER

For many, the retirement years are the most stressful of all because they can bring a whole new set of strains, like unexpected financial concerns or the loss of loved ones. And you don't bounce back as quickly at 65 as you did at 25. This spicy drink is a tasty way to help speed up the process.

1 medium peach, pitted

2 tsp. of apple cider vinegar

2 tsp. of honey

1/2 tsp. of grated fresh ginger

1/2 tsp. of nutmeg

1/2 cup of crushed ice

1 cup of chamomile tea, cooled

Put the ingredients in a blender, and whirl on high until the mixture is frothy. Drink half of it immediately and store the rest, tightly covered, at room temperature for up to four hours. Or share it with a pal or two and drink to smooth sailing.

Track your power surges. Our energy levels can be lower at some times of the day than others, and the lower your energy level is, the more susceptible you are to stress. Here's how to put yourself on a more even keel: For three or four days, every two to three hours, write down whether your energy level feels high, moderately high, moderately low, or low. You should see a pattern emerge that will tell you when to make important decisions, run errands, or schedule appointments—and when to take a nap. This technique works especially well for folks over 60, who tend not to have the energy reserves they once had.

EARLY BIRD SPECIALS

Not only is yoga a top-tier way to sidestep stress and anxiety, but its physical benefits are so powerful that some health insurance companies reimburse the cost of classes for older adults. Many community colleges, senior centers, and YMCAs offer free or low-cost beginner classes for folks in their 50s, 60s, 70s—and beyond. To find a class near you, just search for "yoga classes for seniors [name of your town]."

Take it in stride. For anyone of any age, regular exercise is a renowned stress reliever. But the older you get, the more effective it is. That's because it can get your blood circulating more efficiently, improve your mobility and muscle strength, and give a big boost to your mental cognition and memory. What's more, exercise increases your energy reserves. So the more you move, the younger and more vigorous you'll feel, and the better able you'll be to cope with stress and its kissin' cousin, anxiety. The simple Rx for quick relief: When you're feeling stressed, worried, or not yourself, take a brisk 10-minute walk. It doesn't have to be at a power-walking pace; just move along as though you were running late for an appointment—but don't tense up and charge all-out as if you really were late!

Sit up straight! Yes, your parents, grandparents, and teachers were right on the mark when they issued that command. Now, as adults, we all know that habitual slouching, whether you are sitting or standing, can lead to poor posture and back pain. But according to numerous scientific studies, it can also increase your production of the stress hormone cortisol, hinder mental cognition and recall ability, lower self-esteem, reduce your energy reserves, encourage negative thinking, and dampen your mood. The bottom line is, by simply summoning your inner drill sergeant on a regular basis, you can start feeling calmer, happier, healthier, more alert, and generally younger in body, mind, and spirit.

Money Saver

A major benefit of being retired or pursuing a second-prime career at home gives you an easy way to stop stress attacks before they start, without resorting to medications or costly counseling sessions. What is it? The ability to stay in your cozy, comfy abode when younger workers must confront rush-hour traffic, dangerous road conditions, or temperatures that are unusually frigid or sweltering. Likewise, you can dodge the stress-raising hassle of weekend crowds by running errands; visiting entertainment venues; and enjoying sports like bowling, golf, or tennis on weekdays, when more folks are otherwise occupied.

SPRITZ AND BE CALM BLEND

When stress or anxiety has you all but climbing the walls, this quick, easy-does-it mixture can put you back on the ground fast. Best of all, you can tuck it into your purse or pocket and take it wherever you go, so you'll always have calming relief at your fingertips.

1 tsp. of apple cider or white wine vinegar

10 drops of chamomile essential oil

10 drops of clary sage essential oil

10 drops of lavender essential oil

3 1/2 oz. of distilled water

Add all the ingredients to a 4-ounce dark blue or amber glass spray bottle and shake it until everything is combined. Then whenever you're feeling stressed, anxious, or tense, spritz the mixture liberally on your skin, being sure to shake the bottle vigorously before each use.

Milky oats oust anxiety. Just buy some dried milky oats in bulk at a health-food store, or order them from a reputable online herb supplier. Make a tincture following the directions on page 41. Then three times a day, take 1 to 2 teaspoons, straight or in water, until your anxiety and nervous tension are under control.

Accept what happens... And stay younger longer! If you've fallen into the all-too-common habit of joining the crowd at the office watercooler, or the golf club's 19th hole, to complain about everything from traffic congestion to poor service in a restaurant, do yourself an anti-aging favor: Stop that complaining cold turkey! There's extensive scientific evidence that's shown chronic complaining can lead to elevated levels of stress and anxiety—which in turn can put you on the high road to dementia.

SAFE & SOUND Physical signs of anxiety often include chest pressure, tightness or heaviness in the throat, headaches, and shortness of breath. But if you experience chest discomfort and/or shortness of breath accompanied by nausea or sweating, you may be having a heart attack—so call 911 pronto!

Flaxseed foils hot flashes. Hot flashes, night sweats, and other menopausal annoyances are producers of stress and anxiety. To make this powerful tea, stir 2 tablespoons of finely ground flaxseed into 1 cup of just-boiled water. Let it cool to a drinking temperature, and add 2 tablespoons of apple cider vinegar. Enjoy a cup three times a day to help stabilize the churning hormones causing discomfort.

Quell your inner fire. Sensitivities to food vary, but many women find that excess sugar, alcohol, caffeine, dairy products, meat, and spicy foods of all kinds can bring on hot flashes and night sweats. If your diet is high in any of those triggers, cut back on your intake and see if it doesn't result in cooler internal conditions.

> Take your post-menopausal calcium supplements with vinegar diluted in water so your body can assimilate the mineral more quickly.

Water, water everywhere. At least it should be everywhere when you're going through menopause. In addition to all the other benefits of staying properly hydrated, drinking plenty of water decreases bloating and also helps replace vital fluids lost during hot flashes and night sweats.

Go for the gold. During menopause, carrot juice can be a star player on your health-care team. Drinking an 8-ounce glass of this golden treasure several times a week not only prevents water retention but also strengthens your immune system at a time when you're becoming more vulnerable to a number of chronic conditions, including cardiovascular disease and breast cancer.

Labor Saver

Here's an easy and tasty way to reduce the incidence and intensity of hot flashes and night sweats: Mix 1 to 2 tablespoons of apple cider vinegar in a glass of 100% fruit or vegetable juice. Drink a serving two times a day to help ease your menopausal miseries.

LIGHTEN-UP BATH-TIME RECIPE

Whenever you're feeling cranky or down in the dumps, or maybe wallowing in one of those all-too-common funks leading up to menopause, a good soak in this blend can save the day. It'll lift your mood while relaxing your edgy, buzzing nerves—guaranteed!

1 tsp. of Solubol dispersant*

10 drops of bergamot essential oil

10 drops of sweet orange essential oil

5 drops of geranium essential oil

1 cup of apple cider vinegar

Mix the Solubol and oils in a small container, and add the mixture to a tub of warm bathwater. Pour in the vinegar, and swirl the water around with your hand to disperse the ingredients. Then ease in, lean back, and think lovely thoughts. When you get out, your mood will be a whole lot rosier! **Available at essential oil suppliers.*

Perk yourself up with an herbal tea bath. In many herbal circles, chamomile, lemon balm, and peppermint have earned A+ marks for their ability to boost low spirits and ease worried minds. Tap into that feel-good power by mixing 2 tablespoons of each herb in a heat-proof container, and pour 2 cups of boiling water into it. Let the mixture steep, covered, for 10 to 15 minutes. Then strain out the herbs, and pour the tea into a tub of warm water. Settle in and soak for 10 to 20 minutes. A cheerier, more chipper you should emerge!

HELP WANTED?

A growing number of natural health practitioners are adding flower essence therapy to their repertoires. They've found that these plant derivatives (not to be confused with essential oils) can be highly effective in alleviating many mental gremlins. For example, gentian helps people who feel dragged down after a setback, such as failing a test or not landing a coveted job. To learn more about flower essences and where to buy them, or to find a therapist near you, visit the Flower Essence Society's website at www.flowersociety.org.

Beat the winter blahs. No one is quite sure why only some folks are troubled by seasonal affective disorder (SAD) while others are not. But one thing is certain: The older you get, the less you want to spend a full quarter (or more) of the year in a funk. One of the most effective SAD foes is orange essential oil. It has an almost magical knack for lifting low spirits at any time of year, but especially during the dark days of winter. To send its uplifting scent wafting through your home, simply dab the oil onto several lightbulbs. But first, make sure the bulbs are turned off and cool to the touch!

Snag some sun. While older SAD sufferers may be more resentful of the symptoms than their younger counterparts are, those who are retired or work on a flexible schedule have one major advantage: the ability to catch the sun at whatever time of day it appears in the sky. So use every opportunity you can to get out and soak up those mood-lifting, vitamin D–filled rays. Maybe go for some early-morning or early-afternoon walks. Play in the snow with your dog or your grandchildren. SAD is no match for the blues-bashing team of sunshine and a little bit of exercise.

Fennel fights seasonal fat. One of the most bothersome and very unhealthy side effects of SAD can be an increased appetite and cravings for sweets and starches. To curb your appetite, buy a bottle of fennel essential oil (make sure it's food grade!). Then before each meal, and whenever you're tempted to grab an unhealthy snack, add 2 drops of the oil to a cup of warm water, and drink up.

Money Saver

We all know the old adage "The best things in life are free." And when it comes to your mental and physical health, one of the very best of those freebies is laughter. It releases torrents of feel-good brain chemicals that boost your spirits. What's more, it raises your supply of immune-boosting growth hormones and endorphins. So every single day, make it a point to share jokes, watch a funny movie, read a funny story, or check out your favorite comic strips, either online or in your local newspaper.

DOUSE THE FLAMES TONIC

Science has linked chronic inflammation to health conditions such as rheumatoid arthritis, cancer, heart disease, diabetes, asthma—and even Alzheimer's disease. This tonic can help keep your internal " engine" cool and aids digestion, promotes healthy weight loss, balances blood sugar, reduces pain, and encourages healthy skin.

1 cup of warm (not boiling) water

2 tbsp. of apple cider vinegar

1 tsp. of fresh-squeezed lemon juice

1 tsp. of honey (or more to taste)

1/2 tsp. of ground turmeric

1/4 tsp. of ground ginger

(or 1/2 tsp. of grated fresh ginger)

Pour the water into a mug, and stir in the remaining ingredients. Taste, and add more honey if desired. Then sit back and drink to cooler internal temperatures—and a longer, healthier life!

Boost your immune system with coconut vinegar. This delicious mocktail gets its protective power from coconut vinegar. It's packed with compounds that not only strengthen your immune system, but also fight infections, regulate blood pressure, and help stabilize your blood sugar levels. To make it, muddle 5 or 6 mint leaves in a glass with 1 tablespoon of coconut vinegar. Add 6 or 8 ounces of seltzer and the juice of half a lime, and stir. Garnish with a lime slice, and drink to your long life and good health!

ANTI-AGING MATTERS

Q: Is it true that papaya is a perfect superfood for seniors?

A: It sure is! These tasty fruits are loaded with vitamins, minerals, and other nutrients that are especially crucial for folks over 50. Papayas aid digestion, reduce inflammation and stress, lower your risk for heart disease, boost your immune system, protect against cell-damaging free radicals, keep certain toxins out of your colon, and promote better eye health. Plus, the low sugar content in papayas makes them an ideal addition to a diabetic's diet.

Make a super-simple super syrup. This formula will not only reduce inflammation throughout your body, but it also supports kidney and liver function, promotes cardiovascular health, prevents or fights urinary tract infections, and helps guard against bacterial, fungal, and viral attacks of all kinds, including the common cold. To produce this wonder drug, just mix 2 cups of apple cider vinegar with 1 cup of honey and 2 teaspoons of cinnamon in a jar. Shake or stir well, and store the mixture in a cool, dry area (not the fridge; that will make the honey harden and settle to the bottom). To enjoy all the anti-aging benefits of this heroic blend, simply take a couple of sips in the morning and again at night.

Pile on the pineapple. Why? Because the bromelain it contains has been proven to pack a lot of powerful anti-inflammatory power. Not only is it more effective than many commercial products at relieving pain caused by inflammatory conditions like osteoarthritis, but it can also help to reduce chronic inflammation throughout your body, thereby helping you protect yourself from just about every deadly disease under the sun.

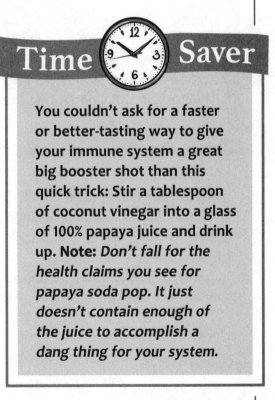

Time Saver

You couldn't ask for a faster or better-tasting way to give your immune system a great big booster shot than this quick trick: Stir a tablespoon of coconut vinegar into a glass of 100% papaya juice and drink up. **Note:** *Don't fall for the health claims you see for papaya soda pop. It just doesn't contain enough of the juice to accomplish a dang thing for your system.*

Move!! I know this is beginning to sound like a broken record, but one of the most effective ways of all to reduce chronic inflammation is also one of the simplest: Keep your body in motion, just as Mother Nature intended. And one of the easiest and most pleasant ways to do that is to walk as much as possible as you go about your daily routine. So if you're looking for a retirement destination, do yourself a major anti-aging favor by choosing somewhere you can take the good old shoe-leather express to most of your frequent shopping and service venues: grocery, hardware, and pet-supply stores, as well as your hairdresser, dentist, and veterinarian.

BRAIN-BOOSTING GREAT-GUT TONIC

New scientific research strongly suggests that our gut health is directly connected to our mental health. That means that one of the most important things you can do to keep your brain firing on all of its cylinders is to keep your digestive system in tip-top shape. This bracing beverage can help.

1 cup of filtered or distilled water, divided

1 tbsp. of apple cider vinegar

1 tsp. of honey

1/4 tsp. of ground cinnamon

Pinch of sea salt

Bring 1/2 cup of the water to a boil. While it's boiling, pour the other half cup into a mug, and stir in the remaining ingredients. Add the just-boiled H_2O to the mug, stir again, and drink up. Don't boil all of the water, or you could end up destroying some of the beneficial bacteria in the vinegar and honey (see "Hold the heat and save the good guys," below).

Hold the heat and save the good guys. If you're among the many folks who like to drink apple cider vinegar in tea or hot water, here's a factoid you should know: If you add the vinegar—or raw honey—while the water is still at or slightly below the boiling point (212°F), some of the beneficial bacteria will die off. So to preserve all the health-giving power of your drink, let the brew cool down to a comfortable drinking temperature before you stir in anti-aging additives.

EARLY BIRD SPECIALS

We all know that in order to keep your brain young and sharp your whole life long, you need to use it. And, if you're age 60 or over, you have a golden opportunity to do that. Thanks to the program Lifelong Learning with No Tuition, public colleges and universities in every state allow anyone in the 60+ age bracket to audit classes at no cost. To learn more, do a search online, or check with the school closest to you.

Dance for your brain's sake. Scientists tell us that whether you waltz in elegant Viennese style or just cut a rug to a swing, tango, or polka tune, moving rhythmically with a partner can reduce your risk for dementia by a full 76%. But beyond the mental stimulation involved, it also helps you maintain muscle mass, which researchers have found to be crucial to avoiding dementia.

As for your body... Ballroom dancing roasts the same number of calories as swimming or cycling (200 to 400 per hour); lowers cholesterol and blood pressure; increases lung capacity and stamina; helps maintain bone density; improves balance; conditions your cardiovascular system; and tones and strengthens the muscles in your legs and buttocks. Plus, guys, if the choreography entails dipping or lifting your partner, you get a darn good upper-body workout. **Note:** *Orthopedic surgeons tell us that because of its low-impact nature, ballroom dancing is a really effective way to help rehabilitate your knees after replacement surgery.*

Don't forget to remember. As unlikely as it may seem, this simple concoction can actually improve your memory: Bring 1 quart of water to a boil, and add 7 teaspoons of aniseed. Reduce the heat to low, and simmer until the water reduces to about 3 cups. Strain the brew, and while still warm, stir in 4 teaspoons each of honey and glycerin. Store the mixture in a jar with a tight-fitting lid at room temperature. To give your gray cells a boost, take 2 tablespoons three times a day and say, "Thanks for the memory!" **Note:** *For the ultimate in health-giving potency, bypass the little glass jars at the supermarket and buy your aniseed, and other herbs and spices, in bulk from a reputable organic-herb supplier.*

Labor Saver

If you commonly sleep on your back or your stomach, you have an easy way to keep your brain healthy. What is it? Just start sleeping on your side. Researchers have found that snoozing in this position appears to improve your brain's ability to clear out harmful chemicals through its glymphatic pathway. That, in turn, can lower your risk for neurological diseases like Alzheimer's and Parkinson's.

CREAM OF THE CROP IMMUNITY BOOSTER

It's no secret that the commander in chief of your anti-aging fighting forces is a strong immune system. And you couldn't ask for a more effective way to boost it than with this luscious libation.

1 cup of vanilla Greek yogurt

1 tablespoon of apple cider vinegar

1/2 medium orange, peeled

1/2 cup of blueberries*

1/2 cup of hulled strawberries*

1/4 cup of chopped pineapple**

1/2 cup of crushed ice

Blend all ingredients in a blender until thoroughly mixed. Pour the mixture into a glass, and drink it immediately, or refrigerate it, tightly covered, for up to four hours. *Fresh or frozen **Fresh or unsweetened canned*

Eat more fiber and beat the big four. Eating a healthy, well-balanced diet is crucial to keeping your immune system strong. And that includes packing in plenty of fiber. Researchers tell us that the average American eats just 15 grams of fiber a day, but in order to stay healthy and fend off premature aging, we need to eat a minimum of 25 to 29 grams each day. And the more high-fiber foods you put on your plate, the more you reduce your risk for four major diseases that strike older adults: heart disease, stroke, type 2 diabetes, and colon cancer. So get with a healthy anti-aging program, and fill up your diet with high-fiber foods like fruits, vegetables, nuts, and whole grains.

ANTI-AGING MATTERS

Q: Every time a friend of mine hears me make a negative comment, she scolds me and says I'm damaging my physical health. Isn't that a bit of a stretch?

A: Actually, your friend is right on the money. Medical science has proven that even mild sadness can weaken your immune system, and the more negative and pessimistic you are, the more likely you are to get sick. On the other hand, happy, cheerful, optimistic souls have an army of battle-ready, infection-fighting T cells in their bodies.

Tap into teamwork. Dietary teamwork can help slow, or even reverse, the aging process. When you eat the delicious combo of bananas and yogurt, a fiber called inulin in the bananas intensifies the growth of the yogurt's healthy bacteria, which improves your digestion while strengthening your immunity. Likewise, when you pair chicken with carrots, the zinc in chicken helps enable your body to convert the carrots' beta-carotene into vitamin A. The result is a rugged immune system, stronger eyes, and healthier skin.

> Maintaining an optimistic outlook on life can boost your physical health and cut your risk for dementia by 30%.

Go with immunity Italiano. Oregano essential oil contains high levels of carvacrol and thymol, which happen to be two of the strongest substances for supporting overall health and maintaining a strong immune system. And all it takes to reap the benefits of this team is to add 1 drop of oregano essential oil to a large pot of your favorite pasta sauce. Just make sure the oil you use is an FDA-approved, certified food-grade brand.

Boost your system gingerly. Ginger essential oil is another immunity-enhancing superstar, thanks to its high concentration of gingerol, zingiberene, and beta-phellandrene. To use, mix 2 or 3 drops of the oil with a teaspoon of jojoba or apricot kernel oil, and rub the mixture onto the bottoms of your feet or the back of your neck. Or mix a drop or two with a spoonful of honey or coconut oil, and swallow. Again, as with any essential oil you intend to ingest, make sure you use a food-grade version.

Money Saver

One of the most effective ways of all to strengthen your immune system and keep it strong is absolutely free, and a whole lot of fun. All you need to do is mix and mingle with congenial companions. The more human (and critter) connections you have, and the more often you get out and about, the better you will be at fighting off illnesses of all kinds.

WINNING WAYS & MEANS

There is almost no limit to the anti-aging tricks using vinegar and its all-star teammates like herbs, spices, honey, and essential oils. But to get a big bang for your buck and your efforts, whether you're using the end product for health or beauty purposes, it pays to keep these basic guidelines in mind.

GO WITH GLASS. When you're buying vinegar that you intend to consume or use on your skin, make sure it's in a glass bottle. The reason is that vinegar (or any other acidic liquid) that's stored in plastic can leach undesirable chemicals out of the container and into the fluid itself—and you don't want that potentially toxic stuff in or on your body! For that same reason, when you make your own vinegar from scratch or infuse it with fruits, herbs, or vegetables (for example, the hot-pepper vinegar on page 61), always use glass or ceramic containers.

OILS NEED GLASS, TOO. Like vinegar, essential oils are strong substances that can pull chemicals right out of plastic containers. In this case, though, to retain the potency of the oils, it's important to store them in dark-colored glass containers. Herb and essential oil suppliers sell inexpensive cobalt blue and brown (a.k.a. dark amber) bottles and jars in numerous sizes, with dropper, mist-spray, and pump-style lids.

ONE EXCEPTION TO THE NO-PLASTIC RULE. When you mix up a bath blend, shampoo, or other formula for use in the bathroom, you sure don't want to risk breaking a glass container. If your DIY creation is for one-time use, a plastic bottle or jar is fine. But for larger quantities, look for leach-proof PET plastic containers (also available from herb and essential oil retailers).

STERILIZE GLASS CONTAINERS. To eliminate the possibility of bacterial buildup in DIY health, beauty, or culinary vinegars that will not be used right away, it's important to sterilize the jars or bottles. To do that, simply fill the container with boiling water, and let it sit for 10 minutes. Then empty the water, and let the container cool down to room temperature before pouring in the potion. Also soak lids or caps for 10 minutes in boiling water.

AVOID REACTIONS. Whenever you heat vinegar, always use nonreactive cookware, such as stainless steel, heat-proof glass, enamel-coated iron, or (in a microwave) plastic. Also, if you must use a metal, rather than plastic, lid on a bottle or jar, cover the opening with plastic wrap before you put the lid on.

CHAPTER 5

HAIR & NAILS

The folks who study such matters tell us that virtually across the board, seniors who take care of their looks remain happier and healthier than their counterparts who slack off in that regard. It is also true that the most visible part of your body is also the one that shows the signs of aging the earliest and most clearly—namely, your hair. The good news is that by adopting a few savvy strategies, you will keep that mane as a mood- and health-boosting asset your whole life long. And that's what this chapter is all about. Plus, you'll also discover a passel of terrific tips, tricks, and tonics that'll help keep your finger- and toenails disease-free and ready to show off for many years to come.

Fortunately, you have a pretty powerful ally in the mission to keep your hair, nails, and your entire body, looking healthy, vibrant, and young. It's none other than infused vinegar. And it couldn't be easier to whip up your own supply (see recipe at right), that's enriched with health- and beauty-enhancing herbs, such as those on page 100.

Pack 1 cup of dried herbs, or 2 cups of fresh ones, into a sterilized 1-quart jar. Heat 1 quart of good-quality apple cider or wine vinegar until it's just warm (don't let it boil!) and pour it over the herbs. Cover the jar with a non-metallic lid and let it sit for a few weeks in a dark place at room temperature. Then take a sniff. If you detect a rich, herbal aroma, it's ready. When the scent is just right, strain the flavored vinegar into clean, sterilized bottles.

ULTRA-NOURISHING SHAMPOO

In order to stay at its peak of health and good looks, mature hair demands extra-strength nourishment. And that's exactly what this multitasking blend provides.

1 1/2 cups of coconut milk
1 tbsp. of honey
1 tsp. of apple cider vinegar
1/2 tsp. of castor oil

1/2 tsp. of vitamin E oil (or the contents of 1 capsule)
6 drops of rosemary essential oil

Combine all the ingredients in a blender, and whirl on high until the mixture is thoroughly combined. Pour it into a 16-ounce plastic bottle (an empty, clean shampoo or conditioner bottle works perfectly). Use it twice a week instead of your regular shampoo. **Note:** *The coconut milk in this recipe does make the shampoo somewhat perishable, but tightly capped, it should be fine in the refrigerator for 7 to 14 days.*

Get the gunk out. Over time, even light-hold hair sprays, gels, and other styling products can build up in your hair, making it dull, drab, and older-looking. This slick trick will rout that residue, at a fraction of the cost of clarifying shampoos: Just mix 3 parts coarse sea salt with 2 parts mild shampoo and wash your hair as usual. Use it once or twice a month, as needed, to thoroughly clean your hair and scalp.

SAFE & SOUND Everyone's hair gets thinner, drier, and more brittle with age. And using aggressive styling techniques along with harsh chemical treatments will make your hair even stiffer, weaker, and more prone to breakage. The key to having the youngest-looking mane possible is to be gentle. Keep heat at a moderate level in the shower and from styling devices like hair dryers. Also bypass any hair sprays that boast mega-holding power. The heavy load of alcohol that they contain can be brutal on mature hair. Instead, seek out or make hair-care products with easygoing, natural ingredients.

Reach for a sun-kissed hair spray. Hair-care products don't come any gentler than this zesty DIY formula. In fact, it's so safe, you could drink it! Just squeeze the juice of one orange or lemon into 1 cup of water and mix well. Pour the mixture into a spray bottle, spritz your hair, and style it as you like. Store the leftover formula in the refrigerator.

A healthy body equals healthier hair. In Chapter 4, you discovered a passel of pointers for maintaining a robust, disease-defying immune system your whole life long. Well, guess what? Those same tips, tricks, and tonics will also help keep your hair and nails looking their best at any age. The mantra: Eat a healthy, nourishing, well-balanced diet; get plenty of fresh air, sunshine, and exercise; drink only in moderation, and above all else, don't smoke! (In addition to its other evils, smoking reduces circulation, which can hinder the growth of your hair and rob it of many youth-enhancing nutrients.)

Wash less and glow more. No matter what kind of shampoo you use, the water removes some of your hair's natural oils, and the older you are, the more of those you want to hang on to. The easiest way to reduce dryness is simply to go longer between washings, and use a dry shampoo as needed to keep your hair looking its best. To make a quick DIY version, just mix 1/4 cup of either cornstarch or arrowroot powder (available at health-food stores and online) with 4 to 5 drops of your favorite essential oil. Store the mixture in a small jar with a tight-fitting lid. To use it, simply rub the powder through your strands and onto your scalp, wait for about five minutes or so, then brush it out.

Money Saver

One of the most effective and cheapest anti-aging hair-care techniques of all is to stay well hydrated. The simple reason is that hair shafts are composed primarily of water. But you don't need to confine your guzzling to H_2O. Beverages of all kinds, including juice, milk, tea, and (yes, nutritionists now tell us) coffee, deliver the elixir of life to not only your hair, but the rest of your body, too.

HEALTHY-SCALP SHAMPOO

Strong, healthy hair starts with a healthy scalp. And the older you get, the more important it is to use products that not only clean your hair, but also improve its native soil (so to speak). In this winner, the apple cider vinegar helps restore a healthy pH balance, the peppermint oil works as an anti-inflammatory agent, and the vitamin E oil nourishes your scalp and hair follicles while promoting growth.

- **1 tbsp. of castile soap**
- **2 tsp. of apple cider vinegar**
- **1 tsp. of vitamin E oil (or the contents of 2 capsules)**
- **6 drops of peppermint essential oil**
- **1/3 cup of distilled water**

Combine all the ingredients in a bowl or measuring cup and pour the mixture into a plastic squeeze bottle. Use the shampoo two or three times a week for a healthy scalp and soft, shiny hair.

Scrub-a-dub-dub your scalp. Even though the skin on your scalp wears an overcoat of hair, it still benefits from periodic exfoliating treatments, just as your facial skin does. This five-minute anti-aging marvel tones your scalp and clears off dead skin cells—thus promoting healthy hair growth and helping prevent dandruff outbreaks. So in a small, nonreactive bowl, mix 2 tablespoons each of apple cider vinegar, brown sugar, coconut oil, and fresh-squeezed lemon juice. Using your fingers, scoop out small amounts of the mixture at a time, and work it into your scalp with small circular motions. Continue for five minutes, then rinse thoroughly, and follow up with your regular shampoo and conditioner.

EARLY BIRD SPECIALS

A number of hair-salon franchises offer senior discounts, as do many locally owned beauty and barber shops. The details vary from one business to another, but a search for "senior hair discounts [name of your town]" will bring up the information. Beyond that, many ultra-chic salons and hairstyling schools are always on the lookout for hair models in every age bracket. If you check with those establishments in your area, you just might wind up with an expert "do" for free!

Rub irritation away. Just like the skin on the rest of your body, your scalp becomes thinner and more delicate with age. As a result, it's more easily irritated by shampoos and conditioners. Here's a simple remedy: Rinse your hair with a solution of 3 tablespoons of white vinegar in a cup of warm water. Work it in well and follow up with a clear water rinse until the vinegar is gone.

Ditch the itch. When a reaction to hair-care products makes your head itchy, this remedy is for you: Blend 2 tablespoons each of lemon juice, olive oil, and water in a blender or food processor. Massage the mixture into your scalp and cover your head with a shower cap or a plastic bag. Then go about your business for 30 minutes. During that time, the lemon will polish off dead skin flakes, while the olive oil delivers much-needed moisture to your scalp. When the half hour is up, wash and condition your hair as usual. You should notice an improvement right away! You can use this treatment every other week, as needed, until you're itch-free. **Note:** *If you prefer, you can put the juice, oil, and water in a bowl, and use a wire whisk to blend them thoroughly, as you would if you were making salad dressing.*

> Whenever you use eggs in a DIY hair formula, rinse it out with cool—not hot—water, or your treatment will cook on your head.

Get egg on your head. It's a one-stop "shop" for a healthier scalp and a thriving head of hair. Just beat an egg and rub it into your scalp and through the length of your hair shafts. Let it sit for 30 minutes, while the fats and proteins in the yolk nourish your scalp, deliver deep-down moisture, and help fight any lurking scalp diseases. Repeat the procedure two or three times a month, and you should see a big difference in your crowning glory!

Labor Saver

One easy way to give your scalp more grow power is to give it a mini massage every time you wash your hair. The circular pressing action increases the blood flow to the area, and that increased circulation results in more, and stronger, hair growth.

DANDRUFF-DEFEATING RINSE

Technically speaking, dandruff is not a hair problem. Rather, it's a scalp condition that arises when the skin on your head becomes ultra-dry and flaky. As a result, your hair can wind up looking like you've just emerged from a snow globe. This rinse will deep-cleanse your scalp and "shovel" off the dead skin cells lickety-split.

1/2 cup of red wine or apple cider vinegar   **1 cup of boiling water**
1/2 cup of fresh mint leaves or 1 tbsp. dried

Combine the vinegar and mint in a heat-proof bowl or measuring cup and pour the boiling water over them. Let the mixture cool to room temperature, then strain the liquid into a clean container. After you're done shampooing, apply the solution to your scalp as a final rinse. Then rinse well with cool water and follow up with a rich conditioner.

Don't go begging for dandruff. When you need to cover your graying strands, it's only natural to want the dye job to last as long as possible. But beware of shampoos that are especially made to increase that staying power. In order to retain the dye color, most of these products are formulated to be weaker than their conventional counterparts. As a result, in a great many cases, they fail to sufficiently clear the oil and product residue out of your scalp, which can put you on the high road to dandruff and other scalp woes. So choose your shampoo wisely.

A no-frills dandruff remedy.

Once or twice a week, simply mix 1/2 cup of white or apple cider vinegar in 2 cups of water and use it as an after-shampoo rinse. The vinegar will restore the pH balance of your scalp and inhibit the growth of the yeast or fungi that may have caused the problem in the first place.

SAFE & SOUND If you're having trouble getting rid of dandruff, cast an eagle eye on your diet. In particular, consuming too much sugar can promote the overgrowth of dandruff-causing *Candida* yeast. Excess sugar depletes your body of B vitamins, which are the key to any anti-dandruff diet.

A DIY hot-oil treatment for extra-dry or damaged hair. Just heat 1/2 cup or so of full-fat mayonnaise (don't boil it!), and rub it into your hair. Wrap your head in a warm towel, wait 15 to 30 minutes, and then shampoo with warm—not hot—water. Repeat every week or two until your tresses can freely lie about their age (so to speak).

A rosy way to restore youthful shine to dull hair. And to reduce dandruff worries. Simply warm up 1/4 cup or so of rose hip oil, and massage it into your hair and scalp. Wait 30 minutes, then shampoo as usual. It works because rose hip oil is rich in vitamins A, C, and E, which are essential for maintaining vibrant hair and a healthy scalp well into your golden years.

Say yes to yogurt! It's probably safe to say that there isn't a woman on earth who doesn't want to keep her hair looking young and shiny for as long as possible. It's also true that if you're pursuing an active retirement or a second-prime venture, you may not care to spend a lot of time whipping up hair-care formulas. If that's the case, and your hair is looking dull and dry, this solo superstar is for you: Simply massage 1/2 cup of plain whole-milk yogurt into your hair. Give it 30 minutes or so to soak in (maybe while you enjoy your morning coffee and plan the day's schedule), then wash and condition your hair as usual. Repeat every other week, as needed, until your tresses are gleaming again. It works because the milk fat moisturizes your hair, while the lactic acid removes dulling dirt and product residue.

Money Saver

Simply spending 10 to 15 minutes in the sunlight each day, or as close to it as possible, can sometimes clear up dandruff or at least lessen its severity. The reason could be that the flakes are your body's way of showing that you need more vitamin D, in which, stats show, most Americans are deficient. It's essential for maintaining vibrant, overall good health—including that of your scalp.

HAIR'S TO MORE HAIR RINSE

Throughout our lives, hair falls out and regrows, but as we age, the regrowth process tends to slow down. This rinse can help speed it up.

1/4 cup of dried rosemary **1 cup of distilled water**
1/4 cup of apple cider vinegar **20 drops of peppermint essential oil**

Combine the rosemary and vinegar in a glass jar, close the lid, and shake. Set it in a cool, dark place for two weeks, shaking it daily. Strain out the solids. Mix 1/8 cup of the infusion (for normal or dry hair) or 1/4 cup (for oily hair) with the distilled water in a spray bottle. Add the oil and shake well. Once or twice a week, wash and condition your hair as usual, towel dry, and spray on the potion. Either wait two minutes and rinse it out or, for more intense action, leave it in.

Kick the stress and keep your crop. Stress is infamous for its ability to bring on or worsen just about every health condition known to mankind. But what many folks don't realize is that both chronic stress and specific stressful events can trigger the loss of hair—sometimes as much as 70 percent of your strands. In fact, one of the most common causes of hair loss in folks in their 50s, 60s, and beyond is the stress caused by the death of loved ones, or by the ongoing strains of caring for elderly parents or ailing spouses. The good news is that when the problem results from a specific event, your hair will grow back once you've recovered from that experience. In the case of chronic stress, the tips in chapters 4 and 16 can help you ease that load and get your "crop" growing and glowing again!

Shedding up to 100 strands of hair a day is perfectly normal, but if you're dropping more than that, or if you're developing bald spots, see your doctor. Certain health conditions and medications can contribute to hair loss. If that's what's happening in your case, changing your prescription(s) or tweaking the dosages could solve the problem.

Grab the horse by the tail. The herb horsetail (*Equisetum arvense*), a.k.a. shavegrass and scouring rush, is the most abundant known source of silica in the plant kingdom. (Yes, I'm referring to the same moisture-absorbing stuff contained in those little packets that come in so many product packages these days.) So what does that have to do with your hair? Just this: Silica can play a major role in improving the overall health of your hair by strengthening the collagen it contains. It's especially effective at adding luster to dull, aging hair and reducing the rate of thinning.

Get on your high horse. You don't need to take my word for this hair helper's seemingly magical powers—try this ultra-simple tonic and see for yourself. To make it, bring a quart of water to a boil, then reduce it to a simmer and add 2 tablespoons of dried horsetail. Steep it, covered, for 20 minutes, then strain. After shampooing as usual, pour the cooled liquid over your hair, and wrap your head in a warm towel. Go about your business for 20 minutes or so, then rinse. Repeat once or twice a week. You'll be amazed at the results!

Call on internal horsepower. You can also make horsetail part of your hair-improvement plan by brewing it

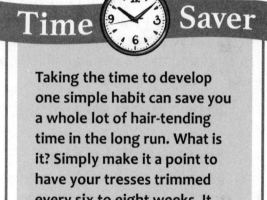

Time Saver

Taking the time to develop one simple habit can save you a whole lot of hair-tending time in the long run. What is it? Simply make it a point to have your tresses trimmed every six to eight weeks. It helps promote healthy hair growth—and also gives you a great opportunity to try out a new style that can make your hair appear thicker.

into a tasty tea. This way, your nails also benefit from the silica-rich herb. Even more importantly for folks of a certain age, silica is essential for maintaining the overall health of your bones. Working more of it into your life could help protect you against osteoporosis and other bone problems. To make the tea, simply pour boiling water over dried horsetail (2 to 3 teaspoons per cup of H_2O). Let it steep for 5 to 10 minutes, then strain. Add honey if you like, and drink to your good looks and good health!

A SAGE SOLUTION FOR GRAYING HAIR

If gray strands are increasing in your dark hair, this rinse can charge to the rescue. Used consistently, it'll darken the gray and impart a gleaming shine to your still-dark brown or black tresses.

1 heaping handful of fresh sage leaves,   **2 cups of boiling water**
torn into pieces, or 2 tbsp. of dried sage   **1/4 cup of apple cider vinegar**

Put the sage in a heat-proof container, and pour in the water. Steep, covered, for 15 to 20 minutes. Strain the infusion into a clean bottle, let it cool to room temperature, and add the vinegar. Lean over a basin or a tightly plugged sink after shampooing, and pour the rinse on your hair. Let it drain, and repeat the procedure two or three times, using the excess liquid in the basin. Then use a towel to dry and style your hair as usual.

Spruce up lighter hair. If your graying invasion is taking place in naturally blonde hair, use A Sage Solution for Graying Hair (above), but replace the sage with chamomile. To add a honey-toned sparkle to light brown tresses, add 2 tablespoons of turmeric powder to the mix. Unlike commercial dyes, these natural formulas will actually help improve the strength and texture of your hair.

ANTI-AGING MATTERS

Q: Can stress and worry make your hair turn gray? And are there any foods or supplements that can delay the graying process?

A: The answer to both questions is no. Pigment-producing cells called melanocytes are genetically programmed to stop manufacturing hair pigment when you reach a certain age. There's nothing that your emotions, your diet, or your overall health has to do with it. It's not uncommon for people to start graying in their 30s; in some cases, even their 20s. Whether you choose to cover your silver strands or embrace them is your call—but don't let this natural, and perfectly harmless, process make you feel any older than you are!

When your gray hair turns yellow... It's easy (and common) to pin the blame on hair-care products. The fact is, though, that once the pigment has flown the coop, your hair becomes more porous. It absorbs all kinds of things that you come into contact with every day. For example, hard-water deposits, second-hand smoke, and even UV rays can all skew the hue.

Whiten up! To put the silvery shine back in your hair, mix 2 tablespoons each of baking soda and water in a plastic container to make a thick paste. In a plastic spray bottle, mix 1 cup each of water and apple cider vinegar. Wet your hair, then rub the paste through the strands and massage it into the roots and scalp until your whole head is covered. Rinse thoroughly, then spray the vinegar solution through the strands until they're saturated. Rinse well, pat your hair with a clean towel, comb with a wide-tooth comb, and let your hair air-dry. If you like, follow up with a conditioner. Repeat the process as needed.

> If you're letting your hair go gray, get frequent trims to speed new growth; the shorter you're willing to cut, the faster the transition will be.

Dial the doc. If you've suddenly noticed a change in the color and texture of your hair, call your doctor. These changes could be caused by an Rx you've recently started, and your doc might be able to help solve the problem. To ensure the best chance of success, carefully describe both the timing and the nature of the change. Say, for example, "My hair started looking brassy about three weeks ago. Since then, it's felt brittle, too."

Labor Saver

When your hair's gold has turned to silver (as the old song goes), keep your tresses sparkling white with this old-time trick: Add a few drops of laundry bluing (available in supermarkets) to a quart of water. Use it as a final rinse after every shampoo, or only when you feel the need for a whitening boost.

NOURISHING CONDITIONER

Over time, sun, wind, and chemicals can take a toll on your hair. This gentle formula can repair the damage and, if used routinely, head off future trouble.

1/4 cup of aloe vera gel

10 drops of lavender essential oil

5 drops of eucalyptus essential oil

5 drops of geranium essential oil

2 tsp. of coconut oil

2 tsp. of apple cider vinegar

1/4 cup of distilled water

Combine the gel and essential oils in a bowl and whisk to create an emulsion. Add the coconut oil and whisk again. Stir in the vinegar and water until the mixture is smooth. Pour the conditioner into a plastic dispensing bottle. After shampooing with a gentle shampoo, apply the conditioner to your hair, wait for about five minutes, then rinse. If your hair is severely damaged, repeat the conditioning step again.

Beware of buzzwords. When you're shopping for commercial shampoos and conditioners, check the labels for words like *smoothing*, *moisturizing*, or *silkening*. Yes, of course you want smooth, moisturized, silky hair. But in reality, these products are generally made for women with thick, dense hair. They'll only make thinning hair look even sparser.

HELP WANTED?

If you've chosen to cover your gray hair with a dye job at home, then stop. You're actually defeating the purpose. Natural hair color is never just one color; it's a combination of many different shades. But DIY commercial hair dyes don't provide this multidimensional effect. So not only does the color look fake, but it also does nothing to help conceal the thinning of your aging hair. Ditch the box and find a skilled professional hairstylist who can give your hair highlights and lowlights that create dimension and the illusion of more volume. Yes, it will cost more, but the payoff will be hair that looks thicker, more natural, and younger!

Bypass bangs. At least, that is, if you want your hair to look fuller and thicker. The reason is that for many older women, hair loss begins at the crown. When you create bangs, you remove hair from the spot where you need it most. If you have your heart set on bangs, an expert stylist can perform some strategic texturing that will give the illusion of bangs without compromising fullness and volume.

"Hire" a berry good repair crew.

If you enjoy the sweet aroma of strawberries, you'll love using this hair mask and love the results even more. It helps deliver deep-down, youth-enhancing moisture to damaged hair. To make it, puree three fresh or frozen strawberries, one egg yolk, and 2 teaspoons of olive oil in a blender or food processor. Apply the mixture to your hair, working it into the roots and strands. Cover your head with a shower cap or plastic bag, leave it on for half an hour, then wash the mixture out with your usual shampoo.

Pass your mane some mayo.

For generations, women have been using mayonnaise to hydrate their hair while making it shinier and more voluminous. It works just as well as it ever did—and when you team up that classic condiment with the right essential oil, the combo can deliver even better results. To see for yourself, mix a few drops of an anti-aging essential oil with 1/4 cup of mayo (see "Heroic Hair-Care Herbs & Oils" on page 100). Massage the mixture into your hair, let it sit for 15 minutes or so, and shampoo as usual. Just make sure you use real mayonnaise, not a low-fat type or the miracle salad dressing; it's the eggs and oil in the full-fledged version that deliver the benefits you're looking for.

Time Saver

Believe it or not, simply by reversing your usual shampoo routine in the shower, you can add volume to your hair and enable it to hold a style better. That's because the same conditioner properties that make your hair silky and smooth can actually just encourage it to lie down, and that exposes any thinning areas. But when you condition first, the volumizing effects of the shampoo make your hair stand up better.

A BERRY NUTTY HEALTH BLAST

Your hair and nails can only stay at their peak of good health and good looks when you fuel them with a nutritious, well-balanced diet. This luscious drink delivers all of the nutrients that are most crucial for maintaining thick, lustrous hair and strong, healthy nails.

1 cup of plain Greek yogurt	1/2 cup of raw whole almonds
1/2 cup of blueberries	3 tsp. of apple cider vinegar
1/2 cup of raspberries	1/2 cup of crushed ice

Combine all the ingredients in a blender and run it on high until the drink is creamy and frothy. Pour the mixture into a glass and drink it all up immediately. Or store it, tightly covered, in the refrigerator for up to four hours.

To perk up your hair and nails, bring on the beef. To hear some folks talk, you might think that eating red meat is guaranteed to put you on the high road to a shorter, sicker life—and make you pack on pounds galore besides. Well, friends, it just ain't so. Granted, it is true that beef in large quantities is far from the healthiest stuff you could put on your plate day after day. But the fact is (as any nutritionist will tell you), it is the most potent source of three nutrients that are essential for the health and appearance of your hair and nails—namely protein, zinc, and iron. The bottom line: Unless you're a dedicated vegetarian, or you simply don't care for the taste of red meat, don't hesitate to help yourself to a steak, burger, or slice of roast beef every now and then when the mood strikes you.

SAFE & SOUND While iron is essential for healthy hair and nails, don't get carried away with upping your intake—and avoid iron supplements. In fact, with the presence of iron in most multivitamins and scads of processed foods, virtually all adult men and postmenopausal women get as much iron as they need in their daily diets. And too much of this mineral can cause more harm than good.

Chase your burger with a beer. It's one of the richest dietary sources of silicon there is. If you have any doubts about the importance of that mineral, consider the results of this study published in the *Archives of Dermatological Research*: A daily 10-milligram silicon supplement was shown to reduce hair and nail brittleness after 20 weeks. And most single servings of beer contain more than 10 milligrams of silicon.

Buy a brush that means business. For women over 50, or whose hair is thinning at any age, hair-care pros recommend going with a soft brush made from natural materials. Boar-bristle versions are especially good because they won't tear or split your hair. They're also effective in increasing blood flow to your hair follicles, which stimulates growth. Shape makes a difference, too. If you blow-dry your hair, go with a round brush that's vented in the center. The holes allow heat to pass through, which makes it easier to get lift while you're drying, and more lift equals more volume.

Healthy hair demands a clean brush. And the cleaning routine is simple: Remove as much hair as possible, using a comb or your fingers. Soak the brush for 15 minutes in a basin of warm water with 1/4 cup of white vinegar and 2 teaspoons of shampoo mixed into it. Pull off any remaining hair and use an old toothbrush to scrub any stubborn residue from the bristles. Rinse the brush under warm running water. Then, to keep the bristles from breaking as they dry, lay flat brushes on their backs, and stand round ones, heads up, on their handles in a glass or similar container. If you use commercial styling products, perform this routine two or three times a week. Otherwise, clean your natural-bristle brushes once a month and synthetic brushes three or four times a month to get rid of airborne dirt that your hair picks up.

Labor Saver

One of the easiest routes to a healthy scalp is to get yourself a scalp massage brush (available online and from many hair salons). This tool unblocks pores, promotes circulation, and helps draw essential nutrients to your hair follicles, thereby leading to better hair growth.

FUNGUS-FIGHTING TOENAIL SOAK

Nail fungus is generally brought on by moisture trapped in a warm, dark place. It most often affects toenails, and it's most common in people over 60. This formula can polish it off and help prevent its return.

1 tsp. of Solubol dispersant*

5 drops of tea tree essential oil

1 cup of white or apple cider vinegar

5 tbsp. of baking soda

Warm water

Fill a basin with warm water. Mix the Solubol and oil in a small container. Pour the mixture into the basin, followed by the vinegar. Swish the water around, then soak your feet for 10 to 15 minutes. Dry thoroughly. Then mix the baking soda in a fresh basin of water and soak your feet for another 10 to 15 minutes. Repeat twice a day to kill existing fungi and inhibit the growth of more. *Available from essential oil suppliers.*

Clip before you soak. Before using any antifungal footbath, trim back as much of the affected nail as you can with sterilized nail clippers. Don't peel it! Then immediately after you've finished soaking your stricken tootsies, disinfect the clippers to avoid reinfecting yourself with the fungus or spreading it to someone else who might use the tool.

Money Saver

At pharmacies and beauty salons, you can buy special solutions intended to sanitize nail clippers as well as scissors, nail files, combs, and other grooming gear. Don't waste your money. Instead, simply soak your tools in isopropyl (a.k.a. rubbing) alcohol for at least 10 minutes. It will kill all pathogens known to science. Let the items air-dry completely or, if you like, use a hair dryer to speed up the process. In the case of active weapons in your fight against dastardly disease germs, tuck the clippers into a resealable plastic bag until you need them again.

Speed up the action. A toenail fungus can take its good old time to heal completely. In some cases, it can hang in there for a year or even longer. The good news is that simply exposing your feet to the air as much as possible can make the process go much faster. That's because the foul forces thrive in warm, moist, dark places like your shoes. They fare poorly in open, well-lit surroundings—even when the light is coming through your closed windows or even lamps. Chalk up another advantage to being retired or semi-retired: It gives you more opportunities to go barefoot or wear sandals or flip-flops, even in the cold depths of winter!

Don't let your shoes do you in. Even a tiny wound on a foot, or minor repetitive trauma, like that caused by wearing ill-fitting shoes, provides an open invitation to toenail fungus. The same goes for wearing a pair of shoes too often or for too long at a time. That's because, even if your feet don't actively sweat, excess humidity can build up inside of your footwear. So always wear shoes that are comfortable and fit well. Then at the end of the day, change into a fresh pair or, better yet, let your tootsies stay in their birthday suits.

Give 'em time off. To further help fend off foul fungi, give each pair of shoes a rest period of at least 24 hours before you wear it again. This is especially important for sports shoes or work shoes of any kind. For example, if you routinely take brisk walks, play tennis, or work in your yard several days or more each week, invest in at least two or three pairs of designated shoes so that you're always giving your active feet the freshest surroundings possible. As a plus, your footwear will last longer, so your finances will benefit too.

Q: I'm fighting a nail fungus that won't quit. My doctor warned me about some dangers of using prescription antifungal medications for any more than a short time. Are there any foods that can help get rid of these foul fungi safely?

A: There sure are! One of the most powerful fungus fighters of all is extra virgin coconut oil. Eating just 3 tablespoons of it a day should help enormously. Simply upping your intake of garlic, onions, carrots, and apple cider vinegar will also deliver tons of antifungal power and give a big anti-aging boost to you at the same time!

ANTI-AGING MATTERS

LEMONY LAVENDER FINGERNAIL FORMULA

When funky fungi and their ilk strike your fingers, this is the recipe to reach for. It'll ditch the pain and itch—and have your unsightly digits looking their best again before you know it.

2 tbsp. of olive oil
1 tbsp. of apple cider vinegar
1 tbsp. of jojoba oil

1 tsp. of vitamin E oil
2–5 drops of lavender essential oil
2–5 drops of lemon essential oil

Put all the ingredients into a glass bottle. Cap it tightly and shake vigorously. Then dab the mixture onto your fingertips with a cotton pad. Rub the blend thoroughly into your skin, paying special attention to your nail beds and cuticles. The formula will kill any fungus, yeast, or mold that may be present and help deter future problems. It'll also increase blood circulation, thereby promoting the health and growth of your nails.

A seedy solution for aging nails. As you age, your fingernails grow more slowly and may become dull and brittle. Carrot seed essential oil can help you retain more of your nails' youthful shine, smoothness, and strength. It's especially powerful when you team it up with olive oil and vinegar in this simple soak. To make it, mix 3 drops of carrot seed oil with 12 drops of Solubol dispersant. Pour the duo into a bowl of warm water, along with 1 tablespoon each of apple cider vinegar and olive oil. Then insert your fingers into the mixture and soak them for 10 minutes. Repeat the process weekly, and you should notice a big difference in the health of your nails.

SAFE & SOUND It's normal for aging nails to develop vertical ridges that run from the cuticles to the tips. But check with your doctor or a dermatologist if you notice changes in nail color, shape, or thickness or have unexplained bleeding, swelling, or pain around the nails. These symptoms can indicate nutritional deficiencies or an underlying health condition.

Bring on the big B's. Baking soda and borax (a.k.a. boric acid) both pack powerful antifungal properties. To put them to work on your finger- or toenails, mix equal parts of baking soda and borax with enough water to form a thick paste. Gently rub it into the affected area(s). Let it sit for 10 to 15 minutes, then rinse with warm water and pat dry. Repeat the process twice a day until your afflicted digits return to normal.

Ditch the emery board. Using this tool can cause your nails to peel and snag. So replace it with a glass (a.k.a. crystal) nail file. They're modestly priced and available in beauty-supply stores, many beauty salons, and (of course) online. Best of all, a glass file will produce a smooth, even edge on weak, brittle, or damaged nails. The key to the smoothest results is to file in one direction, going with the grain of the nail.

> If your nails develop horizontal, rather than vertical, ridges, see your doctor because these often indicate an underlying health condition.

Leave your cuticles alone! They're on your fingers for a reason: to seal the area at the base of each nail. When you cut or remove a cuticle, it breaks that protective seal, leaving your nails vulnerable to bacteria and infection. If you're dead-set on fussing with your cuticles, use this routine once a week (not any more often!): Immediately after getting out of the shower, use a wooden orange stick to gently push each cuticle back. Then throw the stick away and massage a creamy hand lotion into the base of each finger.

Time Saver

When you polish your nails, this quick and easy two-step trick can save the time and frustration of having to repeat the process prematurely. Before you start, dip a cotton ball in either white or apple cider vinegar, and wipe it over your nails. This will remove any oil that might disrupt the sticking power of the polish. Then after you've finished your paint job, spritz your nails lightly with nonstick cooking spray. It will set the polish, help it dry faster, and also moisturize your cuticles.

HEROIC HAIR-CARE HERBS & OILS

Take a look at some herbs and essential oils that can help keep your hair at the peak of good health. Use them alone or combine two or three, but no more than that. If you do, that'll reduce the benefits of each individual herb.

HERBS

These power plants deliver winning results in herbal teas or infused vinegar.

Basil delivers a load of vitamins and flavonoids that promote hair growth.

Calendula and **chamomile** both offer soothing relief for an irritated scalp.

Hibiscus contains vital vitamins that condition your hair.

Horsetail has hair-strengthening silica, and vitamins and minerals to soften hair.

Lavender soothes irritated scalps, reduces inflammation, and boosts circulation.

Licorice root imparts moisture and helps keep your hair soft and smooth.

Marshmallow root is a natural detangler and also conditions your hair.

Nettle is full of hair-strengthening vitamins and minerals and nourishes dry hair.

Rosemary boosts circulation, stimulates hair growth, and is great for dry hair.

ESSENTIAL OILS

Use these oils in your shampoo, conditioner, and hair-styling products.

Cedarwood is antibacterial and antifungal, making it ideal for treating scalp conditions. It also helps to increase hair growth and prevent hair loss.

Clary sage speeds up the rate of hair growth and also makes the hair shafts stronger, thereby reducing breakage.

Lavender boosts hair growth and promotes the overall health of your hair.

Peppermint increases circulation to the scalp, encouraging thicker hair growth.

Rosemary boosts cellular generation and smells great mixed with peppermint.

Tea tree has what may be the most potent antibacterial and antifungal properties of any essential oil. It also helps increase hair growth.

Ylang ylang ramps up oil production, which makes it fabulous for moisturizing and soothing dry scalps and reducing hair breakage. Don't use on an oily scalp!

CHAPTER 6

BEAUTIFUL SKIN

When you step into the cosmetic section of any upscale department store, you're confronted with a mind-boggling assortment of lotions, potions, and creams that claim to perform every anti-aging feat under the sun. And for good reason: It seems just about everyone over the age of 40 is trying to smooth out wrinkles, lose laugh lines, lift sagging skin, and eliminate dark spots. A lot of them are even willing to spend a small fortune to do it. Luckily, you don't need to join that crowd, folks.

This chapter is filled with fabulous formulas and anti-aging strategies that'll get, and keep, your skin looking younger than you ever thought possible and at a fraction of the cost of those commercial products. What's even better is that, unlike many store-bought versions, these simple DIY treatments improve the long-term health of your skin, along with the rest of your body.

A key ingredient in many of these formulas is (surprise!) vinegar. Just one example of the highly effective and inexpensive treats you have in store is this anti-aging toner. To make it, mix 1 tablespoon of apple cider vinegar with 6 tablespoons of pure spring or distilled water. Then add five crushed, uncoated aspirin tablets, and stir well. Pour the mixture into a glass bottle. Apply the toner to your freshly washed face and follow up with a natural moisturizer. It'll clean out your pores, remove dead skin cells, help balance the pH of your skin, and leave it softer, brighter, and revitalized. Store the bottle, tightly capped, in the refrigerator, where it will stay fresh for a month or so.

EXTRA-GENTLE FACE WASH

This facial cleanser is specially formulated for mature complexions. It's mild enough to use twice a day for major anti-aging benefits.

1/4 cup of liquid castile soap
2 tbsp. of distilled water
1/4 cup of honey
1 tsp. of apple cider vinegar

1 tsp. of argan carrier oil
5 drops of lavender essential oil
5 drops of peppermint essential oil

Pour the soap into a dispenser bottle with a pump-style cap. Add the water, close the bottle, and shake well. Then pour in the honey, followed by the vinegar, argan oil, and essential oils, and shake again. Wash your face with the mixture every morning and night, shaking the bottle before each use. You'll be amazed at the results!

A honey of a homemade cleanser. One benefit of making your own facial cleanser is that you can dodge sulfates. They're added to many commercial products to produce lather, but they provide no cleaning action. In fact, they strip off the lipid layer that naturally protects your skin from dirt and other airborne junk. Enter this DIY dynamo: Just add 1/2 cup of vegetable glycerin, about 3 tablespoons of honey, and 2 tablespoons of liquid castile soap to a container that has a tight-fitting lid, then shake to combine. Twice a day, massage the mixture into your face and neck for at least 30 seconds, then rinse well with warm water and pat dry. The honey draws impurities from your pores and also helps guard against damage from UV rays, and it retains moisture in your skin.

If you find the process of making skin-care products confusing, or if you simply want to gather ideas and improve on your technique, consider taking a class or a DIY hands-on workshop in your area. You might be inspired to turn your DIY pastime into a second-prime business venture. In 2018, global demand for organic personal-care products topped $13 billion—and it's still growing!

Rejuvenate your face and hands. Day in and day out, these body parts bear the full brunt of just about everything thrown their way by your daily routine and Mother Nature. About once or twice a week, mix 1 tablespoon of white vinegar with 2 tablespoons of coarsely ground rice in a bowl, and massage the mixture into your face and hands. Your skin will look and feel smoother, younger, and healthier. **Note:** *Use either a coffee grinder or a smaller food processor to grind the rice for this recipe.*

To help prevent the natural thinning of aging eyelashes and promote growth, rub castor oil on the base of your lashes each night.

Give your face a break. As odd as it may seem, being retired or working from home could help shave years off your appearance. When you no longer need to look your professional best every day, you can skip your makeup routine. According to dermatologists and skin-care pros, that's one of the most effective anti-aging ploys of all. When your skin isn't covered in layers of pore-clogging concealer, foundation, and blush, it has a chance to breathe. Oxygen can flow freely in and out of your pores, replenishing your natural moisture level and expelling any lingering cosmetic residue. Going barefaced for even a few days a week can make a big difference in the health of your skin.

Hold the mascara, too. Applying and removing it day in and day out can irritate your lashes and make them look thinner. But when you take some periodic time-outs from that routine, your hair has a chance to regain its strength and put on a fuller, thicker show.

Time Saver

Another reason to ease off the daily makeup grind is that it gives you more time to do the things that can *really* make you look and feel younger, like walking your dog, taking up a new pastime, or playing with your grandchildren. You'll also have more money for youth-enhancing activities because you'll spend less at the cosmetic counter.

NOT-JUST-FOR-BABY WIPES

These wipes are gentle enough to use on an infant's tender skin—which makes them ideal for a delicate, mature complexion.

- **1 roll of premium paper towels**
- **1 plastic container with a tight-fitting lid**
- **1/2 cup of aloe vera juice**
- **1/2 cup of pure witch hazel**
- **1 tbsp. of liquid castile soap**
- **1 tbsp. of olive oil**
- **1 tbsp. of white vinegar**
- **1 cup of boiled water, cooled to room temperature**

Cut the roll in half horizontally with a serrated knife. Place half the roll, cut end down, in the container. Mix the liquid ingredients, pour the solution into the container, and close the lid. Then let it sit for 10 minutes. Next, flip it upside down for another 10 minutes. Return it to its upright position, remove the lid, and pull the tube out from the roll. As you need them, pull the wipes up from the center.

On with the milk, off with the makeup. To remove your makeup and soften your skin at the same time, put 1 tablespoon of evaporated milk into a small bowl and stir in a few drops of almond oil. Pat the mixture onto your face with a cotton pad, then wipe it off with a second pad. Rinse with lukewarm water, then follow up with your usual cleansing and moisturizing routine.

EARLY BIRD SPECIALS

Judging from the hoopla in online beauty circles, you might think that spas only cater to the ultra-hip, young professional crowd. Not so! In virtually every mid- to large-size city and an ever-increasing number of small towns, there are spas offering services especially geared to the particular concerns of folks in the 50-and-up age bracket. Many of these establishments even have senior discount days at least once a week. To find a place near you, simply search for "spa treatments for seniors [your area]."

Is that Grandma's garden I smell? If you like the sweet, nostalgic scent of violets, you'll love this cleanser. And you'll love the results even more because it's a match made in heaven for dry, aging skin. It's a snap to make. Just put 1/4 cup of evaporated milk, 1/4 cup of whole milk, and 2 tablespoons of sweet violets (fresh or dried) in the top half of a double boiler, and simmer for about 30 minutes. Don't let the milk boil! Turn off the heat, and let the mixture sit for about two hours. Then strain it into a sterilized glass bottle, secure the cap, and store it in the refrigerator. To use the cleanser, pat it onto your face with a cotton ball, massage it gently with your fingers, and rinse with cool water.

Hit very high C with a citrus cleanser. It's no secret that vitamin C has a proven ability to reduce wrinkles and generally improve the overall health and appearance of older skin. That's why it's a key ingredient in many high-end anti-aging cleansers, creams, and serums. To put that power to work, at a fraction of the cost of any commercial product, simply grind the peel of whatever type of citrus fruit you have on hand in a blender or coffee grinder. Then mix about 1 tablespoon of the grounds with enough plain whole-milk yogurt to make a paste. Wash your face with the mixture, rinse with cool water, and pat dry.

Money Saver

One of the most effective and least expensive cleansers of all for mature skin is honey. It locks in moisture that helps keep your complexion smooth and glowing. More importantly, it also supplies powerful antioxidants that penetrate your skin to protect your internal organs against damaging oxidative stress. To reap the benefits, all you need to do is rub a teaspoon or so of the "bee juice" into your face and neck, massage for about five minutes, then rinse with warm water.

Consider two fruity factoids.

All citrus fruits are good for your skin, but here are two tidbits you may not know: First, the antioxidant action is highest in oranges, followed closely by lemons and grapefruit. Second, in each case, the content is higher in the peel than it is in the pulp.

AMAZING ANTI-AGING TONER

This moisturizing, anti-inflammatory blend is one of the best friends a mature complexion could ever ask for, and it couldn't be any more simple to make.

20 drops of Solubol dispersant　　**1 tsp. of apple cider vinegar**

5 drops of sandalwood essential oil　　**Organic rose water***

Mix the Solubol and sandalwood oil in a 4-ounce brown or cobalt blue glass bottle. Add the vinegar and fill the remainder of the space with rose water. Then secure the cap tightly and shake well. Gently dab the potion onto your skin after cleansing and follow up with your regular moisturizer. *If you buy a commercial version, check the label to make sure you're getting 100% pure rose water.*

Tee off with a two-timing moisturizer. When you've gone over the 40-year hump, your skin couldn't ask for a stronger DIY skin ally. It delivers deep-down moisture without clogging your pores and also (believe it or not) can actually help reverse sun damage. To make it, melt 1 cup of extra virgin coconut oil over medium heat in a double boiler. Then stir in 2 tablespoons of loose green tea. Cover and simmer on the lowest heat setting for 60 minutes. Strain the oil into a bowl and let it cool until it's almost solid. Then whip it with a wire whisk until it's creamy (typically three to five minutes). Pour the mixture into a glass jar with a tight-fitting lid, store it at room temperature, and use it after cleansing and toning, as you would any other moisturizer.

Labor Saver

How's this for a quick and easy anti-aging facial toner? Just mix 1 part herb-infused vinegar with 3 parts distilled water. Moisten a cotton pad with the mixture and wipe it over your freshly washed skin. It'll remove any residual makeup or dirt and deliver the designated benefits of whatever herbs you've used in the vinegar (see "Five-Star Skin-Care Allies" on page 120).

Perform three grow-younger feats at once. This multitasking marvel removes makeup and both cleanses and softens mature skin. And it's a snap to whip up. Just mix 1/2 cup of full-fat mayonnaise with 1 tablespoon of melted butter and the juice of one lemon or lime. Store the cream in the refrigerator in a tightly closed jar. Use it as you would any facial cleanser, and rinse with cool water.

Everything's coming up rose water. Simply put, it's one of the best and most versatile elements in any anti-aging skin-care kit. To make your own supply, put 1/4 cup of dried organic rose petals or 3/4 cup of fresh petals into a saucepan. Add 1 1/2 cups of distilled or spring water. Cover the pan, bring the water to a boil, reduce the temperature to low, and then simmer until all the petals' color has faded (5 to 10 minutes). Remove the pan from the heat, keeping the lid on, until it's cooled completely. Then strain out the solids and pour the rosy-colored liquid into a sterilized glass bottle with a tight-fitting cap. Store it at room temperature for up to a week, or for several weeks in the refrigerator.

It's what's on the inside that counts. You can buy high-quality dried organic rose petals from reputable herb suppliers. If you opt for fresh rose petals, avoid any from plants that have been sprayed with pesticides or foliar fertilizers. But organic or not, before you use the petals, rinse them thoroughly to remove any dust, tiny bugs, residue, or other debris.

Q: Why does Solubol appear in so many essential oil bath blends?

A: For the simple reason that oils are not water soluble. Pouring them directly into a bath will result in a film of undiluted oil on top. Not only will that fail to give you the full-body (or, in some cases, full-foot) results you want, but your skin will also bear the full brunt of the undiluted oil, and that could be highly irritating. Solubol, which is made from ingredients that are health-giving in their own right, binds and safely disperses the oils evenly through-out a tub or basin of water. It performs this important action in body mists and sprays that are high in H_2O. It's inexpensive and available from essential oil suppliers and other retailers that cater to DIYers.

ANTI-AGING MATTERS

BEAUTIFUL BALANCING TONER

The key to a more youthful-looking complexion is retaining, or restoring, your skin's natural pH balance, which is slightly acidic. This enables it to shed dead skin cells and fend off blemish-causing bacteria. This terrific toner does exactly that along with moisturizing, refreshing, and purifying your skin.

2 heaping tbsp. of linden flowers   **4 oz. of apple cider vinegar***

8 oz. of just-boiled spring or distilled water

Put the flowers in a heat-proof glass container and pour the water over them. Cover, and steep for 10 to 15 minutes. Strain out the solids and let the infusion cool to room temperature. Add the vinegar, stir, and pour the blend into a glass bottle with a tight-fitting cap. Store it at room temperature, and dab it onto your face with a cotton ball or pad. *For very sensitive skin, substitute less-acidic rice vinegar.*

How sweet it is! Anti-aging exfoliating (a.k.a. scrubbing) routines don't come any easier, or gentler, than this one: Once a week, wet your face, then massage about a teaspoon of olive oil into your skin. Then put a teaspoon or so of sugar into the palm of your hand and scrub your face. The oil and sugar work together to help moisturize your complexion and remove dead skin cells at the same time. Wipe off any excess with a warm, damp washcloth, and you'll be grinning ear to ear!

SAFE & SOUND When you're making DIY skin-care products, it can be tempting to use fractionated coconut oil because unlike the extra virgin variety, it retains its liquid consistency at room temperature. Well, think twice about that time-saving ploy. While the fractionated oil is perfectly safe, it lacks the full load of fatty acids, vitamins, minerals, and antioxidants that make extra virgin coconut oil so beneficial for your skin—and hair, too.

Exfoliate and glow. Most exfoliating treatments are scrub-it-on-and-rinse-it-off routines. This one is different because it's also a rejuvenating mask. To make it, mix 3 tablespoons of baking soda, 1 teaspoon each of honey and vitamin E oil, 1/4 teaspoon of cinnamon, and 3 to 4 teaspoons of milk to make a paste. Apply it all over your face in a thick layer. Then gently massage the mixture into your skin using circular motions. Let the mask dry for 10 to 15 minutes. Then rinse it off with warm water, again working in circular motions. Pat dry, and follow up with your normal toner and moisturizer.

The glowing fine print. Here's the secret behind the exfoliating mask above: The baking soda gently scrubs away dead skin cells; the honey supplies intense moisture and antioxidants; the vitamin E repairs and protects your skin; and the cinnamon brings fresh, oxygen-rich blood to the surface to kill bacteria, remove toxins, and give a healthy, rosy radiance to your complextion.

Be a two-way winner. As you will see on page 116 (in the Safe & Sound box), using cosmetic products that contain any unhealthy ingredients can also damage your internal health. The reverse is also true: When you treat your skin with nourishing foods, you also deliver their anti-aging benefits to your body's inner workings. Here's one fine way to put that food force to work: Whirl 1 cup each of shelled almonds, shredded orange peel, and uncooked oatmeal in a blender or food processor to form a fine powder. Store it in an airtight glass container at room temperature. Then scoop some of the powder into the palm of your hand, add a few drops of water, and rub it onto your face. Rinse with warm water, pat dry, and apply your usual toner and moisturizer.

Time Saver

If you use a commercial liquid soap or cleanser, here's a slick trick that'll instantly enhance its softening power: Simply add 1 tablespoon of vinegar per cup of the product. It works on both facial and all-over body cleansers. Whatever kind of vinegar you use—plain or infused with herbs or flowers—will make your skin feel silky soft and look younger.

SKIN-LIVENING LIBATION

This bracing beverage is a fountain of youth for skin. The grapes serve up tons of anti-aging antioxidants, and the tea contains one superstar called EGCG. It reactivates dying skin cells by causing them to produce DNA and start dividing again. The apple cider vinegar adds enzymes that promote the healthy functioning of your body and your brain.

1/2 cup of Concord grapes

1/2 cup of green seedless grapes

1/4 cup of brewed green tea

1 tbsp. of apple cider vinegar

1 cup of pure spring or distilled water

Put all of the ingredients into a blender and whirl them on high speed until the mixture is thoroughly combined and frothy. Pour it into a glass and enjoy it immediately, or store it, tightly sealed, in the refrigerator for up to four hours.

Reduce wrinkles and shore up sagging skin. You could pay mega-bucks for commercial products that help to produce those fabulous feats. Or, for pennies on the dollar, you could make your own anti-aging serum this way: Mix 1 ounce of jojoba oil with 4 drops each of carrot seed, rose, and sandalwood essential oils. Store the mixture in a cobalt blue or dark amber glass bottle in a cool, dark place. Then, every evening after washing your face, wipe a few drops of the serum onto your skin. It will minimize fine lines and wrinkles, and also help tighten your skin.

ANTI-AGING MATTERS

Q: I've heard that exfoliating treatments are damaging to aging skin. Is this true?

A: No. In fact, it's exactly the opposite. Exfoliating stimulates both blood and lymph flow, and helps speed up cell turnover. That's important because, as you age, the process of forming new skin cells and shedding the old ones naturally slows down and your skin can start to look dull. Since mature skin is thinner, exfoliate less frequently and more gently using a product formulated for your skin type.

By golly, glycerin's great! And it's just what the doctor ordered for aging skin. That's because it's a powerful humectant that pulls water from deeper skin layers up to the surface and also draws in moisture from the air to slow down its evaporation on your skin. To make your own marvelous moisturizer, simply combine 1 part vegetable glycerin and 4 parts organic rose water in a glass dropper-style bottle. Close the cap tightly, and shake. Then twice a day, morning and night, put 3 or 4 drops into the palm of one hand, and massage the mixture into your face and neck.

> If you use liquid foundation, use what's settled in the cap as concealer—it's just the right consistency and a perfect color match.

Deliver deep-down moisture to desert-dry skin. Keeping dry, aging skin soft and smooth can be a challenge, but if you live in a parched climate like the Southwest or Intermountain West, it can seem like an impossible dream. This mask can make your dream come true. To make it, mix 2 tablespoons of mashed strawberries, 1 tablespoon each of almond oil and extra virgin coconut oil, and 1 teaspoon of vitamin E oil (or the contents of two capsules) in a bowl. Smooth the mixture sparingly onto your face and go about your business for a few hours. Then rinse with warm water, moisten a cotton pad with pure witch hazel, and pat it onto your face. Refrigerate any leftover formula in a covered glass container and use it within a week.

Labor Saver

You couldn't ask for an easier way than this to reduce puffiness and dark circles under your eyes: Just pour leftover brewed coffee into an ice cube tray, and pop it into the freezer. Then whenever the need arises, grab a cube and gently rub it onto your under-eye skin. This trick is also great for soothing dry, itchy, or irritated eyes. In this case, rub a cube over your eyelids, being careful not to get the chilly java into your eyes themselves.

EASY AS PIE REJUVENATING MASK

Pumpkin is packed with the antioxidant vitamins A and C that help minimize signs of aging and with fruit enzymes and alpha hydroxy acids that perform two anti-aging feats: They remove dead skin cells and boost the growth of collagen, which fills in wrinkles.

1/4 cup of pumpkin puree (not pumpkin pie filling)	**5 drops of orange essential oil**
	1/2 tsp. of ground cinnamon
1 tbsp. of apple cider vinegar	**1/2 tsp. of ground ginger**
1 tsp. of vitamin E oil	**1/2 tsp. of ground nutmeg**

Mix all the ingredients in a bowl and spread a smooth layer of the mixture onto your freshly washed face. Let it dry for about 10 minutes, then rinse with cool water. Pat dry and apply your usual toner and moisturizer. Repeat two or three times a week or as needed to keep your skin vibrant and looking young.

Hang 'em all! You can dry makeup brushes by laying them flat on some paper towels or a lint-free cloth. But here's a better way to do the job: Attach each brush, bristle side down, to a plastic clothes hanger, using a twist tie or a Velcro® strip. Then suspend the hanger from a shower rod or towel bar. This suspension allows the brushes to dry much more quickly and also stay fluffier than they would if you left them in a prone position. Plus, they'll last a lot longer!

EARLY BIRD SPECIALS

Once you pass the 40-year mark, the makeup routine that you used even a few years ago is likely to make you look older, not younger. For that reason, there are scores of online makeup tutorials aimed at senior women. But if you'd prefer a more personal approach, check with cosmetician schools and beauty spas near you. Many of them offer classes or individual lessons— often at senior discount prices—that can help you look your best as the years march on.

Bathe your brushes. Every time you apply foundation, concealer, blush, or powder, the bristles hold on to some of the particles—along with any oil, dirt, or bacteria they pick up from your skin. And the next time you use the brush, you transfer that gunk to your freshly washed face. So once a week or so, wash each brush in a cleaner made from 2 cups of hot (not boiling!) water, 1/2 cup of white vinegar, and 10 drops of tea tree oil mixed with 1/2 teaspoon of Solubol dispersant. Gently, but thoroughly, rinse the bristles under lukewarm water. Swirl them around in the cleaning solution, then rinse under the spigot until the water runs clear. Let the brushes air-dry thoroughly before using them again.

Establish a brush-protection policy. It's no secret that good makeup brushes don't come cheap. So whenever you wash yours, no matter what they're made of, proceed with caution. To be specific, take care that only the bristles get wet. If any liquid gets in between the handle and the bristles, it will loosen the glue that holds the brush together, and eventually it will fall apart.

Money Saver

To make a toning, nourishing facial treatment at almost no cost, mix about a handful of coffee grounds with enough whole milk or half-and-half to form a paste. Apply the mixture to your freshly washed face and relax for 20 minutes. Then rinse with warm water, and admire your firmer, brighter skin!

Tell toxins to take a hike. Day in and day out, your face is bombarded with airborne particles that speed up the aging process. But don't just stand there and take it. Fight back this way: Mix 1 tablespoon each of activated charcoal and bentonite clay in a small nonreactive container. Then stir in enough apple cider vinegar to form a paste (1 1/2 to 2 tablespoons). Spread the mixture onto your skin in a thick layer, avoiding the eye area. Wait until it's dried (about 15 minutes). Then rinse it off with warm water, pat dry, and apply toner and moisturizer. Repeat once a month or as needed. This mask is especially useful during those hot, stifling periods when the air is so humid and crud-filled that you can almost cut it with a knife.

AGE SPOT REMOVAL REMEDY

Brown splotches (a.k.a. age, sun, or liver spots) can start appearing on your skin as early as your 40s, or even younger. They rarely pose health concerns, but they are unsightly. Here's how to send 'em packin'.

1/2 cup of pure aloe vera gel

1 tbsp. of apple cider vinegar

1 tbsp. of lemon juice

1 tbsp. of orange juice

10 drops of frankincense essential oil

Mix all of the ingredients in a bowl and pour the mixture into a clean glass bottle with a tight cap. Keep it refrigerated and shake well before each use. Using a cotton ball or swab, gently rub the formula onto each spot twice a day. How long it takes for the marks to vanish depends on many factors, but they may begin to lighten within a couple of weeks.

Toss the tags. One of the most annoying afflictions of an aging complexion can be the appearance of skin tags. These are small, often dark-colored growths that appear to hang off your skin. The good news is that while they are unsightly, skin tags are really harmless from a health standpoint. The bad news is that, for this reason, many of the insurance companies will not cover their removal. But fortunately, there are plenty of effective DIY remedies that will do that job, and this is one of the best: Three times a day, mix 3 drops of oregano essential oil with 1 teaspoon of extra virgin coconut oil, and rub it onto the tag. Within three to four weeks, it should dry up and fall off.

If a skin tag develops on one of your eyelids, or near an eye, don't even think of trying to remove the growth yourself. Instead, have a medical pro do the job. If you try any DIY measures in that delicate area, you could damage your vision or, in a worst-case scenario, even lose it. Safety aside, professional removal methods are a lot faster than DIY versions. So if you're in a hurry to get rid of the blasted little bumps, consult your family doctor or an ophthalmologist.

Use a rummy-good spot remover. This mixture is especially effective for getting rid of age spots and freckles on your hands and arms: Just mix 2 tablespoons of freshly squeezed lemon juice, 1 tablespoon of light rum, and 1 teaspoon of vegetable glycerin. Store the mixture in a glass bottle with a tight-fitting cap, and dab the potion onto the troubled areas once or twice a day. Before long, the blasted blemishes will be history!

Run, spots, run! Removing skin spots with any DIY remedy requires some patience. After all, it took them some time to build up, so you can't expect them to vanish overnight. But this formula seems to act more quickly than most: Mix 1 teaspoon each of grated horseradish, lemon juice, and vinegar and 3 drops of rosemary oil in a small bottle. Then dab the mixture onto the marks once a day. Just be forewarned that it is quite aromatic.

Enlist antioxidants in your anti-age-spot army. They're your body's best defense against aging on the inside and the outside of your body. So do as your mother always told you and eat plenty of antioxidant-rich fruits and vegetables. While this ploy may not fade the splotches you have now, it can help prevent more from developing. Don't fret about heaping your plate with specific "superfoods" day after day. Instead, simply make sure your diet includes a variety of produce that's high in beta-carotene and vitamins C and E.

Time Saver

To nix either age spots or skin tags with no muss, no fuss, and no mixing, reach for a bottle of apple cider vinegar. In the case of age spots, dab the vinegar directly onto the marks at bedtime, leave it on overnight, and rinse it off in the morning. Repeat as needed until the splotches are gone. For simple skin-tag removal, wash and dry the growth, then soak a cotton ball in vinegar, and squeeze it over the tag until it's saturated, and leave it on—no rinsing needed. Repeat three times a day until your skin is clear as a bell.

FOUNTAIN OF YOUTH BATH BLEND

Literally hundreds of products claim to reverse signs of aging in your skin, and some of them do help in that regard. But this one goes a step farther: In addition to making you look younger, it helps relieve a major internal cause of older-looking skin—namely stress.

- 2 tbsp. of meadowfoam carrier oil
- 3 drops of frankincense essential oil
- 3 drops of sandalwood essential oil
- 1/2 tsp. of Solubol dispersant
- 1 tbsp. of baking soda
- 1 tbsp. of pink Himalayan salt
- 2 tbsp. of apple cider vinegar

Mix the oils and Solubol, then combine the mixture with the baking soda and salt in an unbreakable container. Add the vinegar and stir to achieve an even consistency. Pour it under the tap as the water flows into the tub. Stir it with your hand to disperse the goodness. Then get in, lean back, and enjoy!

Soften your skin the way Grandma did. This simple and nourishing hand and body lotion hearkens back to the time when these products were thinner than the brands you can buy today. As a result, it will be absorbed into your skin faster and feel much less greasy. To make it, mix 2 tablespoons of vegetable glycerin with 1 tablespoon of freshly squeezed and strained lemon, lime, or orange juice (whichever you prefer). Store it, covered, in the refrigerator for up to five days or so.

SAFE & SOUND

Here's a sobering factoid: Roughly 60% of almost any substance that you put on your skin is absorbed into your bloodstream. So when you're shopping for commercial beauty products, read the labels carefully to avoid potential troublemakers. In particular, bypass anything that contains sulfates—especially sodium lauryl sulfate (SLS) and sodium laureth sulfate (SLES)—as well as parabens, triclosan, dyes, or fragrance (a.k.a. parfum).

Build a better body wash. This ultra-softening blend is perfect to use in either the bath or shower, and it's an extra-special skin-pleasing treat during the cold, dry winter months. To make it, put 2 cups of unscented liquid castile soap in a 1-quart jar. Add 1 cup of rose water, 3 tablespoons of melted extra virgin coconut oil, and 15 to 20 drops of lavender essential oil. Tighten the lid, shake to combine the ingredients, then pour some of the mixture into a smaller plastic squeeze bottle and use it as you would any other body wash. Store the remainder in a dark place at room temperature.

> To make a softening body wash, add 1 tablespoon of vinegar to 1 cup of your favorite liquid soap or cleanser.

Battle aging below your neck. During the ongoing effort to maintain a youthful-looking face and neck, it can be easy to overlook the skin on the rest of your body. That's where this super-softening and ultra-nourishing trio comes in. Simply add 1/4 cup each of cold-pressed avocado oil, cold-pressed sweet almond oil, and melted extra virgin coconut oil to a bottle with a tight-fitting cap, and shake well. Then every day, rub the mixture into your skin from your shoulders to your toes.

Out of the kitchen and into the tub! Youth-enhancing bath blends don't come any simpler, or more effective, than this: Mix 1 cup of apple cider or rice vinegar and 1/2 cup each of baking soda and uncooked oatmeal in a tub of warm water. Then ease into the tub for a soothing, softening soak. **Note:** *Be sure to cover the drain with a piece of fabric to snag the oatmeal particles!*

Labor Saver

For centuries, savvy women have been using a quick, slick trick to soften their skin and restore its natural acid balance. What is it? Just pour a cup of wine vinegar into a warm bath, and soak for 15 minutes or so. Either red, white, sherry, or champagne vinegar works like a charm, so use whichever kind you prefer or happen to have on hand.

SOFTENING, FIZZY FOOT SOAK

Treat your feet to this beautifying, and refreshing, bath. (The festive fizzing action comes from the carbon dioxide that's formed when you mix vinegar and baking soda.)

2 qts. of warm water   **1/4 cup of white or herb-infused vinegar**
1/4 cup of baking soda   **2 tbsp. of chopped fresh herbs (leaves or flowers)***

Fill a large, nonreactive container with the water (multiply the ingredients as needed to suit the size). Stir in the rest of the ingredients. Soak your feet for 15 to 20 minutes, then use a pumice stone to smooth especially rough areas and remove any calluses. Pat almost dry and massage a rich cream into your skin. *Either matched with the infused vinegar or not. Calendula, lavender, rose, sage, sweet marjoram, and thyme are great foot-soothing and deodorizing choices.*

Feed your feet some berries. This sweet treat performs the same feat for your feet that a facial mask does for the skin on your kisser. Not only will it make your feet softer and smoother, but it also delivers the youth-enhancing antioxidant power of strawberries. Simply mash 1/2 cup of fresh, hulled strawberries with 3 tablespoons of sugar and 2 tablespoons of olive oil. Rub the mixture all over your bare feet, then lean back and relax for 10 minutes or so. (Just make sure there's a nice, thick towel covering whatever your tootsies are resting on!) Rinse with warm water and follow up with your favorite foot cream.

HELP WANTED?

If your aging skin is so dry that it actually cracks and bleeds when you perform simple movements like flexing a hand, arm, or foot, you need something a lot stronger than DIY remedies. First, march off to the drugstore and get an over-the-counter 1% hydrocortisone cream, and use it according to the package instructions. If you don't get any relief, call your family doctor or a dermatologist, who can get to the root of the problem and help you resolve it.

Hair's to softer feet! When the skin on your feet is a little rougher than you'd like, but your schedule leaves no time for foot soaks or masks, this remedy needs no extra time and has your name written all over it. Before you go to bed, coat your feet with hair conditioner. Then pull on a pair of cotton socks. Keep them on overnight, then come morning, rinse off the conditioner. Repeat the procedure as needed until your skin has softened up, or until you have the time and inclination for more elaborate routines. (Just make sure you perform this process before you hop into the shower, so the soles of your feet aren't slippery!)

Pull an overnighter for extra-dry chapped hands or feet. When either set of appendages calls out for intensive softening action, a classic kitchen staple can come to your aid. At bedtime, rub vegetable shortening into your skin. Then, to protect your sheets and force the oil to penetrate deeper into your skin, put on rubber gloves or, in the case of your feet, thick socks or plastic bags. Repeat the process the following night if necessary.

Get lemon aid for rough elbows. Frequently, your hardworking arm joints are the first body parts to show unwelcome signs of the passing years. But when they start to get rough and dark, don't fret. Simply slice a lemon in half, bend your arm, and hold the cut side of the fruit firmly against one elbow. Then push and twist the lemon as though you were trying to juice it. Repeat the process on your other elbow, using the other half of the lemon. Rinse off the pulp and juice with warm water and apply a rich moisturizer. After a few rounds of this tart treatment, you should notice your elbows returning to their natural color.

Money Saver

You could pay big bucks for a fancy hand exfoliator. Or, for pennies on the dollar, you could get rid of layers of dead skin cells this way: Mix cold-pressed vegetable oil (like sunflower or safflower) with enough salt to make a gritty paste. Rub this mixture over your wet hands, and rinse well. It works like a charm!

FIVE-STAR SKIN-CARE ALLIES

Many herbs and essential oils can not only help you reduce the effects of future aging, but also, in some cases, reverse the damage that you may have already suffered. These rank among the best of the best.

HERBS

These superstars work like magic in facial formulas, body lotions, and bath blends. Use them alone, or combine two or three types. Don't use more than that, or you'll reduce the benefits of the individual herbs.

Calendula flowers cleanse, soothe, and reduce inflammation.

Chamomile supplies anti-inflammatory, antifungal, and anti-aging agents.

Elderflowers cleanse, tone, and act as gentle astringents.

Lavender soothes, cleanses, and helps to reduce inflammation.

Mallow can help reduce the visibility of age spots and wrinkles.

Mint cools, refreshes, and supplies plenty of antioxidant vitamin A.

Rosemary tones and improves anti-aging blood circulation to the capillaries.

Thyme fights bacteria and is especially effective on acne and eczema.

Yarrow is really good at toning, cleansing, and healing aging skin.

ESSENTIAL OILS

Combine these winners with a carrier oil or include them in an anti-aging recipe. Again, limit the number to two or three kinds to retain individual potency.

Carrot seed nourishes, tightens, and rejuvenates your skin.

Frankincense enhances the health and promotes the regeneration of skin cells.

Geranium helps tighten your skin, soothe irritation, and balance oil production.

Lavender hydrates dry skin, helps remove wrinkles, and soothes irritation.

Neroli sheds old skin cells and stimulates the growth of new ones.

Rose supplies a load of vitamin A that is essential for the health of aging skin.

Sandalwood tightens skin and helps prevent sagging.

CHAPTER 7

KITCHEN CLEANING

If you're becoming increasingly sensitive to ingredients in commercial cleaning products, you're not alone: It's an almost universal occurrence, especially once you cross the 60-year threshold. As your immune system becomes more delicate, even the least toxic of those substances can cause more trouble for your health and well-being. In this chapter, you will discover tons of terrific tips and fabulous formulas that'll help keep your kitchen and everything in it sparkling clean, without the harsh chemicals. I will also share some secret techniques to help make that space more user-friendly, now and for many years to come.

As always, vinegar plays a key role in this scenario, both as a solo performer and as a companion to many other natural, health-giving ingredients. However, in this case, when you're using vinegar for cleaning, deodorizing, or even pest-control purposes, don't even bother choosing a high-quality, unprocessed product. Instead, use the cheapest white or apple cider vinegar you can find. It'll do a fine job.

On a related note, the recipes and tips in this chapter call for the same white or apple cider vinegar that your mother and grandmothers likely used, not the newer, super-strength "cleaning" vinegars. Their actual acid concentration is 20 percent greater than that of "regular" vinegar. So that's not something you want to keep within reach of a grandchild or pet, or get on your own skin. If you feel the need to use one of these superpowered vinegars, be sure to handle it with care!

TILE-FLOOR CLEANER CONCENTRATE

This formula works as well as any commercial product, with no harsh chemicals. And you can make it in less than five minutes.

3/4 tsp. Solubol dispersant*
10 drops of grapefruit essential oil
10 drops of lavender essential oil

1 cup of white vinegar
1/4 cup of rubbing alcohol
Water

Mix the Solubol and oils, then combine the mixture in a glass jar with the vinegar and alcohol. Put the lid on, shake, and store it in a dark place. To use it, mix 1 part concentrate with 1 part water in a spray bottle. Spritz it onto the floor, and wipe with a cloth, sponge, or mop—no rinsing necessary. Or, if you prefer, mix 1 cup of the concentrate per gallon of hot water in a bucket, and mop as usual, rinsing the mop as you go along. *Available from essential oil suppliers.*

Take your floor to tea. Correction: Take tea to your floor. Just mix 1/2 cup each of peppermint tea and white vinegar in a measuring cup or bowl with 2 table-spoons of unscented liquid soap or detergent. Pour the mixture into a bucket of hot water and mop your floor as usual. Your kitchen will look like a dream and smell like an old-time candy store!

ANTI-AGING MATTERS

Q: What's the best kind of kitchen flooring for folks who want to age in place with grace? We are remodeling our home with that goal in mind.

A: Rubber tile tops the list. It's easy on the legs and feet and slip-resistant even when it's wet. Plus, if you do take a tumble, rubber cushions the blow better than any other material. It's also resistant to burns and stains and prevents the growth of mold, mildew, or bacteria. Add general ease of maintenance, and you'll see why rubber has become the flooring of choice in many restaurants and senior- or assisted-living facilities.

Join the anti-fatigue league. Standing in one place while you work in the kitchen can take a toll on your body, regardless of the material underfoot. On a hard surface, like ceramic tile, just a brief period can be quite agonizing, even with minor joint pain. For that reason, an anti-fatigue mat could be your first-class ticket to happier mealtimes. The right choice can greatly reduce stress on your feet and legs, and relieve or help prevent back and knee problems.

> A terrific addition to an aging-in-place kitchen is a motorized, adjustable sink that can go from standard to chair height as needed.

Take a test drive. Like most products, anti-fatigue mats are widely available online, and the Internet is a good place to research your options. GelPro® and SmartCells® are two popular brands, but there are many others. But I recommend shopping in person if you can. That way, you can try out several versions before you make what could be a fairly sizable investment.

Ponder before you shop. Finding the best anti-fatigue mat for you can depend on many factors, including your current physical condition, the kind of flooring you have, and how long you normally spend on your feet in the kitchen. Be sure to measure the length of the work surface where you spend most of your time, and choose a mat that spans the whole distance. That's because having to step on and off the padding, or stand with one foot on and one off can lead to posture and joint problems. Also consider mat upkeep. In some cases, your warranty will be voided unless you follow the precise cleaning and general maintenance guidelines in your owner's manual.

Time Saver

To make an all-purpose deodorizing cleaner, mix equal parts of white vinegar, rubbing alcohol, and water with 3 drops of dishwashing liquid in a spray bottle. Spray it on a floor or wall, and wipe the dirt away. Thanks to the alcohol, the surface will dry in a flash!

VINEGAR-LEMON CLEANING GEL

It's not always easy to keep up with liquid cleaners as they run down vertical surfaces, but this winner solves that problem. It packs the heavy-hitting power of vinegar with a big bonus: It stays put long enough for you to carry out the task at hand.

3/4 cup of white vinegar   **5–10 drops of lemon essential oil**
3 tbsp. of cornstarch

Combine the vinegar and cornstarch in a pot, and heat it on low, stirring constantly, until the mixture starts to thicken (5 to 10 minutes). Remove it from the heat and continue to stir until a paste forms, adding more vinegar or cornstarch, as needed, to achieve the right texture. Let the blend cool to room temperature, then stir in the oil. Store the gel in a tightly closed glass container at room temperature, and use it as you would any other gel cleanser.

Clean your cleaning gear. No amount of elbow grease will get any surface clean if you're trying to do the job with an implement that's less than pristine. So immediately after using any brush, mop, or sponge, soak it for five minutes or so in a half-and-half mixture of vinegar and hot water. Then rinse it thoroughly with clear water, and let it air-dry.

EARLY BIRD SPECIALS

After decades of feeding a family, the process of preparing healthy and appetizing meals for just one or two people day after day can be daunting. For that reason, cooking classes for seniors are becoming popular, and many classes are free or very low cost. Some focus on adjusting recipes and food-prep techniques to feed fewer, and older, mouths. Others concentrate on the challenges of people who are cooking for elderly loved ones. Either way, you can refine your culinary skills while making friends. To find classes near you, check with local organizations, churches, and adult-ed facilities, or search online for "senior cooking classes [your area]."

Choose cutting boards with care. Many folks assume plastic cutting boards are safer than wooden versions, when actually, just the opposite is true. According to scientific studies, any bacteria that appear on wood will migrate below the surface, where they cannot reproduce and so eventually die off. Conversely, every time you use a plastic board, your knife creates grooves where bacteria collect and multiply. These slits are nearly impossible to clean out, either by hand or in a dishwasher. So if you prefer to use a plastic board, replace it frequently.

Double up for safety. Regardless of whether you opt for wood or plastic, keep two cutting boards, or two sets of them: one for use with raw meats, poultry, and fish; and another designated for produce and prepared foods. This way, you'll eliminate the chance of cross-contamination.

Cut some canny cutting board capers. Whether you choose to do your chopping, slicing, and dicing on wood or ungouged plastic, it's essential to keep that surface sanitary—and it becomes even more vital as your aging immune system becomes more sensitive to all the unhealthy stuff you encounter. For that job, this simple routine kills virtually all *Salmonella*, *Shigella*, and *E. coli* bacteria, even on heavily contaminated food-prep surfaces. All you need are two spray bottles, one filled with undiluted white or apple cider vinegar; the other with 3% hydrogen peroxide. Spray the board with the vinegar, then immediately spray the area with the peroxide. Rinse with clear water, and you're good to go!

Labor Saver

If you use plastic cutting boards, you know that grooves aren't the only things they collect. Even after washing, the surface retains the odors of the foods that you cut on it. But there is a surefire way to keep the aromas from mixing and mingling: Keep a quartet of color-coded boards on hand. Use one color for meat, a second for bread, a third for strong-smelling vegetables like onions and garlic, and a fourth for less-aromatic produce.

FOOD-SAFE KITCHEN CLEANER

The older we get, the more sensitive we become to the chemicals in commercial cleaning products. So the last thing you need is to have food exposed to lingering toxins in your refrigerator, on countertops, or on your grandbabies' high-chair trays. That's where this DIY cleaning spray comes in.

1 qt. of white vinegar   **2 tbsp. of dried food-grade lavender buds**
3 tbsp. of dried thyme

Pour the vinegar into a clean glass jar with a tight-fitting plastic lid. Add the herbs, and let the mixture steep in a cool, dark place for one to two weeks, shaking the jar every day or so. Then strain the liquid into a clean glass jar. For routine cleaning, mix the formula with an equal amount of water in a spray bottle. To tackle tougher jobs, use the mixture straight from the bottle.

Use a glass act for cabinet doors. Glass doors can make kitchen cabinets look as classy as all get-out. And they're perfect for showing off treasures that you don't use every day. A good example is the family-size platter your granddaughter made for you in pottery class. Unfortunately, while these display "windows" keep the cupboards' contents crystal clear, they seem to collect more than their fair share of the grease and other sticky stuff that goes airborne in every kitchen. To clear the crud away, simply wipe the glass periodically with a mixture of 2 cups of water, 1/2 cup of white vinegar, and 1/4 cup of rubbing alcohol.

SAFE & SOUND

Never use vinegar on granite, marble, or any other natural stone. The same goes for citrus juices or other acidic substances. Stone is highly susceptible to damage from acid, and it doesn't take much to cause trouble. For everyday cleaning, all you need to do is wipe the countertop with water and a soft cloth. To tackle a soiled surface, go with denatured alcohol or cheap vodka.

Say it with citrus—safely. Judging from the scads of citrus-scented cleansers lining supermarket shelves, a whole lot of folks love that fresh, sun-country aroma. The problem is that most of those products contain chemicals that you can't even pronounce, much less want near your food. So forget 'em! Instead, make your own superpowered and super-safe version this way: Wash and dry a large glass jar, and fill it with peels from five or six citrus fruits. Use whatever kind you prefer—orange, lemon, lime, tangerine, grapefruit, or any combination thereof. Add enough white vinegar to completely cover the peels. Cover the jar, and give it a good shake. Let it steep in a cool, dark place for two to three weeks, shaking it every day or so and sniffing it occasionally until it's reached your desired aroma. Then strain the liquid into a fresh container.

Put your power player to work.

For any routine cleaning chore, combine equal amounts of your infused vinegar and water in a spray bottle, and go to town using a sponge, soft cloth, or paper towels. To tackle tough jobs, you can use the citrusy potion straight from the bottle, with no water added.

Fast first aid for a burned broiler pan. It doesn't take much to make a burned-on mess in one of these babies. And it doesn't take much to clear it off, either. Here's all you need to do: While the pan is still warm, pour in 2 cups of white vinegar and 1/4 cup of sugar. Stir lightly, let the pan sit for about an hour or so, and then wash it as usual. Presto—end of the mess!

Money Saver

It's no secret that granite and marble countertops can cost megabucks. But as you get older, dodging these and other materials like ceramic tile, terra-cotta, quartz, and concrete, for countertops and floors both, can save you money in another way. That's because, as your reaction time naturally slows down, and your grip tends to weaken, you become more prone to dropping things. And these substances are unforgiving. For example, a glass or plate that might survive a tumble on a vinyl floor or laminate countertop is all but guaranteed to shatter on a harder surface.

ALL-PURPOSE CLEANING SCRUB

This foaming formula makes ranges, laminate or ceramic-tile countertops, and porcelain appliances shine like nobody's business. Plus, the tea tree oil provides antiseptic, antimicrobial, and antifungal action, and its slight medicinal undertone is overshadowed by the pine oil.

1/2 cup of baking soda	**5 drops of pine essential oil***
1/4 cup of white vinegar	**5 drops of tea tree oil**

Just before you start cleaning, mix all of the ingredients in a bowl. Apply the mixture to the surface at hand using a cotton cloth, sponge, or scrub brush. Then rinse with warm water. *Or other scented oil of your choice (see "Mean, Green Cleaning 'Machines'" on page 140).*

Lose the labels—fast. Removing labels and price tags from glassware and ceramics can be a nuisance for anyone. If you have arthritic fingers, it can be a time-consuming nightmare, unless you use this trick: Fill a sink or large pan with warm water, stir in a scoop of OxiClean™ stain remover, and insert the sticker-decked pieces. Then go about your business for 30 minutes. When you come back, simply rub the labels off.

Time Saver

A lot of budget-conscious folks keep an eagle eye out for supermarket flyers and website ads that list the prices of various products, and then drive from one store to another to save money on groceries. But there are a couple of good reasons to find a convenient, reasonably priced store and do most of your shopping there. One is that all the driving can actually wind up costing you more on car maintenance and gas than you save on food costs. Another is that your golden years give you time to do things like play with your grandchildren, learn a new sport, or putter in your garden. So do you really want to spend those precious hours behind the wheel of a car?

Add some labels—pronto. Does it seem that you're forever tossing out over-the-hill food because you can't remember when you put it into the refrigerator? Well, here's a simple solution to that common aging-brain dilemma: Whenever you put leftovers or just-opened jars or food packages into your refrigerator, write two dates on the container: the current date, and the one by which you want to use the contents. If the container is one you want to keep, use an adhesive label or sticky note.

Don't play guessing games. While food does not become inedible on its "best if used by" date, it does begin to decline in flavor and overall quality. So if there is no date on the package, do an Internet search for "food storage chart." You'll find a passel of sites filled with expert advice on storing food safely, including how long you can keep everything from hot dogs to hard cheese and egg yolks to eggplant.

Banish food-spoiling brain fog in the pantry. It's not only refrigerated and frozen foods that can fall victim to the all-too-common middle-age muddle. Crackers, cereal, and other perishable and semi-perishable edibles in your cabinets can easily get lost and forgotten among your kitchen gear. The solution to this dilemma should be a no-brainer, but in many homes it isn't: No matter how small your kitchen is, keep the food and the equipment in separate places.

Q: We just received a set of lead crystal wineglasses for our 40th wedding anniversary. I'd love to use them on a regular basis, but I've heard the lead can cause health problems. Is this true?

A: Technically speaking, yes—but for all practical purposes, no. It is true that the long-term ingestion of lead can have health consequences, and if (for example) you store wine or liquor in a lead crystal decanter for weeks or months, the liquid could absorb a fairly sizable number of particles. But it is unlikely that enough loose lead would leach out of glasses to cause any risk to people who are using them. But before using new lead crystal for the first time, it's a good idea to soak the pieces (along with any carafes or decanters) in white vinegar for at least 24 hours. Any loose lead that may be present will be absorbed by the vinegar.

ANTI-AGING MATTERS

FRESH AS A DAISY DRAIN DE-CLOGGER

When your kitchen sink isn't emptying out as quickly as it should, this routine will help clear it out in a flash. It even gives the drainpipes a fresh, clean scent.

1/2 cup of white vinegar   **1/4 cup of baking soda**
5 or 6 drops of lemon essential oil   **Hot water**

Pour the vinegar into a glass jar, add the oil, put the lid on, and shake vigorously. Then pour the baking soda into the drain, followed by the vinegar-oil mixture. Let it sit for 20 to 30 minutes, then rinse with hot water. Bingo! You'll have free-flowing pipes again.

Shine up your stainless steel sink. These babies are durable all right—and much gentler on dropped glasses or dishes than their porcelain counterparts are. The one downside is that these sinks seem to lose their shine in a New York minute. To bring back the sparkle, first wipe away any loose grime or food particles. Next, sprinkle baking soda over the surface, and gently scrub it with a soft sponge, using circular motions. Rinse with white vinegar, which will bubble and fizz as it works to disinfect the sink and remove any hard-water marks. Lightly rub with the sponge again, and rinse with clear water. Then, to help the revived shine linger longer, rub the entire sink with a section of orange or lemon peel (pith side down). Finish by buffing the surface with a paper towel lightly moistened with olive oil. That metal should gleam like a dream for several weeks before needing a refresher!

SAFE & SOUND If you have trouble bending over, or lifting things from below waist level, one simple kitchen hack could go a long way toward increasing your comfort, and possibly heading off major back problems. What is it? Raise the height of your dishwasher. Even if that means hiring a handyman or plumber to move the machine to a new location, it should be well worth the cost because it will greatly reduce the strain of loading and unloading the racks.

Silence a chattering dishwasher. When your dishwasher's spray arm starts sputtering, chances are it's gotten jammed with mineral deposits and some food residue. To clean out the crud, remove the dish racks, and then take out the screws that hold the arm in place. Lift it off, and lay it flat on a counter. Then poke a strand of thin wire into each hole. When you're through, give the arm a gentle shake to make sure nothing else is caught in there, and then scrub the mineral deposits away with a solution of vinegar and hot water.

Don't let your can opener share the "wealth." Dang! You're cooking dinner and find that your can opener's wheel is just filled with gunk—and you don't want it transferred to the food inside the tin you're about to open. The quick and simple solution: Immerse the business end of the opener in white vinegar, and scrub the mechanism with a retired toothbrush.

> Before you pour tomato sauce into a plastic food-storage container, spritz the inside with cooking oil spray to prevent staining.

Chill out side by side. Buying a new refrigerator? Whether you're gearing up to age in place, you simply don't move as smoothly as you once did, or someone in your household is disabled, a side-by-side (a.k.a. French-door style) could be your best bet. First, it provides easy access to both fridge and freezer sections. What's more, the slimmer doors let out less cold air than traditional top-and-bottom-mount versions do. If it takes you some time to find and retrieve what you're looking for, that factor can translate into less electric usage and enhanced food quality. Finally, the smaller swing radius of side-by-side doors can be a plus for saving space in a small kitchen.

Labor 👍 Saver

Always keep a tray of vinegar ice cubes in your freezer. Then once a week or so, pop a couple of cubes into the dishwasher just before you start a cycle. The vinegar will keep the machine's interior both stain- and odor-free—saving you the hassle of cleaning it.

GARBAGE-DISPOSAL CLEANING CUBES

These easy-to-make, aromatic nuggets combine the cleaning power of vinegar with the antibacterial and antifungal properties of rosemary. And the citrus peels deliver a one-two punch: They offer up a full load of antibacterial oils and help sharpen the machine's blades, too!

1/2 cup of diced citrus peels   **White vinegar**

2 tbsp. of dried or diced fresh rosemary

Mix the peels and rosemary in a bowl, and distribute the mixture evenly in an ice cube tray. Fill the compartments with vinegar, and pop the tray into the freezer until the cubes are frozen solid. Then transfer them to a freezer container. To get your disposal clean and smelling fresh, simply toss a cube or two down the drain, turn on the cold water, and flick the power switch.

Put your garbage disposal back to work. When a hardened mass of who-knows-what has the mechanism so clogged up that it won't dispose of anything, try this simple remedy: Mix equal parts of vinegar, salt, and baking soda. Pour the concoction directly into the drain, and let it sit for 10 to 15 minutes. Then rinse with 2 cups of boiling water. That should clear out the crud and get things flowing again. If it doesn't, call a plumber, who can install a new disposal if need be.

EARLY BIRD SPECIALS

When you think about senior discounts, appliance repair may not be the first category that pops into your mind. But many locally owned repair shops give price breaks to folks above a certain age (which can vary from one establishment to another), and to military veterans of any age. So do your bank account a favor: Before trouble strikes, in your kitchen or anywhere else in your house, search for "appliance repair discounts [your town]." Then check out your options. That way, you won't find yourself scrambling for help, or paying top dollar, when your freezer stops turning out ice cubes, or your washing machine quits cold turkey.

Wash greasy dishes on the cheap. Contrary to popular belief (and Madison Avenue marketing hype), you don't need to use those special grease-cutting dishwashing liquids to get intensive cleaning power. Whether you are out of your usual brand, or you have grown sensitive to the chemicals it contains, you have an option that works just as well and at a lower cost. Just buy whatever kind you prefer (choosing a fragrance- and dye-free version if you like). Then when you fill up the sink and squirt the soap in, add 1/4 cup or so of white vinegar. That should give you all the oomph you need to get even the greasiest pots and pans sparkling clean—even if you use less than the amount of detergent recommended on the label.

Keep a heavy-duty cleanser on hand. You never know when you have to tackle an extra-tough kitchen-cleaning job. So to save yourself a lot of time and hassle, combine equal parts of baking soda, salt, and borax, and store the mixture in a closed container. It'll get gunky grease and grime off of pots, pans, appliances, tile floors, and just about every other hard surface you can think of.

Scrub softly and thoroughly. When you've got a grimy, but delicate, surface to clean, this is the DIY formula to reach for. Mix 1/8 cup of baking soda with enough of your favorite grease-cutting dishwashing liquid to get a creamy consistency. Apply the mixture with a sponge or soft brush, and rinse with clear water. Voilà! A spotless and scratch-free surface.

Money Saver

When you're shopping for kitchen gear, it's true you may be able to snag a senior discount at a hardware or housewares store, but there's an even better place to save money on pots, pans, and utensils of all kinds. That's a restaurant-supply store. Whether you're in the market for a new frying pan, you need duplicate gear for a getaway cottage, or you're helping to outfit a first kitchen for a child or grandchild, you'll spend a fraction of the price you'd pay in a big-box store. Plus, you'll get the kind of quality that professional chefs bank their careers on!

MIGHTY MICROWAVE CLEANER

What's worse than a microwave oven that reeks of baked-on food? Food that winds up reeking of the chemical concoction you used to clean the nuker—that's what! So forget that toxic stuff and use this safer, and much more appetizing, approach.

2 or 3 lemons, chopped   **Water**
1/4 cup of white or apple cider vinegar

Put the lemon chunks in a microwave-safe bowl or baking dish. Pour in the vinegar, and fill the rest of the container with water. Nuke it on high for three to four minutes, or until the water starts to boil. Let it sit for another 10 minutes or so to let the steam loosen the crud. Then remove the dish and wipe the compartment clean with a damp sponge.

Start every morning with top-notch coffee. When your electric coffeemaker starts producing java that tastes bitter or sour, fill the well to capacity with a half-and-half solution of water and white vinegar. Install an empty filter to catch any crud that comes out, and run the machine through a normal brewing cycle. "Brew" three or four batches of clear, fresh water to remove all traces of vinegar. Repeat the process as needed (your taste buds will tell you when it's time).

If you're looking for ways to make your home safer to live in as you grow older, you're far from alone. In fact, the fastest-growing segment of the residential remodeling industry is modifications for maturing and older adults who want to age in place. The National Association of Home Builders (NAHB®), in collaboration with AARP, has developed a training program that awards the designation Certified Aging-in-Place Specialist (CAPS). Whether you're thinking of making major changes to your current home or building a new one in the future, these experts can help you decide what fits your needs now and what can be tweaked as conditions change. To find an adviser near you, visit www.NAHB.org and search for "CAPS [your area]."

Keep your Keurig® "kettle" clean. If you're a fan of the multitasking Keurig brewers, you should know that one key to keeping your machine crankin' out flavorful cuppas is to de-scale it on a regular basis. To do that, fill the water reservoir halfway with white vinegar and run the brewer (minus any K-Cups) through several brewing cycles until the container is empty. Then rinse it, fill it with clear water, and run it again until all the water is gone. As with a regular coffeemaker, how often you need to perform this chore depends on how much you use the device and how hard your water is. Some models have an indicator light that goes on when it's time for de-scaling. If your machine is lightless, let your taste buds be your guide.

Read before you clean. While vinegar is generally safe to use in any coffeemaker, don't take chances: Before you run it or any other DIY cleaner through the coffee machine, consult your owner's manual. If the technique is not officially approved, you could void the manufacturer's warranty.

Clean your oven the elbow-greaseless way—with no chemicals and without the foul odor that those ultra-hot self-cleaning cycles can toss at you. Start by vacuuming the bottom of the oven to remove any loose debris and some of the stuck-on grime. Next, mix 2 parts baking soda with 1 part water to make a paste, and spread it all over the oven. Let it sit for at least 20 minutes, or even overnight if the surface is extremely dirty. Go over it with a damp cloth or sponge, working in circular motions. Then spray the entire treated area with white vinegar. It will react with the leftover baking soda, so you can easily wipe out the bubbling residue. Finally, dampen a clean sponge with white vinegar, and wipe down the whole oven to help prevent future greasy buildup.

Time Saver

Like just about every other problem under the sun, a clogged drain is less time-consuming and a whole lot easier to prevent than it is to fix. In this case, here's all you need to do: Every three months or so, pour 1 cup of white vinegar down the drain, wait for about 10 minutes, then flush with hot water from the spigot.

HANDS-OFF INTENSIVE COPPER CLEANER

Nothing compares to copper cookware for top-notch performance and classic good looks. Unfortunately, though, when you don't use a pan for a while, it can develop a thick coat of tarnish. If you have big pots that you only use on special occasions, this formula belongs in your repertoire.

3 tbsp. of flour   **White vinegar**
3 tbsp. of salt

Mix the flour and salt with enough vinegar to form a paste that's thick enough to cling to the metal. (Start with about 2 tablespoons, then gradually stir in more as needed.) Using a soft cloth, spread the paste thickly onto the copper, buffing lightly as you go. Put the pan into a plastic bag, secure the opening with a twist tie, and let it sit for 6 to 12 hours. Rinse the coating off, and dry the pan. Repeat as needed.

Treat your teakettle tenderly. Chances are, it "lives" on top of the stove, where it picks up splatters and splotches galore. To get rid of them, spritz the outside with either white or apple cider vinegar. Then sprinkle baking soda on a soft, damp cloth, and wipe the marks away. Just make sure you follow the grain of the metal to avoid scratching the surface.

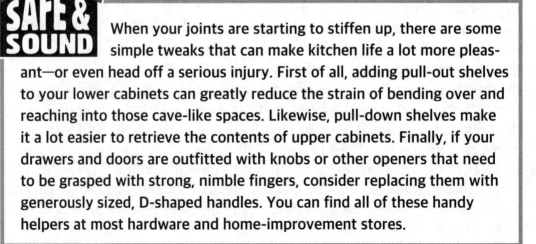

SAFE & SOUND

When your joints are starting to stiffen up, there are some simple tweaks that can make kitchen life a lot more pleasant—or even head off a serious injury. First of all, adding pull-out shelves to your lower cabinets can greatly reduce the strain of bending over and reaching into those cave-like spaces. Likewise, pull-down shelves make it a lot easier to retrieve the contents of upper cabinets. Finally, if your drawers and doors are outfitted with knobs or other openers that need to be grasped with strong, nimble fingers, consider replacing them with generously sized, D-shaped handles. You can find all of these handy helpers at most hardware and home-improvement stores.

Spray your copper clean. A light to medium coat of tarnish on a pan is no match for this good-riddance routine: Mix 1 cup of white vinegar with 1 1/2 teaspoons of salt in a spray bottle. Shake, and spray the potion generously onto the copper. Give it 30 minutes to work its magic, and then rub the surface clean with a soft cotton cloth. Unless the crud has been building up for a long time, that should do the trick, but if any smudges remain, repeat the process.

When you're remodeling a kitchen for the long haul, consider a wall oven installed at a height that reduces lifting and bending.

Say bye-bye to brown stains. For a whole lot of folks, coffee and tea are two of life's greatest pleasures. But there's nothing pleasing about the ugly brown stains they leave on ceramic cups, mugs, and teapots. Fortunately, wherever the stains have settled, it's a snap to get rid of them. If the marks are on cups and mugs, just mix equal parts of salt and white vinegar, and scrub the blemishes away. To clean a teapot, rub the inside with a half-and-half mixture of salt and vinegar, then rinse with warm water.

De-fog your glasses. When you're getting ready for a big party, and you discover that your wine and cocktail glasses are all looking hazy and dull, don't fret! Just fill a pan with vinegar, and heat it until it's almost (but not quite) too hot to put your finger in. Pour it into a tub big enough to hold all your glasses, and set them into the bath. Let them soak for about three hours, and then wash them as usual. They'll sparkle like stars! **Note:** *If the "cloud cover" is extra-thick, you may need to use a plastic scouring pad instead of a dishcloth.*

Labor Saver

To spruce up stainless steel appliances or countertops, don't bother making or buying any special formulas. Instead, just wipe those babies down with plain white vinegar. Believe it or not, it works as well as any commercial cleaner or DIY formula—if not better!

BREATH-OF-SPRING FRUIT-FLY CATCHER

If spring tends to fill your kitchen with fruit flies, snag 'em using this clever variation on a classic trap. It'll polish off the pesky pests and leave the whole room smelling fresh.

1/2 cup of apple cider vinegar   **5 drops of your favorite essential oil**
3 or 4 drops of dishwashing liquid

Pour the vinegar into a bowl and mix in the dishwashing liquid. Then add the oil. There are no right or wrong choices here. Go with whatever aroma you like best or happen to have on hand. For example, rose, geranium, chamomile, lavender, or peppermint will all disguise the vinegar smell and send a fresh, light, and relaxing scent wafting through the air. In fact, no one will even guess that you're trapping bugs!

Rout the roaches. Although cockroaches are prevalent in the South and in densely populated cities like New York, they can show up virtually anywhere. And some types can spread dangerous bacteria, including *E. coli* and *Salmonella*. So if you spot even a single roach, make some DIY traps that'll polish the villains off without a trace of toxic residue, and with no risk to any grandchildren or pets who may be around. Here's the drill: Fill a small jar or expendable glass with moistened coffee grounds and set it inside a larger bowl that's filled about a quarter of the way with water. Place the trap against a wall in your kitchen or anywhere roaches are lingering. The irresistible coffee aroma will lure them to the jar, but before they get there, they'll fall into the water and drown.

Money Saver

To make a cheap and easy fruit-fly trap, simply pour a bit of apple cider vinegar into a jar (just a thin layer on the bottom will do). Cover the opening with plastic wrap, and secure it with a rubber band. Then poke a few small holes in the covering. The flies will flit in through the holes to get at the vinegar, and they won't be able to fly out.

Make kitchen- and kid-safe mouse poison. Just like roaches, mice can spread serious diseases. And the older you grow, and the more susceptible you become to bacteria and viruses of all kinds, the more important it is to keep the menaces out of your kitchen. This formula will deal a death blow to mice (or rats) without harming a toddler grandchild or pet who might decide to sample it. To make it, mix 1 cup each of baking soda, flour, and sugar in a bowl, and put just a tablespoon or so of the mixture into jar lids or similar containers. Then set them where you've seen droppings or other signs of rodent visitations. The baking soda will mix with their stomach acids to create carbon dioxide. Because the critters can't burp, their stomachs will swell up and squash their lungs.

Use a sour-and-sweet ant-deterrent strategy. If a colony of ants has set up camp near your house, and keeping them out of your kitchen is driving you nuts, lay out a sour unwelcome mat this way: Mix equal parts of white vinegar and water, and use the combo to spray or wipe down all of the pests' entrances, as well as counters and any other surfaces that are near food sources.

Keep 'em out with sweetness. To employ part two of your anti-ant strategy, mix equal parts of sugar and water in a shallow paper bowl and set it outside where the ants are likely to find it—preferably on the far side of their nest from your house. Chances are that once they've discovered the sweet stuff, they'll happily sip from that rather than make the trek to your kitchen.

Q: My adult children and grandchildren are prone to dropping in unexpectedly. I like to keep plenty of pasta, rice, beans, and other dried foods on hand so that I can whip up meals on the spur of the moment. But I'm always concerned that insects might get into the packages. How can I keep them out?

A: The answer couldn't be simpler: Store all your dried foods in airtight glass, metal, or plastic containers instead of their original packaging. Also, clean your pantry and other food-storage areas often and thoroughly. Bay-infused vinegar is great for this job because wily weevils, beastly beetles, and other pesky pantry pests will all keep their distance.

ANTI-AGING MATTERS

MEAN, GREEN CLEANING "MACHINES"

We've already shined the spotlight on herbs and essential oils that are effective in health and beauty formulas of all kinds. Many of those heavy hitters can also perform yeoman's work getting and keeping your appliances and kitchen surfaces as clean as a whistle without toxic chemicals.

ESSENTIAL OILS

These oils have prodigious cleaning powers, either used as simple water-based mists or mixed with vinegar. When earlier pages mention substitutions, you can feel free to use any of the following:

Cinnamon leaf is naturally antibacterial and antiseptic.

Eucalyptus is a powerful germicide, odor eliminator, and insect repellent.

Lavender has a clean, fresh scent that soothes and relaxes. It's popular for cleaning supplies, used alone or in combination with more germ-fighting oils.

Lemon is the top oil in natural-cleaning circles. It's antibacterial and antiviral, has grease-cutting power, and is famous for its light, clean scent.

Peppermint has antibacterial properties, along with a cool, invigorating scent.

Pine delivers antimicrobial properties, but is also used for its deodorizing power.

Rosemary is antibacterial and antiseptic, with an aroma perfect for a kitchen.

Tea tree is one of the strongest antifungal, antimicrobial, and antiseptic oils of all. To cover its somewhat medicinal scent, it's most often used in combination with another oil, like pine or lavender. **Caution:** *Tea tree oil is highly toxic to pets and should not be used in their vicinity. Nor should it be ingested by adults or children.*

Thyme is effective against *Salmonella* and safe to use around kids and pets.

Wild orange has a happy, mood-lifting scent and is a powerful grease fighter.

HERBS

The following plants offer the same benefits as their essential oil counterparts, but in a milder form. Use them alone or in combinations of two or three, either brewed into strong teas or infused in vinegar. They work equally well fresh or dried and can be substituted for the herbs listed in the recipes on earlier pages.

Cinnamon, Cloves, Eucalyptus, Lavender, Marjoram, Mint, Rosemary, Sage

CHAPTER 8

BATHROOM CLEANSERS

It seems that in just about every book or website devoted to the topic of senior living, the bathroom gets the lion's share of attention. And for good reason: For anyone whose balance, eyesight, or gripping power is at all compromised, it can seem more like a battlefield than a room that once beckoned you to soothing baths or invigorating showers. Aside from the hard surfaces that need to be navigated with care, most of the cleaners used to keep those floors and fixtures in pristine shape rank among the most toxic products on supermarket shelves. Well, friends, in this chapter, you'll find heaping helpings of tips, tricks, and people-friendly potions that'll help you turn your bathroom back into welcoming territory.

Sneak preview: Here's a DIY cleaner that will not only spruce up every surface in your bathroom, but will also deliver the double-barreled, mood-lifting scent of oranges and cloves—without the long steeping time of most infused vinegars.

Chop the peels from three or four oranges (enough to fill a quart-size glass jar about halfway). Put them in the jar, and add about 1/4 cup of whole cloves. Heat about a quart of white vinegar just to the boiling point, and pour it into the jar. Attach the lid, and let it sit for 24 hours. Then strain the liquid into a fresh jar or spray bottle and discard the solids. Bingo! You've got a superpowered cleaner that's so safe that if a curious grandchild or pet should happen to take a swig, the only consequence would be a rather unpleasant jolt to the taste buds…which is a good thing!

TOUGH, GENTLE, ALL-PURPOSE CLEANER

This helper can tackle tough cleanup jobs in your bathroom, or anyplace else in your home. And it has none of the mysterious, unpronounceable ingredients that most commercial cleaning products contain.

1 tsp. of Solubol dispersant*

1/2 tsp. of lemon essential oil

1/2 cup of white vinegar

1/2 cup of witch hazel

2 1/2 cups of water

Mix the Solubol and oil, then add the blend to a 32-ounce spray bottle. Pour in the vinegar, witch hazel, and water, and shake to thoroughly combine the ingredients. Use the mixture as you would any spray cleaner—no rinsing needed. **Available from essential oil suppliers.*

Keep cleaning power at your fingertips. How? Simply put 1/3 cup of baking soda in a bowl, and using a wire whisk, mix in 15 drops of spearmint essential oil. Transfer the mixture to a shaker container, and store it with your bathroom cleaning supplies alongside a spray bottle filled with white vinegar. Then, when you need to clean (let's say) a shower, sink, or toilet, sprinkle the powder onto the surface, spray the vinegar over it, and scrub the dirt away.

ANTI-AGING MATTERS

Q: I've heard that essential oils never go bad. Is this true?

A: They don't spoil like food, but over time the oils break down and become unsafe to use. Shelf life can vary greatly among oils. The heavier an oil is, the longer it retains its full strength and vitality. Remember, though, that even when an oil has passed its peak for use in DIY skin-care products or topical remedies, it may still work just fine in cleaning, laundry, and room-deodorizing formulas. Let your eyes and nose be your guides: If the oil still looks normal and smells good, then it's okay to use (for more on how to extend the life of essential oils, see "Make Your Oils' Power Last Longer" on page 160).

Clear the air. This DIY blend gives bathrooms a much needed blast of air freshener. Just pour 1 cup of distilled water and 1/2 cup of the cheapest vodka you can find into a spray bottle. Shake well, then add 10 drops of essential oil, either fresh or slightly outdated, and then shake again. The alcohol will sanitize the air and any surfaces the spray touches, while the oil offers up its natural aroma, along with its own particular health-giving, anti-aging properties (see "Mean, Green Cleaning 'Machines'" on page 140).

> Make a DIY air freshener by dabbing pine cones with a drop or two of essential oil, and group them in a pretty basket.

Eradicate swamp gases. Instead of using those extra-strength, commercial air-freshener sprays, simply light a candle—or several if need be. But don't bother with the fancy scented kind. Just like air-freshener sprays, all they'll do is launch potentially dangerous, odor-masking chemicals into the air that you (and maybe your young grandchildren) breathe. On the other hand, a pure candle flame will burn even the nastiest odors away safely.

Light the way. If you've found that as you grow older, your nocturnal bathroom visits become more frequent, do yourself a favor: To make sure a trip to the privy doesn't result in a trip to the ER, tweak your lighting. To be specific, make sure you put night-lights in the bathroom and along any hallways that may lead to it. Avoid them in the bedroom, though, because as dim as they are, they still interfere with sound sleep. Instead, opt for bedside lamps that turn on and off by touch.

Money Saver

If you have a bottle of essential oil that's past its prime for topical use, place it close to the toilet. Then before or after using that fixture, put a drop directly into the water. Tip: You might want to label your expired oils so you remember to use them for this and any other deodorizing purposes before the aroma declines.

TRUE GRIT MULTI-SURFACE CLEANER

When a cleaning job calls for major firepower, this is the recipe to use.

- **1 tsp. of Solubol dispersant**
- **1/4 tsp. of tea tree oil**
- **8 drops of lavender essential oil**
- **8 drops of rosemary essential oil**
- **8 drops of tangerine essential oil**
- **4 cups of water**
- **2 tsp. of borax**
- **1 tsp. of washing soda**
- **4 tbsp. of white vinegar**

Mix the Solubol and oils in a small container. Heat the water until it's almost boiling. Pour 2 of the 4 cups of water into a heat-proof measuring cup. Add the borax and washing soda, and stir until they're dissolved. Pour the mixture into a 32-ounce spray bottle, add the reserved oil mixture and the vinegar, and shake thoroughly. Top it off with more hot water, and shake again. Use it as you would any other spray cleaner (but first test it on an inconspicuous spot).

Decorate for fresher air. Just fill an attractive glass spray bottle with white vinegar and add a few drops of your favorite perfume, extract, or essential oil. Keep it on top of the vanity or in another easy-to-reach spot. Then, whenever the need arises, grab the sprayer, give it a shake, and spritz the air. You can find decorative spray bottles in solid colors and patterns galore in craft shops and on craft-oriented websites like Etsy.com.

EARLY BIRD SPECIALS

When wanting to age in place, renovating your bathroom and the rest of your home can cost a bundle. The good news is that there's plenty of help available, including low-interest loans, as well as grants from county, state, and federal agencies. Beyond that, many local charities, churches, and other nonprofit groups supply volunteer labor to perform senior-friendly upgrades. Other organizations make no-cost, long-term loans for portable ramps and other home-modification equipment. To learn how to benefit from some of this aid, search for "financial assistance for aging in place."

Soften up below. Far and away, the most popular flooring surface in many bathrooms is ceramic tile. It also happens to be one of the most senior-unfriendly materials on the planet for a couple of reasons: One, it's extremely slippery when it's wet. Two, if you slip and fall, you'll crash down on an ultra-hard surface that's bound to cause major discomfort, if not a serious injury. If you're remodeling your current house for the long haul, or building a new "forever home," consider rubber tile. The same soft texture and non-slip surface makes it a top choice for kitchens and also makes it ideal for bathrooms.

Stay on the up-and-up. While nothing can soften a ceramic-tile floor, there are DIY coatings that can greatly lessen your chances of taking a tumble on slick, wet surfaces, including bathtubs and shower stalls. As you might expect, these products vary in price, ease of application, and suitability for particular flooring materials. A search for "slip-resistant floor coatings" will bring up numerous choices. Or visit the Safety Direct America website (safetydirectamerica.com), where you can compare the features, and slip-resistance test data, for many brands.

Slip off the no-skid stickers. Before you apply a coating to a bathtub or shower stall, you'll need to remove any non-slip decals that may already be there. To do that, simply fill the fixture with an inch of very hot water and 1 cup of white vinegar. Let it sit until it's cool enough to stick your hand in, then slide a plastic scraper under the decal, and pry it up. To remove any residual adhesive, soak paper towels in hot vinegar, and lay them over the spots. Wait 10 minutes or so, then scrape the glue away, and rinse thoroughly.

Time Saver

If you're planning to move in the near future and don't care to spend the time or money it could take to apply a non-slip coating to your tub or shower, consider heavy-duty, cushioned anti-slip tape. It's available at some of the same places that sell the coatings (including Safety Direct America). It comes in various thicknesses, in transparent versions, as well as various colors, takes just minutes to apply, and gives you more secure footing than the light-weight decorative stickers.

SUPER-SIMPLE GROUT CLEANER

The grout in many bathrooms seems to pick up dirt and stains in the blink of an eye. There are plenty of commercial grout cleaners and whiteners, but the chemicals they contain can be highly irritating. Enter this mighty powerful, senior-friendly alternative.

1/2 cup of baking soda **1/2 cup of white vinegar**
1/2 cup of borax

Mix the ingredients in a nonreactive bowl to form a thick paste. Wipe it onto the grout, and scrub with a retired (but clean!) toothbrush. Rinse with warm water, and dry with a clean towel. **Note:** *This mixture does a great job of removing hard-water stains from glass shower doors.*

Wage war on mold and mildew. It's no secret that bathrooms are prime breeding grounds for mold and mildew. And the older you get, the more damage they can do to your immune system. When you spot the spores on sealed grout, soak three or four paper towels in white vinegar, and lay them over the mortar, pressing firmly to ensure full contact. Leave them for eight hours or so, spraying with more vinegar as needed to keep the paper saturated. Then remove the towels, scrub away any remaining crud, and rinse with clear water.

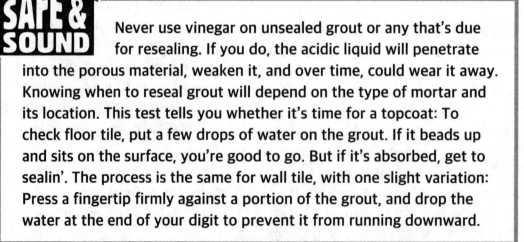

SAFE & SOUND Never use vinegar on unsealed grout or any that's due for resealing. If you do, the acidic liquid will penetrate into the porous material, weaken it, and over time, could wear it away. Knowing when to reseal grout will depend on the type of mortar and its location. This test tells you whether it's time for a topcoat: To check floor tile, put a few drops of water on the grout. If it beads up and sits on the surface, you're good to go. But if it's absorbed, get to sealin'. The process is the same for wall tile, with one slight variation: Press a fingertip firmly against a portion of the grout, and drop the water at the end of your digit to prevent it from running downward.

Clean first—seal later. Before you seal grout, it's crucial that you remove all dirt or stains, especially mold or mildew. Otherwise, it's all but guaranteed that you'll never get rid of those marks unless you scrape out all of the mortar and replace it with a fresh batch. Here's how to do that cleaning job without exposing yourself to the noxious fumes of chlorine bleach: Just mix 1 cup of baking soda and 10 drops of tea tree oil with enough water to form a thick paste (multiplying the ingredients as needed to suit the size of the soiled area). Apply it to the grout using a cloth, sponge, or small plastic scraper. Let it sit for one to two hours, scrub with a stiff nylon brush, then rinse with clear water. If any marks remain, repeat the process as needed.

For faster, easier grout cleaning, use your head. To be specific, attach a retired brush head to your electric toothbrush, apply your cleaner of choice, and brush away! This trick also works like a dream on small areas and tight spots all through your house. That's especially the case if you have even mild arthritis in your fingers or hands. In fact, you may want to pick up a cheap electric toothbrush (not one of the superstar sonic models!), and add it to your housekeeping tool kit.

Make a tip-top tile cleaner. When it's time to spruce up the tiles themselves, you can't beat this super-simple and super-safe scrubbing paste: Just put 1/2 cup of baking soda in a bowl, and slowly pour in pure liquid castile soap, stirring constantly until the mixture looks like cake frosting. (Dr. Bronner's peppermint soap is especially great for bathrooms!) If you like, add 5 to 10 drops of whatever essential oil you prefer (see "Mean, Green Cleaning 'Machines'" on page 140). Then scoop the cleaner onto a sponge, scrub the tile clean, and rinse with clear water. The tiles will look like they're brand-new!

Labor Saver

One easy way to reduce the workload in your bathroom is to keep the curtain and the liner fully drawn across the tub or shower stall. This way, they'll dry out faster, which will help fend off mold, mildew, and germs, and lessen your cleaning chores.

FRESH-AS-A-DAISY FLOOR CLEANER

Not only is this potion thoroughly nontoxic, but thanks to the prodigious powers of lavender and rosemary essential oils, it also fights germs. Plus, according to aromatherapy gurus, it produces an aroma that helps combat both physical and emotional fatigue and helps enhance your immune system. The mixture works equally well on rubber, vinyl, cork, linoleum, and ceramic-tile floors. Talk about anti-aging cleaning partners!

1 tbsp. of Solubol dispersant

1 tsp. of lavender essential oil

1 tsp. of rosemary essential oil

1 cup of white vinegar

1 gal. of hot water (at least 130°F)

Mix the Solubol and oils together. Then combine them with the vinegar and water in a bucket, and mop your floor as usual. No rinsing needed.

Polish your walls. It's important to know that even the smallest bit of oily residue is downright dangerous in a bathtub or the bottom of a shower stall. But on the walls of a shower, it's a whole different story. There, a very light layer of oil will actually slow down the formation of stubborn scum. But you don't have to take my word for it—try it yourself. Just pour a small amount of mineral oil or baby oil on a soft, dry cloth, and lightly rub it on the shower walls, using circular motions. You'll be amazed at the difference it makes!

HELP WANTED? Or, in this case, maybe help *not* wanted. It's probably safe to say that cleaning a bathroom does not rank high on anyone's list of favorite pastimes. And once you reach middle age and your joints don't move as smoothly as they once did, it can be mighty tempting to get hired help for this job, if not for all of your housecleaning. But if you're trying to lose weight, here's a factoid that might give you the incentive to continue your DIY routine: Scrubbing your bathroom can burn up to 400 calories an hour, while toning your arm and shoulder muscles and helping retain mobility in your joints.

Sure doesn't look like a scrub brush! As quirky as this may sound, one of the most effective bathroom cleaning tools of all might be right in your refrigerator's produce drawer. What is it? A lemon. Just slice one of the fruits in two, and use the cut sides as scrubbers. All by itself, the pulp will put a gleaming shine on chrome fixtures. It also makes an efficient delivery mechanism for many DIY cleansers.

Grandma knew best. At least it's all but guaranteed that she used one of the most powerful and least expensive bathroom cleaners that ever came down the pike. To make your own supply, mix 1 cup each of baking soda, borax, and salt, and keep the mixture in a tightly closed container. Then use it as you would any other powdered cleanser. It'll remove the toughest grime from tile floors, bathroom fixtures, and just about any other surface in need of a good scrubbin'.

Clean soft, clean deep, and clean safe. Soft-scrub cleansers may seem like the bee's knees when it comes to gently cleaning delicate surfaces in your bathroom. But these chemically laden products are anything but gentle to aging respiratory and immune systems. So forget 'em! Instead, whenever you need the strength of a heavy-duty, powdered cleanser, but don't want the ugly scratches left behind, make your own supply this way: Just mix equal parts of liquid castile soap and cream of tartar in a bowl to form a paste. Using a sponge or soft cloth, smooth it over the soiled surface, and overspray with hydrogen peroxide. Let it sit for three to five minutes, then scrub down as usual, and rinse with clear water. That's all there is to it!

Money Saver

A leaking flush tank can waste hundreds of gallons of water each day—without you even knowing about it. Fortunately, there's an easy way to find out if this is happening in your bathroom. Just drip a little food coloring into the tank. If the water in the toilet bowl turns color, call a plumber, who can dash right over and repair the seal.

HARD-HITTING SINK & TUB SCRUB

For best results, make a fresh batch of this ultra-powerful cleaner just before you use it, and discard any leftovers. This recipe should give you enough ammo to get one bathtub and two bathroom sinks (or the equivalent amount of square footage) spankin' clean.

1/2 cup of baking soda	**5 drops of lemongrass essential oil**
2 tbsp. of liquid castile soap	**5 drops of pine essential oil**
1 tbsp. of white vinegar	**5 drops of tea tree oil**

Mix the baking soda and soap in a bowl. Pour in the vinegar, stirring as you go. Whisk in the oils until the ingredients are thoroughly blended. Then, depending on the size of the surface you're cleaning, dip a microfiber cloth, scrub brush, or retired toothbrush into the mixture, and scrub-a-dub-dub. When you're finished, rinse with cool water, and dry the tub with a clean cloth.

Turn your shower into an anti-aging sauna. Eucalyptus has been renowned for its ability to help enhance your immune system. One of the easiest and most pleasant ways to tap into that power is to pick up two or three sprigs of fresh eucalyptus at a local florist or greenhouse and tie them to your showerhead. Then step into the tub or stall, and turn the water on at a comfortably hot setting. When the heat and steam hit the greenery, its health-giving oils will be released and you'll breathe in all the benefits. **Note:** *In addition to boosting your immune system, this trick is a great way to relieve any congestion that's caused by bronchitis, allergies, or cold and flu viruses.*

Time Saver

To polish off any flying insects that happen to wander right into your bathroom (or anyplace else, for that matter) reach for a can of aerosol hair spray. It'll kill airborne bugs on contact, both indoors and out.

When spiders are entering through unknown portals ... Mix 5 to 10 drops of a spider-repelling essential oil, 1/4 teaspoon of dishwashing liquid, and 12 ounces of water in a spray bottle. Once a week, spray the areas where you've seen spiders, as well as all possible entrances, until you no longer notice arachnid activity. **Note:** *While peppermint gets the most "airplay" in natural pest-control circles, spiders keep their distance from several other aromas, including cedar, cinnamon, citronella, eucalyptus, lavender, tea tree, and any of the citrus oils. So use whichever kind appeals to you, or that you happen to have on hand.*

Say "Sayonara, silverfish!" These harmless, but hideous-looking, insects rank among the most common bathroom pests because they love dark, damp areas. Silverfish multiply rapidly, so to get rid of 'em, tuck a piece of bread in a tall glass. Then wrap the outside with masking tape. This provides traction as the bugs scamper up the side of the vessel in pursuit of the bread. But once they're inside, the slick interior will prevent them from getting out. Then jump right into vacuuming thoroughly, using your crevice attachment around any baseboards and plumbing pipes, and dispose of the full vacuum bag (inside another bag) in your outside trash can. To play it extra safe, clean your vacuum, inside and out, to get rid of any eggs you might have picked up.

Good smells keep silverfish away. Luckily, these pests hate two of the aromas that many humans enjoy most: orange and lavender. Using either essential oil in DIY cleaning formulas (like the Tough, Gentle, All-Purpose Cleaner on page 142) can deter most of the little buggers.

Q: I've been finding spiders in my bathroom. What's the best way to get rid of them without using toxic pesticides?

A: To kill them—with no possible collateral damage to you, your pets, or your grandchildren—simply dissolve 1/8 cup of salt in a gallon of warm water, and pour the mix into a spray bottle. Spray the saline solution directly onto the spider. As for keeping the varmints out, if you know, or even suspect, that they're coming in through cracks around your windows, wipe the sills with rubbing alcohol once a week.

ANTI-AGING MATTERS

PORCELAIN PERK-UP POTION

There are lots of commercial cleansing powders that can get a porcelain sink or bathtub clean. Unfortunately, most of them contain abrasives that can scratch the fixtures' surfaces, and harsh chemicals that are unfriendly to an aging immune system. This DIY powder tackles the toughest grime with no damage to your porcelain or to your health.

1/2 cup of white vinegar   **1/4 cup of borax**
1/4 cup of baking soda   **10 drops of peppermint essential oil**

Mix all the ingredients in a bowl or small pail. Then dip a damp sponge into the mixture and go to town. Rinse with clear water. If you like, dry with a soft, clean cloth to avoid any water spots. Repeat the process if necessary—but it's highly unlikely that will be needed.

De-stain your tub. Got an aging bathtub that's sporting some rust spots? If so, this is the remedy to use. Mix equal parts of hydrogen peroxide and cream of tartar to form a thick paste. Apply the mixture to the marks, and let it sit for 10 minutes. Then scrub with a nylon brush until the stains are gone, and rinse with clear water.

Leave room to roam. When you're remodeling your bathroom or building a new home, make sure you provide as much space as feasible for the easy use of wheelchairs, scooters, walkers, or similar assistive devices. In particular, allow plenty of room for maneuvering around the toilet, bathtub, or shower stall, as well as the areas around cabinets, closets, or freestanding storage furniture.

SAFE & SOUND If you have a bathroom scale out in the open, move it now! Just about anyone can easily stub their toes or trip over the things as they wander into the bathroom in the middle of the night. For older adults whose mobility and vision are beginning to decline, having a scale on display is all but begging for a serious accident. So either put your scale into the closet, slide it under the vanity cabinet, or store it in an out-of-the-way spot in your bedroom.

Give hard-water stains the heave-ho. We all know that getting a steady supply of minerals like calcium and magnesium is essential for maintaining good physical health as you age. But the danged chemicals produce a major pain in the neck when they leave their grimy residue on just about every surface in your bathroom. Well, those nasty splotches are no match for this simple, but hard-hitting, ploy: Mix equal parts of vinegar and hot water in a spray bottle. Shake it hard, and spray a generous amount of the mixture onto the stains. Let it sit for about four to five minutes, then wipe the surface clean.

Shave clean, and shave fresh.
Cleaning most newer electric shavers, for both men's faces and women's legs, is a simple matter: After each use, you just turn the device off and rinse the shaving head and hair chamber with hot water. The downside is that this procedure fails to remove any stale, unpleasant odor that tends to build up in the shaver's innards over time. To solve that dilemma, once or twice a month, simply rinse both the shaving head and the hair chamber with a solution of 1 part white vinegar to 10 parts tap water.

Bid good riddance to bad rings. Bathroom staples like shaving cream and hair spray that come in metal cans have one glaring drawback: the ugly rust rings they can leave on sink countertops and bathtub ledges. Well, there's a super-simple way to save yourself the hassle of getting rid of those marks. When you first bring the cans home, coat the bottoms with nail polish. Problem solved! **Note:** *This is a great way to use up polish in a color that you no longer wear, or maybe the last, thin layer in the bottom of a bottle.*

Money Saver

If you keep makeup in the bathroom, do yourself a favor and get that stuff outta there! This is an especially smart maneuver if you're retired, or you work from home and no longer need to deck yourself out in your professional "war paint" every day. That's because the life spans of foundations, powders, and other cosmetics can be greatly shortened if these products are not stored properly—and to stay at their peak, they require cooler, drier conditions than a bathroom can provide.

EXTRA-STRENGTH SOAP SCUM REMOVER

It doesn't take long for soap scum to build up in bathtub soap holders and on tub ledges. And it's not just unsightly in its own right. It can attract dirt and mold like nobody's business. Fortunately, it's no match for this kitchen-counter formula.

1 cup of white vinegar

1 tbsp. of cornstarch

2 tbsp. of grease-cutting dishwashing liquid

Mix the vinegar and cornstarch in a microwave-safe bowl, then heat the mixture in the microwave on medium power for 2 minutes. Pour it into a spray bottle, add the dishwashing liquid, and shake to combine the ingredients. Spray the concoction onto the soap scum, let it sit for 5 to 10 minutes, and wipe the nasty mess away with a damp cloth. That's all there is to it!

Clear the tracks! Do the channels that carry your shower doors to their destination seem to clog up in a New York minute? Then try this trick. To provide smoother—and faster—sailing, make it a point to perform this routine every few weeks: Before you go to bed, pour white vinegar into the tracks and let it sit overnight. The next day, wipe it out with a damp sponge.

The single most effective way to prevent falls, in your bathroom or anyplace else, is to retain or regain good balance. One of the best and most enjoyable ways to accomplish your up-and-up mission is to engage in an activity that promotes both coordination and stability. Ballroom dancing happens to be a champ in that regard. If it's been a long time since you last tripped the light fantastic, you might want to take to the floor again. In small towns and big cities all over the country, there are groups that sponsor regular senior dance parties and also provide lessons. A search for "ballroom dancing for seniors [your town]" should bring up choices galore.

EARLY BIRD SPECIALS

Get tough with your shower doors. The same toothpaste that can help keep your teeth clean can also cut through even the most stubborn water marks and soap scum on glass shower doors. Just squeeze some white, non-gel toothpaste onto a cloth or sponge, wipe it onto the stain and splotches, and let it sit for 10 minutes. Then mix equal parts of white vinegar and warm water in a spray bottle, and spritz the area well. Wipe the gunk away, rinse with clear water, and dry the glass with a soft, clean cloth.

When you are in a hurry to de-scum shower doors, spray a soft cotton cloth with cooking oil spray, and wipe the gunk away.

It'll all come out in the wash. At the first sign of mildew on a shower curtain or vinyl liner, wash it in equal parts of baking soda and your usual laundry detergent. Then add 1/2 cup of white vinegar to the rinse cycle. To prevent creases, take it out and hang it back on the shower rod to dry before the spin cycle starts. Or put a large bath towel into the machine with the curtain, and let 'er rip for the duration.

For scratchless cleaning, bag it! Plastic mesh produce bags make for perfect bathroom scrubbers, whether you are using alcohol or any other cleanser. They won't scratch porcelain, tile, or marble surfaces, yet they're tough enough to clear off even the most stubborn grime, like mildew and soap scum.

Give it one last tweak. When you've finished cleaning your bathroom, give the fixtures a final rubdown with a little rubbing alcohol on a soft, clean cloth. It'll kill germs, shine mirrors and chrome, and remove all traces of soap, deodorant, hair spray, and toothpaste.

Time Saver

Polishing chrome faucets, spigots, and showerheads doesn't get any quicker or easier than this: Just give 'em a rubdown with wax paper. In the blink of an eye, they'll have a shine you can see yourself in!

SENIOR-SAFE TOILET BOWL CLEANER

Many commercial toilet bowl cleaners are toxic, and that can be especially troublesome for older adults. Enter this ultra-safe DIY formula.

1 cup of baking soda　　**1 cup of white vinegar**

1/4 cup of salt　　**10 drops of tea tree oil**

Mix the baking soda and salt in a container that has a sprinkler top (a glass jar or the kind used for Parmesan cheese works perfectly). Then combine the vinegar and tea tree oil in a spray bottle. Shake thoroughly, then spray the mixture generously over the inside of the toilet bowl. Immediately sprinkle the wet surface with the baking soda and salt mixture. It should start fizzing to beat the band. If it merely bubbles a little, spritz it with more of the vinegar mixture. Give it 10 to 15 minutes to work, then scrub with a toilet brush and flush.

Add high-rise storage. If your vanity is long enough that you've got space to spare on the countertop, simply perch a freestanding cabinet or bookcase there. Then haul all of the things you use most often out of the cave-like space that's below the sink, and place them on the shelves.

Look to the tank.

Don't forget about that space above your toilet's flush tank. To prevent clutter on it, get a unit that's designed to fit over it, or mount a cabinet or shelves to the wall. In a flash, the things you need will be a lot easier to get at.

HELP WANTED? As you get older, bending and stretching to fetch items from a bathroom vanity cabinet can be a real pain—literally. To provide a whole lot of storage without losing any space from the room, have a carpenter build shelves that are recessed into the walls between the studs. The opening should be deep enough for six-inch shelves because it's the perfect size for most of your storage needs. Best of all, you can have them placed at a height that is comfortable for you to access.

And the freed-up vanity caves can hold… Anything you don't use very often, and that can safely withstand the warm, humid conditions in the room—or any leaks that could spring from the plumbing pipes. This is the perfect place to store things like bathtub toys that you keep on hand for visiting grandchildren or even your dog's shampoo. But you needn't limit the inventory to bathroom gear. For example, you can use the space to hold Christmas decorations that are made of glass, ceramic, or plastic; or even extra dishes and glassware that only get pressed into service for parties.

Let Susan help. If your vanity lacks the countertop space for a shelf unit, you can at least make it a whole lot easier to fetch things from inside the jam-packed vanity cabinets. Just tuck a two- or three-tiered lazy Susan into the space, and load 'er up. Better yet, if space permits, install two units—one for toiletries and one for cleaning supplies. (Don't put both on the same carousel!) Granted, you'll still have to lean over or stoop down, but you won't have to stretch into the depths, or move a bunch of stuff out of the way to reach the item you need.

Display the toilet paper. No, I'm not suggesting that you start keeping your bargain-priced 12-packs stacked up on the counter! But it is a good idea to keep a few rolls out in the open so that you won't have to dive down deep every time you need one. You have plenty of easy and attractive options for storing your supply. Either heap the rolls in a basket, big bowl, or ceramic planter; stack them, one on top of another, in a cylindrical glass vase; or slide them over the post of a vertical paper-towel holder. In addition to relieving you of some uncomfortable bending and reaching, any of these maneuvers will ensure that guests won't have to fish through your cabinets to retrieve a roll if the need arises.

Labor Saver

It's a fact that eliminating tough toilet stains can require some elbow grease. But for the ultimate in toil-less routine toilet cleaning, simply drop a couple of Alka-Seltzer® tablets into the bowl. Give the antacids 20 minutes or so to work their fizzy magic, then brush and flush.

STREAK-FIGHTING WINDOW CLEANER

Glass shower doors and frequently fogged bathroom windows both have one thing in common: They collect streaks that can be a royal nuisance to get rid of—unless you use this magic weapon.

1/4 tsp. of Solubol dispersant   **1/3 cup of vinegar**

5 drops of sage essential oil   **3 cups of distilled water**

Mix the Solubol with the oils, then add all of the ingredients to a spray bottle. Shake it vigorously, and spritz the solution onto the glass. Wipe it with a soft, dry cloth, and those smears will be history! Stored at room temperature, any leftover mixture will retain its full power for about six months or so.

Clear the decks! A bathtub is intended to be used for bathing, not for storing your toiletries. In addition to creating visual clutter that sends your stress level up, all that stuff can pose a serious tripping hazard when you step into or out of the tub. So take all bottles, jars, brushes, sponges, and what-have-you off ledges, and put them in a cabinet or a shower caddy. In the minute or two it takes you to do that, you'll create a more relaxing atmosphere and greatly enhance your bath-time safety.

One of the most effective and economical ways to dramatically enhance bathroom safety is to install grab bars around the toilet, as well as in and just outside the tub or shower stall. If the mere idea of doing that immediately brings up mental images of nursing homes and hospitals, put those thoughts out of your mind right now. Today, you can find grab bars in styles and colors to match any taste and decor. A search for "decorative grab bars" will bring up scads of them. Just bear in mind that to ensure the maximum security, the bars' finish should have some texture that allows for a good, firm grip.

Plan ahead for grab bars. If you're about to embark on a remodel for your bathroom, it's a good idea to install the necessary wall bracing now. Typically, these safety aids need to be capable of supporting 250 to 300 pounds, and having the essential structure in place will save you the cost and hassle of additional construction work. At the very least, you'll eventually want grab bars around the tub, shower, shower seat, and toilet, and possibly other locations, depending on the size of the room and the placement of any storage areas—built-in or freestanding.

To freshen the aroma in your bathroom, fill a spray bottle with vinegar and add a few drops of your favorite essential oil, and spritz the air.

Get ready to walk and roll. For older adults who want to cover all future circumstances, the best choice for a shower is what's known in the aging-in-place biz as a roll-in model. This simply means that the stall has a seamless, bumpless entrance and an opening, with or without a door, that's at least 36 inches wide. This configuration allows access for a wheelchair, while also eliminating a major tripping hazard for anyone who walks into the shower. That can be a big plus for someone at any age!

Money Saver

If you don't require an entirely curbless shower, consider this option: Have your current bathtub modified to permit easier access. There are several national franchises, like TubcuT® and Shower Ease™, that provide this service. A contractor comes to your house and cuts an opening that leaves you with just a 4-inch threshold to step across. Granted, this ploy will limit the fixture to shower use, but it'll cost a fraction of the price you'd pay for a full-service walk-in tub. To find a quick-change artist near you, check the websites of the companies mentioned above, or search for "modify bathtub for elderly people."

MAKE YOUR OILS' POWER LAST LONGER

As the old saying goes, all good things come to an end—including the effectiveness and safety of essential oils. Over time, their components break down and they become unusable. The life spans vary greatly, but you can extend them as long as possible by fending off the oils' three major foes: oxygen, heat, and light.

Oxygen. When you've poured out the desired amount of oil, recap the bottle quickly and tightly. The longer it remains open, the more air gets in.

Heat. The ideal temperature is between 35° and 38°F. For this reason, your refrigerator provides the perfect "living" quarters.

Light. Store essential oils in dark-colored glass bottles in a dark place. No room in the fridge? Use a cabinet in the coolest part of your house.

TWO OTHER KEY FACTORS

Contamination. Inadvertently getting carrier oils or any other ingredients into a bottle of essential oil can shorten its life span, so make sure any spoons or droppers you use are clean and have not touched any other substance.

Safety. Essential oils are quite flammable, with a low flash point. So keep them away from heat and flames, including candles. Also, because essential oils can be extremely toxic to children and pets, store your bottles in a secure spot.

EXPIRATION TIME FRAMES

In general, the lighter an oil is, the sooner it loses its potency. Your essential oil supplier can give you the estimated life span of any particular oil, but here's how long you can expect some common ones to last under ideal conditions:

1–2 years: All the citrus oils

2–3 years: Frankincense, helichrysum, lemongrass, pine, Roman chamomile, rosemary, spearmint, tea tree

3–4 years: Bergamot, black pepper, citronella, clary sage, cypress, eucalyptus, fir, jasmine, lavender, thyme

4–5 years: Cinnamon, clove, geranium, marjoram, oregano, peppermint

6–8+ years: Birch, cedarwood, ginger, patchouli, sandalwood

Carrier oils will go rancid over time. The basic rule is if the oil smells or looks different, throw it out. FYI—coconut oil lasts the longest of 'em all.

CHAPTER 9

LIVING AREAS

In the previous two chapters, we discussed two very specialized parts of your house—namely the kitchen and bathroom—and how you can adapt them to suit your needs as the years march on. Now, we'll broaden our scope to the rest of your home sweet home. In these pages, I'll share scads of savvy strategies, tons of sound solutions, and plain old good ideas to help you age in place happily, safely, and comfortably. You'll also learn some super-simple tweaks that you can make to your present abode, as well as tips for finding a new "forever home."

We'll zero in on vinegar as a key ally in making the rest of your life the best of your life. If that notion sounds over the top, consider this fact: Not only do the passing years make you more sensitive to all the toxins that are surrounding you, but once you are retired, or trying out a second-prime venture from home, you'll be exposed to various household cleaning products, which rank high among the tip-top sources of trouble-causing crud.

Here's a vinegar mix that can tackle a mighty tough challenge: cleaning a mirror without breathing in any toxic fumes, or leaving ugly streaks behind. Mix 1/2 cup of white vinegar, 1/4 cup of rubbing alcohol, and 1 tablespoon of cornstarch in a spray bottle. Add 10 drops each of lemon and lavender essential oils, and shake the bottle. Spritz the solution onto the glass, and wipe with a soft cloth. Presto! Clean, shiny glass, and a fresh, invigorating scent in the air!

WONDERFUL WOOD-FLOOR WASH

The powerful team of players in this potion will disinfect both solid wood and wood-veneer floors, leaving them spanking clean and shiny with a fresh, woodsy aroma. You'll love it!

1 tsp. of Solubol dispersant*

1/4 tsp. of cedarwood essential oil

1/4 tsp. of lemon essential oil

1/2 cup of white vinegar**

1 gal. of warm water

Mix all the ingredients in a bucket. Vacuum or sweep your floor to remove any dust and debris. Then dip a mop, sponge, or cleaning rag in the solution, wring it out, and go to town, rinsing and wringing your implement of choice as you move along. *Available from essential oil suppliers. **Don't use any more than 1/2 cup of vinegar per gallon of water, or it'll ramp up the acidic action and could dull the wood surface.*

Pamper your paneling. Depending on a room's furnishings, wood paneling can evoke the atmosphere of either a rustic lodge or an elegant men's club in Merry Olde England. Either way, this DIY cleaner and polish can keep the wood at its peak of good looks. To make it, mix 1/4 cup of white vinegar, 2 tablespoons of olive oil, and 2 cups of warm water in a glass jar that has a tight-fitting lid. Give the container a good shake, and rub the mixture onto the paneling with a soft, clean cloth. Let it sit for a few minutes, then buff the wood dry with a fresh cloth. The polish will remove any grime and make the wood gleam.

SAFE & SOUND

If you're in or approaching your 60s when, for most folks, senior tripping season starts, get rid of as many of your area rugs as you can bear to part with. Why? Because they have a spot of dishonor in Trip-and-Fall-Hazards Hall of Infamy. In particular, if you have area rugs at the tops of stairways or on landings, get 'em outta there now! Even if they're securely attached to the floor, their raised edges make them disasters waiting to happen.

Go gunnin' for safer throw rugs. When a lightweight throw rug rests on a bare floor, one little misstep can send you, or maybe even a scampering grandchild, on a magic carpet ride in a New York minute. If you need to keep any of these skittery things around, a hot-glue gun can help increase your margin of safety. Use it to make squiggly lines across the back of each rug, and let it dry thoroughly. The raised glue will provide more secure footing, without the sticky residue you'd get from double-sided carpet tape.

Sometimes, glue won't do.
Larger area rugs can demand stronger measures than a glue gun is able to provide. You certainly don't want to "open fire" on (let's say) the needlepoint rug you made decades ago, when you were expecting your first child, or the treasured Orientals that have been in your family for generations. And don't even think of sticking tape onto a floor covering that has any real financial or sentimental value! Instead, stop trouble in your tracks by simply keeping these textiles in place. Use sturdy, non-slip pads underneath and place furniture either on top of or close enough to the edges that you can't get an accidental toehold.

Time Saver

When wood paneling picks up a scratch or gouge, your favorite morning wake-up beverage can repair the worrisome wound in a hurry. Just mix coffee grounds or used tea leaves with some spackling compound or (in a pinch) white glue until you get the right color. Shove the mixture into the crack or hole, smooth it over with a damp cloth, and you're good to go!

Take the stairway to success.
Contrary to what a lot of folks assume, stairways are not the prime locations for senior tumbles. Rather, most falls are caused by tripping while walking on flat surfaces. Having said that, it is crucial to make your stairways as travel-worthy as possible. For starters, arrange the furniture at the top to provide a wide-open path to the steps. And if you have pets or small grandchildren in the house, even if they're only occasional visitors, keep an eagle eye out for any toys they may have left on the stairs.

EASYGOING BASEBOARD CLEANER

When you're mopping or vacuuming floors, it's all too easy to ignore the baseboards. And once grime builds up on those vertical surfaces, removing it can be a hands-and-knees scrubbing job. To give your aging joints a break, each time you tackle the floor, vacuum the baseboards with a soft brush attachment. Then wipe them down with this spray.

2 tsp. of Solubol dispersant   **2 cups of boiling water**

1 tsp. of orange essential oil   **1/3 cup of white vinegar**

1 tbsp. of cornstarch

Mix the Solubol and oil, and set it aside. Put the cornstarch in a heat-proof measuring cup, pour in the water, and stir until the cornstarch has dissolved. Add the Solubol-oil blend and vinegar, then stir again. Pour the mixture into a spray bottle, fire away at the baseboards, and wipe 'em clean with a soft cloth or damp sponge.

Take it long and easy. One reason that so many folks tend to neglect their baseboards is the simple fact that even routine wiping becomes a major undertaking when you have to do it on your hands and knees. And the older you grow and the stiffer your joints get, the harder the job becomes. The simple solution: Get a long-handled mop with a swivel head (like the popular Baseboard Buddy®) that's specially designed for cleaning baseboards. These tools are widely available in hardware and home-improvement stores and online.

EARLY BIRD SPECIALS

One of the biggest boons of all for older adults who want to age in place is an organization called Village to Village Network®. It's a consortium of local support systems dedicated to helping seniors retain their independence. It started in Boston in the 1990s, when a group of like-minded neighbors banded together to form what they called Beacon Hill Village. Since then, hundreds of villages have sprung up throughout the country, each based on the particular needs of its members. To find one near you, visit www.vtvnetwork.org.

Off with the tape! And the goo, too. When you pull up an area rug that's been held in place with double-sided tape, part of the adhesive will stay behind on the wood floor. To remove the residue, first vacuum up any loose debris. Then mix 2 tablespoons of baking soda with 1/4 to 1/2 teaspoon of water to make a thick paste. Wipe the mixture onto the sticky area, and let the spot dry for 10 minutes or so. Then dampen a lint-free cloth, and rub it firmly over the dried paste to remove it. The adhesive gunk should come away with it.

To make getting dressed easier as you age, put your dressers close together near your bedroom closet, so you won't have to dart around the room.

Remove the goo, take two. To oust an extra thick layer of tape residue, apply the baking soda paste as described above (see "Off with the tape!"). Remove as much adhesive as you can with a plastic scraper, going gently to avoid gouging the wood. Brush the remaining adhesive with a half-and-half solution of white vinegar and hot water. Let it sit for three to five minutes, then scrub it away using a soft-bristled brush and working in the direction of the wood grain. Sop up any remaining solution with towels, and go over the area with a cloth or sponge dampened with clear water. Finally, dry the floor thoroughly.

Baby your pseudo hardwood. That final drying step (above) is crucial if your floor is a contemporary "hardwood" version. These products are actually made of a composite material covered with a thin veneer of real wood. If they're left to air-dry, they can buckle, warp, and eventually squeak every time you step on them.

Labor Saver

One of the easiest ways to freshen up a carpet is to sprinkle baking soda over the surface, let it sit for five minutes or so, and then vacuum. The only problem is that it can be tricky to distribute the soda evenly. So instead of sprinkling the stuff from the box or your hand, use a flour sifter. It'll deliver neat results every time!

CRACKERJACK CARPET CLEANER

Shampooing your own carpets is a lot cheaper than hiring a pro to do the job. But many of the cleaning formulas made for DIY use leave a sticky residue that attracts dirt like a magnet. So next time, fill your cleaner's tank with this fragrant formula. It will clean 'em as well as commercial versions for less money and with no harsh chemicals.

1/4 tsp. of Solubol dispersant	**1 part white vinegar***
7 drops of lavender essential oil	**1 part warm water**

Mix the Solubol and oil in a small container. Then add the mixture to a bucket with the vinegar and water, and stir well. Pour the solution into your shampooer's tank, and get to cleanin'. You'll love the results!
You want enough vinegar-water solution to fill your shampooer's tank.

Bid good riddance to bad residue. If you've used a commercial DIY carpet shampoo in the past, before you use the Crackerjack Carpet Cleaner (above), remove all traces of the previous product this way: Fill your shampooer's tank with a solution of 1 cup of white vinegar per 2 1/2 gallons of water. Run the machine over the floor, and let the vinegar lift out the sticky soap—and who knows what else—that's built up on the fibers. Then empty the reservoir, fill it with clear, warm water, and make another pass to ensure that all of the residue is gone.

HELP WANTED?

If your carpet has some serious, set-in stains, call in a professional carpet cleaner right from the get-go. Why? Because in addition to taking more time and energy than you probably want to expend (especially if you're retired and have more pressing, leisure-time matters on your plate), there's a good chance that your DIY efforts won't work. They could even make the problem worse. So don't worry about nasty chemicals; there are plenty of companies that use safe, nontoxic products. Your best bet: Ask neighbors for personal recommendations. If you don't get any, search online for "all-natural carpet cleaning companies [your town]."

End the scorched carpet policy. When a steam iron, fireplace poker, or other hot object leaves a light scorch mark on your rug, don't get all hot and bothered. There's a good chance it'll come right out if you treat it with this kooky-sounding, but effective, formula: Mix 1 cup of white vinegar; 1/2 cup of unscented, talc-free bath powder; and two coarsely chopped onions in a pot. Bring the mixture to a boil, stirring constantly. Remove it from the stove, let it cool to room temperature, and spread it over the mark with a sponge. When the area is dry, vacuum up the residue. Your carpet should look as good as new!

Bring new life to worn rugs.
It doesn't take long for a steady stream of foot traffic and your grandchildren's ride-on toys to make a carpet or area rug look dull and matted. Well, don't rush out and try to replace it. Instead, mix 1 cup of white vinegar per gallon of warm water in a bucket. Then dip a good, stiff broom into the solution, and brush that floor covering briskly. No need to rinse. When you're finished, the rug should be standing at attention again, and the colors will be their original bright (or maybe soothing neutral) selves.

Money Saver

Once you've used a bag of frozen vegetables or berries to harden gum or perform any other non-culinary task, tuck the package into the fridge and use it within a day or so. Produce that's been thawed and refrozen loses valuable nutrients—and often a fair amount of flavor to boot.

Get the gum out. Oops! Your youngest grandchild was showing off his bubble-gum-blowing prowess, when the air-filled goo shot out of his mouth and onto your carpet. Don't fret, but do act fast! Grab a bag of frozen vegetables and set it on top of the gum. Wait 15 minutes or so to let the blob harden. Then slide it off with a plastic scraper or old credit card. Vacuum the area to remove any small particles. If a stain remains, put 1/2 cup of white vinegar in a microwave-safe bowl, and nuke it until it's warm (about 30 seconds). Use a sponge to wipe the spot away, then make another pass with a damp cloth. And consider declaring bubble gum blowing an outdoor sport.

MAGICAL MYSTERY-STAIN REMOVER

What do you do when you discover that an unknown substance has made its mark on your carpet? Well, as long as the "crime" occurred very recently, have a go at it with this spot lifter.

1/2 cup of white vinegar   **2 tbsp. of salt**
2 tbsp. of borax

Mix all of the ingredients to make a paste. Rub it gently into the stain. Let the mixture dry, then vacuum up the residue. If the mark simply won't budge and your attempts at getting a positive ID have failed, you might want to call a carpet cleaning service. And act fast because the longer any stain has time to set in, the harder it is for anyone to remove.

Can the candle wax. Morning-after miseries are not always caused by over-imbibing. It can also be a bummer to wake up and discover that wax from the candles you burned at last night's party has dripped onto your carpets or upholstered furniture. The good news is that removing the drippings is a lot easier than curing a hangover. Start by softening the wax with a hair dryer set on high. Soak up the melted material with paper towels. Then wipe the remaining spot with a cloth dipped in a half-and-half mixture of white vinegar and water. Just go very gently to avoid driving the wax into the fabric or the carpet fibers.

EARLY BIRD SPECIALS

When you've got serious carpet stains, but you're hesitant to call in a pro because you think it might be a budget-busting proposition, think again. Many local carpet cleaning companies offer cut rates to seniors and to veterans (and often active military and law enforcement personnel) of any age. The specific senior designation varies from one firm to the next, and sometimes it does not appear in any advertising. So if you're calling a firm based on a personal recommendation, or if the website doesn't mention discount pricing, ask whether you qualify. You might be surprised!

Drip no more. The simplest way to avoid having wax dripped onto your floor coverings and furniture is to buy dripless candles. But they can set you back by a mighty pretty penny, especially if you're stocking up for parties or future power outages. So give the pricey things a pass. Instead, buy the cheapest versions you can find. Then when you get home, grab a container that's deep enough to submerge the candles completely, and fill it with a mixture of 1/2 tablespoon of salt per 2 cups of water. Let 'em soak for about 24 hours, then let them air-dry. You'll be all set to let the good times roll—or to ride out a spell of heavy weather.

> If it's getting hard to stretch across your bedside table, set a lazy Susan on top so anything you need is just a spin away.

Choose your carpet with care... And with future mobility in mind. When it's time to replace your current floor covering, get a low-pile carpet and have it installed so that it will cling tightly to the floor. The higher the pile is on any carpet or area rug, the more likely you are to catch your foot in the fibers and go tumblin' down. Low pile is also much easier to navigate for anyone who is confined to a wheelchair or scooter, or uses a walker.

Run(ner) down the stairs. To prevent slips and slides, install a low-pile carpet runner, and secure it in place so that it lies perfectly flat and wraps neatly around the rounded front of each tread. In addition to offering more secure footing, it'll provide a softer landing should a fall occur.

Time Saver

Let me take a stab in the dark and guess that dusting does not rank among your favorite pastimes. So here's how to make that chore easier and quicker: Use an empty spray bottle, either a new or clean, dry one that once held a spray solution. Then take aim, pull the "trigger," and blow the dust out of hard-to-get-at places, like the nooks and crannies in figurines, fancy picture frames, and carved furniture.

LOVELY LEATHER FURNITURE CLEANER

This fabulous formula works well on chairs, couches, and leather-topped desks and tables. It's also just what the antique doctor ordered for babying vintage leather suitcases—either ones you've collected recently or treasured grips that bring back fond memories of your travels long ago.

1 cup of extra virgin olive oil	**1 tsp. of liquid castile soap**
1 cup of white vinegar	**15 drops of citrus essential oil***

Add all the ingredients to a spray bottle, and shake it vigorously. Spray the cleaner directly onto the leather, and wipe with a soft cotton or microfiber cloth. Repeat as needed to keep your treasures shiny and clean. *Whatever kind you prefer or happen to have on hand.*

Liven up your leather furniture. Over time, even the most lovingly tended leather upholstery loses its youthful luster. If that's finally happened to your favorite couch or chair, here's a simple way to bring back its glory days: Mix equal parts of white vinegar and boiled linseed oil (available at hardware stores) in a spray bottle. Shake it well, and spritz the surface as evenly as you can. Then wipe the mixture into the leather with a soft, dry cloth, and buff it out with a fresh cloth. Bingo! Happy days are here again!

SAFE & SOUND Before you use any cleaner on furniture, carpets, or window treatments for the first time, read the attached manufacturer's label to make sure it doesn't warn against using any of the ingredients in the cleaner. Then test it on an inconspicuous spot, like the back side of a curtain hem or chair skirt, or a section of carpeting in a closet. Let it dry thoroughly. If you see no change in color or texture, you'll know it's okay to move on to broader territory. Needless to say, this potentially money-saving advice applies to any commercial products as well as DIY formulas.

When it's shampoo time for your fabric upholstery ... This simple routine will do the job quickly, gently, and for a fraction of the price you'd pay for a store-bought, chemical-laden product. Simply mix 1/4 cup of dishwashing liquid or liquid laundry detergent and 1 cup of warm water in a bowl. Using a wire whisk or a handheld electric mixer, whip the solution until dry suds begin to form. Then, with a soft cloth or brush, slowly massage the suds into the material. Let it dry, then wipe it with a soft cloth dipped in warm water and wrung out thoroughly. Make sure the fabric is completely dry before you let anyone take a seat. Otherwise, it'll get dirty all over again! (To speed up the drying time, open some windows or aim a fan at the wet wonder.)

Only you can prevent beer stains. Dangnabbit!! You came home after your best round of golf all year, kicked back a tad too enthusiastically with a cold beer, and wound up sharing it with the couch. Not to worry! You can save the day in a flash. Just grab a sponge or soft cloth, and sop up as much of the liquid as you can. Then saturate the area with a half-and-half solution of white vinegar and water. Blot it with a clean absorbent towel, and that seating piece will look as good as new—or at the very least better than it did before you cracked open your celebratory brewski.

Let the show go on—briefly. Where there are small children, there are crayons. If your visiting grandtykes have presented you with artwork on your walls or hard-surface floors, first photograph the masterpiece (so you can share a good laugh about the episode in years to come). Then dip a soft brush in white vinegar, and scrub the marks to dissolve the wax. Wipe it away with a soft, clean cloth, and you'll have a clean, bare "canvas" just waiting for the next exhibition.

Labor Saver

To remove ballpoint ink from upholstered furniture or painted walls, simply dampen a cloth or sponge with white vinegar. Then rub the area gently until the marks are gone. Rinse with a clean, damp cloth, and you'll be good to go!

DARN GOOD WOOD-DUSTING SPRAY

Chronic exposure to dust can lead to the development of allergies, asthma, and toxins in your body, as well as a compromised immune system. Older adults and young children are at the biggest risk. Unfortunately, many commercial sprays contain chemicals that can cause just as much trouble as the dust itself. Instead, clean and nourish your wood furniture with this safe spray. (Just don't use it on non-wood surfaces because the oils will leave a residue.)

1 cup of water **10 drops of lemon essential oil**

1/2 cup of white vinegar **5 drops of cedarwood essential oil**

Pour the water and vinegar into a spray bottle. Add the oils and shake thoroughly. Shake again before each use. Watch as the dust and grime vanish, and a beautiful shine appears.

Polish off the polish. Regular polishing helps keep wood furniture at its peak of good looks, all right. But when that coating builds up on the surface, it can cast a kind of yellowish tint. In order to remove it and prevent future buildup, just clean your wood pieces occasionally with a half-and-half mixture of white vinegar and water. Dip a soft cloth into the liquid, squeeze it dry, then give the surface a rubdown, moving with the grain of the wood. Then wipe it dry with a soft, dry towel. How often you need to repeat this process depends on the wood and the type of polish you use, so let your eyes be your guide.

HELP WANTED? When you're selling your home and buying one where you can age in place, your requirements will differ from those of a young couple just starting out. So the National Association of Realtors® created a category for agents called Seniors Real Estate Specialist® (SRES). They are trained in the needs of buyers and sellers in the 50-plus age bracket. To find the nearest SRES agent in your city, visit seniorsrealestate.com/why-use-sres.

Make wood furniture upkeep a breeze. You'll never have to scramble to find dusting spray or rags when you have a supply of grab-and-go cleaning cloths on hand. Just mix 1/2 cup of lemon juice and 1 teaspoon of olive oil in a bowl. Soak squares of soft, all-cotton fabric in the mixture for a few minutes (cloth diapers are perfect; so are pieces from old flannel sheets). Squeeze out the excess oil, and store your future helpers in a tightly covered container. Then use them to dust all your wooden furniture. You'll clean and nourish the wood at the same time.

Spruce up painted floors or furniture. You can find plenty of cleaners that are specially made for that purpose, but this DIY version works as well as any of them, at a fraction of the cost. To make it, mix 1 cup of borax and 2 tablespoons of dishwashing liquid per gallon of warm water in a bucket. Gently rub the solution onto the surface with a natural sponge. Tackle one small section at a time, slightly overlapping the just-cleaned areas. (If you're cleaning a wall, start at the bottom and work toward the top.) Then rinse with clear water, and dry with an old, soft, all-cotton towel.

Less is more. It only stands to reason that the fewer pieces of furniture you have, the less time you'll need to spend on their upkeep. It's also true that the more open space you have in each room, the easier and more comfortable it is to move around in. That's true for anyone of any age, but it's especially important if you or anyone else in your household uses a walker, wheelchair, or scooter—or if you're simply a little unsteady on your feet. So take a cold, hard look around each room, and do yourself a favor: If there's anything you don't need, use on a regular basis, or love for whatever reason, get it outta there!

Money Saver

To remove light dirt and smudges from painted furniture or painted-wood floors, don't run out to spend money on a fancy, single-purpose cleaner. Instead, just sprinkle baking soda on a clean, damp cloth or sponge, and lightly rub the soiled area. Follow up by wiping the clean surface with another cloth or sponge dampened with clear water. That's all there is to it!

GENTLY SCENTED GLASS CLEANER

If you prefer to use a glass cleaner that has a pleasant and not over-whelming aroma, you've come to the right place. This fabulous formula will make your windows, mirrors, glass-topped tables, and glass doors sparkle to beat the band. Plus, its light, all-natural scent will lift your spirits and freshen the air all around you!

1/4 tsp. of Solubol dispersant	1 1/2 cups of white vinegar
3 – 7 drops of grapefruit essential oil	1/2 cup of distilled water
3 – 7 drops of lemon essential oil	

Mix the Solubol and oils in a small container. Combine the mixture with the vinegar and water in a spray bottle, and give it a good shake. Spritz the cleaner onto the glass, then wipe the surface clean with a soft cotton or microfiber cloth.

When menopause leaves you with a drawerful of maxi pads... Add them to your cleaning arsenal. For example, spray the Gently Scented Glass Cleaner (above) onto a pad that you've stuck to the palm of your hand, and use it to clean your windows. Or you can team up the soft, absorbent pads with the appropriate cleaners and spiff up furniture, ceiling fans, slatted window blinds, or even hard-surface floors.

ANTI-AGING MATTERS

Q: I just snagged a sterling silver candelabra at a flea market for peanuts—probably because it's so tarnished most people walked right by it. Do you know a good polishing method that my arthritic fingers can handle?

A: You bet! Just mix 1/2 cup of powdered milk, 1 tablespoon of lemon juice, and 1 1/2 cups of water in a container that's big enough to hold your fabulous find. (Multiply the ingredients as needed to cover the piece completely.) Let it sit overnight, or for 8 to 12 hours. Then rinse and dry it thoroughly. It'll shine like the Milky Way on a dark summer's night!

Get your fireplace ready for Santa. Cleaning a fireplace is no picnic. But with your family about to arrive for Christmas, the job has to be done. Start by brushing down the walls so soot and other debris fall onto the hearth floor. Then sprinkle some used, moist tea leaves or still-moist coffee grounds, or a combination of both, over the soot. This helps prevent the noxious particles from flying into the air when you sweep the stuff up with a broom. Follow by vacuuming any of the remaining loose material from the walls and floor. Then mix 1 cup of vinegar per gallon of warm water in a bucket. Dip a large sponge into the solution, and wipe down the bricks. Now Santa will have a clean, soot-free landing pad on Christmas Eve!

> To keep newly cleaned brass from tarnishing, apply a very light coat of boiled linseed oil, and let it dry before handling the piece.

Brighten up your brass. Produce a flawless finish on candlesticks, or anything else that's made of unlacquered brass, with this easy, down-home routine. Dissolve 1 teaspoon of salt in 1/2 cup of white vinegar. Then stir in 1/2 cup of flour or more, as needed, to make a thick paste. Dip a soft-bristled toothbrush in the mixture, and scrub the tarnish away. Then rinse with clear water, and dry the metal thoroughly to keep water spots from forming.

Darken up your brass. Vinegar can give brass a patina of tarnish so it looks antique. Simply dissolve 1 teaspoon of salt in 1/2 cup of white vinegar, and wipe the solution onto the metal. Let the object(s) sit for a couple of hours, and rinse. If the color isn't dark enough, repeat the process until you're pleased with the results.

Time Saver

Got a treasured glass vase that's turned hazy? To clear it up in a flash, mix 1/3 cup of lemon juice with 1 cup of cool black tea, then pour the solution into the vase, and let it sit for a few hours. Empty the vase, wipe the inside surface with a soft cloth, and rinse with clear water.

SANITY-SAVING BUG-OFF SPRAY

Even beneficial bugs can drive you nuts. This spray will send them elsewhere without hurting them at all. In fact, it'll save many from ending up as splatters on your windows and save you from having to scrape them off.

4 tbsp. of citronella essential oil   **1/4 cup of white or apple cider vinegar**
4 tbsp. of Solubol dispersant   **3 cups of water**

Mix the oil and Solubol in a small container. Pour the mixture, along with the vinegar and water, into a spray bottle. To keep bugs away from closed windows, clean the outside of the glass with the potion. If the little guys seem to be bouncing off the screens, thoroughly spray the mesh, too. Just make sure you spray from the inside out, so you don't wind up with puddles on the floor!

Go away, lady! Even if you love ladybugs and appreciate the work they do in your garden, you'd probably rather they didn't move into your house, as they have a tendency to do when winter's looming on the horizon. Here's a simple, safe way to send them scurrying back outdoors: Sprinkle whole cloves in the infested areas. Ladybugs don't care for the strong scent, and they'll evacuate quickly. When you're sure the gang's all gone, vacuum or sweep up the cloves.

Bedbugs cause the most trouble in apartment buildings, where they move readily from one unit to another, but they can show up in any home. These tiny terrors are as clever as all get-out, and they're highly creative at finding unreachable hiding places. They also move at lightning-like speed. So at the first sign of trouble, call an exterminator who uses integrated pest management (IPM) techniques. These pros know where to look for the wily devils, and they will use the least toxic methods possible to actually get rid of them—instead of just sending them to other hard-to-reach hidey-holes, as any DIY attempts are likely to do.

De-mouse your house. And make it snappy. Unlike many pests, mice are not simply nuisances. Not only do they spread diseases that are especially dangerous for older adults and young children, but mice can start house fires by chewing on wiring or on matches that they've collected and dragged back to their nests. For years, folks have tried to build a better mousetrap, but forget that idea. As professional pest controllers will tell you, nothing beats the old-fashioned Victor® snap trap. It's been eliminating mice, and their rat cousins, since 1898.

Do not use 'em again, Sam!
Whatever you do, don't try to economize by using reusable plastic snap traps. For one thing, they can spread diseases when you wash or reuse them. But, because they don't snap as hard as the original metal versions, they don't always deliver a death blow to the prisoner. And a wounded, squirming rodent is the last thing you want to deal with!

Stage a full-scale blitz. Instead of setting out a few mousetraps each night over a period of time, invest in as many as your budget will allow and set them out all at once. Mice normally travel close to walls, so put plenty of traps along those routes, as well as in any places where you've seen evidence of mice. Repeat the process until your bait has no more takers. And speaking of bait, this trio is tops: chunky peanut butter, cucumber pieces with the rind left on, and dryer lint. (Mice covet the stuff for nest-building material.)

Money Saver

Retailers are doing a brisk business in detergent- and essential-oil-based sprays that claim to get rid of bedbugs safely, and the Internet is awash with DIY versions. Well, don't waste your money. It is true, as scientists have found, that some of these formulas can kill the pests, but here's the clincher: These studies were conducted in laboratories, where the pesticides were sprayed directly on the targets. In a home, it's difficult to spray anything directly on bedbugs because of their ability to hide in tiny cracks and crevices to lay their eggs. And when you are able to make direct contact, either white vinegar or rubbing alcohol will work just fine. They don't have any residual power—but neither do any of the pricier concoctions.

ROOTS-OF-THE-MATTER PLANT HELPER

When you see tiny gnats flitting around your houseplants, it means that they're fixin' to lay their eggs in the soil. And soon, the hatchlings will start sucking the juices from the roots and lower stems. So spring into action fast with this simple trap.

Apple cider vinegar **Small piece of ripe fruit**
Dishwashing liquid **Transparent tape**

Pour about 1/2 inch of vinegar into a disposable plastic cup, and stir in a couple drops of dishwashing liquid. Set the fruit into the container so that it sticks out above the surface of the liquid. Cover the cup with the tape, leaving a 1/8-inch opening in the center. Set the trap close to your plagued plant(s), and check it daily. Don't disturb any gnats you see on the tape. They'll find their way to the hole and be gone in a few days.

Pine for your houseplants. If you're busy living an active retirement, it's easy to forget little things like watering your plants. So try this trick: Stick a pinecone into the soil. When the pinecone's petals open up, it means the soil is dry, and the plant needs a drink. When the petals are closed, then everything's hunky-dory.

SAFE & SOUND Whether you're shopping for a new home or modifying your current one, make sure the place has windows that open easily. As we've noted, the older you get, the more sensitive your system becomes to toxins and allergens in the air. Simply by letting balmy breezes blow, you'll make the great indoors a whole lot healthier. If your house was built with non-opening windows, replace at least some of them with functioning versions. And for good measure, ease off a bit on the weather stripping. This is especially important if you live where you tend to move from the heating season into AC season with little or no time for an open-window respite.

Give your houseplants vim and vinegar. If your plants look unhealthy, despite your best efforts, and you have hard water, that's all but guaranteed to be the problem. Hard water is highly alkaline, and most plants prefer soil with a pH in the neutral range. The simple solution: Every time you water, add about 1 tablespoon of apple cider vinegar per gallon of H_2O. This will enable the roots to absorb more nourishment. The vinegar will also provide trace nutrients that will help boost the plants' overall growth.

Keep cut flowers at their peak. Nothing can make them last forever, but this routine will keep the show on the road for as long as possible: Mix 1 part lemon-lime soda pop and 3 parts water to make a quart of solution. Then add 1/4 teaspoon of bleach, and pour the mixture into a vase. Add another 1/4 teaspoon of bleach every four or five days, and you'll be amazed at how long your posies will stay pretty and perky!

Provide spud security. Here's another trick that—kooky as it sounds—will keep flowers fresh longer: Simply cut slits in a raw baking potato, and push flower stems into the slits, making sure they're secure. Set the spud in the bottom of an opaque vase, and pour in the water. If you keep the arrangement out of direct sunlight and away from heat sources, it'll keep its good looks for up to two weeks.

Give 'em clean living quarters. It doesn't take much time for gunk to build up in the bottom of a vase. Instead of trying to scrub it out with a brush, pour in enough water to cover the residue about 3 inches, and then pop in two denture-cleaning tablets. Let it stand for about an hour or two, then rinse well. Repeat the process as necessary.

Labor Saver

Anybody who thinks tending houseplants is a headache apparently doesn't know about this slick trick: Just feed each of your plants once a month with an aspirin tablet dissolved in water. It's just the ticket to keep them looking and feeling their very best.

HOW HOUSEPLANTS KEEP YOU YOUNG

More and more scientific research is showing that adding a few houseplants to your home can actually help you stay healthier and happier longer. Here's a sampling of what a little greenery can do:

IMPROVE YOUR SLEEP. As we all know, plants take in carbon dioxide and give off oxygen, and more oxygen can enhance the quality of your slumber. Both gerbera daisies and snake plant (a.k.a. mother-in-law's tongue) are great choices. They keep producing oxygen even after the sun goes down.

RELIEVE ALLERGIES. Researchers have found that rooms with plants in them have less dust and mold than those without any foliage. Plants act as natural filters to snag allergens and other airborne crud, but those with textured leaves, like African violets, are especially effective trappers.

LIFT YOUR SPIRITS. Studies show that people who work in offices with plants (especially flowering types) tend to feel better about their jobs, worry less, and take fewer sick days. And the same benefits are conferred upon retired folks or those who work from home.

HELP FIGHT OFF VIRUSES. Furnaces dry out indoor air, and that can increase your chances of catching a cold or flu. Houseplants add moisture to the air to a healthier level. One study found that a few spider plants helped raise the relative humidity in a bedroom by a full 10 percent.

REDUCE STRESS. Numerous studies have found that being around plants has a calming effect. It tends to lower your blood pressure and heart rate, as well as levels of the infamous stress hormone cortisol.

SHARPEN YOUR MENTAL FOCUS. Studies performed in classrooms show that the presence of plants can enhance concentration and strengthen your memory—and the older you get, the more help you can use on that score!

SPEED HEALING. Research shows that people who have plants around after surgery recover more quickly, tolerate pain better, and require less medication.

ENHANCE MENTAL AND EMOTIONAL HEALTH. Nurturing a living plant, indoors or out, can lower anxiety, improve attention, and relieve depression.

CHAPTER 10

LAUNDRY & STORAGE

If it seems that even with your children grown and gone, you still have an awful lot of laundry to do, there's a reason for this: The average person generates more than 500 pounds of dirty clothes each year. Even in a one- or two-person household, that means major work—and as with any other household chore, the older you get, the more challenging it all becomes. To make matters even less senior-friendly, many detergents, fabric softeners, and other laundry aids rank among the most toxic products on supermarket shelves. Well, friends, in this chapter, you'll find help on both fronts. I'll share a ton of terrific tips to ease the physical burden and simple DIY formulas that will keep your wardrobe and your health in fine fettle. In these pages, you'll also discover wily ways to organize and safeguard your home's storage areas, so they can serve you well as the years march on.

As always, you'll find vinegar at the front and center of the action. As an example, here's an ultra-easy, ultra-safe fabric softener that's every bit as effective as any commercial version, and at a tiny fraction of the cost:

Simply mix 30 drops of lavender or peppermint essential oil with 1/2 teaspoon of Solubol dispersant (available from essential oil suppliers). Add the mixture to a 1-gallon jug of white vinegar, and shake well. Then use it as you would any other liquid fabric softener, at a rate of 1/2 cup for top-loading washers and 1/4 cup for HE machines. Believe you me, life in the laundry lane doesn't get any easier than this!

HERE'S TO YOUR HEALTH DETERGENT

Commercial laundry detergents are among the most toxic products of all. This version is entirely free of noxious chemicals.

1 1/4 cups of white vinegar   **1 cup of washing soda**

1 cup of baking soda   **1/4 cup of liquid castile soap**

1 cup of borax

Pour the vinegar into a large bowl. Add each dry ingredient gradually, stirring with a wooden spoon, breaking up any clumps. Add the soap last* and stir again until the mixture is about the texture of a soft, rather crumbly loaf of bread. Store it in a large non-metallic container with a lid. To use it, break off about 1/4 cup of pieces, and toss them into the washer before adding your clothes. *Timing is crucial; if you add the soap before the vinegar is mixed with the solids, you'll have a gooey mess on your hands.*

Don't take "hand wash" at face value. Unless you're dealing with a treasured heirloom, ignore that instruction that appears on so many fabric-care labels. Instead, simply tuck special-care items into mesh lingerie bags and wash them in cold water on your machine's most delicate cycle. It's all but guaranteed they'll fare just fine. Not only will you save time and trouble, but if your hands are at all stiff, you could also spare yourself some major discomfort.

EARLY BIRD SPECIALS

When your washer, dryer, or any other appliance goes on the blink, don't forget to ask about available discounts when you call for help. Many local repair shops offer them to seniors as well as veterans and active-duty military personnel. As always, age requirements and exact dollar figures vary from one establishment to the next—but unless you are a repeat customer, the staff won't know that you're eligible for anything unless you remember to speak up!

Soften up below. If you prefer a liquid detergent to a crumbly version (see Here's to Your Health Detergent, at left), give this formula a try. Start by bringing 4 cups of water to a boil. Put 2 cups of washing soda into a large nonreactive bowl, and add 2 cups of the boiling water, stirring continuously until the soda is fully dissolved. Follow up by stirring in 1/2 cup of Dr. Bronner's Sal Suds (available online and at supermarkets) until it's well combined. Then stir in the remaining 2 cups of boiling water. Finally, let the mixture cool to room temperature, and store it in a tightly capped bottle at room temperature. Use it as you would any liquid detergent, at a rate of 1/4 cup per load. For extra softness, add 1/2 cup of white vinegar to the rinse cycle.

End bottle cap drips. Tired of having detergent drip everywhere after you pour the liquid out of the lid and into the washer? If so, then simply toss the cap into the wash along with the clothes. It'll come out squeaky clean and dripless. (Just remember to fish the cap out of the mix before you throw the load into the dryer!)

Time Saver

When possible, run your dryer loads back to back. The reason is because when the machine is already warm, the second load and all the loads after that will dry more quickly, so you'll get your laundry done in less time. Plus, because the mechanism won't have to go from stone cold to a higher temperature, you will also save some money on your next energy bill.

Location, location, location.
If your laundry room is in the basement, whether you plan to age in place or sell your home when you retire, consider moving your washer and dryer to the first or second floor. Or replace them with new models in a laundry area upstairs. Either way, you'll dodge the hassle and potential risk of navigating the stairs on wash day. Plus, according to professional realtors, having machines in the main living area will add to the value of your property. Conversely, a laundry area that is located in the basement can actually decrease the desirability and sale price of your home.

ULTRA-STRONG, ALL-OVER STAIN REMOVER

There are many ways to tackle isolated stains. But if your grandchildren come in from outside with their clothes covered in who-knows-what, you'll need a broader approach. And this DIY formula can help:

6 drops of Solubol dispersant* **1 cup of white vinegar**
3 drops of tea tree oil **1/2 cup of baking soda**

Mix the Solubol and tea tree oil in a small container. Add the mixture, along with the vinegar and baking soda, to a filled washer. Soak the stained duds for about 60 minutes, drain the drum, and wash the load with your usual detergent. Then examine the clothes carefully. If any marks remain, repeat the soaking and washing process before tossing the garments into the dryer. *Available from essential oil suppliers.*

When you wind up wearing part of your lunch... Reach for the white vinegar. It's dynamite at removing stains left by many foods, including berries, cherries, citrus fruits, grapes, pears, apples, honey, and all manner of syrups and jellies. In each case, dab the spot(s) with a mixture of 1 part vinegar to 2 parts lukewarm water. Blot dry with a clean, colorfast cloth, towel, sponge, or white paper towels. Then rinse with clear water. **Note:** *Do not use paper towels that are imprinted with colored designs because the vinegar could cause the dye to bleed onto the fabric and give you more trouble than you already have!*

HELP WANTED? When you're dealing with stains on really expensive clothes, or on cherished, irreplaceable pieces of any kind, don't even think of trying these DIY treatments. Instead, take any contemporary garments to an expert dry cleaner (a tailor or dressmaker should be able to recommend one). In the case of a real or possible antique—for example, a quilt that you just bought at an estate sale, or your grandmother's christening dress that your new grandchild will be wearing soon—consult a museum curator who specializes in textiles.

A spoonful of sugar makes grass stains go away. Every lawn and garden tender picks up plenty of these green souvenirs. To get 'em out easily, and without toxic ingredients, mix granulated sugar with enough warm water to make a thick paste. Just start with equal parts of each, and add more solid or liquid as needed. Then spread your mixture onto the spots, wait for an hour, and wash the garment as usual. End of problem!

> Just as with the kitchen and bathroom, make sure the laundry area in an aging-in-place home has non-slip flooring with no throw rugs.

Build a better bleach gel pen. If you like the convenience of bleach gel pens, but not the high price tags, make your own. Combine 2 tablespoons of cornstarch and 1 cup of water in a pan, and stir it until the starch is completely dissolved. Then heat the mixture, and continue to stir until it comes to a boil (it will get quite thick). Remove it from the heat, and let it cool to room temperature. Slowly stir in 5 to 6 tablespoons of liquid bleach to form a gel, and pour it into a clean, empty squeeze bottle with a pointed tip. It'll work just as well as commercial versions for tough laundry stains, or other household chores.

Take a load off your joints on laundry day. If your hands are even mildly arthritic, pulling garments out of a laundry hamper and tossing 'em into the appropriate pile can be excruciating. So stop already. Instead, get a multi-bin rolling hamper, and label each section (dark colors, whites, delicates, and so on). Then, when it's time to take your clothes off in the evening, drop each item into the appropriate receptacle.

Money Saver

No matter what stain-removal method you use, always make sure the marks are completely gone before you put the garments into the dryer. The heat could cook the splotches so deeply that they'll be all but impossible to get out. You could wind up spending your hard-earned cash on replacements for clothes that still had plenty of life left in them.

DANDY DIY DRYER SHEETS

Most commercial versions contain toxins that can harm sensitive skin and breathing passages. But this DIY version works just as well as store-bought brands, with no harmful chemicals. Plus, you can reuse them.

1/4 tsp. of Solubol dispersant   **1 cup of white vinegar**
20–25 drops of essential oil   **Squares of soft cotton fabric**

Mix the Solubol and oil in a small container, then combine the mixture with the vinegar in a widemouthed glass jar (with a tight-fitting lid). Shake thoroughly. Dip each fabric square into the solution, and wring out any excess, so the fabric is damp, not saturated. Keep any leftover solution in a glass jar, and store the sheets in an airtight container. Use one sheet per load of laundry until the aroma fades, then dunk them into the drink once again.

Wake up and smell the dryer sheets. Here's a simple way to soften your clothes and eliminate static cling at a fraction of the cost of commercial dryer sheets—and with no nasty chemicals: Dampen a coffee filter with white vinegar, and add a few drops of essential oil (lavender is a laundry-day classic, but you can use whatever colorless scent you prefer or happen to have on hand). Then toss the filter into the dryer with your clothes, and you'll enjoy static-free clothes!

SAFE & SOUND

Undiluted essential oils can stain fabric. So whenever you use them in laundry detergents, fabric softeners, or the At-the-Ready Wrinkle Releaser on page 188, make sure to mix the oil with Solubol dispersant before you add the oils to your recipe. And for good measure, keep your clothing-care arsenal to colorless oils. Lavender, peppermint, clary sage, juniper, and rosemary (among others) will all deliver a light, natural scent, with no risk of staining the fabric. Save your colorful favorites, like orange, lemon, and rose, for household cleaning and pest-control purposes.

Keep scented filters at the ready. Rather than douse a coffee filter with vinegar and oil every time you do a load of laundry (see "Wake up and smell the dryer sheets," at left), make a supply to keep on hand. Just put a stack of filters in a small glass container that has a tight-fitting lid. Then combine your chosen oil with Solubol dispersant at a ratio of about 1 part oil to 3 parts Solubol, add the mixture to a jar with a cup or so of vinegar, and shake the jar vigorously. Pour enough of the blend over the filters to dampen, not saturate, the paper, and fasten the lid. That's all there is to it! **Note:** *The amount of vinegar you need depends on how many coffee filters you're using, and the amount of oil is entirely up to you. Use as much or as little as you need to get your preferred intensity of fragrance.*

To prevent creases, use your noodle. Tired of those lines and creases that form on clothes when you dry them on a rack? If so, then try this slick trick. Cut a swimming pool noodle to the length of the rods on your rack. Then slice along the length of the foam to make an opening. Make as many crease preventers as you're likely to use at one time, and keep them on hand in your laundry room. Then, when you take delicate items out of the washer, cover the rod(s) with the easygoing foam. It'll cushion the fabric so it can dry smoothly.

Sure doesn't *look* like fruit! If you're short on easy-to-access storage space in your laundry room, get yourself a wire hanging fruit basket or two. Stash your small supplies, like clothespins, detergent tablets, dryer sheets, or dryer balls, in the tiered compartments. Everything will be right at your fingertips, no bending or stooping required.

Labor 👍 Saver

You say that static cling is not an issue—you'd just like to give your laundry a fresh, clean scent? If so, then this easy tactic has your name written all over it: Simply drip a few drops of your favorite essential oil onto several cotton balls or pads, and toss them into the dryer along with your clothes or linens. They'll emerge with a light, natural fragrance and with no chemical residue.

AT-THE-READY WRINKLE RELEASER

It's frustrating, all right: You reach for a shirt, dress, or other garment and find that it's sporting some wrinkles, and there's no time to iron it. That's why it pays to keep this dandy helper on hand.

1/4 tsp. of Solubol dispersant   **1 cup of distilled or filtered water**

6–8 drops of colorless essential oil   **1 cup of white vinegar**

Mix the Solubol and oil in a small container, then combine it with the water and vinegar in a spray bottle. Then shake it vigorously. Lightly spray the fabric from side to side, using a sweeping motion. Use your hands to smooth out the material, and let it air-dry. Put woven garments on hangers, and either drape cotton knits over a drying rack or spread them out flat on a towel. **Note:** *Don't use this formula on silk or rayon.*

Fend off creases in the closet. One benefit of growing older is that we learn so many valuable lessons—including the fact that most minor annoyances are easier to avoid than they are to remedy. A prime case in point is the hassle of pulling out a pair of pants that's been hanging in your closet and finding a deep crease made by the hanger. The solution: A variation on the theme of "To prevent creases, use your noodle" (on page 187). In this case, cut and slice the foam to fit the lower hanger rod of a wooden or tubular plastic clothes hanger. Then drape your pants over it. This same trick also works for flat accessories like scarves, shawls, and neckties.

Time Saver

When your clothes are wrinkled, and there's no time to either pull out the iron and ironing board or whip up a wrinkle-release spray, steam the creases out in your dryer. If your machine doesn't have a special steam setting (as some fancy new models have), just toss your afflicted garment(s) into the drum along with a damp washcloth or hand towel. Then run the dryer for 10 to 15 minutes. As the water evaporates, it will create enough steam to eliminate even the most set-in creases.

When good vinegar does bad things to your clothes... Don't panic. While it is true that darker-colored culinary vinegars, including balsamic, malt, red wine, and some fruit-infused types, do stain fabrics, if you act fast you can usually get the marks out. First, immediately blot the spill with white paper towels to soak up as much moisture as possible. Then flood the area with cold water, and wash the item as usual. If any splotches remain, submerge the whole garment in a mixture of oxygen-based bleach (like OxiClean™ or OXO Brite®) and tepid water, and let it soak for 4 to 12 hours. Then, once more, launder it as usual. That should be all she wrote! This method is great for just about any washable fabric, but to play it safe, don't use it on silk, wool, or anything that's trimmed with leather. These all demand the prompt attention of a professional dry cleaner.

Pre-soak gym duds. When they are feeling less than fresh after an especially enthusiastic workout, put your dirty clothes in a sink. Then add enough cold water to completely cover them, and pour in 1/2 cup of white vinegar. Let the clothes soak for at least one hour, then wash them as usual. They will be their old fresh-as-daisies selves again—guaranteed!

What not to soften. When you wash clothes that you wear for sports, workouts, or warm-weather outdoor work, don't use any fabric softener in either your washer or dryer. The reason is that any of these products can make fabric less absorbent and less breathable. That in turn can greatly reduce your comfort level when you're engaged in perspiration-producing endeavors, especially during hot, humid weather when you're sweating up a storm.

Q: Does apple cider vinegar work just as well as plain old white vinegar for laundry purposes?

A: Yes and no. Thanks to their acetic acid content, both types can soften fabrics and remove stains, but apple cider vinegar can sometimes stain white or light-colored fabrics. For that reason, it's safer to use white vinegar for laundry purposes. If you need to tackle a stain quickly, and you only have apple cider vinegar on hand, avoid possible damage by testing a small hidden area first before going all in on the job.

ANTI-AGING MATTERS

LOVELY LEATHER CLEANER

Vintage leather suitcases make versatile and attractive storage pieces. They're especially useful if you've moved to smaller quarters because they can hold anything from out-of-season clothes to Christmas decor, office supplies, and toys kept on hand for visiting grandchildren. This DIY cleaner is perfect for keeping your valises looking their best.

1/4 tsp. of Solubol dispersant   **1/2 cup of warm water**

6 drops of eucalyptus oil   **1/4 cup of white vinegar**

Dust the leather to remove any loose dirt. Mix the Solubol and oil in a small container. Combine the water and vinegar in a bowl, and stir in the Solubol-oil mixture. Dip a soft cotton cloth into the solution, and squeeze out excess moisture. Wipe the surfaces firmly, repeating as needed until they're spankin' clean. Then dry with a fresh cotton cloth.

The older you get... The more important it becomes to heed the golden rule of storage in every part of your home: Keep the things you use most often in the places where they're easiest to get to. When you're dealing with shelves, that easy-grab, easy-replace territory consists of those that are located from about mid-thigh to shoulder height. To keep bending and stretching to a minimum, save the higher and lower shelves for storing items that you only use occasionally.

EARLY BIRD SPECIALS

If you're getting ready to relocate and you lack the time, energy, patience, or physical strength to do the job yourself, don't do it—at least not all of it. Instead, contact the National Association of Senior Move Managers, which, as the name implies, specializes in the particular needs of older adults. They can refer you to a pro in your area who can tackle all or part of your transition, from setting a time line and comprehensive plan for the move to arranging the furniture in your new home and even hooking up all your electronic devices. You'll find this gold mine of expertise at www.nasmm.com.

Consider another aspect of shelf life. Always keep heavier objects on the lower shelves and lighter things on the upper ones. This arrangement will help anchor a freestanding unit, so that if you should bump into it, it's not likely to fall over. Beyond that, it will make your life easier and safer in another way. That's because you'll put a lot less strain on your aging muscles and joints when you reach up to snag your quarry—not to mention greatly reducing the chance of damage if you should lose your grip on the item, only to have it come tumbling down on your head.

Depth matters, too. If you're installing new shelves, whether built-in or freestanding, in a home where you plan to age in place, use versions that are as shallow as possible. Ideally, they should be only deep enough to hold the contents in a single row. This is especially important when some or all of the items you'll be storing are breakable. You are able to avoid having to move things in front to reach the stuff in back, which could send something crashing to the floor in the process. In addition, the more shallow a shelf unit is, the less floor space it takes up. And that will increase maneuvering room for you or anyone in your household who is confined to a scooter or wheelchair, or otherwise has less than full mobility.

If you must store items two or more rows deep… Always put the shortest things in front and the tallest in back. This way, even if your eyesight is somewhat limited, you can see at a glance exactly what you've got, so you'll be less likely to brush something off the shelf by accident.

Labor Saver

One of the most effective ways to freshen up the air in closets, drawers, and storage containers of all kinds is also one of the easiest: Just scoop a few tablespoons of baking soda into a coffee filter, twist the top closed, and secure it with a twist tie or rubber band. These little pouches are also perfect for removing those less-than-pleasant odors from things like athletic shoes and for preventing musty aromas in books (just pop some sacks behind the volumes on the shelves).

WONDERFUL WOOD FURNITURE POLISH

This is perfect for keeping dressers, armoires, and other solid-wood storage pieces looking their best with none of the synthetic fragrances and other nasty chemicals found in most commercial polishes.

1/4 cup of malt vinegar*	**1/4 tsp. of vegetable glycerin**
1 tbsp. of jojoba oil	**30 drops of essential oils****

Combine all the ingredients in a glass spray bottle, shake it vigorously, and lightly spritz the wood. Using a soft cotton cloth, wipe the polish around until the surface is completely covered. Wipe away any excess polish with a second cloth. Store any leftovers in a cool, dark place, and shake the bottle again before each use. *Use white vinegar on very light woods, or any that you think could be stained by the darker malt variety. **An excellent combo for wood is 10 drops each of orange, lemon, and either cedarwood or pine.

A stairway is not a storage space! Many storage experts recommend installing shelves or pegboard on one or even both sides of a stairway. But the fact is that hanging anything there is all but begging for a serious accident, and the older and less steady you get, the greater the risk becomes. But at any age, you—or even your grandchildren—could easily brush against all that stuff on your way down the steps, or bump into it with a laundry basket that you're carrying. If that just so happens (and you're lucky), the mop, coat, bottle, or what-have-you will go flying down the stairs. If you're not so lucky, *you* could go flying down the stairs!

SAFE & SOUND If, like many older folks, you routinely park things on a top or bottom step so you won't forget to take them with you on your next trek, break that habit right now! Granted, this trick probably does work just fine as a memory aid, and it may save you an extra trip. But if you happen to stumble over any of that stuff, you could easily wind up taking a fast ride to the ER!

Picture this. Many sources that specialize in safety advice for older adults tell you it's fine to hang photos or paintings on stairway walls as long as the pieces don't extend out any more than 1 inch. But if you're getting unsteady on your feet, and going up or down the steps requires your full concentration, forget that idea. The reason is that if you happen to glance at the adornments on the wall, it could distract you just enough that you lose your balance and go flying downward. So instead of turning your stairway into an art gallery, hang your pictures on a wall where you can view them safely from the comfort of an easy chair.

Clear out that clutter. Whether you're aiming to age in place, or you plan to relocate after retiring, one of the biggest favors you can do yourself is to get rid of extra stuff (the sooner the better). How so? Well, for one thing, it's a proven fact that clutter can send your stress level soaring, and that can aggravate or usher in just about every physical and mental woe under the sun. For another, the more stuff you have, the more time and effort it takes to care for it. Studies show that decluttering would eliminate 40 percent of housework in the average home. That translates into a lot of time you could spend on the golf course, or playing with your grandchildren.

Money Saver

If you're renting a storage locker to hold things that won't fit in your house, you're throwing hard-earned cash right down the drain. Simply by emptying out that money pit, you could save a bunch to help fund your retirement. In fact, if you sell even some of your cast-off goods at a garage sale or flea market, or through an online venue like eBay or Etsy, you'll not only save your monthly locker fee, but you can also add even more money to your golden-age treasure chest.

If you're planning to sell your house . . . You have another reason to clear out extraneous stuff. Even though clutter may not affect the appraised value of your property, it is all but guaranteed that it will take longer to sell. Most likely, you'll also get less than your asking price, maybe considerably less, depending on the nature and extent of the junk load.

MOTH-AWAY CLEANING SPRAY

This formula is an effective, senior-friendly alternative to those toxic mothballs. It'll clean all the surfaces in your storage areas and repel moths. And it even destroys eggs or larvae that may be hidden in nooks and crannies.

1 tsp. of Solubol dispersant

10 drops of clove essential oil

10 drops of rosemary essential oil

10 drops of thyme essential oil

3/4 cup of water

1/4 cup of white vinegar

First, thoroughly vacuum all the surfaces you'll be treating. Mix the Solubol and oils in a small container, and add them to a spray bottle with the water and vinegar. Shake thoroughly, and use it like any other spray cleaner. Be sure to tackle easy-to-overlook areas like hooks, racks, drawer sliders, and the edges and undersides of shelves. Also, spray the potion in the gaps between the floor and baseboard.

Clean before you store. Both clothes moths and carpet beetles are very attracted to fabric that has food or perspiration stains, as well as odors, oil, or any moisture that we may not even notice. So wash or dry-clean all of your garments and linens before you put them away for the summer or winter.

Stick it to 'em. One of the most nose-pleasing ways to repel moths is to tuck cinnamon sticks into your drawers, and hang bundles of them in your closet. Pieces cut from mesh produce bags make great pouches because they let the aroma circulate freely.

While it can be somewhat easy to terminate casual "visits" from a small gang of clothes moths or carpet beetles, an infestation calls for some serious professional help. If, for example, you haul out your winter clothes, only to find large, ragged holes in more than a few garments, call an exterminator quickly. Look for one who uses integrated pest management (IPM) techniques that will wipe out the invaders using the least toxic methods possible.

Make room to roam in your closets. While a cluttered, disorganized closet can be a time-consuming annoyance for anyone, it's a major danger zone for an older adult whose eyesight or mobility is diminished in any way. And that's true not only in your bedroom, but also in closets throughout your home. One way to help ensure that you can get at the things you need and open up the space enough to provide clearance for assistive devices like wheelchairs, scooters, crutches, and walkers, is to outfit the area with a great commercial organizing system. Many local hardware stores not only stock the necessary components, but also have contractors who can install the whole kit and caboodle for you.

To remove the mothball scent from a wooden trunk or dresser drawers, simply sand the inside surfaces and coat them with polyurethane.

Lighten up! The more iffy your eyesight becomes, the more important it is that any closet or any other storage area is well lit. Not only will you be able to find and grab whatever you need more quickly, but you'll also avoid possibly nasty consequences. For a relatively small outlay of cash, an electrician can install light fixtures and advise you on the most effective placement. If you prefer to take the DIY route, hardware stores and home-improvement centers sell battery-powered, stick-on lights that could give you all the viewing help you need.

Time Saver

To quickly confirm whether or not you have a moth or carpet beetle infestation, pick up some adhesive-lined traps (available at hardware stores and home-improvement centers), and set or hang them in your closets. The artificial pheromones (a.k.a. sex hormones) inside will lure and snag any adults in the vicinity, and you'll be able to make a positive ID. After you've gotten rid of the current population, keep a few fresh traps on the job. That way, you'll know at a glance when any future mothers have arrived, and hopefully stop trouble before it starts.

CARPET BEETLE ELIMINATOR

Clothes moths aren't the only insects that can destroy your garments. Carpet beetle larvae also chew ragged holes in clothing, and anything made of natural-fiber fabrics or natural-synthetic blends. Fortunately, if the voracious multi-legged varmints have moved into your home, you have this powerful weapon at your disposal.

1 cup of white vinegar

10 drops of cedarwood essential oil

10 drops of eucalyptus essential oil

10 drops of peppermint essential oil

Combine all the ingredients in a spray bottle, and shake it vigorously. Then saturate all infested or vulnerable areas. Target all nooks and crannies, such as the tiny gaps between carpeted floors and the baseboards. These are prime beetle breeding grounds. The oils' vapors kill both adult beetles and larvae, while the entire combo repels and helps prevent future parental invasions.

Think anti-acid for plastic. Believe it or not, over time, cardboard can discolor white plastic or light-colored plastic (see "Don't take an acid trip," at right). If you're storing things made of plastic, like small appliances, vintage toys, or Christmas decorations, then it's fine to wrap them in more of the stuff. Depending on how fragile the objects are, you can use bubble wrap or foam packing peanuts. And as long as the entire surface is covered, it's safe to store them in a regular cardboard box.

ANTI-AGING MATTERS

Q: When my husband and I moved to our new retirement home last winter, the movers mistakenly put a box of our summer clothes in the basement. By the time I found the container, mildew was starting to set in. Is there any way to save the things?

A: There is! As kooky as this may sound, here's all you need to do: Brush off the mildew spores outside. Soak the items overnight in buttermilk, then wash and dry them as usual. Your clothes should come out as good as new!

Make the basement a no-cardboard zone. The key to safe storage in a basement is to avoid putting anything in a cardboard box—even things that are totally waterproof, like beach gear. And if at all possible, don't keep empty boxes down there, either, because they tend to harbor mildew spores, bugs, and even mice, all of which can easily spread to other parts of your house.

Don't take an acid trip. The acid contained in cardboard will damage just about anything it touches. So whenever you store items made of fabric, leather, or paper, put them in an acid-free, archival box. Or wrap the article in acid-free tissue paper, and tuck it into a container made of plastic, wood, or metal. Whatever you do, don't use newspaper, packing paper, or regular tissue paper because they also contain acid that will damage your treasures. Likewise, avoid plastic bags or wrappings, which can trap moisture inside, causing mildew to form.

To save your clothes, cook 'em or freeze 'em. If moths or carpet beetles have been at work in your closet, fast action could prevent a lot of expensive damage. Soaking washable fabric in hot water (above 120°F) for 20 to 30 minutes or running it through a dryer, set on high, for an hour or so will kill larvae and eggs. So will tucking your clothes into the freezer for three or four days at a temperature that's below 18°F. The cold treatment also works for dry-clean-only fabrics, but unless you've got a mighty big, empty freezer, you'll want to send coats and other sizable items to the dry cleaner.

Labor Saver

One of the most effective and easiest moth-deterring strategies of all is to put a dehumidifier everywhere you have clothing stored. That's because the adult moths prefer the humidity to be on the high side—between 70 and 80 percent. When you make the air in your closets as uninviting as possible, the mamas will go elsewhere to have babies. If you're put off by the possible cost, don't be. You can buy a mini dehumidifier for less than the cost of an average sweater, and a whole lot less than a coat or a wool blanket.

MIGHTY SAFE MOUSE REPELLENTS

Anything that's stored in a basement or attic is a prime target for mice. And because you may not visit these spaces frequently, the rascals can cause major damage before you discover it. For that reason, the proverbial ounce of prevention these softies deliver is worth a whole lot more than a pound of cure.

1 cup of white vinegar

25 drops of peppermint essential oil

6 – 8 cotton balls

Mix the vinegar and oil in a bowl, and drop the cotton balls into the mixture. Stir them with a spoon until they're soaked. Then stuff them into any spaces that could provide entryways for mice or rats. As the aroma fades, either replace the balls with a fresh supply, or simply mix the vinegar and oil in a spray bottle, and thoroughly spritz the barriers. **Note:** *Multiply the ingredients as needed.*

Install stronger rodent barriers. While fragrant cotton balls are fine to keep mice and rats out of your house over the short term, permanent protection demands tougher stuff. To be specific, get some sturdy, 1/4-inch woven, welded hardware cloth, cut it to fit, and stuff a piece securely into each gap. Then fill the opening with a high-quality patching compound and smooth it out. Both materials are available at hardware stores and home-improvement centers.

SAFE & SOUND When you're filling chinks in your exterior walls to guard against rodent invasions, your rule of thumb should be, "When in doubt, seal it up." The reason is that these vile varmints have an almost magical ability to condense their bodies and glide through what seem like impossibly tight spaces. Believe it or not, an adult rat can slip through a 1/2-inch gap in a wall or floor. A mouse can squeeze through a 1/4-inch opening. So close 'em all up!

Make your attic a hard-hat zone. Is there a part of your attic where the ceiling is too low for you to stand up to your full height? If so, then do your head a favor: Get a hard hat. Hang it right inside the entrance, where you can grab it on your way in. If that idea sounds extreme, bear in mind that if you should forget you're in tight quarters and stand up too quickly, the results could range from a big 'ol bump to a nasty cut from an exposed roofing nail. You can buy construction-worthy hats at lumberyards, home-improvement centers, and many hardware stores for not much more than $10—and that's a small price to pay to protect your aging noggin!

> Only use your basement to store things that can't be harmed by pests, dirt, or dampness (not to mention plumbing leaks or full-scale floods).

Stack with care. Your head isn't the only part of your body that could meet with a mishap in the attic. When you are the least bit unsteady on your feet, it's easy to bump into a stack of boxes and send 'em crashing to the floor—possibly bumping into you on their way down. If possible, store your boxes on shelves (freestanding wire versions are perfect for attics because they allow air to circulate around the cartons). But if you absolutely must stack all or some of your boxes, do it right. Either put boxes of similar size on top of one another so they won't wobble or, safer yet, stack them pyramid style, with the larger, heavier boxes on the bottom and smaller, lighter ones on top.

Money Saver

Once you've gotten rid of extraneous possessions (see "Clear out that clutter," on page 193), photograph everything that has even moderate financial value. That will take some time, but having a photographic record may save you a lot of money if you need to file an insurance claim. Keep the photos in a safe deposit box along with any relevant information like model and serial numbers, dates of purchase, and in the case of antiques or original artwork, appraisal reports.

LIGHTEN YOUR LAUNDRY LOAD

If you're like many folks, doing laundry isn't one of your favorite pastimes. And the older you get, the more of a hassle it becomes. These laundry-area tweaks help make the chore easier, whether you plan to stay where you are, or spend your golden years in a new home:

CUSTOMIZE THE LAYOUT. If your laundry area is a separate room, make sure the doorway is wide enough to accommodate a wheelchair; 36 inches is ideal. Remove obstacles that partially block the entrance or hinder your movements inside the room. Keep cabinets and countertops close enough to the washer and dryer to allow for easy transfers, but not so close that you won't have room to maneuver a wheelchair, scooter, or walker.

GET UP-FRONT APPLIANCES. Front-loading washers and dryers are easier to load and unload, especially from a wheelchair. Also, before you buy any appliances, make sure the controls are clear, easy to read, and will be easy to use if your hand mobility is ever limited.

USE COUNTER INTELLIGENCE. Make it a point to provide as much countertop space as you need for folding and sorting. Adjustable-height counters are the cat's meow for laundry rooms because they allow you to work from either a standing or seated position.

KEEP SUPPLIES AT YOUR FINGERTIPS. Open shelving is ideal because it allows you to see what you want at a glance and grab it without difficulty. If you do have closed cabinets or drawers, install D-shaped handles, which are far easier to use than knobs that must be grasped with nimble fingers.

BE SINK-SAVVY. A wall-mounted sink is a necessity, with space underneath it for a wheelchair or scooter, or a regular chair in case you want to sit while you work. Also, choose faucets with easy-to-use lever or paddle handles.

CHOOSE SAFE FLOORING. The same resilient, non-slip rubber tile that works beautifully in kitchens and bathrooms is also perfect for laundry areas.

IRON WITH COMFORT. Install an ironing board that folds down from the wall and can be adjusted to whatever height you need, and you'll wonder how you ever lived without it!

CHAPTER 11

LAWN & GARDENS

Gardening is good for anyone, but research confirms that the health benefits are downright striking for folks in the 50-plus age bracket. It can boost your mood, self-esteem, and overall mental well-being, while helping to prevent age-related problems like diabetes, hypertension, stroke, and cancer. A University of Arkansas study of 3,300 women aged 50 and older even found that those who gardened at least once a week had higher bone density than ladies who did other types of exercise.

Like any physical activity, gardening requires some modifications as we age, and that's where this chapter comes in. It will share tips and strategies that'll help your green thumb live it up well into your golden years. Naturally, you will find vinegar at the heart of it all. It can keep your lawn and garden beautiful and productive, without harsh chemicals that can harm your ever-more-sensitive immune system, and every living thing in your yard.

To be safe, use food-grade vinegars with 5% acidity. "Horticultural" varieties, with acid levels of 20% or even 30%, are made from glacial acetic acid, which can damage your skin, eyes, and breathing passages. And you sure don't want these products anywhere near your grandchildren or pets! Don't be fooled by the 10% vinegars sold in garden centers. In many cases, they're watered-down versions of the 20% stuff.

WOODY-SEED SUCCESS SOLUTION

Seeds with thick, woody coats, like morning glories, moonflowers, and okra, can be difficult to germinate. To greatly improve your chances of success, give these reluctant starters this preplanting treatment.

1 cup of vinegar (either white or apple cider)   2 cups of water
2 tbsp. of mild dishwashing liquid

Mix the vinegar, dishwashing liquid, and water in a jar (each type of seed needs a separate batch). Nick the seeds slightly with a knife, or rub them gently between two sheets of sandpaper. Drop them into the drink, and soak them for 24 hours. Rinse and plant them according to the directions on the seed packets. **Note:** *Use this formula, but without the nicking step, for nasturtiums, parsley, beets, and parsnips.*

Give 'em blanket power. After you've planted your pretreated woody seeds outdoors, cover the row, or the whole bed, with burlap. It will create a moister, warmer environment that can encourage faster sprouting. Check the scene once a day, and remove the covering as soon as any green shoots emerge.

Put non-woody seeds on a fast track. Before you plant any flower, herb, or vegetable seeds, soak them overnight in a solution made from 1/2 cup of apple cider vinegar and 1 pint of warm water. Come morning, take the seeds out of their bath, rinse them with clear water, and tuck them into the soil or seed-starting mix. If the seeds are fresh, some of them, like lettuce and the whole cabbage family, which includes broccoli, kale, and cauliflower, could germinate within 24 hours.

In the Woody-Seed Success Solution (above), and for plant-care purposes, use clear, unscented dishwashing liquid. And avoid any product that has antibacterial properties, which will destroy the friendly bacteria that plants need for good growth—and could actually prevent seeds from sprouting at all.

Root for more perennials. It's a common experience among retired folks who set out to start their first perennial flower gardens: You walk into a garden center and get a case of sticker shock. Here's an easy and less expensive alternative: Start stem cuttings in a sterilized rooting medium. You begin by dipping the bottom of each cutting in a commercial rooting hormone before tucking it into your medium-filled flat or pot. But for a high-quality rooting medium, you don't need commercial hormones. Just mix 1 teaspoon of some apple cider vinegar in 6 cups of water, and dip your cuttings in that. Your plants will get off to a rip-roarin' start.

> Prepare soil or starter pots before you pretreat seeds because it's important to sow them as soon as possible after they have sprouted.

Make your tools announce themselves.

If your eyesight isn't quite as sharp as it once was, it's very easy to lay your garden tools down, only to have them vanish among their surroundings. The solution: Paint the handles in bright, eye-popping colors. That way, they'll stand out like beacons in the grass and foliage, or against the bare brown soil.

When you're choosing plants, hedge your bets. Whether you're shopping for trees, shrubs, perennials, or turfgrass, remember that plant hardiness zone numbers are based on the coldest temperature in an average winter. So don't take chances. Go with plants that are hardy to at least one zone colder than yours to prevent panic if the weatherman says, "We'll have a record low tonight, folks!"

Money Saver

For lawn and garden uses, you don't need to use pure, unprocessed apple cider vinegar. Any distilled white or apple cider vinegar will work just fine. While mother-rich apple cider vinegar does contain micro-nutrients that plants need, their low quantities won't make much of a difference. There are less expensive ways to keep your garden well fed.

FABULOUS FOLIAR FERTILIZER

By midsummer, flower and vegetable plants can start looking a little frazzled. That's the time to give them a snack they can sink their leaves into lickety-split. This nutritious blend delivers the perfect pick-me-up.

1 cup of compost tea*

2 tbsp. of apple cider vinegar

2 tbsp. of fish emulsion**

2 tbsp. of liquid seaweed**

2 tbsp. of molasses

Mix all of the ingredients in a bucket, multiplying amounts as needed. Then, depending on the size of your "herd," funnel the mixture into either a handheld spray bottle or pump-style sprayer (not a hose-end version, which dilutes the ingredients). Spray the plants until the liquid starts dripping off the leaves. *For the recipe, see "Serve tea and see..."* (*at right*). **Available online and at garden centers.*

Make hard water plant-friendlier. Contrary to what you may have heard, hard water is not harmful to plants. Rather, the issue is that it's usually alkaline, and most plants grow best in soil that has a pH that's close to neutral (roughly 6.5 on the acid-to-alkaline scale). Simply adding 1 tablespoon of white vinegar per gallon of H_2O will lower the pH of the water, thereby enhancing the ability of your plants to absorb essential nutrients from the soil. It doesn't have to be done with every watering, but it can't hurt.

ANTI-AGING MATTERS

Q: My husband and I have reached an age where we no longer want to mow a steep slope in our yard. Can you suggest a good, low-maintenance replacement for the grass?

A: I sure can! Go with an aggressive vine. There are many that'll cascade down a hillside, smothering grass and weeds in the process. Just plant them at the top, point them downward, and let 'em go. Good candidates for this job include English ivy (*Hedera helix*), mountain clematis (*Clematis montana*), and sweet autumn clematis (*C. terniflora*).

Give sourpusses a bloomin' boost. Many popular flowering shrubs, including azaleas, gardenias, rhododendrons, hydrangeas, and camellias, crave acidic soil. One little bit of extra TLC can help them put on a show that's the talk of the town. Every week or so, and after every rain, water the bushes with a solution of 3 tablespoons of white vinegar per gallon of water. Discontinue this routine when the first blooms appear; otherwise, the vinegar could harm the plants or shorten the flowering time. **Note:** *Bear in mind that while an occasional sour cocktail can enhance flowering, the plants still need to be grown in soil with a pH that's below 6.5. Otherwise, no amount of vinegar will make them happy.*

Serve tea and see . . . Your garden grow like gangbusters! Compost tea can deliver a well-balanced supply of the important nutrients that plants need, and also fend off diseases. To make it, pour 4 gallons of warm water into a bucket. Scoop 1 gallon of fresh compost into a burlap sack, tie it closed, and put it in the water. Cover the container, and let the mixture steep for three to seven days. Then pour it into a watering can or mist sprayer, and give your plants a good spritzing every two to three weeks. Or ramp up the action by using it in a vinegar-enriched formula such as the Fabulous Foliar Fertilizer (at left).

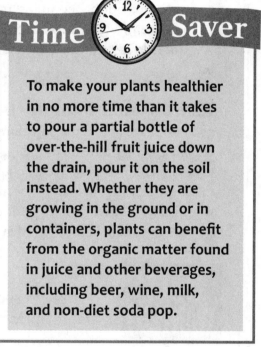

Time Saver

To make your plants healthier in no more time than it takes to pour a partial bottle of over-the-hill fruit juice down the drain, pour it on the soil instead. Whether they are growing in the ground or in containers, plants can benefit from the organic matter found in juice and other beverages, including beer, wine, milk, and non-diet soda pop.

Make compost the senior-friendly way. While it's true that compost is fabulous for plants, making it in a conventional pile or bin can be hard on aging muscles and joints because the ingredients need to be turned periodically. So forget about a pile altogether, and look for a tumbling-type bin that's easy to spin around. They come in a number of shapes, styles, and sizes and are widely available at garden centers and online. Just search online for—you guessed it—"tumbler compost bins" to find the best one for you.

DOUBLE-PLAY GARDEN SPRAY

Talk about versatile potions! This double-action combo can demolish dastardly disease germs and pesky insect pests at the same time.

- **1 1/2 tbsp. of baking soda**
- **1 tbsp. of canola oil**
- **1 tbsp. of insecticidal soap***
- **1 cup plus 1 gal. of water**
- **1 tbsp. of white vinegar**

Mix the baking soda, oil, and soap with 1 cup of water. Add the vinegar, but don't mix it in just yet, or the mixture may bubble over. Pour it into a pump-style or backpack sprayer, and add 1 gallon of water. Shake or stir to thoroughly combine the ingredients. Spray your plants from top to bottom, being sure to coat the undersides of leaves, where many insects love to linger. **Available at any garden center.*

Rise up and be comfortable. Enclosed, raised garden beds provide both good drainage and better moisture retention for your plants. But for gardeners of a certain age, they have an even bigger advantage: easier maintenance. You don't have to reach so far to pull weeds, cut flowers, or harvest crops. Plus, because you can make the sides as high as you want, you can garden comfortably even if you use a wheelchair or have trouble bending over. If you can't build the enclosures yourself, you can buy them at many garden centers and online garden-supply retailers.

HELP WANTED? One key to successful and easier gardening is to find a first-rate, locally owned nursery and buy all, or at least most, of your plants and supplies there. The folks who work in these establishments are usually highly knowledgeable and experienced gardeners themselves. They are able and willing to answer your questions, alert you to any prevalent pest and disease problems, and even help tote your purchases to your car. Even if you pay a little more for your stock than you would online or at a big-box store, you'll get what amounts to an ongoing gardening education and probably wind up saving a lot of time, effort, and money besides!

Freshen up flowerpots. It doesn't take long for soilborne minerals or fertilizer salts to cause those unsightly white splotches on terra-cotta pots. If you catch them in the early stages, simply pour some white vinegar on a rag, and wipe the stains away. To remove a thick, tough, crusty buildup, soak either the whole pot or the affected area (most often the rim) in full-strength vinegar overnight. If you treat the whole pot, soak it in clear water for a few hours afterward to dilute the vinegar absorbed by the clay.

Give your mower blades vim and vinegar. When you have finished mowing your lawn, always wipe the blades thoroughly using a cloth dampened with white vinegar. That way, you will remove any grass that's clinging to the blades. That's important for two reasons: First, stuck-on grass can make the blades tear rather than cut the grass, leaving it with frayed tips that are open invitations to disease and sun damage. Second, there's always a good chance that some of the grass will harbor insects, their eggs, or both. But when you wipe the greenery away, you'll take any potential troublemakers with it.

Go native with woodies. All plants can have problems. But the troubles that befall woody ones tend to be big, expensive, and stressful to cope with. The key to stopping trouble before it starts is to choose trees and shrubs that are native to your region. They're far less susceptible to pests and diseases than any plant that's been brought in from elsewhere, even if the newcomer is a variety that can perform in your growing conditions. To find winners for your yard, just search for "native plant nursery [your state's name]."

Labor Saver

There's no gardening process that is simpler than sowing seeds, unless you have trouble bending over. If that's the case for you, get a piece of PVC pipe that reaches approximately from your waist to the ground. Then send the seeds down through the chute and onto the prepared seedbed. When the seeds are where you want them, use your foot or a hoe to lightly firm the soil over them. Problem solved!

A GOOD KILLER FOR "BAD" PLANTS

From a botanical standpoint, there is no such thing as a "weed." Rather, that term applies to any plant that's growing where you don't want it to be. No matter where your uninvited green guests have appeared, this feisty formula will knock 'em dead without harming the living organisms in your soil, as commercial weed killers can do.

2 tsp. of Solubol dispersant*   **2 1/2 cups of white vinegar**
1 tsp. of clove essential oil

Mix the Solubol and clove oil in a container, and add the mixture to a spray bottle with the vinegar. Screw on the cap, and shake the bottle vigorously. Then take careful aim, and pull the trigger. Remember to be extra careful because the killer combo of vinegar and clove oil will make any plant it touches go belly-up. **Available from essential oil suppliers.*

Sleepy time is weeding time for lawns. If you live in a region where the grass goes dormant in the fall, but some weeds keep growing, you can take advantage of that lull to spray your lawn with A Good Killer for "Bad" Plants (above). That's because it and other nonselective herbicides, with or without vinegar, only work on plants that are actively growing. So you can fire away, knowing that you won't kill the grass right along with the plants you want to get rid of.

EARLY BIRD SPECIALS

One of the best advances to come along for aging gardeners in recent years has been the arrival of tools designed especially for folks whose strength and range of movement are compromised. The roster includes everything from hand tools with extra-long, padded handles to stand-up weed pullers that let you remove even the toughest perennials, like dandelions, without kneeling or bending. These implements are available online, but it's a good idea to buy your own at a local garden center. That way, you can try them out to make sure you get versions that best suit your needs.

Say "So long, Charlie!" Creeping Charlie, plantain, and many other broad-leaved weeds can spread like wildfire through a lawn or garden. To wipe 'em out with ease, duct-tape a foam paintbrush to a 2- to 3-foot branch or dowel. Then dip the brush in vinegar, and dab it onto the leaves. The pesky plants will bite the dust, and you won't even have to bend over!

Use a weed killer that's safe enough to drink. Back on page 141, I shared a great recipe for an extra-strength cleaner made from citrus peels, cloves, and vinegar. Well, guess what? That formula can not only get just about every surface in your house spic-and-span, but it can also wipe out the toughest weeds your yard can produce. In this case, instead of having to dilute it with water as you might for cleaning purposes, use it straight from the jar. Just remember, though, that while this is perfectly safe for people and pets, it will kill garden plants right along with the irritating invaders.

> For simple lawn feeding, overspread it with top-quality compost in spring and fall, at a minimum rate of 50 pounds per 1,000 square feet.

To mow more comfortably, get in the swim. Many older folks enjoy the relaxing process of cutting their grass, but they find that the vibration from the mower's handle aggravates the arthritis in their hands. If that's your case, cut a piece of swimming pool noodle to fit the size of your mower's handle. Then slit it down the middle, fit it over the handle, and attach it with double-faced tape.

Time Saver

Here's a great way to get rid of crabgrass without tedious hand-weeding and without using herbicides: Cover the crabgrass with either black plastic or black paper mulch (available at garden centers), and leave it on for 10 days. When you pull it off, that ol' crabgrass should be dead as a doornail. Any covered grass will be yellow, but it'll green up again once you take the mulch away and let the sun shine in.

ULTRA-STRONG WEED KILLER

When you're battling weeds that just won't take "No!" for an answer, this is the formula to reach for. The oil helps break down the protective coverings on the plants' stems so that the double-barreled acidic combo of lemon juice and vinegar can move in for the kill.

2 qts. of lemon juice   **1 tbsp. of cooking oil**
2 qts. of white vinegar

Combine all of the ingredients in a bucket, and pour the mixture into a spray bottle. Saturate the entire plant to the point of runoff, paying special attention to the stem. Any plants soaked with this powerful solution should die back to the ground within a few days. Any annuals will be gone for good, and perennials will be weakened to such an extent that they'll be far easier to pull or dig up.

Serve weeds a fatal cocktail. When your vegetative invaders just won't quit, mix 1 tablespoon each of white vinegar, dishwashing liquid, and cheap gin or vodka in 1 quart of hot water. Pour the mixture into a spray bottle, and drench the invaders to the point of runoff, taking care not to get any of the beverage on other plants.

When you're spraying in close quarters like a flower bed, it can be all but impossible to saturate weeds without getting any of the fluid on plants that you want to keep, especially when your hands are a little stiff and your aim isn't as sure as it used to be. Here's an easy way to put the killing power of vinegar right where you want it: Slice the bottom off a 1- or 2-liter soda pop bottle (but save the top). Sink the bottomless bottle into the soil over your target weed, shove your sprayer nozzle into the top, and let 'er rip. Then screw the top back on the bottle, and walk away. In a week or so, check back. The weed should have shriveled up. But if it hasn't, give it another blast.

Deliver a death blow to dandelions. Plan your attack for a hot day—the hotter the better—when the sun is at its brightest and no rain is predicted for the next 48 to 72 hours. To assemble your weaponry, mix 1 cup of salt and 1 teaspoon of dishwashing liquid in 1 gallon of white vinegar. Pour the mixture into a spray bottle, and turn the nozzle to the straight-stream setting. Don't use the mist- or fan-type spray because you want to strike the most powerful blow possible. First, blast the center of each flower. This will prevent it from setting seed and kill any seeds that may be starting to form. Then spray the foliage from top to bottom. Finally, saturate the base of the stem, so the vinegar can soak down into the roots. After a few days, the dandelions should all be dead ducks.

Make moss move on. If moss keeps cropping up in your lawn, no matter how many times you rake it away, simply drench it with white vinegar. Just be aware that if your unwanted greenery is growing in the kind of damp, shady spot that it craves, and you can't or don't care to alter those conditions, you will have to repeat this routine periodically.

Transplants help win the war on weeds. That's because, whether you grow your own seedlings indoors, or buy them at a garden center, those young plants will take off like gangbusters the minute you set them into the ground. That means they can start shading out weeds right from the get-go. There's also another big advantage to this head start: Even if your eyesight is no longer crystal clear, when something green does appear, you'll know it's a weed. So you can pull it right up, without a worry in the world that you might be ousting a future friend.

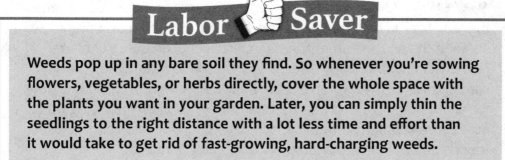

Labor Saver

Weeds pop up in any bare soil they find. So whenever you're sowing flowers, vegetables, or herbs directly, cover the whole space with the plants you want in your garden. Later, you can simply thin the seedlings to the right distance with a lot less time and effort than it would take to get rid of fast-growing, hard-charging weeds.

A SWEET TREAT FOR THE NOT-SO-SWEET

Although codling moths are infamous for ruining apple harvests, they also target crabapple, pear, quince, plum, and walnut trees. Before the blossoms open, hang one of these traps in each vulnerable tree. The moths will fly in for a sip, and they won't get out.

1 cup of sugar	Water
1 cup of vinegar	1/8-inch wire or plastic mesh
2 or 3 chunks of ripe fruit	

Put the sugar, vinegar, and fruit into a 1-gallon milk jug. Add water to almost fill the bottle, secure the cap, and shake well. Remove the cap, cover the top with wire or plastic mesh so that the material extends down an inch or so all around the opening, and secure it with tape (so honeybees can't get in). Then tie a cord or piece of wire around the handle, and hang the bottle from a tree limb.

Go soak your hands. If you have arthritis in your hands, even the simplest garden chores, like pulling the trigger on a spray bottle, can be painful. This trick can help in that regard: Soak your hands in warm water, laced with a few teaspoons of apple cider vinegar, for a few minutes before you put on your gloves. You will be amazed at the difference it can make!

HELP WANTED? It's no secret that chemicals in pesticides and fertilizers can be highly dangerous to both humans and animals. And the older you get, the more sensitive you become to those toxins. Well, studies show that, contrary to marketing hype, some of the souped-up nutrients in fertilizers can actually hinder, rather than help, plant growth. If you decide to outsource your yard-care chores, or if your current provider uses chemical products, look for an all-organic company. There are more of them springing up all across the country, so a quick Internet search, or referral queries to friends and neighbors, should bring in a few winners.

Vinegar vanquishes slugs. There are countless ways to kill slugs. But one of the safest weapons of all is to fill a spray bottle with white vinegar, and let 'em have it. Or if your aim's not so great, pour a cup or so of vinegar into a bucket, latch on to the slugs with a pair of retired, long-handled tongs, and dump the demons into the drink. Or put a bounty on the slugs' heads and deputize a posse of grandchildren to do the honors. **Note:** *In each case, you want to strike shortly after dark, when the slimers slink out to feed.*

Slam snails and slugs. One of the most effective slug and snail baits of all is a mixture of 1 teaspoon of brown sugar per cup of apple cider vinegar. But to make sure that only slugs and snails can get to it, not your pets or toddlin' grandchildren, you can forget the oft-recommended shallow cans. Round up some widemouthed pint bottles, like the kind many juice drinks come in. Pour about an inch of the potion into each one, then sink it into the ground so the top is just at ground level. Then the villains will slither up to the edge and dive right in, and the beverage at the bottom will lie beyond the reach of small human hands and long canine tongues.

Go to spring training. When a long, cold winter has kept you confined mostly indoors, it can be mighty tempting to celebrate the year's first balmy breezes by grabbing your tools and rushing out to the garden. Well, don't do it! Instead, do what baseball players do every spring: Hold your horses, and gradually work your way back into shape. For several days to a week before you plunge into action, do some gentle stretching exercises for your arms, back, and torso. This way, you'll be better equipped for a winning, injury-free season.

Money Saver

You don't need to drop big bucks on fancy products to keep your plants free of foul fungal diseases. Just provide them with good air circulation in the beds and use plenty of compost in the soil. Then once a week throughout the growing season, spray each plant with a mixture of 3 tablespoons of apple cider vinegar per gallon of water. That's all there is to it!

APHIDS-AWAY SPRAY

There are more than 1,300 species of aphids. And they all do the same deadly deed: drain the life-giving fluids from plants, leaving them wilted, discolored, and stunted. This cocktail can save the day and the whole growing season.

1/4 tsp. of Solubol dispersant	1 cup of vinegar
10 drops of lemon essential oil	1 tsp. of unscented dishwashing liquid
10 drops of rosemary essential oil	3 cups of water

Mix the Solubol and oils in a small container. Combine the mixture with the remaining ingredients in a larger container, and stir thoroughly. Pour the solution into a spray bottle. Shower the plants with water from the garden hose, wait 10 minutes, then spray them from top to bottom, paying special attention to buds and young shoots. Repeat in four days.

Yes, have some bananas. And then toss the peels on the ground under your plants. Aphids can't stand them. As an added attraction, as those skins break down, they'll infuse the soil with valuable potassium and phosphorus. Roses are especially fond of banana peels. So this factoid should be music to your ears: A pal of mine feeds her bushes nothing else, and each year they put on a bloomin' show that's the hit of her neighborhood.

EARLY BIRD SPECIALS

Whether you're new to gardening and want to learn the basics, or you're an old hand at the game and simply seeking ideas that can make the pastime more enjoyable as you grow older, check out your closest botanical garden. Most of them offer senior discounts for memberships, daily admission, or both. Many conduct adult gardening classes, and some even sponsor tours that let you visit horticultural sites around the world. In addition to greening up your thumb, you'll have a chance to strike up friendships with fellow gardeners from just about anywhere.

Get ants outta Dodge. Ants don't directly damage plants. But they sometimes "ranch" aphids in trees, so they can have a steady supply of the honeydew the little villains produce. If that's happening on your spread, don't pull any punches. Boil a 50-50 solution of white vinegar and water. Then scrape the top off the ant mound, and quickly pour the mixture into the ant nest. If the potion reaches its target, the queen will be an instant goner, and any workers that do survive will soon die of old age. Check back in a week or so; if the colony still shows signs of activity, give 'em another hot-and-sour shower.

Keep ants out of a hummingbird feeder.

Hummingbirds can do a whole lot more than provide hours of visual entertainment for you and your grandchildren. Once you have enticed them to your yard with a nectar feeder, they will hang around to polish off destructive insects galore. But unfortunately, ants also crave that sweet nectar. To keep them out of it, mix 1 tablespoon of ground cloves in 1 cup of white vinegar in a spray bottle, and spritz it on the trail leading to the "chuck wagon."

Make a move on mealybugs.

Aphids aren't the only tiny sap suckers that can cause major mischief in your yard. Mealybugs will also target a wide variety of plants. Fortunately, if their victim is small, or you catch the invasion in its early stages, it's easy to head off an attack: Just dab every cottony-looking bug with a cotton swab dipped in white vinegar. Game over.

Time Saver

Spending just a little less time on your outdoor chores can save you a lot of time on your pest-control efforts. For example, let some flowers and vegetables go to seed, thereby offering up a fine-dining experience to bug-eating birds. Don't clean up too thoroughly under trees and shrubs, and let some weeds spring up here and there. Both leaf litter and uninvited plants provide food, shelter, and maternity wards for many kinds of birds, butterflies, and beneficial insects, which will devour many times their weight in pesky little pests.

A GARDENER'S SUIT OF ARMOR

An old-time saying goes, "He who is bitten by the 'gardening bug' gets bitten by garden bugs." This easy-to-make repellent can stop those buggy thugs in their tracks. They all hate it—but it's mild enough to use on young grandchildren, or on your own mature skin.

1/2 cup of fresh basil	**1/2 cup of fresh thyme**
1/2 cup of fresh lavender	**1 cup of white vinegar**
1/2 cup of fresh mint	

Put the herbs in a heat-proof bowl. Heat the vinegar just to the boiling point, pour it over the herbs, and cover the bowl. When the vinegar has cooled to room temperature, strain it into a spray bottle. Spritz all your and the youngsters' exposed skin before you head outdoors, and reapply it every couple of hours. **Note:** *The repellent will keep for about two months in the refrigerator.*

Hang 'em up. While growing plants in raised beds is a fabulous, easy-does-it ploy for older gardeners (see "Rise up and be comfortable" on page 206), here is another simple and decorative way to reduce strain on your muscles and joints: Plant in hanging baskets. To make your tending chores even less strenuous, use the baskets that have retractable hangers. That way you can lower the containers to a comfortable working height. Then send them back "home" when you're finished and enjoy a new, pain-free way of gardening.

Labor Saver

For anyone, watering with a coiled garden hose is a whole lot easier and more convenient than dragging a conventional hose around, then having to wind it back up. But for seniors, these light-weight wonders are a true godsend. To make your irrigation chores much easier, get a water wand with a telescoping handle, and attach it to the end of your hose. Even hard-to-reach plants will be a snap to spray!

Win the beetle battles. Beetles and weevils can be the very dickens to eliminate because they wear a natural coat of armor that withstands most natural insecticides. But these tough guys are no match for neem oil because it dissolves that hard, waxy covering, then dehydrates the pests. It also kills their eggs and larvae on contact. To use it, simply mix 2 tablespoons of Solubol dispersant and 1 tablespoon of neem oil per cup of white vinegar in a spray bottle, take careful aim, and then let 'er rip! The operative word is *careful* because you don't want to hit ladybugs or any other beneficial insects by mistake.

Bark back at bark beetles. These nogoodniks produce larvae that can cause fatal damage to trees and shrubs. The bad news is that once they've tunneled into the bark, no insecticide can reach them. The good news is that it's a snap to snag 'em on the fly. Just set jars of white vinegar (no other kind!) among your troubled woodies. The beetles will dive right in and die. This works well because the odor from the vinegar is the same as the distress signal sent out by ailing trees, which are bark beetles' targets of choice.

Please pass the salt. Epsom salt, that is. Simply by mixing it with the right essential oil(s) and spreading the mixture on the ground under your plants, you can perform four fabulous feats: Prevent destructive insects, attract pollinators, help fend off diseases, and give your green pals a health-giving dose of magnesium. About 4 drops of oil per cup of salt will do the trick. As for which oil or combination of oils to use for any of the tasks at hand, you'll find a veritable trove of the best on page 220.

Q: I'm looking for a DIY repellent that will protect my tomato plants from bugs without risk to my pets or grandchildren. Do you know a good formula?

A: You betcha! Just make an extra-strong batch of basil-infused vinegar (see "Give the gift of good health" on page 356). Then spray it on and around your tomato plants. Besides making them off-limits to all kinds of pests, the basil will boost the overall health of your crop.

ANTI-AGING MATTERS

HOMEGROWN HARVEST BATH BLEND

Tiny insects lurk on fresh vegetables, but they're most common in crops that have a lot of nooks and crannies, like broccoli and cauliflower. To make sure your vittles are varmint-free, treat them to this bath.

1/4 cup of salt　　　　　**Cold water**
1 tbsp. of white vinegar

Pour the salt and vinegar into a sink filled with cold water. Completely submerge the vegetables, and let them sit for 15 minutes. Any bugs that are present will float up to the surface, where you can easily skim them off with a paper towel. Rinse their former homes with fresh, clear water, and get to cookin'! **Note:** *Use this on produce that you've bought at a farmers' market or plucked from the vine at a pick-your-own field.*

Establish a strict containment policy. In the blink of an eye, rabbits, raccoons, or other critters can turn a lovely container garden into a major mess. Here's an all-but-invisible way to keep the rascals out: Saturate small pieces of wood with white vinegar, and set them on the soil. The diners will take their appetites elsewhere, but the repellents will blend right in with the scenery.

Make it look a lot like Christmas. One of the surest ways to keep four-legged feasters of all kinds from ravaging plants on your deck or robbing your bird feeder is to string up blinking Christmas lights. White or multicolored versions will work best. It's the constant on-again, off-again light that sends warning signals into animals' minds and, unless they're literally starving, makes them scurry in a hurry.

SAFE & SOUND The older you get, the more important it is to invest in a pair of high-quality gloves that you can keep on regardless of the task at hand. That's because, as we discussed back in Chapter 3, we pick up more scratches, scrapes, and cuts as we age, which can take longer to heal, and hand wounds are especially vulnerable to infection.

Put your soil to the test. If you've just moved to a newly built house, and you have no idea what kind of soil you have, here's a quick way to find out: Put a tablespoon of dried garden soil on a plate, and add a few drops of white vinegar to it. If the soil fizzes, that means it's extremely alkaline, most likely above 7.5 on the pH scale. To check for the opposite problem (severe acidity), put about a tablespoon of wet soil on a plate, and add a pinch of baking soda to it. If the soil fizzes, then the pH is most likely below 5.5.

> One secret to enjoying gardening in your golden years is to farm out any essential, labor-intensive task that becomes a strain.

Don't play guessing games. Whether your ultra-simple test (above) reveals that your soil is either highly alkaline or highly acidic, a more exact laboratory test is called for. That's because very few garden plants will tolerate soil with a pH that's above 7.5 or below 5.5. Your closest county extension service should be able to perform a soil test, or direct you to a lab that can.

Kneel comfortably. If you have knee or back issues, kneeling down to tend or harvest your crops can be agonizing. The simple solution: a garden kneeler bench. Your knees rest on a thick cushion while you work. Then, when it's time to stand up, a handrail on either side makes the process smooth and easy. To find a model that's just right for you, consider shopping at a local garden center or hardware store.

Money Saver

One of the best ways to save big bucks on yard care is to replace some or even all of your turfgrass with groundcovers. Your monthly water bills will drop dramatically. And the more lawn you get rid of, the more your retirement account can benefit from the savings on mower fuel and maintenance, as well as fertilizers and pesticides or their DIY ingredients. And that's not to mention any hired help you employ.

OIL'S WELL IN YOUR GARDEN

Essential oils, used alone or mixed with other ingredients, can be some of your best garden allies. You can put the power of scent to work in several ways:

- For container plants, put a drop or two of oil on a cotton ball, and tuck it into the pot (for large planters, use two or three balls).
- Put drops of oil on strips of cloth (one or two drops per strip), and hang them from shrub or tree branches.
- Spray plants with a solution made from 3 drops of essential oil and 6 drops of Solubol dispersant per gallon of water.
- Soak lightweight cotton cord in the oil-water spray and tie the ends to stakes between plant rows or beds.

Here's a rundown of which oils work best for what gardening purposes:

REPEL PLANT-MUNCHING PESTS

Aphids: Cedarwood, peppermint, spearmint

Beetles: Peppermint or thyme

Caterpillars: Peppermint or spearmint

Moths: Cedarwood, lavender, peppermint, spearmint

Slugs: Cedarwood

Snails: Cedarwood, garlic, patchouli, and pine

Weevils: Cedarwood, patchouli, sandalwood

ATTRACT INSECTS TO TRAPS

Cinnamon lures Japanese beetles, leaf miners, and thrips.

Lemon sends out a y'all-come signal to fungus gnats, Japanese beetles, mealybugs, scales, and thrips.

Melissa draws fungus gnats and thrips.

WELCOME POLLINATORS

Bees make a beeline to orange, lavender, hyssop, marjoram, helichrysum, basil, sage, and rosemary.

Butterflies flutter by to lavender, fennel, helichrysum, and sage.

CHAPTER 12

OUTDOOR PROJECTS

In the last chapter, we focused our attention on the plants in your yard and how you can keep them healthy and vibrant, while the process of doing that performs the same service for you. In these pages, we'll zero in on your home's exterior, and the various structures and non-living surfaces in your personal piece of the great outdoors—what landscape architects and garden designers call "hardscape." I'll clue you in on simple solutions and fantastic fixers that will help you keep these parts of your green scene looking and functioning at their peak. Plus, you'll find a passel of ingenious ideas for making the outside of your home sweet home suit your evolving needs as the years go by.

Yet again, vinegar plays a starring role in this energizing enterprise. It can help you do everything from sprucing up your patio furniture to keeping bothersome pests from putting a damper on your outdoor fun, with no risk to your health or that of your grandchildren or pets. Just as an example (speaking of pets), if wandering tomcats leave aromatic offerings on your fence or the walls of your house, just fill a spray bottle with white vinegar, and regularly spritz the places where the boys are making their mark. The scent will confuse and repel the rascals.

> As a reminder, for outdoor spruce-up and maintenance purposes, there is no need to seek out mother-rich unprocessed apple cider vinegar, much less the superpowered and highly acidic white versions. For the sake of your pocketbook (and, in the latter case, your safety), be sure to use the cheapest apple cider or distilled white vinegar you can find. It'll do a yeoman's job every single time—guaranteed!

POWERFUL PAINTED-PORCH CLEANER

If you have an old-fashioned porch, you know how quickly the painted floors, stairs, and railings can pick up a major load of dirt and grime. Well, that crud is no match for this fabulous formula.

1/2 tsp. of Solubol dispersant*   **1/4 cup of baking soda**

1/4 tsp. of lemon essential oil   **1 gal. of water**

1 1/2 cups of white vinegar

Mix the Solubol and oil in a small container. Then combine the mixture with the remaining ingredients in a bucket, and use the solution to clean your porch, and all your other painted wood surfaces, including fences, doors, and window frames. **Note:** *For easier use on vertical surfaces, pour the mixture into a spray bottle. *Available from essential oil suppliers.*

Paint 'em safe. Especially as you grow older, wet steps are a disaster waiting to happen, whether they're made of wood or concrete. For that reason, even if you're planning to move in the next year or so, do yourself a favor and paint all your outdoor stairways using 1/2 cup of clean builders sand per gallon of paint. The little bit of time it takes could literally save your life. **Note:** *Use the grittiest sand you can find, not the fine-textured type used for sandboxes and decorative plantings. The rougher the texture is, the better your traction will be.*

SAFE & SOUND

Never use an oil- or soap-based cleaner on painted wood flooring or steps because even a tiny bit of residue can make the surface a little slick. And if you're even a smidgen stiff in your joints or unsteady on your feet, one slight misstep (especially on stairs) could lead to big trouble. Instead, tackle major jobs with the Powerful Painted-Porch Cleaner (above). For routine cleaning, simply damp-mop your porch or painted deck using a mixture of 1/4 cup of white vinegar in a bucket of warm water. No rinsing needed.

Give your deck stairs some traction. When it rains, the stairway to a wooden deck gets so slippery that it's a disaster waiting to happen. Thankfully, you have two easy fixes at your beck and call: You can coat each step with a mixture of a clear sealer and builders sand (see "Paint 'em safe," at left). Or you can attach self-adhesive anti-skid tape (available online and in home-improvement stores). Note that some brands come in clear versions, so once the strips are in place, you'll hardly notice them.

To avoid introducing bacteria to DIY cleaners, always make sure any spray bottles, mixing containers, and tools are clean as a whistle.

Pre-wash your porch. Over the course of a long, messy winter, even a covered porch can pick up a lot of dirt and grime. So before you tackle the first cleaning of spring, wipe the wood surface down with a soft cloth or mop that's been dipped in rubbing alcohol. It'll help dissolve the greasy dirt, so the Powerful Painted-Porch Cleaner (at left) can really get in there and do its job.

Keep your deck on duty. A well-built deck is highly durable but still needs an occasional cleaning to remove unsightly and potentially damaging residue. Here's the drill: Sweep away any loose debris with a broom, and use a garden hose to blast away any stuck-on dirt. Then fill a bucket with 1 cup of white vinegar per gallon of water, dip a broom into the solution, and scrub the boards following the direction of the wood grain. Rinse thoroughly, and let the surface air-dry. The vinegar will remove garden-variety dirt and any mold and mildew growth.

Leaves, branches, and other yard debris that lodge in between the boards on a deck are like an invitation to moisture and decay. To get that junk out easily, duct-tape a putty knife or screwdriver to a dowel or an old broom handle, and poke the stuff through the cracks so it falls safely to the ground.

CRACKS & CREVICES WEED KILLER

There are few more annoying hardscape happenings than weeds that continuously pop up in tight spaces. This ultra-strong formula is tailor made for eliminating those rascals.

1 gal. of white vinegar　　　　**1 tsp. of dishwashing liquid**
2 cups of table salt

Mix the vinegar and salt in a bucket, stirring until the salt is dissolved. Add the dishwashing liquid, and stir again. Pour the solution into a spray bottle or a backpack or pump-style sprayer. Saturate the weeds once a day until they're dead as doornails. **Note:** *Don't use this potion on a larger area where you may want to grow plants in the future. The high concentration of salt can destroy the soil's fertility.*

Hose-end sprayers are mighty convenient, but ... Bear in mind that they are intended for use with ultra-potent tonics (most often for lawn-care purposes) that need to be diluted with plenty of water. For the Cracks & Crevices Weed Killer (above), or any other formula that should be applied at full strength, always use a handheld spray bottle or either a backpack or pump-style sprayer. Otherwise, you won't get the results you're looking for, and the time, effort, and money you've spent will be wasted.

ANTI-AGING MATTERS

Q: My husband and I are in our fifties, and if we plan to remain in our home rather than move when we retire, we'd like to start making some gradual exterior changes. Now, just in case we opt to stay, any ideas on a good place to start?

A: You might begin by adding or expanding a deck or porch, or paving over part or even all of your lawn and replacing it with a terrace. You could start reaping the benefits immediately because virtually all hardscape features are easier, less time-consuming, and less expensive to maintain than turfgrass is. These changes can also add to the value of your property if you decide to sell the place and move 10 years or so down the road.

Make moss meander. For many, there's nothing like a little moss to soften up the appearance of a brick or stone wall. But if you don't care for that furry green stuff, or you simply have more of it than you want, here's a first-class removal remedy: Fill a spray bottle with 2 cups of water and 2 tablespoons each of cheap gin and vinegar. Then thoroughly drench the moss. **Note:** *If the green-bedecked structure is in a damp, shady spot, you will have to repeat this process periodically.*

Make more moss. What can you do if you have a little bit of moss, and you would like to increase your supply, maybe to impart a relaxed, old-time look to a stone pathway in your newly built retirement home? Here's what: Mix 1/2 quart of buttermilk, 1 cup of moss, and 1 teaspoon of corn syrup in an old blender. Then dab the mixture onto the ground where you want to encourage moss. Once it starts growing, keep it in good health by "watering" it with plain buttermilk every few weeks.

Time Saver

When a wayward charcoal briquette or toppled candle leaves its ugly brown "signature" on your brick patio, don't panic. Sponge white vinegar onto the spots and rinse with clear water. Then get back to enjoying the festivities!

Don't cry over water marks. Granted, the splotches that mineral-laden water leaves on patios, driveways, water spigots, and other hard outdoor surfaces can be mighty unsightly. But they're easy to get rid of. Just dissolve 1/2 cup of borax in 1 cup of warm water, and stir in 1/2 cup of white vinegar. Sponge the mixture onto the spots, let it sit for 10 minutes or so, and wipe the blemishes away. **Note:** *For thicker, longer-standing deposits, you may need to repeat the process a time or two.*

Bid good riddance to bad rust. Whether the brownish-red blotches have arrived courtesy of rain falling on unsealed iron furniture or forgotten tools, you have an easy removal remedy at your disposal: Pour full-strength white vinegar onto the spots and wait for about five minutes. Then, while the vinegar is still wet, scrub it with a stiff nylon brush. Rinse with clear water, and repeat the process as needed until the spots are gone.

MAGICAL MOLD & MILDEW REMOVER

Mold and mildew can trigger respiratory problems and allergic reactions, and also make decks, walkways, stairways, and other surfaces as slick as the dickens. This nontoxic potion will rout the slimy stuff from wood, concrete, brick, or stucco without the dangers of chemicals.

2 tsp. of Solubol dispersant   **1 qt. of white vinegar**
1 tsp. of tea tree oil

Mix the Solubol and tea tree oil in a small container, and combine the mixture with the vinegar in a spray bottle.* Apply the solution liberally to the affected surface. Let it sit for 15 minutes or so, then hose it off thoroughly. Repeat the process until the sinister spores are history.
To treat larger areas, multiply the ingredients as needed, and use either a backpack or pump-style sprayer.

Don't put your deck under wraps. A lot of folks think rugs or mats make a deck or porch look nice and homey. Well, that may be, but they also pose the same slipping hazards as indoor area rugs. Beyond that, outdoors, they can trap moisture beneath them, and moisture spells early death for any wooden surface. So save the floor coverings for your indoor rooms, not for your deck or porch.

HELP WANTED? With the aging-in-place concept booming as it is, more and more landscape designers and contractors are catering to the needs of older adults who want to stay put throughout their golden years. A search for "landscaping for aging in place" will bring up plenty of pros who can help make your outdoor living spaces safer to move around in, and easier to maintain. In most cases, you can opt for a brainstorming session or have the experts draw up a plan that you can implement as your time and budget permit. Or you can have the firm install the whole kit and caboodle, including lighting and low-maintenance plantings, as well as pathways and other hardscape.

Get a positive ID. Any outdoor surface that's in a damp, shady site can be plagued by mold or mildew. But that doesn't mean that every discolored patch is a menace in the making. To find out exactly what you're dealing with, perform this test: Dab a few drops of chlorine bleach on the area in question. If the color stays the same, it's plain old dirt. But if it gets lighter or changes color, then it's mildew, so swing into removal mode pronto.

Oil-based paint promotes mold and mildew. The spores feed on the oils in the paint, which makes their colonies grow by leaps and bounds. So, for the sake of your health (especially as you grow older), and your pocket-book, use non-oil-based exterior paints, preferably formulations that contain a mildewcide. Don't try to pinch pennies because top-tier paints are far more mildew resistant than bargain-basement brands. And go with a gloss or semi-gloss finish, either of which will help prevent mildew penetration. Finally, especially if you live in a cool, wet climate, consider painting exterior surfaces a dark color. Darker tones absorb more sunlight, and therefore the surface will dry faster after it's been exposed to rain, dampness, or morning dew.

Don't put your fence under pressure. When your vinyl fence falls prey to mold or mildew, it may be tempting to reach for a pressure washer. Well, don't do it. Instead, mix 2 cups of dishwashing liquid and 1/2 cup of white vinegar in a container, and then add 1/4 cup of the mixture to a bucket filled halfway with water. Dip a rag, sponge, or soft-bristled brush in the vinegar solution and scrub the spots away. Hose the suds off with clear water. Use the remainder of the mixture added to fresh buckets of water until your entire fence is clean and has been hosed off.

Money Saver

Before you clean a vinyl fence or any other manufactured landscape feature with vinegar, check the manufacturer's guidelines to make sure that it's rec-ommended for use on your brand. Otherwise, you could be in for an unpleasant and possibly expensive surprise and a voided warranty.

HEAVY-DUTY OUTDOOR WINDOW CLEANER

Even the grimiest outdoor windows or glass doors are no match for this simple but powerful formula.

1/4 cup of cheap vodka*   **3 cups of warm water**
1/4 cup of white vinegar

Mix the ingredients in a bucket, multiplying the recipe as needed. Then dip a natural sponge in the solution, wring out the excess, and wash the glass. Then pull a squeegee over the wet pane in whatever pattern you prefer. Overlap passes, and at the end of each stroke, wipe the blade clean with a lint-free cloth. Finish by drying the glass and frames with a fresh lint-free cloth. *Or you can substitute with 1/4 cup of rubbing alcohol.*

Keep your hot tub happy. Hot tubs (a.k.a. spas) earn kudos in senior circles not only because they instantly soothe and relax stiff muscles and joints, but also because they're less expensive than swimming pools, they take up much less space in the landscape, and they're a lot easier to maintain. Manufacturers generally recommend that once every three months or so, you drain the tub and wipe down the liner with white vinegar on a warm, damp sponge. Then fill 'er up with fresh water—no rinsing needed.

SAFE & SOUND

In addition to installing grab bars next to exterior doors (see "Grab on!," at right), there's another way you can help ensure smooth, safe sailing on your return home: Make sure that just outside every entrance (at least the ones you use most often) there's a table, bench, or shelf to set down whatever you're carrying while you search for your keys and open the door. Otherwise, with your arms full of packages, you could easily stumble as you unlock the door and shove it open, especially if you need to navigate a step or two on your way in.

De-scale ceramic pool tile safely. A lot of swimming pool "experts" would have you believe that the only way to remove the scale that builds up at the water line is to spray it with muriatic acid. Well, forget that stuff! It'll clean your ceramic tiles all right. But in the process, it can also hand you a heap of trouble, especially when you're spraying it on at roughly your eye level, which is where the deposits collect. Instead, reach for white vinegar. Heat it on the stove, then either sponge it on straight from the pot you've heated it in, or pour it into a spray bottle. Then wipe the crud away with a soft cloth. Your tile will sparkle like the stars!

Grab on! If you only think of grab bars as bathroom safety aids, think again. If you're the least bit unsteady on your feet—or planning for the time when you might be—these balance enhancers can also help prevent falls in your yard, or as you leave or enter your house. It's a good idea to install them beside all exterior doors, on the inside and outside, as well as garage entrances and (of course) at the tops and bottoms of porch stairways. At home-improvement stores and online, you can find bars that are designed especially for outdoor use, including models made of weatherproof plastic with a sturdy aluminum core and soft grip moldings that reduce the risk of your hands slipping when the bar is wet.

Keep the jets jumpin'. One other chore will ensure that your spa remains in full therapeutic-action mode: Once a year, empty a gallon jug of white vinegar into the tub, and run it through a cycle. This will help clear out any soap residue or calcium deposits that have built up in the pumping system.

Time Saver

Whenever you're using vinegar, either straight or in a mixture, to clean windows, fences, or any other outdoor structure, always take one precaution: Move all container plants away from the work site, and cover any inground plants that are within splashing reach of the solution. Otherwise, you could wind up spending considerable time and money replacing your stricken vegetation.

AMAZING ALUMINUM FURNITURE CLEANER

This powerful formula can keep your aluminum chairs, tables, and other outdoor pieces sparkling clean—no matter how much dirt Mother Nature tosses their way. Best of all, it is free of all the mischief-making chemicals found in most commercial cleansers.

1/2 cup of baking soda	**1/2 cup of white vinegar**
1/2 cup of cream of tartar	**1/4 cup of soap flakes**
5 drops of orange essential oil	**(such as Ivory Snow®)**

Combine the baking soda and cream of tartar in a bowl, and stir in the orange oil. Add the vinegar, and mix to form a paste. Stir in the soap flakes, transfer the mixture to a glass jar with a tight-fitting lid, and label it. Rub the cleaner onto the aluminum with a plain steel wool pad, and rinse with clear water.

Don't let your furniture share its "wealth." Aluminum furniture can be a great choice for older adults because its light weight makes it easy to move around. But it has one glaring flaw: Left untreated, the surface will oxidize and develop a powdery, white residue that leaves ugly gray marks on seat cushions, tablecloths, and your clothes. To end that generosity, wipe the metal down with a half-and-half solution of white vinegar and water. Let it dry, then spray on a coat or two of either clear lacquer or exterior latex paint.

EARLY BIRD SPECIALS

If you want to tweak your landscape to make it more user-friendly as you approach your golden years, here's a piece of good news: Throughout the country, many top-notch companies offer senior and veteran discounts for the design, installation, and maintenance of both plantings and hardscape features. Some contractors even specialize in working with clients in the 50-plus set. It's best to seek personal recommendations from trusted friends before you sign on any dotted line, but a search for "seniors discount landscaping" will bring up lots of choices to start you off.

Slam the slime! In a naturally damp climate, or during extended periods of wet weather anywhere, algae can create a slimy green film on wood lawn furniture and other outdoor wooden surfaces. To remove the scummy stuff without resorting to toxic chemicals, simply mix equal parts of both white vinegar and warm water in a bucket. Then dip a scrubby sponge in the mixture, and rub the marks away. Rinse with clear water, and repeat the process if necessary until the green goo is gone.

> When you are planning a landscape for aging in place, ensure your ongoing comfort by incorporating plenty of seating.

Save the seats. When algae, mildew, or mold blossoms on nonwashable cushions, spray undiluted white vinegar onto the front, back, and sides. Let it sit for 10 minutes. Then using a sponge, scrub all the surfaces with a mixture of 1 teaspoon of dishwashing liquid per 3 cups of warm water. Rinse with a soft, clean cloth dampened with cool water, and let the cushions air-dry. Finally, spritz 'em with vinegar once more to remove any lingering spores and help prevent new ones from growing.

Take your patio umbrella to a self-service car wash. Yes, you read that right. It's a super-simple way to give the "brolly" a jolly good scrubbing in a lot less time than it would take at home. Just open it, lay it on its side, and spray it down just as you would your car. Hold the hose at least two feet away from the fabric so the force of the water doesn't damage it. Rinse thoroughly, but skip the wax cycle. Then take your spankin' clean sunshade home to air-dry.

Labor Saver

If your washable outdoor cushions or removable covers are attacked by mold, mildew, or algae, the remedy couldn't be easier: Launder them according to the directions on the fabric-care label, with 1 cup of white vinegar added to the wash and (for good measure) rinse cycles. Then set them outdoors in a sunny spot to dry.

DOUBLE-DUTY TRASH DEODORIZER

Nothing will make an outdoor trash can smell like a rose garden. But this minty-fresh spritzer will make that receptacle a lot more pleasant to have around. As for the double-duty part, the peppermint aroma will repel ants, mice, and raccoons. Quite simply, they all hate it.

2 tsp. of Solubol dispersant*

1 tsp. of peppermint essential oil*

2 tbsp. of white vinegar

2 cups of water

Combine the Solubol and oil in a small container. Add the mixture to a spray bottle along with the vinegar and water, and shake well. After each trash pickup, give the empty can three or four spritzes, and add a fresh bag. For pest-repellent purposes, also spray the lid and outside bottom of the can. *If you are having problems with any four-legged foragers, double or even triple the amounts until the visits end.*

Clean the can. When your nose tells you that your trash receptacle is ripe and ready for a thorough cleaning, launch into this routine: Mix 1/2 cup of white vinegar, 2 tablespoons of dishwashing liquid, and 2 cups of water in the empty can, and swish the mixture around with a long-handled brush or sponge. Rinse the can, and let it dry thoroughly. Then sprinkle a generous layer of borax over the bottom before inserting a fresh bag.

SAFE & SOUND

Accidents happen. And they happen frequently when you're working in the yard, especially once you've reached a certain age. So keep a first-aid kit in a prominent place in your shed or another easily accessible spot. (Some folks like to install a separate mailbox to use for this purpose.) Make sure that the kit is always stocked with antibiotic ointment, bandages, and any product you use for treating insect bites. Include a pair of tweezers for pulling out ticks and bee stingers. And if you live where poisonous snakes pose a threat, make sure you have a snakebite kit in your mini ER.

Wooden it be wonderful... If there was an easy-to-make formula that would clean your wooden outdoor furniture and also help preserve it? Well, there is. Just pour 1 tablespoon of white vinegar into a nonreactive bowl. Then slowly and thoroughly whisk in 1 tablespoon of olive oil, 4 drops of arborvitae essential oil, and 2 drops of lemon essential oil, just as though you were making salad dressing. Dip a soft cotton cloth in the mixture, wipe down all the wood surfaces, and let them air-dry. That's all there is to it!

A positively pleasing plastic ploy. Outdoor plastic furniture is tough stuff, but it can sure pick up its share of dirt! To spruce up either solid, mesh, or tubular versions, mix 2 cups of white vinegar and 2 tablespoons of dishwashing liquid in a bucket of hot water. Then wipe the solution onto solid surfaces with a sponge or soft cotton cloth. Use a soft-bristled brush to really work the mixture into any flexible materials. Rinse with clear water, wipe with a clean towel to avoid streaks, and set the pieces in the sun to dry thoroughly.

Tweak your teak. This stuff is worth every penny it costs because it will stand up to decades of wear and tear with barely any maintenance. But the chairs and tables still require one little piece of TLC: Once a year, you should coat the legs with a water repellent (the ones made for decks work fine). It's a simple process: Pour about 3 inches of the product into a clean coffee can. Place one leg of a table or chair into the can and leave it there for two or three minutes. Repeat the process until each leg of each piece has had its turn in the tin.

Time Saver

For reasons I've never been able to understand, a lot of squirrels love to chew on redwood furniture. If you see they are getting up to those shenanigans at your place, here's a quick fix: Rub all the furniture's surfaces with chili sauce, then buff with a soft cloth. The color of the sauce will blend right into the wood, so you won't even notice it. But after one tasty lick of the fiery stuff, any squirrel is guaranteed to hightail it outta Dodge!

INTENSIVE VINYL VITALIZER

More and more folks are installing vinyl storage sheds in their yards, and for good reason: They're less expensive and easier to maintain than either wooden or metal versions. But they still attract their fair share of dirt, bird droppings, and windblown debris. This formula will keep your handy store-all looking its best for years to come.

2 cups of white vinegar   **Warm water**
2 tbsp. of dishwashing liquid

Mix all the ingredients in a bucket. Wash off loose dirt with a garden hose. Then either spray the mixture onto the surfaces or wipe it on with a soft cloth or sponge, scrubbing away any stains or stubborn dirt. Use a toothbrush or bottle brush to reach nooks and crannies. When you're done, rinse with a garden hose, and dry the structure with a towel to prevent water marks from forming.

Give your metal shed a better paint job. If you have a galvanized metal storage shed and you're getting ready to paint it, then this tip is for you: To make sure that protective coating hangs in there for the long haul, rather than peeling, give the surface a primer coat of white vinegar. Either brush it on or wipe it on with a cloth, as you prefer. Let the vinegar dry completely, then grab your brush, roller, or spray can and get to paintin'.

Money Saver

Here's a cost-free way to extend the life of your porch or deck: On a porch, suspend hanging plants from the outer (not the inner) edge of the eaves. If you attach planter boxes to the rails of a porch or deck, make sure they hang out beyond the floor surface. This way, when water drips from the containers, it'll hit the ground, not your floorboards.

It's what's inside that counts... Regardless of whether your shed is made of vinyl, metal, or wood, the golden rule for reaping its full benefits is the same as it is for any other storage space: Keep the things you use most often where you can get at them easily. Of course, the criteria will change with the seasons. In the spring and summer, you'll want the lawn mower, garden hose, and watering cans in prime territory. Come fall, leaf rakes and plant-protection gear need to move up front. Then in the winter, retire all those out-of-season things to the back to make room near the door for snow-removal gear and ice-melting substances.

If you have small grandchildren on the scene. Even if they're only around on occasion, store all fertilizers and pesticides, even "food-safe" organic products and any DIY formulas, in a locked cabinet if you can. At the very least, these things should be well out of reach of the kiddos and any animals (wild or domestic) that could happen to wander into the shed.

Rout out rust. Metal furniture, like barbecue grills and forgotten tools, can leave nasty rust stains on patios, walkways, and even driveways. But those malevolent marks are no match for (what else?) white vinegar. Simply pour it generously onto the afflicted area. Then to retain the moisture, cover it with a cloth that you've dampened with vinegar. Let it work its magic for 15 minutes or so, then use a stiff brush to scrub the blotches away. Next, rinse thoroughly with a garden hose. This is one case where much more is better. You want to dilute the vinegar as much as possible so that the runoff doesn't harm your grass or other nearby plants.

Q: I've always loved gardening and working with hardscape features, and I enjoy helping friends in their yards. Some of them are encouraging me to pursue landscape design as a second career when I retire in a couple of years. Is that really feasible at my age?

A: Yes! While we all get a little too creaky and stiff for the hard physical work, you're never too old to design and plan a landscape. Many community colleges and even some botanical gardens offer certificate programs that, along with your years of hands-on experience, will give you everything you need to hang up your consultant shingle.

ANTI-AGING MATTERS

SUPER-SAFE SNOW & ICE MELTER

The older you get, the easier it becomes to slip on an icy surface, fall down, and go "Boom!" This down-home mixer melts snow and ice with none of the harm salt can cause to concrete, wood, or metal surfaces, not to mention your plants, your pets' paws, and your shoes.

2 cups of wood ash   **2 cups of white vinegar**
1 gal. of water

Put the wood ash and water in a bucket, and let it sit for 8 to 12 hours. Clear off any floating bits and pieces, and then pour the mixture into another container, being careful to leave the sediment in the bottom of the original bucket. Add the white vinegar, and stir well. Then either splash the melter directly from the bucket onto the ice, or funnel the solution into a backpack or pump-style sprayer, and let 'er rip.

Stay upright and get your tires rolling—safely. The same wood ash that melts ice can also help you get a grip on icy surfaces, with no nasty side effects to your yard. You say you don't have a fireplace to supply you with ashes? No problem! Sand, birdseed, cat litter, or even a commercial organic fertilizer can help you stay upright while actually improving your soil and therefore, benefiting your turfgrass and any other plants in the vicinity.

SAFE & SOUND It's no secret that chemical ice melters can sicken pets and cause major damage to turfgrass, plants, concrete, asphalt, and wooden surfaces. But what many folks don't realize is that these products also corrode the metal fasteners that hold decks, porches, and outdoor stairways together. So if you've routinely used salt or other harsh chemicals on your outdoor wooden surfaces, carefully inspect all metal hardware on your walking or sitting areas, and replace any pieces that are showing signs of corrosion. Or you can decide to have a contractor do the job for you.

Evict the efflorescence. The snowy-looking, chalky-white salt crystals (a.k.a. efflorescence) that can build up on outdoor bricks don't cause any structural damage. But the deposits sure make a visual mess of a wall or patio. To send the stuff packin', spray the affected surface liberally with a half-and-half solution of vinegar and water, and scrub the marks away with a stiff brush. Then, to neutralize the acid (which could damage unsealed brick if it's left on), spray again with a solution made from 1 tablespoon of baking soda per cup of water. Finish with a fresh-water rinse from the garden hose, and you'll be good to go. **Note:** *For best results, choose a hot, sunny day for this job.*

Bundle up! The older you get, the harder it becomes for your body to warm itself. In the winter, that puts you at greater risk for potentially fatal hypothermia. So when you go outdoors in frigid weather, even if it's only for a few minutes, make sure you're covered in warm, weather-resistant outerwear from the top of your head to the tips of your toes. And stay out only long enough to do the job at hand. **Note:** *If you start shivering, it means that your body is losing too much heat, so high-tail it inside, and have a hot drink to warm up.*

Stay vertical. When it's not only cold, but also the least bit snowy or icy, pay special attention to your winter footwear, especially if your joints are getting stiff, or your balance isn't as sure as it once was. Guard against a tumble by wearing sturdy, slip-resistant boots—yes, even if you're only venturing far enough to fetch the mail from the box or to spread a little ice melter on the sidewalk.

Time Saver

When you need to banish a small patch of ice now, and you have no melter on hand, baking soda can charge to the rescue. Just rush to the kitchen, grab that trusty orange box, and sprinkle a generous amount of the contents onto the site. It will melt the ice without harming anything else (living or otherwise) that it touches.

SKUNK-ODOR ELIMINATOR

When a skunk opens his "spray guns" on your deck, house walls, or other outdoor surfaces, the result is never pleasant. But it can be dangerous because the sulfur-rich chemicals released from the critter can aggravate asthma and other respiratory woes. If your place has been on the receiving end of a fragrant blast, reach for this remedy—ASAP!

2 tbsp. of Solubol dispersant

1 tbsp. of lemon essential oil

1 qt. of white vinegar

1 tbsp. of dishwashing liquid

2 gal. of warm water

Combine the Solubol and oil in a small container. Add the mixture to a bucket with the remaining ingredients and mix well. Then thoroughly saturate walls, stairs, or any other object your local skunk has left his mark on. **Caution:** *Use this formula only on non-living things.*

De-skunk fabrics. Skunk "perfume" contains an oil that makes it cling to most fabrics. To remove the ugly odor, mix 1 cup of baking soda and 1 teaspoon of grease-cutting dishwashing liquid with 1 quart of white vinegar, and then pour the mix into a spray bottle. Then, while wearing rubber gloves, saturate the smelly spots. Blot up the liquid with an old, dry towel, and continue to spray and blot until the odor is gone.

Give them some rags. When it comes to giving off a distinctive aroma, skunks are the champs. But one odor can make them scurry in a hurry: white vinegar. So, if they wander where they're not wanted, soak some clean rags in the potent liquid, and hang 'em in the trouble spots.

When DIY repellents fail to end visits from skunks or other unwelcome wildlife, call your local animal control for help. They may transport the critter(s) to an appropriate location, or refer you to a licensed relocator. Just don't try to trap and release an animal yourself. A wild creature could turn on you, and you could then find yourself on the wrong side of the law. In many places, it's illegal to trap and transport wildlife without a license.

Go one, go all . . . Skunks aren't the only four-legged invaders that shy away from vinegar. Rabbits, raccoons, deer, squirrels, rats, and mice also tend to take off when they get a whiff of the pungent stuff. Best of all, unlike many other theoretically "safe" repellents (ammonia is one example), vinegar is entirely harmless and safe to use around pets, grandchildren, and your own increasingly sensitive system.

> To find out if a skunk has vamoosed, stuff newspaper into his entrance hole; if it's gone within 24 hours, it means he's still there.

Clean your grill—fast. After your next barbecue, lay a sheet of aluminum foil on the still-hot grill. When it's cooled completely, peel off the foil, crinkle it into a ball, and sprinkle white vinegar onto it. Then start to rub-a-dub-dub. All the burned-on burger residue will be gone faster than you can say, "Make mine medium rare, please."

Clean your grill, take two. If you'd rather make this a hands-off chore, this method has your name written all over it: Once the grill has cooled, put it into a plastic trash bag. Set it on the ground, and pour in enough hot water to cover the grill when the sack is lying flat. Then add 1/4 cup of dishwasher detergent (not dishwashing liquid) and 1/4 cup of white vinegar. Close the bag tightly with a twist tie, and shake it to mix the ingredients. Let the grill soak for about an hour or so, then rinse and dry it thoroughly.

Labor Saver

Few things can put a worse damper on a summer afternoon than flies that keep buzzin' at you while you are trying to relax on your deck, porch, or patio. But this all-but-effortless maneuver will help keep the buzzers at bay: Mix equal parts of vinegar and mouthwash in a spray bottle, and spritz the liquid around your furniture, on planters, and even on yourself. Then get back to chillin' out!

AGE-PROOF THE GREAT OUTDOORS

At least your personal piece of it. We've discussed some of the changes that can make your home's interior safer, more comfortable, and more efficient as you approach your second prime of life. But when you're aiming to age in place, it's also important to tweak the outside of your abode. Start some of these improvements now because they're simple and can benefit anyone of any age. For more elaborate structural alterations, like installing ramps, it's a good idea to consult with a remodeling expert first. That way, you'll have a solid game plan in place and ready to go when (and if) the need arises.

REPLACE DOORKNOBS WITH LEVERS. This is one of the easiest and least expensive alterations of all. Plus, in addition to being great for stiff-jointed hands to open, they offer a major advantage for anyone: They enable you to elbow your way inside even if your arms are full of packages.

LOWER THE THRESHOLDS. The flatter you can make them, the better. But for the utmost in safety and comfort, the step up (and down) at an entrance should be no more than 1/2 inch high.

WIDEN DOORWAYS. Thirty-six inches is the ideal width because it will easily accommodate anyone who's in a wheelchair or using a cane or walker. (The bare minimum for a wheelchair is generally 32 inches.) If you can't change the size of the opening, replace the current door hinges with offset versions to provide sufficient clearance.

LET THERE BE LIGHT—AND PLENTY OF IT. Make sure that all stairways and entrances are well lit, preferably with lights set on automatic timers. It's also a good idea to install security lighting at corners and other areas that could harbor would-be troublemakers. On a more positive note, well-lit walkways and outdoor sitting areas can keep good times rolling a whole lot longer on warm summer evenings.

LEVEL THE "PLAYING FIELD." If possible, eliminate any abrupt changes from one part of a wooden deck or walkway to the next. In cases where a few stairs have been included in a brick or stone walkway to accommodate sloping ground, pull the steps out if you can. Then grade the soil and replace the masonry with as gentle a slope as the terrain permits.

CHAPTER 13

ON THE ROAD AGAIN

If you're one of the many folks who love that iconic "new car smell," this factoid will not be music to your ears, but here goes: That aroma is the result of hundreds of chemicals off-gassing into the air. The typical car contains literally dozens of volatile organic compounds (VOCs) used in the manufacture of the carpeting, upholstery, and other parts of the vehicle. Some of these substances continue emitting their gases for extended periods of time, so even when a car is far from new, the air can be less than healthy, especially for older adults whose systems have naturally become more sensitive to environmental "additives" of various kinds. And when you go to use any of the many chemical-laden commercial products to clean your car (inside or outside), you increase your toxic intake.

That's where this chapter comes in. These vinegar-centric tricks, tips, and tonics will help keep your car, truck, SUV, or boat in tip-top shape. And the best part is, using these tricks causes no collateral damage to you or any of your passengers, including your young grandbabies or pets.

Here's an example of how you can use vinegar to help remedy a self-induced but highly annoying automobile dilemma—namely an old bumper sticker that refuses to budge: Saturate a paper towel with white vinegar, then press it onto the site and let it sit for three to five minutes. Then pull up one corner with your fingertips, and peel it right off.

AMAZING AUTO UPHOLSTERY CLEANER

Many folks find fabric-covered car seats more comfortable than vinyl versions. Granted, they do demand a little more attention, but this formula makes it a snap to deliver.

8 drops of Solubol dispersant*   **1 cup of rubbing alcohol**
4 drops of lemon essential oil**   **1 cup of white vinegar**

Mix the Solubol and oil in a small container. Then add that mixture, along with the alcohol and vinegar, to a spray bottle that has a fine-mist option. Shake the ingredients, spray generously onto the upholstery, and let it sit for a minute. While it's still wet, scrub briskly with a sponge or clean towel, then let it air-dry. Repeat when needed to remove any stubborn stains. *Available from essential oil suppliers. **Use more if you like, but stick with the same ratio of 2 parts Solubol to 1 part oil.*

Get the dad-blamed gum out! When a small grandchild or any other passenger accidentally deposits a wad of chewing gum on your car's cloth seat covers, deliver this fast first aid: Put ice cubes in a plastic bag, and hold it to the site until the blob is solid. Then scrape off as much as you can, using a plastic scraper or expired credit card. Dampen any remaining particles with a sponge dipped in white vinegar, and scrape again. Repeat as needed until the upholstery is spotless. Afterward, consider declaring your car a gum-free zone.

SAFE & SOUND There is no nest-building material that mice covet more than car insulation—the stuff on the underside of your hood, and between the passenger compartment and the engine wall. And there's nothing mice hate more than mint. So to keep your car's "underwear" safe from four-legged foragers, arm it with anti-mouse mints. Just dribble peppermint essential oil onto a few cotton balls and tuck them in among the insulation. The tiny terrors will find a less aromatic place to get their nest-building supplies.

Keep your vinyl vivacious and your leather lovely. To banish routine dirt from leather or vinyl upholstery, start by mixing equal parts of white vinegar and water in a nonreactive container. Dip a soft, clean cloth in the solution, and wipe it firmly across the surface. The result: Fresh, clean seats in just minutes!

Freshen up the fabric. Just like any other upholstery, the material that covers your car's seats can start smelling stale, even when it's not actually soiled. To remedy that little dilemma, put 1/2 cup of baking soda into a shallow bowl, and add 20 drops of whatever essential oil you prefer. Mash it into the soda with a fork and stir in another 1 1/2 cups of baking soda. Pour the mixture into a flour sifter, and sift away, distributing the blend onto your car's freshly vacuumed upholstery. Let it sit for at least an hour or, better yet, overnight, then vacuum up the powder, and breathe in the fresh aroma.

Bid goodbye to grease stains. Hands down, vinyl wins top marks as a tough, easy-care upholstery for car, truck, and boat seats. But it can collect its fair share of grease and oil stains. That is where this fabulous formula comes in. To make it, mix 2 tablespoons of baking soda, 2 teaspoons of liquid castile soap, 20 drops of lemon essential oil, and 2 cups of warm water in a spray bottle. Then spritz the mixture onto the affected spot(s), wipe it down with a damp towel, and shine up the surface with a fresh, dry towel.

Money Saver

Unless you're a farmer, you may not know that baking soda is commonly used as a filler in livestock feed. So when you're using it in large quantities to clean your car, garage, or boat, buy sodium bicarbonate in bulk at your local feed store. It'll cost a fraction of the price you'd pay for a couple of orange boxes at the supermarket. Just don't use farm-grade bicarbonate in health formulas or cooking recipes because it's not meant for humans to consume and it could contain a few little creepy-crawlies, or other things that you don't want to put in your or your grandchildren's mouths.

DARN GOOD DASHBOARD CLEANER

This fabulous formula is tailor-made for spiffing up your dashboard, between-seat console, and other hard surfaces in your car's interior. The oil ramps up the action by imparting a little shine, while helping to repel dust.

1/2 cup of olive oil **6 drops of non-chemical cleaner concentrate***

1 tbsp. of white vinegar **1 cup of distilled water**

Combine all the ingredients in a spray bottle, and give it a good shake. Dampen a soft cotton or microfiber cloth with the mixture, and wipe down all of the smooth surfaces in your vehicle. A retired toothbrush makes a perfect tool to clean out textured areas. *Like Dr. Bronner's Sal Suds or Branch Basics, both available online.*

Don't let a car ride make you sick. When you're prone to motion miseries, even a trip to the supermarket can turn into an unplanned adventure. So do yourself a favor and stop trouble before it starts. How? Thirty minutes or so before you start out, drink a glass of warm water with 2 tablespoons of apple cider vinegar and 1 teaspoon of honey (or more to taste) mixed into it. That should keep your stomach stable for the duration.

EARLY BIRD SPECIALS

A great way to keep you and your passengers safe on the road (and most likely get a discount on your auto insurance) is to have your driving skills assessed and, regardless of the diagnosis, take some courses that are especially designed for senior drivers. AAA has many of them, including Roadwise Driver™, which you can take either online or in a classroom setting. Among other potentially lifesaving techniques, you'll learn how to adapt your own driving style to your body's age-related changes—and also how to defend everyone in your car from the shenanigans of distracted, drowsy, aggressive, and road-enraged drivers. To learn more, visit www.AAA.com or call your local AAA office.

Keep the kiddos road-worthy. If your grandchildren suffer from car sickness, here's a simple way to make their road trips more fun (and potentially a lot easier on you): Five to 10 minutes before you hop in the car, even if you're only headed for a playground across town, serve each tyke a cup of peppermint tea. **Note:** *Keep a supply of peppermint tea bags on hand just for this purpose.*

Baby, these come in handy! No matter what kind of gunk has gotten onto your vehicle, just clear it off with a baby wipe. They work like magic on cars, trucks, bikes, boats, and more, all without damaging the paint. The DIY versions on page 104 are great for these automotive tasks, so keep a batch in the car and another in the garage. That way, help will be close at hand whenever the need arises.

When remodeling a garage, leave at least five feet between vehicles to accommodate wheelchairs or other assistive devices.

Before you load your roof rack, use your noodles. Pool noodles, that is. Cargo like bicycles, luggage, ladders, and construction material can make a scratched mess of your vehicle's luggage rack. The simple solution: Cover the rack's bars with pool noodles. Just cut them to the length you need, slit the foam lengthwise, and fasten them on with tape. The resulting cushion will keep everything neatly in place and scratch-free.

Time Saver

To make a dandy car deodorizer quickly, poke a dozen or so holes in the lid of a small container (one that formerly held throat lozenges or hard candies is perfect). Dribble essential oil onto a few cotton balls, and tuck them inside. Snap the top closed, and shove your air freshener under a seat. The aroma is entirely up to you, but a blend of juniper berry and cypress (2 drops of each per ball) delivers a scent that eases drive-time stress and anxiety without hindering your alertness.

CRACKERJACK CAR CARPET CLEANER

Having the right cleaning solution can spell the difference between a job that's a breeze to perform and one that's a royal pain in the bumper. This heroic helper puts the chore firmly in the first category.

1 cup of club soda　　　　**1/2 cup of dishwashing liquid**

1 cup of white vinegar

Mix the ingredients in a large spray bottle, and thoroughly spritz the carpet. Let it sit for a few minutes to fully penetrate the fibers, but not dry out. Then scrub with a brush using a circular motion, and pay special attention to any stains. Rinse using a second spray bottle filled with warm water, and suck up the mixture with a wet/dry vacuum. Finally, open all doors and windows, and in the case of a convertible, put the top down so the material can dry completely.

For isolated spot-cleaning... Mix 1 tablespoon each of white vinegar and baking soda to form a thick paste. Work it into the stains using a scrub brush or retired toothbrush. Let it dry, then vacuum. Repeat as needed until your carpet, floor mat, or upholstery is spotless again.

SAFE & SOUND If you think that you only need winter tires on snow- and ice-covered roads, think again. In cold weather, the rubber compound that all-season and summer tires are made of starts to lose its elasticity. The lower the temperature gets, the less pliable these tires become, until they're so hard that your traction and handling ability are reduced to dangerous levels. However, winter tires stay pliable down to the lowest temperatures. That's especially important as you grow older and your reaction times naturally slow down. So change from all-season tires to winter versions when the temperatures can drop below 45°F. Summer tires, which can withstand ultra-hot temps, need to take a winter vacation at the 50-degree mark.

Banish bloodstains. Even a minor cut on a grandchild's finger or Fido's paw can drip a surprising amount of blood onto your car's upholstery or carpet. Here's a foolproof way to get it out: Mix equal parts of cold water and dry laundry starch to make a paste (adding more of one or the other as needed). Then apply it generously to the stain using a sponge or scraper. As the starch dries, it will pull the blood out of the fabric. When the mixture has dried completely, vacuum up the residue. If any traces of red remain, repeat the process.

Paint your car clean. Well, in a manner of speaking. To get stubborn dust and dirt out of your car's air vents or other challenging spaces, dampen a small foam paintbrush with a half-and-half solution of white vinegar and water, and have at all the little nooks and crannies.

See through your glass clearly. Nothing is more crucial to automotive safety than crystal-clear windows. As odd as it may seem, the commercial cleaners that can work fine on your house tend to leave auto glass full of vision-impairing streaks. So forget 'em. Instead, to keep your car windows dirt-free and fully transparent, mix 1 cup of distilled water, 1 cup of rubbing alcohol, and 2 tablespoons of white vinegar in a spray bottle. Spritz the glass, and wipe it clean with a soft, lint-free cloth. **Note:** *This same potion works just as well on another key safety feature—namely your tail- and headlights.*

Labor Saver

A toothbrush is an ideal tool for cleaning textured surfaces inside your car or getting stubborn dirt out of hard-to-reach places. But to ramp up that spruce-up power, and make the process easier on stiff hands and fingers at the same time, add an electric toothbrush to your automotive tidy-up kit. You can pick up a cheap version for next to nothing at a pharmacy or supermarket, along with both soft- and stiff-bristled brush heads. That way, you are sure to be well equipped to tackle any kind of surface.

DANDY DIY CAR WAX

The next time you give your car, truck, or SUV a top-to-bottom cleaning, follow up with a coat of this whiz of a wax. It'll make that old chariot look almost as good as the day you drove it out of the showroom.

2 cups of linseed oil

2 tbsp. of beeswax pellets*

2 tsp. of carnauba wax

1/2 cup of white vinegar

Heat the oil and waxes in a double boiler until the waxes have melted, stirring to blend the ingredients. Remove the pan from the heat, pour the mixture into a metal container, and let it cool to room temperature. Apply it to your freshly washed car using a soft, clean, lint-free cloth. When the wax dries, lightly dampen a second soft, clean cloth with the vinegar and gently wipe the vehicle's surface. Then stand back and admire your smiling face in the hood! *Available at craft-supply stores.*

Nix the nozzle. Whenever you wash your car, resist the temptation to blast it clean with the hose. Instead, detach the hose nozzle, and let the water wash the bubbles away in a gentler, free-flowing sheet. The result will be a much more thorough rinsing job and a whole lot shinier vehicle.

The Internet is awash with hacks for removing various stains and discolorations from the inside and outside of your car, as well as fixing scratches and minor dents. A few of these slick tricks work just fine—at least some of the time. But when you try any of these DIY maneuvers, your motto should be, "If at first you don't succeed, don't try again." Instead, take your buggy to a reputable auto detailer or body shop because your well-intentioned efforts could actually make matters worse. At the very least, get an estimate for what the work will cost. The price might be lower than you think. And if you plan on selling your vehicle or trading it in at some point, investing in a professional spruce-up job could more than pay for itself.

Make road deicer stains hit the road. Stains left on your car by both salt and other ice melters not only look nasty but can also cause major damage to the chassis. So as soon as you get home from a drive on sloppy winter roads, inspect Old Betsy from head to toe, and wipe off any deposits with a soft cloth dipped in a half-and-half solution of white vinegar and water.

Auto-supply stores sell oversized rearview mirrors that hook over your current version and greatly increase your sight lines and your road safety.

Wipe off wayward wax. You say you washed and waxed your car, and then a few days later you notice a chalky white film on parts of the plastic trim? That is a common dilemma that indicates your waxing cloth went astray and left part of its "cargo" where it didn't belong. If you act quickly, removing the stuff is a fairly straightforward process. Just spread smooth peanut butter over the discolored area, scrub it into the plastic with a toothbrush, and wipe the surface clean with a wet towel. If traces of the film remain, repeat the process. Finish by applying a trim protectant (available at auto-supply stores), following the directions on the label.

Bug off! Even the shortest of summer road trips can leave your windshield splattered with dead bugs. To get them off the glass and other affected parts of your car, just sprinkle some baking soda on a wet sponge and wipe the surface clean.

Money Saver

Taking your vehicle to a commercial car wash will not only save you time and effort, but it'll also trim your water bill. These establishments use less than half the water that a do-it-yourself job requires. Depending on how big and dirty your vehicle is, washing a car at home typically uses between 80 and 140 gallons of water. On the other hand, a professional wash generally uses anywhere from 32 to 45 gallons per car. Depending on where you live, that could result in big savings.

DOWN-DEEP OIL-STAIN REMOVER

When you need to get oil stains out of your garage floor, or your concrete driveway, this is the formula to reach for. It will penetrate deep below the surface to pull out even old, set-in spills.

Baking soda   **Borax**
White vinegar

Cover the stain with a generous layer of baking soda. Let it sit for three or four minutes, then pour vinegar over the soda. When the mixture starts to fizz, add a generous amount of borax. Scrub the stain with a stiff-bristled brush,* then rinse the area, using as much force as your garden hose can deliver. Repeat the process as needed until the marks are gone. *Never use a wire brush on unsealed concrete (or brick). If you do, bits of the bristles could become embedded in the surface, and then you'll have rust stains to remove.*

Clean up a fresh oil spill. When you're changing your car's oil, and a petro-puddle winds up on the pavement, quickly cover it with a thick layer of clumping cat litter heavy enough so that you can't see the concrete or asphalt underneath. If there's no feline in the house to lend you some litter, use cornmeal or sawdust instead. To remove any grease that's left behind, pour baking soda onto the spot, and scrub it away. Rinse with clear water, and you'll be good to go!

Time Saver

How much time do you spend fishing around in the spaces between your car's seats and the console for dropped keys, cell phones, or your grandchildren's tiny toys? If the answer is "too much," here's a way to fix that: Cut a pool noodle or a length of foam pipe insulation into appropriate sizes. Then wedge the flexible chunks into the gaps. The almost-invisible barrier will snag your wayward treasures.

If you decide to paint your garage floor… First clean the concrete using straight white vinegar, applied with a rag or sponge mop. No rinsing needed. The pungent fluid will remove all traces of grime and grease, and will also slightly etch the floor surface so the paint will adhere better.

Put an end to your ice-scraping days. Waking up to frosty or icy car windows is no fun when you're twenty, and the older, stiffer, and more cold-sensitive you get, the more of a damper it puts on your day. So every time you need to park your car outdoors on a frosty night, mix 6 cups of white vinegar and 2 cups of water in a bucket or pan, drench a cloth with the solution, and give all your car windows and mirrors a once-over. Or, if you'd prefer, pour the potion into a spray bottle and spritz the solution all over the glass. The next morning, you'll wake up to ice- and frost-free windows!

Say "paper, please." Chances are, you have never even thought of a brown paper shopping bag as a handy automotive accessory. Not surprising enough, these handy hold-alls can help you weather the weather all year round. In the winter, you can keep your windshield from freezing over by cutting a bag open, spreading it across the glass, and securing it in place with the wiper blades. Come morning, strip off the bag and toss it into the trash. In the summertime, lay a sliced-open bag against the inside of your windshield, and lower the visors to hold it snug and keep out the hot sun.

Q: I turned 55, and my car insurance premium suddenly shot up, despite the fact that I've never had an accident or even a moving violation. What gives?

A: This is business as usual, for the simple reason that senior drivers as a group are more accident-prone than their middle-aged counterparts are. On the flip side, individual companies differ in their policies, and also, many states mandate that drivers over 55 be given discounts for good driving records and for taking approved driving courses. One place to do some comparison shopping on both counts is www.insurance.com.

ANTI-AGING MATTERS

ULTRA-STRONG MOLD & MILDEW REMOVER

A garage is prime territory for the growth of mold and mildew. That space is especially vulnerable if it's part of your home's basement, as is common in hilly parts of the country. When spores have sprouted in the concrete floor or concrete block walls of your car's domicile, this is the formula to reach for.

4 tsp. of Solubol dispersant*   **2 cups of white vinegar**
2 tsp. of tea tree oil

Mix the Solubol and tea tree oil in a small container, and combine the mixture with the vinegar in a spray bottle. Then saturate the affected areas. Don't rinse—and whatever you do, don't dilute the mixture with water. The hard-hitting, mold-busting combo of vinegar and tea tree oil will kill the spores on contact.

Cutting garage clutter could save a life. Cluttered surroundings can raise your stress level and contribute to health problems of all kinds. Beyond that, extraneous objects can pose tripping hazards galore. But if your garage is too full of stuff to hold your car, a decluttering mission, or at least making room for your car, belongs at the top of your to-do list. If that statement sounds extreme, just imagine having to rush a loved one to the ER some snowy night—but first having to brush away the snow and get the cold engine warmed up. Need I say more?

When mold and mildew appear on any porous surface in your garage, like wallboard, ceiling tile, or insulation, call a licensed contractor to remove, dispose of, and replace the material—pronto. Even if your physical strength is still up to the task, and you have the necessary know-how, once you've reached your fifties, it doesn't pay to take chances. That's because getting up close and personal with those spores for any length of time can compromise your immune system and bring on allergic reactions, flu-like symptoms, or even chronic respiratory infections.

If you don't have a garage ... Buy a car cover, and tuck your buggy into "bed" whenever you're not driving it. While a cover can't keep a car warm in cold weather, it will guard the exterior from snow, ice, and windblown debris, and also discourage vandalism. Cover prices vary greatly, depending (of course) on quality, as well as on the size and shape of your vehicle. But for most automobiles, you can pick up a basic "overcoat" for about what you'd pay for a couple of professional car washes and less than you'd probably have to shell out for a full-scale detailing job. For the full scoop, search the Internet for "car covers," or ask about them at your local auto-supply store.

Get in a rut. Once you've cleared out your garage, one sure way to help fend off creeping clutter is to always park large, bulky things like bicycles, scooters, wagons, garbage cans, and your car(s) in the same spots. One simple maneuver will make it a snap to do that: Just outline a parking space on the floor for each one using fluorescent tape or spray paint.

Separate your tools. As you organize your newly freed-up space, plan to keep your automotive tools as far away as possible from any other tools you keep in the garage. The reason: Car equipment tends to get greasy, and saws, shovels, and the like tend to get dusty. And when grease and dust happen to mix, you've got a huge mess on your hands.

Money Saver

In any part of the country, a vehicle that's kept indoors will stay clean longer than one that spends its nonworking time in the driveway or on the street, thereby cutting back on the money, time, and effort you'll spend on car washing. If you live in cold-weather territory, keeping your buggy indoors is also a super-simple way to save gas (and, therefore, money at the pump). That's because during the first five miles of driving, a car that's spent the night in a warm garage burns fuel twice as efficiently as one that's been left out in the cold.

ONE FINE FIBERGLASS BOAT CLEANER

A fiberglass hull is actually made of fiberglass resin covered with an ultra-thin layer of plastic called gelcoat. Any abrasive cleaner will wear right through that fragile coating to reveal the base color or leave a glaring dull spot. So when you give that baby a bath, be sure to use a gentle formula like this one.

1 cup of ammonia	**1/2 cup of baking soda**
1 gal. of warm water	**1/2 cup of white vinegar**

Mix the ammonia and water in a bucket. Add the baking soda and vinegar, and stir until the soda has dissolved completely. (This is crucial because even this mildest of abrasives will damage the gelcoat.) Wipe down the hull, deck, and any other parts of your vessel that are made of fiberglass. Rinse with clear water, and dry with a soft, clean towel to prevent streaks and water spots from forming.

Out, dang spots! Water spots can make an unsightly mess of a fiberglass boat hull, especially one that's black or another dark color. To banish the blemishes, spray them with a half-and-half mixture of white vinegar and water, and wipe them away with a soft, clean cloth. After that, repeat the procedure every time you take your beloved craft out of the water, and before it's had time to dry. Never again will you see spots before your eyes! (At least not on your boat.)

SAFE & SOUND Abrasive cleaners aren't the only culprits that will damage a boat's gelcoat. Even common household detergents and grease-cutting dishwashing liquids, which commonly have a very high pH, can etch your vessel's tender "skin." And any tough-guy cleaning tools like wire or stiff-bristled brushes or scouring pads will cause major damage. So when you clean any fiberglass surface, on the inside or outside of your vessel, play it safe and only use soft cloths or sponges.

Dispatch the "dust." If you've taken up boating as a retirement pastime, and you've found a steal of a deal on an older model that looks dirty, don't pass it up simply on that account. Over time, oxidation can make fiberglass look dusty, but it causes no damage to the material. And there's a chance you can make that hull look as shiny as new, or close to it. Just wipe it down with a solution of 4 tablespoons of white vinegar per gallon of water. Then immediately spray the surface with a wax that's specially made for gelcoat. There are many good brands available at marine-supply stores.

> To prevent mildew on a wooden boat's interior, wipe wood surfaces with a half-and-half solution of vinegar and water after every cruise.

Save your seats. Boat seats are prime breeding grounds for mold and mildew. When the spores descend, don't panic. Just remove the cushions if you can. If you've got built-in upholstered seats, anchor the boat in a sunny spot. Then tackle one cushion or small section of upholstery at a time this way: Rinse the seat with clear water. Sprinkle the surface with a thick layer of baking soda, and scrub using a soft-bristled brush, focusing on the mildewed areas. Pour or sponge on a half-and-half mix of white vinegar and water. Don't rinse! Instead, leave the seat in bright sunlight until it's dry. The combination of vinegar and sunshine will kill any lingering spores.

Don't use bleach. Never use bleach to clean any of your boat seats. It'll kill the spores all right, but in addition to irritating your increasingly sensitive system, bleach can damage the vinyl and will definitely cause the stitching to deteriorate.

Labor Saver

When mildew starts growing on something as big as a canvas boat cover, removing the nasty stuff can be a major undertaking, especially when you're not as young and spry as you used to be. So save yourself that hassle by using this trick: Every time you wash down your vessel, spray the cover with a half-and-half solution of white vinegar and water.

DYNAMITE DACRON SAIL CLEANER

An annual bath with this formula will keep your wind catchers looking and performing their best for many years to come.

1 cup of white vinegar   **1 gal. of water**
2 tbsp. of non-chemical cleaner concentrate*

Mix the ingredients in a bucket, multiplying the quantities as needed. Spread each sail out on a soft, grassy lawn (not a hard surface), and gently wash the fabric using a soft-bristled brush. Rinse thoroughly with clear water. Hang the sails up in a spot that has good air circulation until they are completely dry. Then fold them, avoiding any windows in the material, and store them in a well-ventilated space away from heat. **Note:** *Never use anything but plain water on nylon sails like spinnakers or drifters.* *Like Dr. Bronner's Sal Suds or Branch Basics, both available online.*

When it's bath time for your canvas cover… Don't go toss it into an oversized washing machine at a laundromat. That could shrink the fabric and damage its water repellency. So can washing it with harsh cleaners. Instead, whenever your mooring or travel cover needs more than a simple hosing off, fill a bucket with 1 part borax, 1 part white vinegar, and 2 parts warm water, and stir to combine the ingredients. Sponge the mixture generously onto the soiled areas, and let it sit for 10 to 15 minutes. Scrub off any stubborn spots, and rinse thoroughly with a garden hose. Then let the canvas dry completely before you fold it up.

EARLY BIRD SPECIALS

Have you always thought you'd like to sail, but lacked the time or discretionary funds (or both) while you were working and raising a family? Here's a great way to find out whether you really want to put yourself at the helm: Take a learn-to-sail vacation. A search for that term will bring up oodles of companies that offer week-long cruises—many in exotic locales—during which time you can master all the basic skills and earn certification from the American Sailing Association (ASA).

Keep your brass bright. If you're the proud owner of a wooden boat, you know that these treasures demand a hefty amount of TLC to keep them looking and performing at their peak. Whether your treasure is a seagoing sailing vessel or a classic Chris-Craft speedboat, this three-part formula will make the brass fittings (a.k.a. brightwork) gleam, with none of the harsh chemicals found in most commercial polishes. To make it, mix equal parts of all-purpose flour, salt, and white vinegar to form a paste. Rub it onto the brass with a soft, clean cotton cloth, and let it sit for an hour or so. Then rinse with warm water, and buff dry with a fresh cloth. That's all there is to making your boat's fittings sparkle like the stars!

Time Saver

Got a water-spotted hull? Simply leave your boat out overnight, with the hull uncovered. Come morning, wipe away the dew with a soft cloth. Because morning dew is distilled water, the spots will vanish like magic!

Row, row, row your boat. If you love being on the water, but you don't want the hassle and expense of caring for a boat of your own, consider plunging into one of the fastest-growing senior sports of all: rowing. It's catching on with health-savvy folks from their forties through (yes, you're reading this right) eighties for a number of reasons. For one, it gives you a whole-body work-out while putting much less strain on your joints than, say, running. It improves muscle tone and physical stamina, increases lean body mass, and slows your heart rate. Plus (attention, ladies!), rowing has been shown to stimulate bone growth and increase bone density.

Learn the ropes. The oars, rather. In river- and lakeside towns throughout the country, both clubs and community groups offer adult beginners' lessons and organized competitions in both sweep rowing and sculling. What's the difference? Just this: Scullers hold one oar in each hand, and the boats (a.k.a. shells) accommodate either one, two, or four rowers. In sweep rowing, each person rows with two hands on a single oar, and the shells are manned in pairs, fours, or eights. To find a teaching venue near you, search for "adult rowing [your area]."

PROLONG YOUR DRIVING PLEASURE . . .

And your safety. As a group, drivers over the age of 55 are more likely to have a serious collision per mile driven than any other age group except for those under 25. But wait—it gets worse! Drivers in their late 70s have roughly the same number of injury-involved accidents per mile as do the notoriously crash-prone early-20s set. These tips can help you stay safely on the road longer.

MAINTAIN YOUR HEALTH. Get regular health checkups to prevent any small problems from turning into big ones. Keep any corrective lenses or hearing aids current, and always wear them.

CONFER WITH YOUR DOCTOR. Ask about the ways in which any health conditions you have or medications you're taking can affect your driving prowess.

GET YOUR FULL QUOTA OF HIGH-QUALITY SLEEP. Sufficient sleep is an absolute must for safe driving. It's been proven that driving when you're drowsy is just as dangerous as drunk-driving.

STAY FIT. In addition to aiding your overall health, exercise from sports, ballroom dancing, and general physical activity helps foster quick reaction times.

ADAPT YOUR VEHICLE. If you have physical limitations, see an occupational therapist or certified driving rehabilitation specialist who can prescribe equipment that makes it easier to operate a car. Even if you're fully able-bodied, choose a vehicle that has automatic transmission, power steering, and power brakes.

BE A STICKLER FOR MAINTENANCE. Find a top-notch mechanic who will keep your car in safe working condition. And keep all windows, mirrors, and headlights spankin' clean.

STAY IN YOUR COMFORT ZONE. If driving in a particular situation makes you feel stressed or uncomfortable, don't do it! If you don't see well at night, drive only during the daytime. If the high-speed traffic and relentless noise of interstates and freeways push your stress buttons to the max, avoid them at all costs.

DON'T DRIVE IN BAD WEATHER. After all, one of the luxuries of being retired or working from home is not having to fight your way through rain, snow, sleet, or whatever other nastiness Mother Nature may be dishing up that morning.

CHAPTER 14

OUT & ABOUT

One of the greatest luxuries that retirement offers is having the time to pick up and take off anytime the travel bug bites you. Whether you've already reached that stage in life, or it's still a bright light on the not-too-distant horizon, this chapter can help you pack an added passel of pleasure into your wanderings. I'll share a steamer trunk's worth of tips that'll save you money, enhance your comfort, and help ensure your safety on the land, on the sea, or in the air, whether you're in five-star resorts, bare-bones campsites, or even at a picnic ground right in your own neighborhood.

Just like the Boy Scouts, experienced travelers live by the "Always be prepared" motto. For that reason, you'll discover scads of reasons that a bottle of vinegar belongs in your luggage—or at the top of your shopping list when you reach your destination. With this old kitchen standby at your beck and call, you'll be prepared to conquer on-the-go challenges ranging from wrinkled clothes to aromatic shoes and any annoying bug bites.

Speaking of bug bites, this chapter is filled with topical remedies that both prevent and cure the nasty afflictions. In each case, before you use the formula for the first time, make sure you're not sensitive to any of the ingredients. To do that, dab a drop of each ingredient onto the inside of your arm before you use it on a larger area. And before you use it on a young grandchild, check with the tyke's pediatrician.

ON-THE-GO STAIN-REMOVER STICK

The sooner you treat any stain and wash the soiled garment, the more likely it is to come out clean. When you're away from home, and quick action isn't possible, this DIY laundry aid can save the day.

1 bar of Fels-Naptha® soap, grated	2 tbsp. of white vinegar
2/3 cup of washing soda or borax	2 tbsp. of grease-cutting dishwashing liquid
4–6 tbsp. of water	2 empty stick-deodorant containers

Combine all the ingredients except the dishwashing liquid in a pan, and heat over low, stirring, until the soap is nearly melted. When the mixture starts to thicken, remove it from the heat, let it cool slightly, and quickly stir in the dishwashing liquid. Fill one of the containers about halfway, tap it on the countertop to eliminate air pockets, then finish filling 'er up. Repeat the process with the second container.

Stick it to stains. As soon as possible after a garment has been "decorated," grab your On-the-Go Stain-Remover Stick (above), and then gently rub it onto the spot(s). Toss the item into your traveling laundry bag. Come wash day, moisten the treated area, and rub the fabric together briefly. Then add it to the rest of the load and say "so long!" to the stain for good.

ANTI-AGING MATTERS

Q: My husband and I just retired. We'd been dreaming of traveling, but lately I'm hearing horror stories about seniors who've developed fatal blood clots on long flights. Should we worry about it or forget this idea?

A: No! While it is true that the older you get, the more likely you are to develop these clots, there are ways to help ensure that you fly safe skies. Get your doctor's okay before you take any flight of four hours or longer. On the plane, wear below-the-knee graduated compression stockings. Also, wear loose, comfortable clothing that doesn't restrict your movement, and while you're seated, move your legs frequently.

Take your chariot to the auto doc. Vehicle problems that are minor annoyances close to home can be major headaches (or worse) when you're hundreds of miles away. So before you hit the road in an RV, car, or truck, have your mechanic perform a top-to-bottom, stem-to-stern examination. Make sure all mechanical systems are "Go" (as the Mercury astronauts used to say); that all fluids are fresh and topped off; and the brakes, lights, tires, and windshield wipers are in tip-top shape.

Internal gas expands on takeoff, so for 24 hours before you fly, avoid eating any gas-producing foods like beans or cabbage.

Love it and leave it at home. In the excitement of planning a trip, it can be easy to forget the golden rule of fret-free traveling: If parting with a particular object would break your heart (say, a necklace your granddaughter made for you) or your budget (like a pricey designer dress), don't even think about packing it. Instead, confine your on-the-go inventory to things that you won't miss if your luggage is lost or stolen.

Get up and go with vim and vinegar. If you routinely drink apple cider vinegar in a glass of water or fruit juice to aid digestion, speed up weight loss, or perform other health-care feats, here's good news: You don't have to deprive yourself of all that anti-aging power when you're traveling. Just pack a supply of apple cider vinegar capsules, and take one or more as needed with your water or juice. You can find these portable powerhouses in health-food stores and online.

Time Saver

To grate Fels-Naptha soap quickly (and easily), nuke it in the microwave for about 2 1/2 minutes until the bar puffs up and gets brittle. Let it cool to room temperature, then break it into chunks and toss them into your food processor. Grind 'em up using the chopping blade, and this classic laundry-day helper will be ready to use in the On-the-Go Stain-Remover Stick (at left), or any other DIY grated soap formula.

TRAVELIN' WRINKLE-RELEASE SPRAY

This marvelous mixer relaxes the fibers of your clothes so that wrinkles fall away like magic. It's a time- and effort-saver on any trip, but it's especially handy on a cruise ship or other place where you don't have access to an iron.

2 cups of water

1 tbsp. of white vinegar

1 tsp. of hair conditioner

Mix all the ingredients together, and pour the liquid into spray bottles of your desired size (TSA-approved versions if you'll be flying). To use the solution, shake the bottle and set the nozzle onto the mist setting. Then lightly spray the wrinkled areas of the garment. You will want to dampen the material, not wet it thoroughly. Gently stretch the fabric to smooth out the creases, and let it air-dry.

Don't paint a target on your back. When you're out in public, whether at home or far away, it's only natural to want to look your best. But avoid the temptation to wear fancy designer clothes or flashy jewelry. Even if you snagged the goods for next to nothing at a thrift shop, they alert potential muggers that there may be gold in them thar pockets or in that thar pocketbook with a big-name designer's initials plastered all over it.

EARLY BIRD SPECIALS

As you grow older, it's only natural to feel more vulnerable to attacks from muggers or other bad apples. For that reason, many police departments and municipalities provide no- or low-cost self-defense training for seniors. And martial arts facilities commonly offer self-defense classes for seniors. In addition to building your defense capabilities, you'll get some great exercise, meet like-minded folks, and boost your confidence. That last benefit alone will make the adventure well worth any price. Begin your search with your local police department. If they don't have classes scheduled, they should know who in your area does have some on their docket.

Lie about where you came from. Just like any other businesspeople, professional crooks pick up leads whenever they can find 'em—including luggage tags that they or their roving accomplices "just happen" to see in airports, hotel lobbies, or anyplace else that travelers gather. So instead of putting your home address on the outside of your suitcase, use your work or destination address.

Be prepared to keep your shoes lookin' lovely. Sturdy leather walking shoes, and even ladies' dress shoes, take up valuable space in a suitcase and can add a fair amount of weight besides. So instead of packing a spare pair or two, mix 1 part white vinegar to 2 parts linseed oil in a spray bottle (TSA-approved if you're flying), and tuck that into your grip. Then whenever the need arises, spray the mixture onto the leather, and rub in circular motions using a soft, clean cloth. Let it sit for at least an hour. Wipe again with a fresh cloth, and you're good to go!

Make friends on the go. Once you've passed middle age, it's not as easy to form new friendships as it was in your younger days. This can be especially true for single folks who are retired or work from home. One excellent way to forge ties that bind is to take a group tour that originates in your hometown or nearby (thereby making it more likely that you and your new buddy will continue meeting after you get home). Even if you're unmarried, though, don't limit yourself to singles' tours. Rather, choose one with destinations or activities that appeal to you for their own sake—maybe an art-themed junket to Santa Fe, or a wildlife-watching trek to a national park.

Labor Saver

Whenever you travel, carry along an index card with all of your emergency contact information written on it. Label it clearly, and include the international symbol of a red cross. Keep the card in your wallet or in a visible, easy-to-access pocket. That way, if something goes wrong and you can't access your phone, you can still reach out to your contacts. Or if there's an emergency and people are trying to help you, they can easily find the details they need.

SMALL-QUARTERS CLEANING INFUSION

If you travel or, like many retirees, even live in a travel trailer, houseboat, or RV, this versatile cleaner belongs in your onboard inventory. Not only does it spruce up any kind of surface, but it's also free of chemicals that can be especially irritating in a small, closed-up area.

1 qt. of white vinegar   **2 tbsp. of dried lavender buds**
3 tbsp. of dried thyme

Combine all the ingredients in a clean, dry glass jar, and fasten the lid. Let the mixture steep in a cool, dark place for at least one week,* shaking it a few times a day. Then strain the infused vinegar into a clean spray bottle, and use it as you would any other spray cleaner. *The longer you wait, the stronger the herbal aroma will be, so let your nose be your guide.*

Vinegar relieves the runs. Nothing can put a damper on a pleasure jaunt—whether it's a simple weekend getaway or long-anticipated European tour—like a bout of diarrhea (a.k.a. Montezuma's revenge). At the first sign of trouble, mix 1 to 2 tablespoons of vinegar in a glass of cool water or fruit juice. Or, if you prefer a warmer cure, mix the vinegar in hot water and add honey to taste. Drink the mixture two or three times a day until your symptoms subside.

HELP WANTED? Common diarrhea (a.k.a. bacterial dysentery) is usually more of a nuisance than a health hazard, and DIY remedies can generally clear it up within a day or two (see "Vinegar relieves the runs," above). But if it strikes while you're in a foreign country, see a doctor to rule out the possibility of either amoebic or viral dysentery, both of which are serious medical conditions. And regardless of your location, get medical help if your diarrhea lasts for more than two days without improvement, you become dehydrated, or you have a fever above 102°F, severe abdominal or rectal pain, or bloody or black stools.

Plan ahead to avoid "plumbing" problems. When you are bound for foreign shores, following this routine can help shore up your inner workings and prevent Montezuma from exacting his famous revenge: Beginning two weeks before you take off, eat one raw onion, weighing 8 ounces or so, every day. You can simply add it to salads, sandwiches, or whatever you eat during the day. Or, to pack an even more potent antibacterial punch, mix a whole, finely diced onion in a cup of plain yogurt. Don't worry—it tastes a lot better than it sounds because the yogurt sweetens the flavor of the onion.

When motion sickness strikes, rinse your mouth with 1 teaspoon of apple cider vinegar in 1/2 cup of water to help prevent further vomiting.

Don't let motion sickness spoil your fun. If you're prone to the movement miseries, vinegar can help. About half an hour before you start out, mix 2 tablespoons of apple cider vinegar and 1 tablespoon of honey in 1 cup of lukewarm water, and sip it slowly. The vinegar has a pH-balancing effect on your body that will help settle your stomach and control nausea. **Note:** *If you're traveling by air, pour the vinegar and honey mixture into a TSA-approved travel bottle. Then, about 30 minutes before takeoff, mix it with water from a restroom tap.*

Money Saver

With the flexibility that retirement brings, you can save a whole lot of money on airfare. That's because the cheapest fares are last-minute deals offered by the various airlines. So sign up for weekly e-mail alerts from the airlines to see the latest low-price offers, regardless of the destination. Or for bargain fares to a specific city, you can sign up for a free, personalized fare tracker at a travel site. You'll get a weekly e-mail with the lowest ticket prices. In both cases, you'll get very short notice to make your plans—too short for anyone still working a full-time job.

HAPPY CAMPER FABRIC REFRESHER

If camping is high on your—and maybe your grandchildren's—list of favorite pastimes, you're well acquainted with the musty smell that sleeping bags, tents, and other gear can pick up in storage. But that aroma is no match for this dandy DIY odor eliminator.

1/2 cup of distilled water　　**1/4 cup of liquid fabric softener**
1/2 cup of white vinegar

Pour all the ingredients into a spray bottle that has a mist setting, and then shake lightly. Spray the fabric from side to side using a sweeping motion. Let everything dry completely before packing it up and hitting the road to your campsite. **Note:** *Be sure to pack a full bottle of the formula, too, because it's just the ticket for freshening up clothes that you've worn around a campfire or barbecue grill.*

Watch the critters, and turn back the clock. Study after study has shown that communing with animals in the wild improves people's mental and physical health, and even increases their productivity at work. What's more, you don't have to become another Roger Tory Peterson, or even take up serious bird-watching, to reap these anti-aging benefits. Something as simple as watching hummingbirds hover around a trumpet vine, or butterflies flit among the zinnias, serves the purpose nicely. In other words, your personal Fountain of Youth could be waiting right in your own backyard.

Whenever you head off on a camping trip or any other outdoor adventure, take along a spray bottle filled with a half-and-half solution of white vinegar and water. Then quickly spray the perimeter of any area where you don't want ants roaming, like your tents, picnic site, or grandchildren's play areas.

Make lantern light linger longer. New propane lantern wicks will burn brighter and longer on the same amount of fuel if you give them this performance-enhancing pre-treatment: Soak the wicks in vinegar for several hours, then let them dry thoroughly before using them, whether at a campsite or at home during a power outage.

Summerfy picnic gear. A long winter in storage can leave picnic jugs and coolers with an unappetizing musty odor. To make them food- and drink-worthy, rinse the inside with white vinegar, then wash with hot, soapy water, and rinse 'em thoroughly. Dry the cleaned surfaces as well as you can using a towel or soft, absorbent cloth. Let the containers air-dry completely (preferably in a sunny spot) before you close them up. They'll be ready for the next day of summer fun.

Keep your powder dry. Correction: your matches. A butane lighter works just fine for lighting a campfire or barbecue grill. But, like any other tiny objects, lighters are easy to lose, not to mention the fact that they can run out of fuel just when you need them most. So cover your bases: Before you head off on a camping trip, stash a whole bunch of old-fashioned wooden matches in a mason jar, and glue some sandpaper to the underside of the lid. You'll always have a dry supply of fire starters at your fingertips, complete with an equally dry striking pad.

Q: Lately, I've been hearing that bird-watching is especially beneficial for older adults because it helps improve your memory. Is that really true?

A: It is. Scientists tell us that birding enhances both long- and short-term memory. That's because you have to pay attention to all the little details that set one bird apart from another. Then you have to remember those identifying marks and shapes, so you can look up your "trophy" in a field guide and maybe write it down on your list of sightings. Finally, you really stretch the old gray cells when you relive the experience by describing it to another person. And take it from me: It works. Since I've taken up bird-watching, I spend a lot less time trying to remember the names of old boyhood pals or where I put my cell phone last night!

ANTI-AGING MATTERS

POP-UP CAMPER CLEANER

Pop-up campers get high marks for their light weight, easy maneuverability, and low prices. But their poor ventilation encourages mildew. Wipe spores out with this fantastic formula.

1/4 cup of soap flakes　　**White vinegar**
1 gal. of water

Working on a bright, sunny day, mix the soap in the water to get a nice, sudsy mix (add more soap if needed). Using an abrasive sponge, scrub away any surface dirt and debris. Then soak a terry-cloth towel in white vinegar, and firmly wipe it onto the canvas to the point of runoff. Let it sit for 5 to 15 minutes, then scrub with a brush and rinse the areas thoroughly with clear water. Dry the camper completely in direct sunlight before you "un-pop" it.

When you've got bigger fish to fry. Just give them a rubdown with a palmful of vinegar before you clean them. This makes the scales easier to remove and also helps reduce that strong fishy smell that naturally permeates any campsite where fishing is on the agenda.

Gladly accept substitutions. Here's yet another reason to take a jug of vinegar along on every camping trip: If you forget to pack deodorant or insect repellent, it makes a dandy stand-in on both counts. The acidity creates a hostile environment for bacteria that cause body odor and bugs that want to bite you!

SAFE & SOUND Before heading out on a road trip, whether you're driving an RV or a car, with or without a trailer or camper behind you, take one simple safety precaution: Check for any rough weather warnings or natural disasters playing out along your driving route. Being caught in a wildfire, flood, or tornado will give you the kind of travel adventure you really don't want and possibly result in food, lodging, and other expenses that you hadn't bargained for.

Play cleaner sports. To remove mud and ground-in dirt from plastic, aluminum, or fiberglass sports equipment, rub the dirty surfaces with a paste made from 1 part vinegar to 3 parts baking soda. Wash the paste off with soapy water. Rinse with clear water, dry with a clean, soft cloth, and let the games begin!

Say "Sayonara, static!" Static electricity doesn't limit its annoying shenanigans to synthetic clothing fabrics. Static cling can also make plastic tarpaulins and outdoor equipment covers a challenge to handle, especially when they're large and your skin is growing more sensitive. To end that problem, just wipe down the material with a solution of 1 tablespoon of white vinegar per gallon of water. It'll stop the tiny sparks from flying—and also help reduce the amount of dust that's attracted to the plastic.

When you buy a tent, think big. For newcomers to camping, it's only natural to think that a "two-person" label on a tent means what it says. But don't believe it. In most cases, a two-camper tent is barely large enough to hold two sleeping bags. Instead, look for a model that has room for nice, comfortable air mattresses, large flashlights or lanterns, backpacks, and whatever other baggage you need to have close at hand to make your sojourn comfortable.

For peace and quiet, camp in the off-season. If you're traveling without grandchildren, book a time after school has started. The weather should still be fine, and the prices will be lower—possibly by a considerable amount. As an extra benefit, many beaches and other attractions that prohibit dogs during the tourist season welcome them after Labor Day. Also, in addition to being able to enjoy Fido's company, you can save on boarding fees.

Labor Saver

To make zippers on your tents, sleeping bags, backpacks, and jackets function more easily, rub candle wax or lip balm over the teeth. Those fastening mechanisms will open and close like a dream, even if your fingers have grown more stiff over the years.

TOODLE-OO, TICKS TONIC

Whether you're hiking in the woods, searching for a golf ball that you've sliced into the rough, or playing with your grandchildren in your backyard, you're a prime target for these disease-carrying demons. Keep 'em away with this liquid weapon.

20 drops of Solubol dispersant*	**1/2 cup of white vinegar**
10 drops of lemongrass essential oil	**1/4 cup of water**

Combine the Solubol and oil in a small container. Add the mixture, along with the vinegar and water, to a spray bottle. Before heading into the great outdoors, shake the bottle to thoroughly combine the ingredients. Then spritz your hair, your clothes, and any exposed skin with the tonic. Ticks will give you a wide berth! *Available from essential oil suppliers.*

Shoo, shoo, shoe odor! Sneaker balls are selling like hotcakes online because they promise to banish unpleasant aromas from hiking boots, walking shoes, and similar footwear. Unfortunately, many balls are filled with the same synthetic fragrances that can cause major physical woes, especially for older adults with sensitive respiratory systems. So forget those things! Instead, dip cotton balls in either white or apple cider vinegar. Stuff them into empty tea bags (one ball per bag), and tuck one sack into each shoe and two per boot. **Note:** *Empty tea bags, in both drawstring and press-and-seal versions, are available online and in herbal-supply shops.*

SAFE & SOUND Whether you're living it up halfway around the world or simply gadding about town, an effective way to stay safe is to equip yourself with an aerosol screech alarm (available online). It fits neatly into a pocket or purse, emits an ear-piercing shriek that can carry up to a quarter mile, and there's no mistaking the fact that it's a call for help. It's virtually guaranteed to send any would-be mugger running away. And if you should meet with any other mishap, the distress signal is sure to bring passersby charging to your aid.

Use a sage solution to make skeeters scram. It's always nice to camp right next to a stream, pond, or other body of water. The downside is that mosquitoes covet that same kind of territory. One way to keep them at bay without having to bathe in toxic Deet, or even safer DIY repellents, is to burn bundles of fresh sage around your campsite. The mini vampires can't stand the scent, and they'll vamoose—guaranteed!

Bar the door on wasps. Unlike mosquitoes, which are after your blood, wasps throng to your campsite to get your food—although they won't hesitate to stick their stingers into you while they're on the premises. One of your best defensive weapons is a soda pop bottle trap. To make it, cut the top third off a 2-liter plastic soda bottle. Pour 2 cups of apple cider vinegar into the bottom section, and stir in a couple tablespoons of sugar. Then flip the top section of the bottle upside down, and shove it into the bottom part. Position your trap close enough to your food so that wasps that were homing in on your vittles will go for the trap on their way. They'll flit right in, but they won't get out alive.

Stop spiders in their tracks.

Most spiders are harmless, but if you are like many folks, you won't want the crawlers wandering around your camp-site. To keep them out, pour about ¼ cup of table salt into a 1-quart spray bottle and add water to within about an inch of the top. Shake well to dissolve the salt, then generously spray around the perimeter of your tent, and any other areas you would like to keep spider-free!

Money Saver

March has earned a reputation in frugal-shopping circles as the best time to buy luggage because stores are eager to make way for their incoming summer inventory. The fact is, though, that in most cases, prices are only reduced by 10 to 20 percent. To snag the biggest bargains, wait until after Independence Day. That's when summer travel begins to slack off, and retailers slash prices to rid their shelves of slow-moving inventory. Your selection may not be as broad as it would have been earlier in the season, but you could save as much as 50 percent on your purchase. You can't beat that!

LIFE OF THE PARTY BUG REPELLENT

A festive outdoor event calls for this extra-strength potion. It shouts, "You were not invited!" to every flying insect you can name.

1 tsp. of Solubol dispersant	6 drops of bergamot essential oil
15 drops of lavender essential oil (preferably *Lavandula angustifolia*)	6 drops of lime essential oil
	1/4 cup of distilled water
10 drops of lemon eucalyptus essential oil	1/4 cup of vinegar (either
10 drops of tea tree essential oil	white or apple cider)

Combine the Solubol and oils in a small container. Add the mixture to the water and vinegar in a spray bottle, and shake the bottle to mix the ingredients. Spritz the air with the repellent, spray it on furniture, and set bowls of it around the space to keep bugs from crashing the party. **Note:** *This formula is not intended for topical use.*

Can the colors and skip the scents. Whenever you're hiking, visiting, or partying in an outdoor recreation area, or simply relaxing in your yard, it's a good idea to wear light-colored clothing, preferably in neutral shades. That is because bright colors and flashy patterns send a loud, clear "Y'all come!" to bees and just about every other stinging or biting insect. So do sweet- or floral-scented skin lotions, perfumes, and soaps.

You can start tapping into the travel benefits of Road Scholar as soon as you've passed the 40-year mark. This not-for-profit organization offers "learning adventures" in 150 countries for groups of 10 to 50 people. The roster includes art classes, language and cultural studies, and expert-guided tours as well as volunteer vacations, giving you a chance to try a potential second-prime venture. Itineraries can be designed especially for grandparents and grandchildren, as well as family adventures for parents, adult children, and grandchildren. To find out more, log on to www.roadscholar.org.

EARLY BIRD SPECIALS

It's good to have old money. Especially when you venture outdoors in the summertime. In this case, the cash in question is a clean, old penny. Keep it in your pocket, along with an adhesive bandage. Then the minute you get stung by a wasp or bee, press the coin over the site, secure it with the bandage, and keep it on for 15 minutes. (If you don't have a bandage or tape on hand, hold the penny to the sting site.) The copper will neutralize the acid in the insect's venom, thereby helping to head off pain and swelling. There's just one caveat: You must use a penny that's dated 1982 or earlier. The ones minted from 1983 on are made almost entirely of zinc with just a thin copper coating, and they aren't worth beans for sting relief.

> To make easy-to-tote fire starters, rub cotton balls in petroleum jelly, and stash them in a plastic container like an empty pill bottle.

Put the oomph back in old pennies. To get a dirt-covered copper penny ready for action as a bug-bite soother, put a tablespoon of salt in a bowl, and mix in enough white vinegar to make a paste. Then insert your coin. Let it sit for five minutes or so, then rub the paste over both sides with a soft cloth. That Lincoln portrait will emerge as sparkly as the day it was minted. Rinse with warm water, wipe it dry, and you're good to go.

Hold your horses! Do not use any formula to clean a coin that is, or might be, considered collectible. Removing the patina from a rare, old coin will greatly reduce its value. The same applies to any other metallic antique.

Time Saver

When you're serving ice cream at a summertime outdoor gathering, the key to success is speed, and the key to that is a bit of preparation. To be specific, scoop individual servings into small bowls, arrange them on a cookie sheet, and stow it in the freezer until it's time for dessert. Then pull out the still-frozen treats, and serve 'em up.

DOUBLE-PLAY OUTDOOR ARMOR

This spray delivers powerful, but gentle, insect protection and makes you all but invincible to poison ivy, oak, and sumac.

Large handful of fresh jewelweed leaves
   and stems (*Impatiens capensis*), chopped*

1 qt. of apple cider vinegar

2 1/2 tbsp. of Solubol dispersant

1 tsp. of citronella essential oil

1 tsp. of eucalyptus essential oil

1 tsp. of orange essential oil

1/2 tsp. of pennyroyal essential oil

Put the jewelweed in a glass jar, add the vinegar, and let it steep, covered, for four days. Strain out the solids. Combine the Solubol and oils in a small container, add the mixture to the infused vinegar, and pour it into easy-to-carry spray bottles. Spray the potion generously onto your clothing and any exposed skin except your face, and reapply it every half hour or so. *Available online and at garden centers.*

When it's too late for prevention... Simply crush freshly picked jewelweed leaves in your hand and rub them over your afflicted skin. You'll feel almost-instant relief from the discomfort of any bug bite, sting, or poison-plant rash. This wild cousin of common garden impatiens grows in damp, shady spots (like stream banks) throughout most of North America. In fact, it's often found growing near poison ivy, so help could be closer at hand than you might imagine.

When you're hankering to go off on a cruise or pamper yourself with a sojourn at a health and wellness spa, choosing the right one is a lot more complex than booking a plane ticket or finding a suitable hotel room, especially when you're looking for a senior-friendly experience. So do yourself a favor: Contact an experienced travel agent (preferably one that's been recommended by a like-minded friend) who can help you find what you're looking for at the best price and, more importantly, help you make the best match in terms of your particular needs.

Pack picnic-perfect sandwiches. When planning your menu, take a tip from sub shops: Build hearty sandwiches on sturdy hoagie rolls, and wrap them snugly in wax paper, parchment paper, or butcher paper—and then again in aluminum foil. This will help protect them from moisture if you'll be toting them in a cooler. It'll also keep the subs from falling apart once you start to eat, since you can fold the coverings back bite by bite. Then when you're done, you can throw the whole thing away, with the drips and drops safely inside the wrapper, instead of on your or your grandchildren's clothes.

Take along a solar-powered cell phone charger. These devices are especially useful for camping trips or other adventures where you don't have easy access to an electrical outlet. But regardless of where you're bound, it makes sense to tuck one of these babies into your baggage. That's because, as long as you have access to some sunshine, you'll be able to stay connected even during a power outage. An online search will bring up numerous brands. So check 'em out and see which one best suits your needs and your budget.

Don't forget dry shampoo! It's perfect for those times when you don't have time to wash your hair, or you're not near a water source. If you have gray or light-colored hair, this DIY version is a one-ingredient fix: All you need is a plastic container filled with cornstarch. For medium-colored hair, use a mixture of 3 parts cornstarch to 1 part cocoa powder. Dark hair calls for 2 parts cornstarch to 1 part cocoa powder. To use your hair cleaner, apply the powder to the roots, and comb it through the strands. That's all there is to it!

Labor Saver

Getting ready to hit the road with children or pets? If so, you can make cleanup a breeze by draping a king-size sheet over the car's backseat and floor. Then when you come to a rest stop, pull it out and shake off all of the hair, cookie crumbs, bits of paper and plastic, and whatever else fell to the floor.

ON THE ROAD TO ANYWHERE

After you've reached a certain age, trotting the globe or road trippin' across the USA can be even more rewarding than it was in your younger days. That's especially true after you've retired and are no longer limited by your employer's vacation policy, or constantly nagged by thoughts of the built-up workload that will greet you upon your return. This handful of tips will help you make the most of your newfound freedom.

PACK YOUR ARMOR. If you use vitamin or nutritional supplements, tote them along and remember to take them on your regular schedule. Likewise, take an ample supply of any prescription or OTC medications you may be on. It's a good idea to carry enough to last several more days than you expect to be gone. This way, you'll be covered in the event of delays. If you're traveling outside the country, be sure to keep all drugs in their original containers to avoid problems with border officials.

THINK LOCATION, LOCATION, LOCATION. In each "landing" spot, choose a hotel that's central to all your plans and easy to reach. At the end of a long day of adventuring, the last thing you need is a hassle to get back to your home on the road. Also, look for accommodations that fulfill all your needs. Many hotels offer special considerations for senior travelers, so always ask!

WALK AS MUCH AS POSSIBLE. It'll help keep you healthy throughout your travels. Plus, strolling along city streets, small-town avenues, or rural pathways gives you the opportunity to see your surroundings better than you ever could from the window of a tour bus, car, or train.

TAKE IT EASY! Don't rush around trying to cross off every item on your must-see list. You'll only raise your stress level, which defeats the whole purpose of any vacation. Instead, keep the schedule loose, and give yourself some time to sit back, relax, and simply soak up the atmosphere of wherever you are.

DON'T BROADCAST AN ONGOING TRAVELOGUE. Sure, it's nice to share your pics with the folks back home. But you can't fully appreciate the sights, sounds, and special delights of a place you're in when your eyes and mind are glued to a smartphone. Once you get home, you'll have plenty of time to regale the gang with wonderful tales of your wanderings.

CHAPTER 15

KIDS & GRANDKIDS

For legions of folks, the most rewarding part of life comes in the form of your kids and grandkids. This chapter is chock-full of fabulous, fun ideas that will help you make the most of every minute you spend with them or with any other kiddos in your life. And, because they and their gear will always demand a certain amount of TLC, you will dicover tips, tricks, and tonics that'll help you do everything from easing the entry of baby's first teeth to keeping toys clean enough to chew on.

Of course, vinegar plays a key role in the work and the fun. In this case, though, there is just one caveat: While vinegar can be perfectly safe for kids to consume in standard culinary quantities, the super-powered and very strong wellness drinks featured in earlier chapters are intended for adults only. Also, be sure to check with a child's pediatrician before even thinking of dosing him or her with any internal or external DIY remedy that contains vinegar.

Likewise, essential oils, which routinely team up with vinegar in previous chapters, can be far too potent to use on anyone whose body is still developing. So regardless of the (often conflicting) advice you read online about which oils are and are not okay to use on children or adolescents, it's best to play it safe: Consider these natural, but also potentially risky, substances in the same league as alcoholic beverages—for adult use only.

ACNE 911 RESPONSE

When an acne outbreak erupts on a visiting teenager's face, deliver a fast first response in the form of this strong, but gentle, remedy. Tip: It works just as well clearing up any zits that may even appear on your own increasingly sensitive skin.

2 tbsp. of apple cider vinegar   **2 cups of water**
1 tbsp. of pure aloe vera gel

Mix all the ingredients in a spray bottle. Then, once or twice a day, either spray it onto your face, taking care to avoid your eyes, or apply it generously to individual blemishes using a cotton ball or swab. Let it sit for a minute or two, then rinse with clear water and pat dry.

Conquer cradle cap. This skin condition can be highly disturbing for new parents and for grandparents who are seeing it for the first time. The good news is that while cradle cap is unsightly, it's both harmless and temporary. It's essentially the infant form of dandruff, and the child will outgrow it. In the meantime, apple cider vinegar can help. Simply combine 1 part apple cider vinegar and 2 parts water, and gently massage the mixture into the tyke's scalp. Let it sit for 10 minutes. Then gently brush the flakes away with a soft brush, and follow up with a natural baby shampoo. Repeat as needed to reduce flaking skin and control any itching.

In this case, it's a teething baby who can use your help in relieving the pain of "hatching" his new choppers. For babies, teething typically occurs between six and nine months of age. Contrary to the popular assumption, though, the teeth do not actually cut through the gums. Rather, the infant's body releases chemicals that cause certain cells in the gum tissue to die off, making room for the teeth to come through, but not without a certain amount of irritation and inflammation. To help ease the discomfort, dip a finger in extra virgin coconut oil, and gently rub it over the affected site. End of tears!

Perform three kiddo-care feats for the effort of one. When you've got a toddler visiting for a spell, you can use all the shortcuts you can come by. Well, here's a trick that'll deodorize and humidify your small guest's quarters and make the space safer at the same time: Just take a damp towel out of the washing machine, spray it generously with white vinegar, then hang it over the door to the temporary nursery. As the vinegar-soaked fabric dries, it'll control odors, add moisture to the air, and keep the door from closing all the way, so the little one won't be accidentally locked in the room.

> When a child loses a baby tooth, stop the scary bleeding by rolling up a moist tea bag and holding it on the vacant spot.

Toss the tangles. It is virtually impossible to keep a little girl's baby-fine hair from getting tangled during a shampoo. But there is a way to loosen up those tresses with no muss, no fuss, and no tears: Simply add a splash of apple cider vinegar to the final rinse water. And chalk up another winning play for Grandma!

Bubble, bubble—no toil, no trouble. Just about every kid on the planet loves a bubble bath. But most of the products that cause the foamy fun are filled with toxins like surfactants, artificial fragrances, and dyes. So forget 'em! Instead, when bath time rolls around, combine 1 cup of liquid castile soap and 1 1/2 teaspoons of vegetable glycerin in a bowl, and pour the mixture under the spigot as the water runs into the bath tub. The bubbles may not be as big as store-bought formulas, but they're still great for splashing, toy-dunking fun.

Labor Saver

Even little kids get out of sorts once in a while, often for no apparent reason. If your visiting child has been grumpy all day, pour 1/2 cup of apple cider vinegar into his or her bedtime bathwater. It should help 'em relax enough to get a sound night's sleep and have him or her wake up feeling a lot more chipper.

BOUNCING APPLE SEEDS

Looking for a new way to entertain your young children? If so, then give this simple magic trick a try. It never fails to produce giggles and grins from kids of all ages—and young-at-heart grown-ups too.

1/2 cup of water   **Seeds from one or more apples**
2/3 tsp. of baking soda   **1 tbsp. of white vinegar**

Pour the water into a tall, thin drinking glass, then add the baking soda, and stir until it's dissolved. Drop in the seeds, pour in the vinegar, and stir gently. The seeds will rise up to the surface, carried by carbon dioxide bubbles, then fall back down as the bubbles burst. Make sure you're prepared to repeat the process because the tykes will probably demand an encore performance!

Make hard water plant-friendlier. Here's a variation on the Bouncing Apple Seeds trick (above). It's a great rainy-day pastime and a mini-science lesson for little kids. Back in my day, we called it "bubble-blowing seashells." All you do is fill a glass or bowl one-quarter of the way with vinegar (any kind will do). Gently drop in two or three seashells, and watch the bubbles rise to the surface. Then explain to your little ones that this happens because the acetic acid in the vinegar reacts with the limestone in the shells to form carbon dioxide, which is the same stuff that gives soda pop its fizz.

SAFE & SOUND

What do you do when a toddler is getting into everything in sight, and you've got a collection of delicate treasures spread out around your living room? Consider yourself lucky because you've got a golden opportunity to pull off a dilly of a triple play. Just by grouping those valuables in one or more display cases with glass doors, you can guard the objects from breakage, protect the kiddo against possible injury, and make the room look less cluttered at the same time. Also remember to keep the cabinet doors locked!

Create a crystal palace. This project has tickled generations of little boys and girls, and it's just as much fun today as it was in days gone by. Start by boiling 1/2 cup of water in a pan. Remove it from the heat, add 1/4 cup of Epsom salt, and stir until it's dissolved. Then put a sponge in the bottom of a shallow bowl, and pour the solution over it. Put the bowl in a sunny spot, and keep a close watch on it. As the water evaporates, crystals will develop all over the sponge, forming what looks like a miniature ice palace. What's best of all though is the fact that, because no two crystals are alike, you'll get a whole different structure each time you repeat the process.

Off to the races! If you're like most of the grandparents I know, you're always on the lookout for simple, wholesome, even downright old-fashioned games you can play with your young grandchildren. Well, in my book, marble racing is a jim-dandy on all counts. And all you need to make a derby-worthy track is a swimming pool noodle. Just cut it in half lengthwise, and lean the two pieces, side by side, against a chair or table, with the inside facing up. Then release your marbles at the top, and see whose glass orb gets to the bottom first.

Money Saver

Phooey! You're baby-sitting your diaper-wearing bundle of joy for a few days, and his mother forgot to pack baby powder in his luggage. What do you do? Well, don't rush out and buy some. Use baking soda or cornstarch instead—either one makes a perfectly safe stand-in!

Kids, meet the amazing self-inflating balloon. For this classic, never-fail child pleaser, you will need a balloon, 2 tablespoons of water, 1 teaspoon of baking soda, a clean empty soda-pop bottle, and 4 tablespoons of white vinegar. First, stretch the balloon a few times in both directions to make it more flexible. Then add the water and baking soda to the bottle. Pour the vinegar into the bottle and then very quickly fit the balloon's opening over the top of the bottle. The carbon dioxide released from the vinegar-soda combo will inflate the balloon right before your eyes, while the youngsters will be amazed and ready for balloon number two.

DOLL DUDS LAUNDRY DETERGENT

During a rough-and-tumble play session, a doll's clothes can get as dirty as those of her young "mother." This strong, but gentle, formula will get them spankin' clean again.

3 tbsp. of white vinegar　　**1 qt. of warm water**
2 tbsp. of baking soda

Combine the ingredients in a sink or plastic basin. Insert Dolly's clothes, move them around gently with your hand, and then let them soak. The length of time depends on how dirty they are, so let your eyes be your guide. When you get a visual all-clear signal, rinse the little garments with clear, cool water and let them air-dry. **Note:** *Before washing doll clothes for the first time, test an inconspicuous area for colorfastness.*

To bathe Dolly herself... Provided that she is made of plastic, as most clothes-wearing dolls are, simply give her a head-to-toes rubdown with some white vinegar. No rinsing needed!

Don't pamper plush toys. Unless the label says otherwise, nearly all plush toys will go through the washing machine in fine fettle. Wash them in warm or cold water on a gentle cycle. If a toy is very soiled, sprinkle baking soda on it before putting it into the washer. Then add a capful of white vinegar during the rinse cycle.

EARLY BIRD SPECIALS

Back in Chapter 14, we discussed the senior-travel group Road Scholar. While that is an excellent and budget-friendly option, it's far from the only game in town. Tour operators are tapping into the ever-expanding market of active, young-at-heart seniors who want to trot the globe with their children and/or grandchildren. In addition, many resorts and high-profile travel destinations offer activities specifically designed to promote bonding. A search for "grandparent-grandchild trips" will bring up scads of organized tours, as well as ideas for planning your own grand adventures.

How dry they'll be. When your clean toys emerge from the washer (see "Don't pamper plush toys," at left), put them in zippered pillowcases and toss them into the dryer. Set it on high, and let 'er rip. They should be dry and ready for cuddling in about 15 minutes. If they're still a little damp, either give them some more spin time, or if you prefer, let them air-dry the rest of the way.

When there's no time for toy washing ... Or in the event that your grandchild's favorite critter is not washable, here's your ultra-easy game plan: Just fill a bag with baking soda, pop the toy inside, and shake the sack until the fabric is completely covered. Wait 15 minutes or so to let the soda absorb all the dirt and oils. Then remove the toy, and shake or vacuum off the excess white stuff. **Note:** *This situation is most likely to occur with less snuggly and more collectible (valuable) stuffed animals, like the highly realistic versions made by the famous Steiff company.*

Get in the swing. Swing sets spend all of their time in the great outdoors. Unfortunately, the seats of these summertime favorites bear the brunt of a lot of dirt from play clothes (and often the shoes) of the little swingers. Whether the seats are made of plastic, wood, or metal, the spruce-up method is the same: For routine cleaning, wipe them down frequently using a half-and-half solution of white vinegar and water. If you need to treat any stubborn stains, use the same formula, but let it sit for about five minutes. Then sprinkle the seats' surface with baking soda, and scrub it well using a rag, scouring pad, or brush. Finish by rinsing the seat with clear water, and you're ready for action! **Note:** *This same routine works just as well on outdoor action toys like teeter-totters, pedal cars, scooters, and tricycles.*

> ## Time Saver
>
> For a battery-powered toy, a broken spring can spell disaster. But aluminum foil can spell quick relief. Just wedge a small piece of foil between the battery and the spring. The result: A real power play! **Note:** *This same trick works just as well with flashlights, battery-powered lanterns, and other small appliances.*

ULTRA-STRENGTH TOY CLEANER

Many toys can go right into the washing machine, or even dishwasher. But those that can't withstand the treatment need to be washed by hand. When their load of dirt and grime is beyond the reach of simple soap and water, this is the formula to rely on.

1 2/3 cups of baking soda **2 tbsp. of white vinegar**
1/2 cup of liquid soap **1/2 cup of water**

Combine the ingredients in a large bowl or small bucket, and mix until all clumps have dissolved. First, remove any batteries from the toy, and set them aside. Then dip a terry washcloth in the mixture, and scrub until each toy is soil-free. Work carefully to avoid getting any moisture inside the toy. Rinse with clear water, and set the playthings on a dish rack to air-dry thoroughly before returning them to their young owner.

Treat plastic toys like dishes. To keep them mouth-worthy for even the tiniest tykes, simply run 'em through the dishwasher. Depending on the size of the toys, either load them into the silverware holder, or corral them in a colander or lingerie bag to keep them from falling off the racks. Then run them through on the gentlest cycle, and let them air-dry.

Water and wood don't mix. Wooden toys will emerge from the dishwasher warped and rough. Instead, wipe 'em clean with a lint-free cloth dipped in a half-and-half mixture of white vinegar and water. Tackle any extra-dirty spots or stains with rubbing alcohol on a cotton ball, then wipe with a damp cloth.

SAFE & SOUND If you have small children who ride their bikes, trikes, pedal cars, or scooters in your driveway, here's a potentially lifesaving tip for you: Lay an extension ladder across the end of the drive to block entrance to the street. You will still need to keep a constant eagle eye on the action, but knowing that the tykes can't suddenly zoom out into any oncoming traffic will give you invaluable peace of mind.

Baby the books. Those colorful picture books that babies and preschoolers love are made of tough stuff, and for good reason: They don't just get looked at and giggled over. They also get dribbled on, nibbled on, and smeared with jelly, and who knows what else. So to keep vinyl, cloth, or board books clean and mouth-worthy, dampen a cloth with a solution of 1 part white vinegar and 2 parts water, and wipe the covers and any pages that are made of the sturdy, baby-resistant material. Then stand the books up, and separate the pages while they air-dry. **Note:** *Do not use vinegar on any thin paper!*

When you no longer need a plastic mesh baby gate you kept on hand for visiting grandchildren, use it as a sweater dryer.

Ensure safe splashing. A splash pool in your backyard can keep the happy times coming all season long. But you need to make sure that pint-size pond stays crystal clear and clean. To do the job quickly, with no harsh chemicals, first empty the pool and dry up any remaining water using old towels. Use a brush to scrub the bottom and sides with a half-and-half solution of white vinegar and water, then rinse the basin with the garden hose, and fill 'er up again.

Keep the water under wraps. Ideally, a splash pool should be cleaned after each use. Unless a child or pet has urinated in the water, that's not really necessary, but do be sure to top the pool with a sturdy cover. It will keep out dirty debris and, more importantly, prevent mosquitoes from using the standing water as a breeding ground.

Money Saver

If you have a big new plastic storage bin, you've got the makings of an almost-free entertainment center for small children. Fill the container with dried beans, and toss in measuring cups, a funnel, and a few well-rinsed lids from detergent bottles or spray-paint cans. It'll provide hours of rainy-day fun for preschoolers (with adult supervision).

A BOMBASTIC BACKYARD VOLCANO

This pretend version works like the real deal, with just a few differences: It's a fraction of the size, it flows faster, and (of course) it's harmless to toddlin' tykes and curious canines.

Empty 1- or 2-liter bottle

Moist dirt

Hot water

Dishwashing liquid

Red and/or orange food coloring

2 tbsp. of baking soda

White vinegar

Set the bottle on the ground, and press dirt up around it in the shape of a volcano, avoiding the opening. Fill the bottle three-quarters full with hot water. Then add a squirt of dishwashing liquid, several drops of food coloring, and the baking soda. To start the eruption, just pour vinegar into the hole. It'll react with the baking soda to produce carbon dioxide. The dishwashing liquid will trap the gas, so instead of escaping into the air, it'll flow down the sides like lava.

Make mini eruptions. These tiny volcanoes deliver the same punch as the backyard version (above), but on a smaller scale. They're ideal for preschoolers and easier for busy grandparents to organize and clean up after. To start the action, set out a tray or rimmed baking sheet, and arrange small, clear cups on top (the disposable plastic shot glasses sold at dollar stores are perfect). Set a bowl of white vinegar next to it. Add 2 teaspoons of baking soda and a few drops of food coloring to each glass. Squirt vinegar into each one with a turkey baster or medicine dropper, or have the kids do the honors. Then listen to the "Oohs!," "Wows!," and giggles as the "lava" bubbles up inside the cups and spills over the sides.

SAFE & SOUND You can make the backyard volcano (above) indoors, using modeling clay for the cone, but be forewarned: Even if you set it in a shallow container, the eruption is likely to make more of a mess than you care to reckon with!

Heat up the action. This project is a great way to get kiddos hooked on science. You'll need white vinegar, a glass jar with a lid, a chunk of steel wool, and a thermometer. Put the steel wool in the jar, and pour in enough vinegar to cover the material. Insert the thermometer, and fasten the lid. After three minutes, remove the thermometer and note the temperature. Drain off the vinegar, and wrap the soaked steel wool around the thermometer. Put the bundle back in the jar, and attach the lid. After five minutes, check the temperature again. It should be much higher than it was earlier. Then have the youngster hold the jar and feel the increasing heat. Scientific lesson learned: Vinegar speeds up the process of oxidation (a.k.a. rust), which is an exothermic reaction—meaning that it produces heat.

It's a gel of a sight, all right! Here's yet another way to introduce the younguns in your life to nature and science—this time in the realm of botany: Mix unflavored gelatin according to the package directions. Then pour it into one or more glass jars or transparent plastic cups to a depth of at least 2 inches. Insert seeds so they sit 1/4 to 1/2 inch below the surface of the gelatin, and cover the container(s). The kids can watch the show as root structures develop and little sprouts emerge. **Note:** *Large seeds, like those of pumpkins, squash, or beans, put on the most dramatic visual performance.*

To keep your seeds healthy... Before you mix up your gelatin (above), sterilize everything you plan to use in the project. To do so, cover glass jars and metal utensils with boiling water for 10 minutes. If you prefer to use clear plastic cups, wash them in one part bleach to nine parts water before beginning the planting process.

Labor Saver

To make fun, foamy finger paint in a flash, mix shaving cream with a few drops of food coloring. The kids can sit or stand outside, creating masterpieces on windows or sliding glass doors. When the exhibit closes, you can spray it away with the garden hose—after you have photographed the whole show for posterity, of course!

FOOLPROOF FOOD-SAFE GLUE

This paste works like a dream for paper crafts. And because all the ingredients come from your food cupboards, no harm will come to any toddler or pet who grabs a taste.

3/4 cup of water

2 tbsp. of corn syrup

1 tsp. of white vinegar

3/4 cup of cold water

1/2 cup of cornstarch

Combine the water, corn syrup, and vinegar in a pan. Heat the mixture on medium-high until it comes to a rolling boil. Meanwhile, combine the cold water and cornstarch in a small bowl. Whisk this blend into the boiling liquid, stirring constantly until it's thoroughly incorporated, then remove the pan from the heat. Let it cool, pour the mixture into a container with a tight-fitting lid, and refrigerate it for at least eight hours before using it. Store the glue in a sealed container in the fridge.

Prevent no-sticker shock. Sooner or later, just about all kids go through a sticker phase. To make sure your nearest and dearest can indulge their hobby during their visits to your place, make a supply to keep on hand. First, cut pictures from gift wrap, magazines, or junk mail. Mix 2 teaspoons of flavored gelatin with 5 teaspoons of boiling water. With a small brush, paint a thin coat of the solution onto the back of each cutout. Let them dry, then store them in a covered box until your grandkids are ready to lick and stick.

Money Saver

An expired bottle of roll-on deodorant might look like potential trash, but it's actually a highly useful and free addition to a child's (or even a grown-up's) craft-supply arsenal. Just pry off the roller ball, wash the bottle thoroughly, and fill it with tempera paint or fabric-painting ink. Then pop the ball back in, and get creative!

What a corny idea! To make colorful, high-gloss paints that are safe enough for even the tiniest tykes, mix corn syrup with a few drops of food coloring in a plastic container. When your young Rembrandt has finished his masterpiece, let it dry flat for a couple of days, until it's no longer sticky. The picture or craft project will have a shiny, glazed look. Be aware, though, that even after the paint has dried, it will retain just a hint of stickiness, so don't use it on something like a handmade bookmark or greeting card that will come into direct contact with another surface.

Have a red-blooded adventure. If you're helping your little ones make monster costumes for Halloween, give them an extra touch of scariness by adding some pretend blood to the scene. To make it, pour corn syrup into a small container, and stir in red food coloring until you have the shade you want. Add a few drops of molasses to thicken the stuff and make it realistically dark.

Let's give a show! When it's time for your pint-size thespians to trod the boards, or Halloween is on the horizon, make up some makeup to suit the script. Mix 2 tablespoons of cornstarch in with 1 tablespoon of solid shortening, and stir in whatever food coloring the role calls for.

Make kid-safe paint. Simply mix 3 parts white vinegar and 2 parts cornstarch in a clean food-storage container or a shallow bowl. Then add food coloring until you get the shade you desire. Just bear in mind that cornstarch naturally wants to separate from any liquid, so you'll need to keep swishing the paint around in the container as you work.

Q: My daughter is pregnant with twins. I'm thrilled, but also nervous because I'll be helping to look after the babies, and I know that infant-care practices have changed since my own children were little. Can you offer any basic guidance?

A: Yes! Register for a grandparent refresher class ASAP. You'll learn the full, cutting-edge scoop on the care of newborns. The class will also bring you up to speed on the latest developments in all maternity matters. That in turn will help you provide invaluable support to your daughter throughout her pregnancy, delivery, and early days of motherhood.

ANTI-AGING MATTERS

HOT-DIGGITY DYED PASTA

Dyed pasta is a hit with youngsters of all ages. Preschoolers love to play with the stuff (with supervision!). For older kids, and crafty adults, it provides material for collages and assemblage art of all kinds.

2 cups of uncooked pasta (for each color)   **Gallon-size plastic bag**
10 or more drops of food coloring   **3 tbsp. of white vinegar**

Put the pasta and the food coloring into the bag. Pour in the vinegar, close the bag, and shake it until all the pasta is covered. If needed, add more vinegar to make the color spread evenly, or more coloring to darken the shade. Shake again, and let the closed bag sit for 10 to 15 minutes, shaking once about midway through. Spread the noodles out on paper towels. Once they're fully dry (six to eight hours), they should keep indefinitely in a covered container at room temperature.

Consider the pastabilities. The best pasta to use for your art material depends on what the end product will be. For example, the tubular kinds, like ziti, penne, and rigatoni, are ideal for stringing into necklaces or even Christmas tree garlands. Exotic shapes, like shells, farfalle (a.k.a. bow ties), and rotelle (wagon wheels), are tailor-made for collages and assemblages. And the tiny types, like orzo and the pearl-shaped acini de pepe, make fabulous filling for sensory bins, where they provide "hiding places" for plastic animals, letters, or numbers that toddlers just love to seek and snag.

SAFE & SOUND It goes without saying (I hope!) that small children should handle dried pasta (dyed or otherwise) only under close and continuous adult supervision. Also, speaking of safety, if your end users are still in the toddler stage, ignore any recipes you may see online that call for rubbing alcohol rather than vinegar to dye pasta. Alcohol does the job just fine, but you sure wouldn't want it going into a curious grandchild's mouth even for a second!

Rice is nice, too. Pasta isn't the only food that makes dandy art material and super sensory-bin filler. Rice also works, either alone or in combination with colored noodles. The dying procedure is the same, but in this case use 1 tablespoon of white vinegar per cup of uncooked rice, along with enough food coloring to achieve your desired shade. Start with a few drops per cup and work up from there.

> To give any drawing or photo a textured finish, paint the surface using a 1-inch-wide paintbrush dipped in clear nail polish.

Equip some undercover agents. If your kids and their pals are going through a "let's-be-spies" stage, give them the supplies they need to write down their secret messages: a sheet of paper, a bowl of white vinegar (a.k.a. invisible ink), and either a small, thin paintbrush or an old-fashioned fountain pen. Once the clandestine correspondence has been written and the "ink" has dried, the recipient can reveal the message in one of three simple ways: ironing the paper, setting it on a radiator, or holding it up to a hot lightbulb.

Blow bombastic bubbles. Every kid on earth loves to blow bubbles, but you don't need a store-bought solution to create a fabulous show. Just mix 2 parts dishwashing liquid, 1 part vegetable oil, and 2 parts water in a shallow pan. Then instead of using a regular bubble blower, bend a wire clothes hanger into a circle, leaving the hook in place to use as a handle. Dip the loop into the "drink," and draw it gently through the air. The result—the biggest bubbles you've ever seen—guaranteed!

Labor Saver

To give your grandkids some real fun on a rainy day, or even a whole rainy week, spread a sturdy plastic drop cloth or a vinyl shower curtain liner over the floor. Then hand out washable felt markers in a rainbow of colors, and let the youngsters go to town. They'll have a ball, and when sunny weather beckons them outdoors again, all you'll have to do is toss the "canvas" into the washing machine.

YELLOW-STAIN REMOVER

Protein-based stains like formula, mother's milk, and urine leave yellow marks on fabric. They can be challenging to remove, but by using this formula and acting quickly, you'll stand a very good chance of making them vanish.

1 tbsp. plus 1/4 cup of　　**1/2 tsp. of dishwashing liquid**
white vinegar (divided)　　**1 qt. of cool water**

Mix the tablespoon of vinegar in a sink with the dishwashing liquid and water. Insert the clothes, and let them soak for 15 minutes. Rinse in cool water, then run them through a regular cold-water wash cycle, with 1/4 cup of vinegar added to the final rinse. If any discoloration remains, wash the garments again. Or, if the marks are fairly faint and weather permits, hang them outside to dry in the sun. Often, Ol' Sol's rays will lift stains right out.

If a grandbaby's high chair "lives" at your house... Clean and disinfect the main structure by spraying or wiping it with a half-and-half solution of white vinegar and water. Then give the tray a thorough going-over with some undiluted vinegar, and let it air-dry. This surface deserves extra-special attention since a lot of food spends time there before it finds its way into a little one's mouth.

HELP WANTED?

It's always nice to have help in the kitchen. But what do you do when a child wants to lend a hand but isn't old enough to use knives or other sharp tools? Just give the budding chef a pair of clean, blunt scissors, and have him cut up salad greens for dinner. Even this simple chore will lessen your workload, and it'll give the youngster the satisfaction of making a genuine contribution to the task at hand. Even more importantly, this active time together can bring the two of you closer and help form memories that you'll both carry through the years.

Vinegar does darn good diaper duty. Contrary to what the folks who sell disposable diapers may say, plenty of folks still use the traditional cloth kind, at least part of the time. If you're among that crowd, white vinegar can be your best pal on laundry day. So keep a jug of it close at hand, and use it in two ways: After you rinse dirty diapers in the tub or toilet, soak them in a solution of 1 part vinegar to 10 parts water before you toss 'em in the wash. Once they're in the machine, add 1 cup of white vinegar to the final rinse cycle. It'll break down both uric acid and soap residue, leaving the fabric softer and more comfortable on baby's tender skin.

Douse diaper rash. A vinegar rinse does more than soften diapers (see "Vinegar does darn good diaper duty," above). It also helps prevent diaper rash by inhibiting the growth of bacteria and bringing the pH of the fabric closer to the neutral pH of baby's skin. And that's a big plus for the potential sufferer and her doting grandma!

Money Saver

When your little ones outgrow the backyard wading pool they've always used at your place, don't be too quick to toss that pseudo pond out. Chances are you can give it a second-prime career as an under-bed storage container—at a cost of $0.00.

Hold on to that baby... Gently! When you're bathing an infant, it's not easy to hang on to that wet, and possibly squirming little body, especially if your joints have grown a little stiff. The simple, comforting solution: Wear cotton gloves. They'll give you a better grip than you'd have with bare hands, and they'll feel a whole lot better on the baby's skin than rubber gloves would.

Make a baby bath formula. To make bath time an extra-soothing treat for visiting grandbabies, whip up this easygoing blend and keep it on hand. Simply mix 1/4 cup each of nonfat dry milk and whole, dry buttermilk with 1 tablespoon of cornstarch. Store the mixture in a covered glass jar at room temperature. So when the occasion arises, pour 1 tablespoon of the powder into a baby bathtub, or 1/4 cup into a full-size tub. Then gently lower the tyke into the drink, and enjoy his smiles and giggles!

VOMIT-STAIN VANISHING SPRAY

After you have removed any "recycled food" from its landing spot, whether it's carpet, upholstered furniture, or clothes, use this simple formula to get rid of any lingering stain.

1/2 cup of rubbing alcohol   **1/2 cup of white vinegar**
1/2 cup of water

Mix the ingredients in a spray bottle, and lightly spritz the stained area. Let it sit for three or four minutes, then blot it up with a soft, clean, and absorbent cloth (an old cloth diaper or section of a retired flannel sheet is perfect). Repeat this process until all traces are gone. The alcohol in the mix teams up with the vinegar to remove the marks and also makes the solution dry quickly. **Note:** *This combo is safe for most fabrics, but test it first in an inconspicuous spot to make sure it doesn't affect the dye or otherwise damage the material.*

When little Johnny drops his pizza on the couch... It, or any other spilled food, can make a mess of the upholstery. But the damage will only be temporary if you spring into action this way: Mix 1/4 cup of liquid laundry detergent and 1/4 cup of white vinegar with 2 cups of water in a spray bottle. After lifting away any solid material, spray the mixture very lightly on the affected fabric, and let it sit for 30 minutes. Then blot with a soft, clean towel. Repeat the process as needed until all traces of the stain are gone.

SAFE & SOUND Like most afflictions, swimmer's ear is simpler, and a lot more pleasant, to prevent rather than treat after the fact. One way to do that is to use the vinegar-alcohol mixture immediately after every dip (see "Stop swimmer's ear quick," at right). Wearing earplugs can help too, but an even more effective solution is to teach kids to dry their ears, first thing, as soon as they get out of the pool, before they dry the rest of their bodies.

Soak sunburn pain away. No matter how careful you are to protect a small child's tender skin (or your own), sunburn can strike. So be prepared to offer a tubful of relief. Mix 1 cup of vegetable oil, 1/2 cup of apple cider vinegar, 1/2 cup of honey, and 1 tablespoon of pure (not artificial!) vanilla extract in a bowl or measuring cup. Pour the mixture into a bottle with a tight stopper, and store it at room temperature. Then, at bath time, shake the bottle, and pour one-quarter of the contents under running water. **Note:** *You don't have to be suffering from sunburned skin to enjoy this soothing blend. At any time, it's a relaxing treat for kids and grown-ups alike. Be careful to avoid slipping when getting out of the tub.*

Stop swimmer's ear quick. Sooner or later, any child who spends much time frolicking in the water comes down with the painful and itchy condition that is known as swimmer's ear (technically, it's *otitis externa*). To relieve the discomfort quickly, rinse the victim's ears with a half-and-half solution of white vinegar and rubbing alcohol. The alcohol acts as a drying agent, soaking up the moisture in the ear canal, while the vinegar kills the bacteria that cause the infection.

Turn tripping hazards into high-flying fun. Okay, so in the interest of staying on the up-and-up, you've eliminated lightweight throw rugs from your living areas. But what do you do if you've got a few that are so beautiful and colorful that you can't bear to part with them? Well, if you've got small grandchildren who visit periodically, tuck those fancy floor coverings into an easy-to-access storage space. Then when the kids arrive, and they need a magic carpet ride—as every youngster does from time to time—one of those pretty rugs can provide their imaginary transportation. **Note:** *This is also a terrific way to give new "careers" to fringed, patterned tablecloths that no longer complement your decor.*

Time Saver

Want to make bath time more fun for a small child in the blink of an eye? Just get a sponge in the shape of a boat, or a favorite animal, and cut a slit in one end. Then tuck in a tiny, hotel-size bar of soap, or some leftover slivers. Bingo—a soaping tub toy!

LIVE IT UP AS GRANDPARENTS!

To a large extent, your role as a grandparent will be determined by personal choice, but also by how close you live to your grandchildren and whether you are retired or still working. Regardless of the circumstances, this roundup of ideas will help you and your young loved ones make the most of your time together.

SHARE SIMPLE PLEASURES. These things fall into "the best things in life are free" category, which you may have learned from your own grandma or grandpa. Show the tykes how to blow the fluff off a dandelion, catch and release lightning bugs, or lie on your back finding critter shapes in the clouds that drift by overhead.

TELL—AND SHOW—THEM WHERE YOU CAME FROM. After all, your history is also part of their history. They'll love seeing the house you grew up in, the grade school you attended, or the church where you married their grandpa (or grandma, as the case may be). Tell them stories about your own parents and grandparents, complete with visits to relevant landmarks.

GET THEM MOVING. Stroll around the block. Play catch in the backyard. Go for walks in the woods, at the shore, or around your neighborhood, and teach them to identify different birds, trees, butterflies, and flowers. If the weather's nasty, head for a bowling alley. Not only does it bring you closer together, but your outings can help encourage a lifelong habit of healthy exercise.

MAKE 'EM LAUGH. Shared laughter automatically draws people closer together. Starting when they're babies, read them funny books with silly pictures. Watch funny movies and classic TV comedy shows. Exchange jokes and riddles. And laugh off minor mishaps, like dropped ice cream cones or broken plates. You'll be teaching the kids to use humor to cope with the unfortunate things that happen to everyone from time to time.

PLAN FOR FUTURE FUN. Don't confine leisure-time activities to standard fare like playgrounds, amusement parks, and the zoo. Introduce the kids to some of your own favorite places and pastimes—perhaps the art museum, the local botanical garden, or young people's concerts at the symphony. These jaunts will help broaden their horizons, maybe even spark a lifelong passion, providing you with a companion who shares your enthusiasm.

CHAPTER 16

SUPER SENIOR CARE

Throughout the course of recorded history, there have always been people who have lived to advanced ages. The difference today lies in the numbers: Folks who are 85 years of age and older represent the fastest-growing segment of the United States population. That fact is the result of the miraculous advances in modern medicine. Many of today's octogenarians and younger seniors are surviving with health problems that would have been fatal just a few decades ago. The bottom line: There are loads of people who need a lot of TLC from their adult children and/or other family members. So if you're one of those caregivers, you've come to the right place. You won't find medical advice in this chapter, but you will find timely tips, tricks, and tonics that'll help make life easier, more comfortable, and more fun for you and your older loved ones.

As always, vinegar plays a central role in the action here. And just as a reminder, when a tip or tonic calls for apple cider vinegar, it's important to use the raw, unprocessed kind. In the case of white vinegar, only use the food-safe, 5% kind that's distilled from edible grain, and not from petroleum-based chemicals.

You'll notice that essential oils are back on the scene in these pages. To play it safe, always check with your loved one's doctor before using essential oils or vinegar in medicinal quantities. Either substance can commonly interact with a medication or nutritional supplement. Or it could simply be too potent for a frail system to handle safely.

APPETITE-BOOSTING MOCKTAIL

Once many folks age, their interest in food tends to decline, and it becomes harder for them to pack in vital nutrients. This beverage can wake up their taste buds.

4 cups of water, divided	**1/4 cup of fresh-squeezed lemon juice**
2 tbsp. of minced, peeled fresh or 1/2 tsp. of ground ginger	**2 tbsp. of apple cider vinegar**
	2 tbsp. of raw honey or pure maple syrup

In a small pan, bring 1 cup of the water to a boil over high heat. Stir in the ginger, and boil for two minutes. Remove the pan from the heat, cover, and let it sit for 15 minutes. Strain the mixture into a jar, and refrigerate until it's well chilled. Stir in the lemon juice, vinegar, honey or maple syrup, and remaining water. The recipe makes two servings and will keep for a week in the refrigerator.

Sniff before you dig in. Ninety percent of taste is actually controlled by our sense of smell. So before you stick your fork into the food on your plate, take a good whiff. The more odor molecules hit the receptors in your nose, the stronger your sense of taste will be, and the more you will enjoy your meal.

ANTI-AGING MATTERS

Q: My father has always had a robust appetite, but now that he's in his eighties, he just doesn't seem to care about eating. I've heard that people actually lose taste buds as they age. Is this true? And could that be the reason for his decreased appetite?

A: In answer to your first question, yes, it is true. We're each born with roughly 10,000 taste buds, but after age 50, the number begins to decline. Most likely that accounts, at least in part, for your dad's lack of culinary enthusiasm. But some prescription and over-the-counter medications can also be powerful appetite suppressants, especially in the elderly. I'd ask your father's doctor whether tweaking the medication regimen might help solve the problem.

Vinegar invigorates taste buds. One of the best ways to perk up a lagging appetite is to douse food and meals with a complementary vinegar. In many cases, using straight-from-the-bottle balsamic will make a reluctant eater's taste buds bounce back. So will herb- or fruit-infused vinegars. You can find oodles of flavors online and also in specialty food stores, or make your own following the directions on page 81.

> For an easy appetite booster, add a few sprigs of peppermint to a glass of lemonade, and let it sit for 10 minutes before sipping.

Head home to comfort food. Very often, you can jolt a reluctant eater out of a slump by serving up foods he loved as a child, or that evoke happy memories of days gone by. Think ballpark hot dogs, macaroni and cheese, Mom's sweet potato casserole, or Dad's steaks sizzling on the charcoal grill. For the short term, don't fret about always providing traditional well-balanced meals. Remember, your goal here is to rekindle the food-loving "fire," and anything that does that (barring allergens and other doctor-declared no-nos) is fair game.

Say "Yes!" to onions again. For legions of folks, there's nothing like raw onions to wake up the flavor of salads and sandwiches. Unfortunately, as we age, even the sweetest of the sweet varieties can become hard to digest. Here's a sweet solution to the problem: Marinate the onions in sherry vinegar for 30 minutes to an hour before you use them. They'll retain their enticing flavor and satisfying crunch with no sassy back talk later.

Labor Saver

Nothing revs up the appetite like hot pepper. It adds a whole new dimension to potato salad and deviled eggs, as well as soups, stews, and other hot dishes. Just a few shakes of powdered cayenne pepper will do the trick. So will a splash or two of hot-pepper vinegar (see page 61 for an ultra-easy DIY version).

A BERRY DELICIOUS DIGESTION HELPER

A decline in taste buds isn't the only reason many elderly folks lose their enthusiasm for eating. Digestive woes, which tend to increase with age, also contribute to the problem. This drink delivers a load of vitamins and minerals that smooth the passage of food through the digestive tract, and also ensure that they're properly distributed throughout your body and effectively absorbed. This recipe makes two servings.

1 cup of blackberries

1 cup of raspberries*

1 medium pear, peeled, cored, and sliced

1 tbsp. of apple cider vinegar

2 cups of water

Combine all the ingredients in a blender. Whirl it on high speed until the mixture is thoroughly blended and frothy. Drink the beverage immediately, or refrigerate it, tightly covered, for up to four hours.
Red, black, yellow, or any combination thereof.

Vinegar tames tummy turbulence. When a bout of indigestion hits, relief is close at hand (or should be). Just mix 2 teaspoons of apple cider vinegar in a glass of water, and drink up. Repeat the process once an hour until the discomfort passes. It shouldn't take long!

As the 60-plus to 80-plus demographic continues to expand, so do courses that target their needs and interests. One of the most popular is cooking, with classes directed at caregivers, at senior cooks themselves, or in many cases, both. Some formats focus on specific techniques, like working effectively within particular dietary restrictions, or packing more solid nutrition into smaller quantities of food. Others encourage students to cook more and to broaden the variety of foods they eat. Formal cooking instruction delivers two big benefits for elderly adults: It increases their confidence in the kitchen and reduces the risk of accidents. A quick Internet search should bring up classes near you.

EARLY BIRD SPECIALS

Enhance digestion from the outside in. Ginger-enhanced beverages, both with and without vinegar added, have gained fame far and wide for their ability to soothe digestive problems, but this tangy spice can also work its wonders in topical form. In this case, it's ginger essential oil that you want to reach for. Just mix 2 or 3 drops of it into olive, coconut, or jojoba oil, and rub the mixture onto your abdomen. Repeat the process every few days until your tummy troubles are history. **Note:** *This gingery rub can also help stimulate a sluggish appetite.*

Turn meals into social events.
It's a very well-known fact that socializing with friends, or even congenial strangers, is absolutely vital for everyone's overall physical and mental health. When elderly folks dine with others, they're much more likely to eat larger amounts and digest their food more effectively. So as often as possible, make mealtime a group affair. Seek out community barbecues, church suppers, and other public events where food is central to the action. Let friends and family members know that brunch, lunch, or dinner invitations are always welcome. And especially if you are caring for someone who cannot easily leave the house, make it a point to invite folks to join you at your dinner table as frequently as possible.

Variety is the spice of life. It can also be the key to rousing the interest of a lackadaisical eater. Even a self-proclaimed, stuck-in-the-mud geezer could be enticed to try something new and nutritious if it contains at least a few ingredients they like. So flip your cookbook open to pages you've never stopped at before, and let 'er rip!

Time Saver

These days, when you visit a doctor, either for yourself or with an elderly relative in tow, you're likely to get three minutes, max, to spend with the doc himself. So to make the most of your brief encounter, skip any initial pleasantries. Just say "hello" immediately, then blurt out your most urgent concern. This way, you'll stand a better chance of getting the help you need on the first try, rather than being plunged into a constant round of recurring visits and trial-and-error remedies.

MAGNIFICENT MAGNESIUM FOOT SOAK

Magnesium is essential for maintaining crucial bodily functions like muscle control, energy production, tissue healing, and the elimination of harmful toxins. Most of us don't get enough of it in our daily diets. One simple solution: Soak it up through your feet!

2 gal. of warm water

1 cup of Dead Sea salt

1 cup of Epsom salts

1/2 cup of apple cider vinegar

1/2 cup of bentonite clay*

Pour the water into a foot basin or other non-metallic container that'll hold your feet comfortably. Stir in the remaining ingredients. Then sit back and relax in a comfortable chair, and soak your tootsies for 20 to 30 minutes. Rinse them with clear water, and dry with a soft towel. You'll feel good all over. *Available at health-food stores and online.*

Create an even feistier foot bath. With one simple tweak, you can turn the Magnificent Magnesium Foot Soak (above) into a multitasking marvel. The slick trick is to add rosemary essential oil to the blend. This senior-friendly superstar is renowned for its ability to elevate moods, relieve stress, stimulate lagging appetites, and improve cognitive performance. All you need to do is mix 8 to 10 drops of the oil with 1/2 teaspoon of Solubol dispersant in a small container, and stir the mixture into the basin with the other ingredients. Talk about an anti-aging power play!

Caution! While magnesium is incredibly essential for good health, it is also very possible to give yourself an accidental overdose—especially if you are taking any medications that contain the chemical. If you're under medical care for any chronic health condition, consult with your doctor before you use Epsom salts. This is especially important in the case of high blood pressure, heart disease, or diabetes.

Keep your cool. As people age, even hot-weather lovers become more sensitive to high temperatures. But that doesn't mean you should hunker down in front of an air conditioner for the duration of the summer. At every age, regular outdoor exercise, or movement in any form, is essential for good health. So when you head out, just make sure to pack a bottleful of cooling comfort like this dandy DIY version. To make it, mix 12 drops of lavender essential oil and 10 drops of peppermint essential oil with 1/4 teaspoon of Solubol dispersant in a small container. Combine the mixture with 2 teaspoons of pure witch hazel in an 8-ounce spray bottle, and fill the remainder with water. Then, every once in a while, pull it out and give yourself and any companions a few refreshing spritzes. You will all stay as cool as those famous cucumbers—or close to it!

Energy going up! When the day's outing ends with your loved one(s), and maybe you, too, weary to the core, serve up tall glasses of this no-fail fatigue fighter: Mix 2 teaspoons of apple cider vinegar and 2 teaspoons of raw honey per cup of water in a big pitcher. Then sit back and drink up as you reminisce about your exploits. Before you know it, you'll be back in the pink and planning your next big action-packed adventure.

Tater water fights fatigue. In fact, it's one of the most powerful energizers of all, especially first thing in the morning. Here's the simple drill: At bedtime, put a few slices of a fresh potato in a glass of water, cover it, and tuck it into the fridge. Come morning, strain out the potatoes and drink up. You can brighten the flavor by mixing the infused water with orange or apple juice.

Money Saver

One of the best ways to heighten your energy level, improve your digestion, and boost brainpower, at any age, is absolutely free. What is it? Guzzle plenty of water. But forget the oft-heard advice to down eight glasses a day. Instead, just keep an eye on your urine. It should be clear or very pale yellow. If it's a darker shade, your system needs an influx of fluid. But again, contrary to conventional "wisdom," it doesn't have to be H_2O. Beverages of all kinds, like juice, milk, tea, and (nutritionists now tell us) coffee, deliver the elixir of life.

GENTLE DENTURE CLEANSER

Both full-mouth dentures and partial plates demand daily cleaning to remove any bacteria and—in the case of partials—to prevent the clasps from degrading. This formula does the job perfectly.

2 tsp. of baking soda	**1 part white vinegar**
2 tsp. of water	**1 part water**

Mix the baking soda and water to make a paste. Apply it to a soft-bristled toothbrush, and gently but thoroughly scrub away any debris. Rinse with clear water, then soak the dentures for 15 minutes in a half-and-half solution of vinegar and water. That's all there is to it!

Rose vinegar rescues receding gums. While advancing age is not the only reason for this serious oral problem, it is more prevalent among the most elderly members of the population. One of the most effective weapons in the effort to both strengthen and help restore the gum tissue is none other than rose-infused vinegar. To make it, fill a glass jar with freshly rinsed and dried rose petals (a clamp-lidded canning jar is perfect). Pour in enough red wine vinegar to cover the petals, and set the jar in a sunny window for seven days. Strain the liquid into another glass container. Then twice a day, add 1 tablespoon of the vinegar to 8 ounces of lukewarm water, swish it around in your mouth for a minute or two, and rinse with clear water. Your gums will be stronger than ever!

Time Saver

You couldn't ask for a tastier way to help reduce blood pressure and lower stress than this no-extra-time-needed trick: Just sprinkle ground cinnamon onto your ground coffee, and quickly mix that in before you press the machine's brew button. There's no specific dose, so use as much as you like, but about 1/2 teaspoon per cup of java always seems to do the trick.

Do a weekly deep cleaning. Every seven days, after brushing your dentures using the baking soda and water paste (at left), put them in a glass of white vinegar and let them soak overnight. This will remove any built-up tartar and, more importantly, kill bad bacteria and help prevent the overgrowth of yeast and fungi—thereby preventing thrush and other oral infections.

Demolish denture pain. Sooner or later, just about every denture wearer under the sun cries out for pain relief. Well, here it is: Mix 1/2 teaspoon of powdered cloves with a few drops of olive oil. Smooth the mixture onto your sore gums, and let it sit for five minutes or so. Then rinse your mouth with lukewarm water. Repeat the procedure twice a day until you can wear your pseudo-teeth with no discomfort.

Nourish and baby ultra-sensitive skin. Contrary to what a lot of folks think, even fragile elderly skin can benefit from the right exfoliating facial scrub every week or so. This effective but ultra-mild winner will gently unclog pores, help soothe irritation, and even deliver a load of anti-aging antioxidants. To make it, mix 1 1/2 cups of ground, uncooked oatmeal and 1/2 cup of melted extra virgin coconut oil in a bowl with 1 teaspoon each of brown sugar, raw honey, and pure vanilla extract (don't use the artificial kind!). Massage the mixture onto your freshly washed face and neck using small circular motions. Let it dry, and rinse it off with warm water. Then pat dry, and follow up with a rich moisturizer. **Note:** *To grind the oatmeal, you can use a coffee grinder, blender, or food processor.*

Q: Now that my father has reached his mid-eighties, his facial skin is very sensitive and becomes irritated when he shaves. I got him a commercial pre-shave product, but it was really expensive. Do you know of a good DIY formula?

A: You betcha! Just mix 2 parts castor oil and 1 part olive oil in a plastic bottle. To use the mixture, your dad should rub a small amount onto his face, let it sit for about 60 seconds, then get to shavin'. By the way, this pre-shave formula works just as well on ladies' legs and underarms as it does on gents' faces.

ANTI-AGING MATTERS

URINE-ODOR ELIMINATOR

Few people reach old age without having at least a few issues with incontinence, and it can be hard to keep a telltale odor out of the air. This superpowered spray can tackle that job with none of the risks posed by the synthetic fragrances in commercial air fresheners.

6 drops of Solubol dispersant

3 drops of essential oil*

1 tbsp. of white vinegar

2 cups of water

Mix the Solubol and oil in a small container. Combine the mixture with the vinegar and water in a spray bottle with a mist setting, and shake thoroughly. Then lightly mist the air. In addition to deodorizing the room, the vinegar will act as a mild disinfectant. *Use whatever scent you prefer, but lavender, peppermint, and citrus oils are excellent cognition-sharpening and mood-boosting choices.*

Ditch the deodorant. Why? Because most commercial brands are actually antiperspirants that (of course) prevent you from sweating—which happens to be one of your body's most effective means of eliminating toxins. So to minimize body odor and keep the detox channels open, simply rub a little white, malt, or apple cider vinegar on your underarm skin. The acid will change your skin's pH, thereby deactivating the odor-causing bacteria.

While everyone's natural aroma alters over the years, a sudden change in the body odor of an elderly adult can point to a major health problem. So when you're spending time with an elderly loved one, and you notice a sudden difference in breath or overall body odor, get medical help. For instance, breath that carries a fruity scent can signal diabetes, while breath that smells like ammonia can point to kidney disease. Beyond that, a general unpleasant body odor can arise if they've neglected basic personal hygiene—and that could indicate the early stages of dementia.

Keep tabs on the odor. Many factors can contribute to the permeating aroma that's often referred to as "old people smell." For example, medications, diet, an underlying illness, and incontinence issues can all play a role. One way to clear the air is to make a supply of odor-reducing tablets. Here's how: In a large bowl, mix 1 cup of baking soda, 1 tablespoon of pure vanilla extract, 20 drops of lemon essential, 10 drops of lavender essential oil, and 1/4 cup of distilled water. Press the dough firmly into a silicone ice cube tray or candy molds (if it's packed too loosely, it'll crumble). Let it dry thoroughly (8 to 12 hours), then pop the tablets out of the molds, and store them in an airtight container. Tuck them into trash cans, dresser drawers, linen closets, or anyplace else that unwanted odors linger.

Be ready for action. As we all know, an emergency can strike anyone at any time. But elderly people are especially prone to sudden trouble. So take a tip from the Boy Scouts and be prepared to respond at a moment's notice, whether you can reach the scene or not. Anytime you're on the go, with or without your loved one, take along a complete list of all her medications, her insurance information, and her doctors' phone numbers. And don't go anywhere without a roster of other important phone numbers, including (for example) her day-care establishment or resident caregiver and any transportation service she may use, as well as the numbers of neighbors, relatives, and anyone else who could help you out in a pinch.

Labor Saver

Don't simply program your loved one's essential data into your smartphone and leave it at that (see "Be ready for action," above). Remember that gadgets, especially small ones, are famous for vanishing or crashing just when you need them most. So play it safe: Type out all of this information on a computer, and reduce it to one or two wallet-size cards. Make several sets, and have them laminated. Then tuck one set into your wallet, purse, or pocket; stick another set in your glove compartment; and just for good measure, keep a spare set at home.

MAGICAL MUSCLE-RELIEF RUB

Most of us tend to equate sore muscles with exercise, injuries, or overuse of the affected body parts. But especially in elderly adults, other factors can trigger aches and pains. These include dehydration; blood-flow problems due to illness or lack of activity; or a deficiency of minerals like calcium, magnesium, and potassium. Whatever is causing the discomfort, a rubdown with this vintage liniment will ease it fast.

> **2 egg whites**
> **1/2 cup of apple cider vinegar**
> **3 tbsp. of olive oil**
>
> **12 drops of black pepper essential oil (optional)***

Mix all of the ingredients in a bowl. Massage the lotion into the painful areas, and wipe off the excess with a soft cotton cloth. Be careful not to get any on sheets, clothes, or upholstery fabric! *Black pepper oil is highly effective at stimulating blood flow and improving circulation.*

Mind the meds. One of the most important tasks for any caregiver is making sure that all medications are served up at the right times and in the right amounts. To avoid any mishaps, keep a current, dated copy of the list posted on the fridge. Make sure it shows the dosage amounts and times for all prescription and over-the-counter preparations as well as any vitamin and nutritional supplements. Don't forget to add phone numbers for the prescribing doctor(s) and pharmacy, and make it a point to replace the list with a new one as soon as any changes occur.

In most cases, DIY treatments work just fine to relieve muscle pain. But there are times when you need to get medical help. See a doctor ASAP if the onset of the pain followed the start or change of any medication; the pain lasts for more than three days, and home remedies aren't helping; there are any signs of poor blood circulation or infection in the sore area; or the pain is in the chest and radiates to the left arm or jaw.

Can the cramps. Anyone of any age can suffer from painful muscle cramps. But as older people lose muscle mass, the remaining tissue can get overstressed more easily and therefore tends to act up much more often. One beverage that can ease the discomfort is an 8-ounce glass of water with 2 teaspoons of apple cider vinegar and 1 to 2 teaspoons of raw honey mixed into it. Three servings total throughout the day should do the trick.

> When a muscle cramp strikes suddenly, drink (or serve your loved one) an 8-ounce glass of tonic water; the quinine should provide quick relief.

Bring 'em home safe. There are few more harrowing experiences than learning that a loved one who suffers from Alzheimer's disease has disappeared, either from home or from a care facility. Well, thanks to the Alzheimer's Association's Wandering Support program, roaming elders are much more likely to have a happy return. For an up-front charge, plus an annual renewal fee, the patient gets a MedicAlert® bracelet or pendant, and caregivers get access to a 24-hour search and rescue network. To learn more about Wandering Support, visit www.alz.org/help-support.

Don't let him leave without it. You say that your dad is in fine fettle physically, but as the old saying goes, he'd forget his head if it wasn't fastened to his neck? If he still ventures out on his own, make a list (in very large type) of everything he needs to take with him, and tape it to the door where he can't miss it as he leaves the house. It could include house keys, cell phone, eyeglasses, wallet, spare cash, and so on. And don't forget to add a reminder to lock the door on the way out!

Time Saver

To get faster action from aspirin, Tylenol®, or other over-the-counter pain relievers, take them in the form of liquid-gel capsules. The active ingredients will reach your bloodstream quicker than conventional tablets, which require more time to dissolve in your stomach.

INTERNAL MUSCLE-MISERY CHASER

This simple, tasty tonic works from the inside to reduce muscle soreness. It's highly effective used either in addition to or instead of the Magical Muscle-Relief Rub (see page 308), and it's just the ticket for delivering almost-instant relief on a hot summer day.

2 tsp. of apple cider vinegar   **8–10 oz. of cold water**
1 tsp. of raw honey (or more to taste)   **Sprig of fresh mint**

Mix the vinegar and honey in a tall glass of water. Bruise the mint sprig slightly, and swirl it around in the mixture. Then sit down, put your feet up, relax, and sip away your pain.

Organize for muscle safety. The golden rule for efficient storage is to keep the things you use most often in the area that's between your upper thighs and your shoulders. But for older adults whose strength is beginning to ebb, tapping into that prime real estate offers more than convenience. It can also help prevent muscle strains, or even serious injuries. So take the time to go through the house and relocate the things your loved one uses on a regular basis to that safe and sane territory.

Corral the documents. Also consider papers that you might have to get at quickly in the event of an emergency. Gather things like passports, wills, insurance policies, and powers of attorney into one secure, locked place. Not only will you be spared a possible "treasure hunt" during a highly stressful time, but you'll also help eliminate the possibility of identity theft by an intruder.

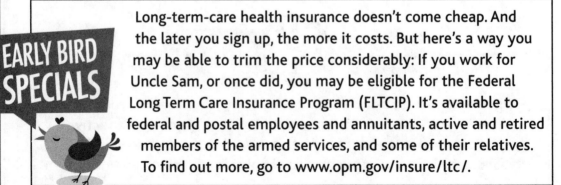

EARLY BIRD SPECIALS

Long-term-care health insurance doesn't come cheap. And the later you sign up, the more it costs. But here's a way you may be able to trim the price considerably: If you work for Uncle Sam, or once did, you may be eligible for the Federal Long Term Care Insurance Program (FLTCIP). It's available to federal and postal employees and annuitants, active and retired members of the armed services, and some of their relatives. To find out more, go to www.opm.gov/insure/ltc/.

Equip your vehicle. When you spend a lot of time driving an elderly person, even if it's only taking him to day care and back, all kinds of mini-disasters can cause mega-headaches. So head off trouble by stocking your car or van with just-in-case supplies like a first-aid kit; plenty of toilet paper, paper towels, and cleaning wipes; and disposable pads for sitting on. It's also a good idea to include a few extra pairs of underwear and an extra set or two of clothes.

Enlist household help. Asking dementia sufferers to help with simple chores is a great way to keep them occupied, as well as physically and mentally stimulated. The key to success is to choose jobs they can perform successfully so they feel like they're contributing to the household. One of the best tasks is folding washcloths or hand towels. Or another is to assign the same food-prep steps that young children enjoy, and can do safely. Tearing up salad greens or even cutting them with blunt-nosed scissors ranks high on this list. So does dumping ingredients into a large pot or bowl. A real winner is sorting forks, spoons, and butter knives (not sharp-bladed types!) into their containers.

It's a puzzle, all right. Here is a no-fail way to help keep an elderly loved one safely occupied and having fun: Print out a copy of their favorite photo, or maybe even a picture of a much-loved place or type of scenery, like a longtime favorite family vacation spot or a beautiful beach. Then laminate the photo and cut it into four puzzle-shaped pieces—or more, depending on the mental state of the future player. They will have a great time putting their beloved photo back together again.

Money Saver

Simple card games, using large-print playing cards, are favorite pastimes for people in the early stages of dementia. And for those folks whose hands have trouble grasping a full hand of cards, here's a no-cost way to solve that dilemma: Remove the cutting strip from a box that once held aluminum foil, plastic wrap, or wax paper. Then close the lid, and slip the cards into the slot between the flap and the side of the box. It works like a charm!

HAIR'S TO HEALTHIER HAIR BLEND

Conditions common in mature and elderly adults, including stress, anxiety, depression, and nutritional deficiencies, can lead to excessive hair fall and dry, brittle hair. To achieve a permanent fix, you need to resolve the underlying problem, but in the meantime, this nutrient-rich mixture can help your hair look thicker and glossier.

2 tbsp. of coconut milk   **1 tbsp. of apple cider vinegar**

1 tsp. of extra virgin coconut oil   **1 tbsp. of water**

Mix the coconut milk and oil in a bowl, then stir in the vinegar and water. Apply the mixture to your hair, making sure that all strands are covered from the roots to the tips. Put on a shower cap, and go about your business for 30 minutes or so. Then rinse with clear water, and dry and style your hair as usual. For the best results, repeat the process three times a week.

Produce photographic memory aids. To help aging adults recall what's inside various cupboards, drawers, or storage containers, photograph the contents, print the pics, and tape them to the outside of the receptacles. Or use pictures, clipped from magazines, that represent the general category of goods—for example, drinking glasses, pajamas, or towels.

ANTI-AGING MATTERS

Q: My mother uses a walker to get around and she's developed painful calluses in the palms of her hands from the constant pressure and rubbing. What's a good way to get rid of them?

A: Just mix 1 tablespoon of mashed avocado with 1 to 2 tablespoons of cornmeal to form a paste. Have your mother take the mixture in the palm of one hand and rub both hands together, working the gritty stuff into the calluses and around her fingers. Then rinse with warm water and pat dry. Repeat once or twice a week, and soon, her skin will be soft and smooth again. After that, a follow-up treatment every couple of weeks should keep the annoying bumps at bay.

Looks just like home! For folks who have been in the family home for decades, moving can be traumatizing. If you're helping elderly relatives relocate, here's how to make the transition a little easier: Before you change anything, photograph the inside of their current home. Then after the move, arrange their belongings in a way that's as similar as possible to the old style. Carry out the plan in as much detail as possible, from placing books on shelves and pictures on walls to arranging furniture. The closer you can come to duplicating the old setup, the sooner your loved ones will start to feel at home.

> When you're washing an elderly person's hair, prevent possible eye irritation by using a gentle, no-tears baby shampoo.

Sock it to sound sleep. As adults age, falling into a deep, health-giving sleep tends to take longer. But believe it or not, wearing socks or gloves, or both, to bed may speed things up. Many studies show that people fall asleep faster when their hands and feet are warm. That's because warm appendages cause your blood vessels to enlarge, which allows more heat to escape your body. This, in turn, lowers your body's core temperature faster and makes you nod off in as little as half the time it normally takes.

Check your meds. Sleep impairment in older adults is often caused by the side effects of a certain drug, or the interaction of several of them. So ask your (or your loved one's) doctor if a change in the medication lineup could pave the way to sounder, healthier shut-eye.

Labor Saver

Anyone who uses a walker or routinely watches the laborious process knows how difficult it is to carry anything from one room to another. Here's a nifty solution: Get a wicker bicycle basket (one that attaches to the handlebars), and hang it from the front bar of the walker. It'll hold a book, magazine, reading glasses, dog biscuits, sweater, or just about anything else the user needs to tote around.

A CALMING CAREGIVER COCKTAIL

When it comes to chronic stress, caring for aging loved ones ranks at the top of the ladder, whether you're on duty 24/7 in your own home or overseeing the action in a nursing home. At the end of the day, relaxing in an easy chair and imbibing this cocktail can put your cares on the back burner, at least for a while.

1–2 oz. of vodka	**1/4 oz. of triple sec**
1 oz. of cranberry shrub*	**Ice**
1 oz. of fresh-squeezed lime juice	**Lime twist (for garnish)**

Add all the ingredients to a cocktail shaker, and shake it. Strain the mixture into a stemmed cocktail glass, and garnish with a lime twist. Then sit back in a cozy chair, and feel the day's pressures fade away.
*You'll find the directions for this and other flavors on page 352.

Take a break! Caring for an elderly loved one may be rewarding, but it's also physically, mentally, and emotionally exhausting. So it's crucial to take a day off once in a while, even if it means calling in a substitute caregiver. Devote the whole day to yourself, doing whatever you find enjoyable and relaxing. Then, when stressful moments come up, think back to that quiet time. When those thoughts no longer rejuvenate you, it's time for another break!

HELP WANTED? When your parents or other elderly loved ones have been in their home for decades, helping them downsize for a move to smaller quarters can be a nightmare for all of you. If there was ever a time to call in a pro, this is it. And the place to find your hero is at the website of the National Association of Productivity & Organizing Professionals (www.napo.net). They can refer you to a specialist in your area who can help you make those often emotionally charged keep-it-or-leave-it decisions—and even help you organize the keepers at the new place.

Try a jarring trick. It may sound corny, but this stress- and anxiety-busting technique can be amazingly effective: Find a large jar or other container. Then every day write down something that makes you happy. It could be a joke, an amusing quotation, the title of a song that always starts you humming, or maybe just a beautiful sight or lyric—the sky's the limit! Tuck each scrap of paper into the container. Then, whenever you are feeling frazzled, sift through your happy thoughts and watch your anxiety level plummet!

Kill ANTS. No, not the annoying but mostly harmless insects. These ANTS are automatic negative thoughts that trigger anxiety and flood your body with stress hormones. And the process is a companion trick to the happy thoughts jar (see "Try a jarring trick," above). Whenever an ANT pops into your mind, write it down either in a notebook or, if you prefer, on a slip of paper that you toss into a container. Then a few weeks or more later (the time frame is your call), review your ANTS, try to figure out where they're coming from, and work out a plan to correct your negative thinking.

Money Saver

When you find yourself running out of steam long before the day is over, and you are tempted to reach for a caffeinated multi-hour energy drink, forget it. Instead, have a club soda with a squeeze of lime juice and a wedge of lime in it. The snappy fizz and light, citrusy aroma will perk you right up for a lot less money than you'd spend on one of those over-hyped drinks.

Save the sound. If an aged loved one is starting to lose his hearing, or you want to preserve your own as the years march on, this exercise can help: First, put on some melodic instrumental music, and turn down the volume to a sensible level. Then practice singling out a particular instrument—say, a clarinet or a flute. According to the experts at the American Academy of Audiology, performing this routine periodically will help you develop the ability to perceive more details in everyday sounds. The more your loved one does this, the longer their hearing will stick around to enjoy the sounds.

SPOTLIGHT ON YOU

Few things in life are more stressful than caring for a spouse, an elderly parent, or other relative—especially when you're coping with Alzheimer's disease or other cognitive impairment. So consider this section your personal tender loving, and possibly sanity-saving, tool kit.

FOCUS ON YOURSELF. The airline flight attendants make the point perfectly when they remind us to put on our own oxygen masks before helping others. After all, if you don't take good care of yourself, you can't do much for anyone else.

GET HELP—AND PLENTY OF IT. Don't be shy about asking relatives and friends to lend a hand whenever the need arises. And get as much professional support as your budget allows.

LEARN THE ROPES. In many communities, the Red Cross offers free classes on general caregiving skills, home safety, healthy eating, and legal and financial issues. To find your nearest local Red Cross branch, search for "family caregiving classes [your town]."

CONNECT WITH OTHER CAREGIVERS. As soon as you can, ask your local doctor's office, local hospital, or the Red Cross about caregivers, support groups. They provide an invaluable way to exchange tips and advice, and also to get backup for some of the hard decisions you'll have to make from time to time in the future.

CONSIDER ADULT DAY CARE. Even one or two days a week in the right setting can provide your loved one with more mental and physical stimulation than you can offer at home. Plus, it will give you time to run errands, do household chores efficiently, or simply get some much-needed R&R.

DO WHAT MOM ALWAYS TOLD YOU. Eat right, get a sound forty winks each night, don't smoke, and get plenty of fresh air and regular exercise. Even on days when all you can manage is a stroll around the block, it'll deliver a boost to your physical, mental, and emotional well-being.

STAY CONNECTED SOCIALLY. Having friendly, supportive people around you is crucial to good mental and physical health. Whether you volunteer in your community, join a bridge club, or take up a sport, the lift to your health and spirits will pay off in big dividends for you and your loved one.

CHAPTER 17

PROPER PET CARE

For the past 25 years, study after study has shown that pet owners generally feel happier, healthier, more independent, and more secure than folks who don't have an animal in the house. Older adults, especially, can benefit from the companionship and unconditional love all types of pets provide.

This chapter is a treasure trove of tips, tricks, and tonics that can help you take care of your pets and enhance the quality of your time spent together. As always, vinegar is front and center in the action. And if you are reluctant to adopt a pet because you or a family member has allergies, or you're starting to develop sensitivities to any of the pets that you have now, vinegar could save the day. It helps relieve allergy symptoms by cleaning out your lymphatic system and also by reducing the buildup of mucus. So for a daily Rx, follow this tip: Mix 3 teaspoons of apple cider vinegar in tall a glass of water, with or without honey added.

As in the case of children, there are specific guidelines to keep in mind when you are dosing pets with remedies that contain vinegar (see page 336). Likewise, you'll notice that essential oils are absent from this chapter. That is because individual animals can have very different reactions to these powerful substances. In particular, they can be extremely toxic to cats. If you feel the need to use essential oils on—or even diffuse them around—pets or livestock, first consult a holistic veterinarian and always err on the side of caution.

SUPER-SAFE DOG SHAMPOO

Many canine shampoos contain harsh chemicals that you really don't want on the four-footed members of your family. Enter this powerful, yet gentle, formula.

1 cup of pure dishwashing liquid*	**1 cup of warm water**
1 cup of vinegar	**2 oz. of vegetable glycerin**

Pour the dishwashing liquid into a large jar with a tight-fitting lid. Add the remaining ingredients and shake the container vigorously. Wet your dog down thoroughly, then pour the shampoo onto his coat, and rub it into his hair and skin. Rinse with clear water, then either dry the pooch thoroughly or follow up with a leave-in rinse (see Multitasking Tea Rinse for Dogs on page 320 and Soothing Winter Skin Rinse on page 322).
*Use a brand that is free of dyes and synthetic fragrances.

Dry-clean your cat. If your pet needs a bath but refuses to go near any body of water that's bigger than her drinking bowl, and there's no time for a visit to the groomer, look for help in your kitchen. Just rub cornmeal into Fluffy's fur, and brush it out. You'll have a squeaky-clean kitty with no hissy fits!

Get the better of burrs. The next time your dog or cat has a run-in with a bush full of burrs and prickles, pour a few drops of vegetable oil on the stickers, then gently comb them out. If any are left, add a bit more oil, and comb again.

HELP WANTED? If your pet hates to be bathed, don't press the issue. Trying to control even a small animal that's bouncing and wriggling can put undue strain on your aging joints and muscles. Instead, take Fido or Fluffy to a groomer, preferably one who comes highly recommended by pet-owning friends. For one thing, the best groomers are trained to work with reluctant bathers. Beyond that, though, most pets tolerate baths and other grooming procedures much more calmly when their human "parents" are not on the scene.

Stop that skunky smell. When your dog has a run-in with a skunk, you can find odor-removal formulas galore online and in pet-care books. But if you live in or are traveling to a place where your pooch stands a good chance of being sprayed, and you've reached the age when you want to solve problems with as little fuss as possible, forget DIY tricks. Instead, buy a commercial enzymatic product that's especially formulated to remove skunk odors. There are several highly effective brands available at hardware and pet-supply stores and online.

Soothe sore muscles with vim and vinegar. Just like us humans, the older your pooch gets, the more often and the harder the discomfort from the achy muscles or stiff joints is likely to strike. For quick relief, soak a soft cotton cloth or towel in warm (not hot!) apple cider vinegar, and apply that compress directly to the ailing body part, or as close to it as Fido will put up with, for five minutes or so. Repeat the process two or three times a day. But if you don't see any improvement within a few days, schedule an appointment with your vet.

Control your dog's weight. Excess pounds can cause the same problems in canines that they do in humans, including arthritis and similar, potentially disabling joint ailments. So feed your pup a healthy, natural food in the right amount for his size, and make sure he gets regular exercise. Long walks with you are ideal, so you'll both reap the anti-aging benefits.

Time Saver

Looking for some healthy pup-pleasing treats to calm him or her after a semi-traumatic event, like a bath? Just put 1/2 cup of finely chopped fruits or vegetables and 1/2 cup of plain yogurt in a blender, and puree them on high speed. Pour the mixture into ice cube trays. Tuck them into the freezer until treat time rolls around. **Note:** *Bananas rank high on the favorite-fruits list, and broccoli is a popular choice in the vegetable category. Avoid avocados, grapes, and onions, all of which are toxic to dogs.*

MULTITASKING TEA RINSE FOR DOGS

This tonic soothes itchy skin and restores its natural pH; calms welts, rashes, stings, and bites; and can help keep fleas, flies, and gnats at bay.

1/2 cup of apple cider vinegar   **1 cup of distilled water**
1/2 cup of brewed green tea, cooled

Mix all the ingredients in a nonmetallic container. After bathing your pooch, sponge the mixture onto his body, and massage it thoroughly into his skin, and pat dry. For the added benefit of bug-repelling action, let the rinse air-dry (weather permitting). **Note:** *You can also whip up this mixture ahead of time, refrigerate it in a glass jar for up to two weeks, and use it to spot-treat bug bites and stings. Just keep an eye on it and discard it if any signs of mold appear.*

Enhance Fido's coat from the inside. Simply adding some apple cider vinegar to your dog's food or drinking water can help deter fleas and improve the condition of his skin and hair. Start with a few drops, then gradually work up to a larger amount. The general recommendation is 1 teaspoon for every 40 pounds of body weight, but ask your veterinarian about the optimum dose for your pet.

EARLY BIRD SPECIALS

Many shelters waive their fees for older adopters, and veterinary clinics offer reduced-cost vaccinations and general care. Scads of pet-supply and feed stores and even some supermarket chains not only give senior discounts on food and gear, but also host periodic events that provide free or low-cost vaccinations and microchipping. At many pharmacies, those prescription discount cards you get in the mail are honored for your pets' medications as well as your own. Hundreds of local Meals on Wheels programs offer pet-care support and pet-food assistance to their homebound senior clients. The list goes on. Search for "senior pet-care resources" or "discounts." You'll be amazed at the results!

Infused vinegar "rides" again. The same vinegar that delivers major anti-aging benefits to your hair and scalp can do the same for your dog. In this case, a half-and-half mixture of water and either rosemary-, mint-, or lavender-infused vinegar helps control dandruff, calms skin problems, adds shine to Fido's coat, and helps to remove odor while issuing a "Keep away!" notice to fleas. Use it as an after-bath rinse as described in the Multitasking Tea Rinse for Dogs (at left).

Lemon aid for flea control. This flea-removal and deterrent method is equally effective and equally safe to use on dogs and cats. It's also super-simple, which can be a big plus if the passing years have reduced your patience for fussing with more complex formulas. All you need to do is slice a fresh lemon, and put the pieces in a heat-proof container (like a 16-ounce measuring cup). Then bring a pot of water to a vigorous boil, and pour it over the lemon. When it's cooled to room temperature, dip a flea comb into the brew, and run it through your pet's hair. You'll get the pests out while leaving a lingering scent of lemon that will keep them from coming back.

Deliver TLC with caution. When you use either lemon juice or vinegar as a topical treatment—alone or in a formula—be careful to keep it away from your pet's eyes and from any open sores or wounds. While it may not cause any permanent harm, it will sting like crazy!

Money Saver

If you think that the natural, ultra-premium dog and cat foods on the market today are a waste of money, think again. The best ones actually save you big bucks. How? Because they lack the non-nutritional fillers found in the common supermarket versions, your pet requires a much smaller quantity of the product. They also contain far more of the essential nutrients that pets need to stay at the peak of good health, thereby heading off trips to the vet and even sparing you the cost of ingredients for DIY treatments. But that's not all! Across the board, veterinarians will tell you that healthy dogs and cats are less likely to be plagued by fleas than their less robust counterparts are.

SOOTHING WINTER SKIN RINSE

Cold, dry winter air makes your dog's skin feel just as uncomfortable as yours does. This gentle rinse can help Rover feel a lot better.

1/4 cup of calendula flowers	**1/4 cup of yarrow**
1/4 cup of dill	**1 1/2 cups of apple cider vinegar**
1/4 cup of lavender buds	**1 cup of warm water**
1/4 cup of rose petals	

Put the herbs into a 1-quart canning jar, adding more as needed to fill it halfway. Heat the vinegar to a gentle simmer, then pour it over the herbs, adding more if needed. Let the mixture cool, strain out the solids, and stir in the water. After bathing your dog and rinsing him with clear water, pour the infused vinegar over him as a final rinse, and let it air-dry (indoors!). **Note:** *Use either fresh or dried herbs.*

When it's too late for tick prevention ... Mix 1 cup each of vinegar and mild dishwashing liquid per quart of warm water in a nonreactive container. Transfer the mixture to a plastic squeeze bottle, and apply it liberally to your dog. Massage it into his fur, and let it sit for five minutes. (If Rover is reluctant to sit still that long, keep rubbing for the duration.) Rinse thoroughly with warm water, and towel the pup dry. The whole blood-sucking gang should be goners.

To sterilize a plastic or glass bottle ... Pour boiling water into it, and let it sit for 10 minutes. Empty the bottle, let it cool, and pour in your chamomile tea (see the Labor Savor box, at right) or other DIY healer.

Whenever you use any shampoo or rinse on your pets, don't get any of it on their faces. Even the most gentle, natural formulas can irritate their eyes or ears. While the shampoo is unlikely to do any lasting harm, it could cause major discomfort for a dog or cat, and that's an all but guaranteed way to turn even the most laid-back critter into a die-hard bath hater.

Make a better bitter spray. Bitter apple sprays sell like hotcakes online and in pet-supply stores for a good reason: They're effective at keeping puppies (at least most of them) from teething on your furniture, shoes, and other stuff that you'd rather not sacrifice to those enthusiastic jaws.

But it's easy and a whole lot cheaper to make your own supply at home. Just mix 2 parts of apple cider vinegar with 1 part of white vinegar in a spray bottle, and spray away on any potential puppy targets. That should make your young Rover keep his distance.

Save your Christmas tree! And maybe have fun with your grandchildren at the same time. Many dogs, including those who are normally fastidious in the house, think that any tree is meant to be peed upon. That can include your Christmas tree. But the aroma of vinegar issues a total turnoff. To put that "Not here, my dear!" power to work in a festive way, dip coffee filters in some white vinegar, and let them dry. Then cut them into strips and form them into garlands. Or create snowflakes or other happy holiday shapes and hang them as individual ornaments. Either way, it's a good bet that Fido will give this privy a pass.

> When you've got a teething puppy, distract him from your belongings by giving him cold, raw, gum-soothing carrots to chew on.

Labor Saver

Chamomile has powerful disinfectant properties that can make quick work of canine rashes and minor skin irritations, without reducing the work of the beneficial bacteria that protect Rover's birthday suit. To keep relief on hand, make a strong batch of chamomile tea, pour it into a sterilized, new (not recycled) spray bottle, and stash it in the fridge. Then whenever the need arises, pull it out and spritz the chilled brew generously onto any red, raw, or itchy skin for an immediate soothing effect—with no sting, and no risk of collateral damage should the pup try to lick it off.

DANDY DOG EAR CLEANER

The all-star team in this tonic not only cleans your dog's ears, but also helps maintain a healthy pH that discourages ear infections. To head off trouble, use this cleaner at least every time you bathe your dog, or as needed to keep dirt at bay.

1/4 cup of vinegar (white or ACV)	**2 tbsp. of boric acid**
1/4 cup of water	**1 tbsp. of non-alcoholic witch hazel**

Mix the vinegar and water in a container that has a tight-fitting lid. Then add the boric acid and witch hazel, put the lid on, and shake well. Dip a cotton ball or a piece of practical cotton right into the solution (see the Money Saver box, at right), and gently wipe away the accumulated crud. Repeat the process using fresh cotton as needed until both ears are spotless. **Note:** *Never try to use a cotton swab to clean your dog's ears because you could easily puncture his eardrums.*

Timing is everything. While it is true that a dog's ears should definitely be cleaned every time he gets a bath, between-bath timing depends on the breed. Floppy-eared types, like cocker spaniels, beagles, and basset hounds, are highly prone to infections, and need to have their ears cleaned about once a week. Breeds with upright ears naturally stay drier, and so they're less susceptible to trouble. This means that dogs like German shepherds, corgis, and huskies can generally wait about two weeks or so between cleanings.

HELP WANTED? If you see any signs of redness and irritation or smell a foul odor while cleaning your dog's ears, or if the cleaning appears to be causing pain, stop immediately and call your vet. It's likely that an ear infection is at work. These maladies are very painful, and you'll need to get your pet started on antibiotics ASAP. Also, don't ever try to treat any infection with an ear cleaner—DIY or otherwise.

For weekly cleanings, think ultra-mild and ultra-simple.

The Dandy Dog Ear Cleaner (at left) is perfect for bath-time use, and for those occasions when you've waited a little too long and there's more buildup than usual. But if you've got a floppy-eared pooch whose ears need to be cleaned every week—or even more often during hot, humid weather—then use a gentler solution. Mix 1/3 cup of apple cider vinegar with 2/3 cup of lukewarm water, and have at it. Besides being easy on Rover's skin, it'll take next to no time for you to mix up. In fact, it's so simple to make that it's a great project for a grandchild who is interested in helping with your pet-care chores.

Flush the crud away. When dirt and wax have collected in your dog's ears, use a bulb syringe (like a turkey baster) to go after the stuff. And do the job outdoors if you possibly can. First, gently squeeze the cleaning solution into each ear, and lightly massage the base. Then let your pooch follow his natural instinct, which will be to shake his head like crazy to expel the foreign substance. When he's finished, all you'll need to do is wipe off any residue.

Money Saver

Instead of spending big money and the time it takes to buy bag after bag of little cotton balls to clean your pet's ears or apply DIY formulas or vet-prescribed topical meds, opt for a roll of practical cotton. It's widely available by that moniker at pet- and medical-supply stores online. Simply tear off as little or as much as you need, and proceed with the task at hand.

When a bee plants its stinger in your dog ... It causes every bit as much discomfort as it would for you. So spring into action fast. First, scrape the stinger out. (A credit card makes an ideal tool for this purpose, and it won't be harmed, so feel free to use a current one if that's all you have on hand.) Then make a solution of 1 teaspoon of Epsom salt per cup of warm water. Soak a soft, clean cloth in the liquid, and apply it to the sting site for 15 to 20 minutes to relieve pain and swelling. If the sting was on a foot, and Fido will sit still long enough, soak the afflicted paw in the solution instead.

CANINE TUMMY-TROUBLE TAMERS

Every dog on earth gets an upset stomach on occasion. While there are plenty of effective DIY remedies, even the simplest ones take a little time to prepare. But with a stash of these nuggets in your freezer, you can deliver soothing and tasty relief instantly.

2 lbs. of bones, cooked or raw (any kind, or a mixture)	**3 tbsp. of apple cider vinegar** **Distilled or filtered water**

Put the bones and vinegar in a slow cooker. Pour in enough water to cover the bones completely. Then turn on the machine and let the mixture simmer for 24 to 48 hours. Strain the contents through a sieve to remove all traces of skin or bones, then refrigerate the broth for 2 hours or so. Skim off the fat, pour the broth into silicone molds or ice cube trays, and place them in the freezer. When the need arises, give Fido a frozen cube or two as a treat, or let them melt so he can drink the broth. **Note:** *These are also perfect summertime treats.*

If you don't have a slow cooker... Or it's otherwise occupied, make Fido's broth in the oven instead. It takes a bit longer but works just as well. Just put the bones, vinegar, and water in a Dutch oven or covered casserole dish, and roast the mixture on the lowest heat for 24 to 48 hours. Then proceed as you would with the Canine Tummy-Trouble Tamers (above).

SAFE & SOUND Just like humans, dogs get an upset stomach at some point, and usually it's no big deal. But if your pup is also vomiting excessively or keeps throwing up for more than 24 hours, see your vet ASAP. This same guideline applies to diarrhea or constipation. Any of these symptoms can indicate that something serious is going on. It could be a condition like allergies or diabetes, or it could be that whatever Rover gulped down is blocking some internal passageways.

Make pill time treat time. If your dog hates taking pills, try these DIY pill pockets. Unlike most commercial versions, they are nutritious, delicious, inexpensive, and easy to make. To start, mix 2 tablespoons of peanut butter, 2 tablespoons of brown rice flour, and 1 tablespoon of coconut milk in a bowl. Form the dough into roughly 1-inch balls. Roll them in a little more flour, and set them on a tray covered with wax paper. Then push a soda straw about halfway into each ball to form a pocket. Pop the tray into the freezer for an hour or so, then store the firmed-up pockets in a covered container in the freezer or the fridge. If you freeze them, let them thaw for 20 minutes before "stuffing" and serving them to Fido.

Buy peanut butter with caution. When you buy peanut butter for your dog, check the label very carefully, and bypass anything that lists xylitol as an ingredient. It's extremely toxic to dogs and can even be fatal. What's more, its use as a low-calorie alternative to sugar is increasing. For the full lowdown on this and other substances that could harm your dog or cat, visit the website of the ASPCA's Poison Control Center at https://www.aspca.org/pet-care/animal-poison-control. In an emergency, at any time 24 hours a day, call (888) 426-4435.

Make pill pockets pussy-cat style. If your reluctant patient is a feline, use the same basic recipe above, but substitute low-sodium chicken broth for the coconut milk. And instead of peanut butter, use an equal amount of either canned pumpkin puree (not pie filling) or tiny bits of chicken or tuna.

Labor Saver

When a dog, cat, or visiting grandchild vomits on your carpet or hard flooring, cover the spot thoroughly with dried coffee grounds. Or in a pinch, use some ground coffee. Let it dry completely, then sweep up the mess. In addition to drying up the recycled food, the java will eliminate the odor. **Note:** *If you don't drink a whole lot of coffee, you might want to buy a big can or two of a cheap brand and keep it on hand for this and any other cleanup and odor-removal purposes.*

MUDDY PAW PRINT REMOVER

When Ruff leaves muddy "autographs" on your carpets or area rugs, don't reach for your cleaning gear. At least not immediately. Instead, cool your heels until the spots are dry before using this tonic.

2 cups of cool water   **1 tbsp. mild dishwashing liquid**
2 cups of white vinegar   **Baking soda**

Mix the water, vinegar, and dishwashing liquid in a spray bottle. Vacuum up as much dirt as possible, then lightly spritz the solution onto the soiled spots. Blot with a clean, dry towel, repeating as needed with fresh towels until you've lifted all the moisture from the carpet. Cover the area with a generous layer of baking soda, then vacuum it up—along with any remaining dirt.

When the pet pee meets the rubber... Reach for a tube of toothpaste. While it is true that rubber tile ranks at the top of the senior-friendly flooring list, it poses one challenge for pet owners: Urine can cause stains impossible to remove with conventional cleaning methods. So when your pet has an accident, think outside the box. Apply a generous layer of white (not gel) toothpaste. Let it dry for 10 to 15 minutes, then wash it off with warm water. Repeat until the marks are gone.

ANTI-AGING MATTERS

Q: Now that I'm in my mid-sixties and recently widowed, I've thought about getting either a kitten or an adult cat for some company. Do you have any advice on that score?

A: First, bear in mind that cats often live well into their teens and sometimes early twenties. If you don't feel comfortable making that kind of commitment, I'd suggest adopting an older animal from a shelter or rescue group. An adult is also your best bet if you lack the patience to put up with a kitten's curious nature and high-speed antics—or if you have young grandchildren who visit frequently. Kittens are fragile, and kids under age six usually can't handle them safely.

Shine light on the scene. After you've finished cleaning pet urine from a carpet, shine a UV pet urine spotter light (available online) on the area. Sometimes, the urine can crystallize and leave minute particles clinging to the carpet fibers. Especially if your sense of smell is beginning to decline, as it normally does after age 50, you may think the area is pristine. But the spotter will show you the whole "crime scene" so you can go back and attack what's left. This time, try using a commercial enzyme-based cleaner that's specially formulated to break down all the biochemicals in their waste product so that your pet will no longer be able to smell the enticing residue.

> When you accidentally clip a pet's toenail too short, dab the bleeding end with cornstarch to speed clotting and ease the pain.

Don't get cross at kitty! When your previously picky cat starts peeing in all the wrong places, don't be too quick to blame her. Instead, schedule an appointment with your vet ASAP because her behavior may signal a health problem. It could be a minor matter, like food allergies, parasitic worms, or impacted anal glands. Or it could be a potentially life-threatening condition, like tumors, bladder infections, or kidney failure.

Deep-clean the bathroom. Some cats only use a pristine litter box. If you forget to clean yours on a regular basis, that could be the root of kitty's problem. To freshen up the scene, remove and dispose of the old litter. Then pour 1/2 inch of white vinegar into the box, and let it sit for 15 minutes or so. Pour out the vinegar, then rinse and thoroughly dry the pan. Sprinkle the bottom generously with baking soda, and add fresh litter. That very well might put your pussycat back on track!

Money Saver

Cats get the same anti-aging benefits from exercise that we humans do, and some of the best workout equipment is stuff that's usually destined for the trash can. Try giving your feline an empty toilet-paper roll or a plastic pill bottle with a few dried beans or buttons inside.

FELINE FLEA & TICK REPELLENT

Many all-natural flea- and tick-fighting substances that are perfectly fine for dogs are toxic to cats. Not only is this formula 100% safe, but it also helps improve the health of Fluffy's hair and skin.

- **1 tbsp. of dried catnip**
- **1 tbsp. of dried lavender buds**
- **1 tbsp. of dried neem leaves**
- **1 tbsp. of dried peppermint leaves**
- **2 cups of apple cider vinegar**
- **1 tbsp. of pure aloe vera gel**
- **Filtered or distilled water**

Put the herbs in a glass jar. Heat the vinegar until it's slightly warm, and pour it over the herbs. Cover the jar with a non-metallic lid, and set it in a dark place at room temperature for two weeks, shaking it daily. Strain the mixture through cheesecloth or a coffee filter into a clean jar, and store it at room temperature. To make the repellent, combine 1/2 cup of the infused vinegar and the aloe vera gel in a spray bottle that has a fine-mist setting, and fill the remainder with the filtered or distilled water. As you groom your cat, spray the potion onto her hair, rub it in, and let it air-dry. Or dab the mixture on with a soft cloth.

Blast the cat fat. When Fluffy seems to be packing on too many pounds, one way to take care of the situation in a safe and gradual way is to add 1 teaspoon of apple cider vinegar to her drinking water twice a day. But just to play it safe, check with your vet before you start this or any other DIY health routine.

HELP WANTED? Because ticks can spread so many vile diseases, it's always wise to see your vet for blood tests after your dog, cat, or horse has been bitten. This is especially the case if you live in Lyme disease territory because its symptoms, like joint stiffness, swelling, lameness, loss of appetite, and lethargy, may not appear until several months after the bite. This same cautionary approach applies to you if you're a bite victim. Bites can be especially dangerous for older adults—and older pets.

Use the ultimate tick repellent. Folks who live, work, and/or play in tick territory swear by old-fashioned pine tar soap as the most effective tick repellent that ever came down the pike. It also turns off many other kinds of insects, and is perfectly safe to use on adults, children, and pets. Plus, it smells just like a Christmas tree! You can put this stuff to work in two ways: Mix 1 tablespoon of the soap (either liquid or shavings from a bar) per cup of warm water in a spray bottle, and spritz your clothes, your skin, and Rover's hair. Or simply use it in the shower, as you would any other soap, or even bathe your pup with it. Whichever method you choose, it'll keep you and yours free from ticks all day long. Pine tar soap is available at health-food stores and online.

Use the candy-cane approach. Another highly effective, time-honored tick repellent calls for some Dr. Bronner's liquid peppermint soap (available online and at health-food stores). Mix 1 tablespoon of the soap per cup of water in a spray bottle. Then before you and your dog head into potential tick territory, spritz your clothes, your skin, and Rover's hair (being careful not to get any in his eyes). It works like a charm and young grandchildren love it because its candy-cane aroma reminds them of Santa.

Time Saver

Fleas are attracted to light, and that gives you a no-fail, almost effortless way to wipe them out by the zillions. Fill the lid from a cottage cheese or yogurt container with soapy water, and set it under a night-light that you've plugged into a wall outlet. The tiny beasties will hop into the water and drown. Depending on the size of the blood-sucker population, a single trap might do the trick, or you might want to make several and distribute them around your house.

Vinegar strikes again. Simply adding unprocessed apple cider vinegar to your dog or cat's diet can help repel fleas and ticks. It creates an internal environment that discourages the blood-sucking menaces. And it also boosts the critters' immune system, thereby helping them fend off external parasites, and almost every disease under the sun.

Y'ALL COME HORSEFLY TRAPS

Horseflies do more than make life miserable for our equine pals. They can also spread internal and external parasites, as well as numerous diseases. You can buy commercial traps to snag the demons, but these DIY versions work just as well and at a fraction of the cost.

1/2 cup of apple cider vinegar	**Water**
1/2 cup of sugar	**2-liter plastic bottle**
1/2 cup of syrup*	**Duct tape**

Cut off the top quarter of the bottle, maintaining a straight line all the way around. Pour the vinegar, sugar, and syrup into the bottom portion of the bottle. Then fill it about halfway up with water, and stir thoroughly. Invert the top of the bottle, and fit it inside the bottom to create a funnel. Seal the pieces together using duct tape. Set a trap in each enclosed area where the flies linger. They'll zoom in to get the cocktail inside and they won't get out. *You can use either corn syrup or cheap pancake syrup.*

Kill horseflies on the fly. Or on a barn wall. Fill a spray bottle with a mixture of 2 parts white vinegar and 1 part water, and add a squirt or two of dishwashing liquid. Shake the bottle, then take aim and pull the trigger. Any flies you hit will be dead ducks.

Labor Saver

To discourage horse-hounding pests from the inside out, simply add a half-and-half mixture of apple cider vinegar and water to your steed's feed. The recommended daily dose is 1/4 to 1/2 cup. As with any changes to the menu, start with just a tablespoon or so and work up to the full amount slowly—ideally over a two-week period. Regular consumption of vinegar causes higher levels of thiamine (vitamin B1) to be excreted through the steed's skin, and that discourages all kinds of biting insects, including flies, ticks, and mosquitoes.

Hair's to easy horse care. Believe it or not, the same product that keeps your hair sleek and shiny can perform similar feats for your horse. To detangle his mane and tail, just rub a little hair conditioner through the strands, and comb as usual. When you want to shine his hooves (maybe to get ready for a parade or a show), rub on a dollop of conditioner, and buff with a soft, clean cloth.

Horse around. Holistic equine vets and experienced horsemen alike swear by unprocessed apple cider vinegar as an all-around health tonic, and for good reason: It delivers all the same benefits to horses as it does to us humans. The Rx for a healthy horse: 1/4 cup of the vinegar that's mixed with an equal amount of water, added to Dobbin's feed grain once a day. Thanks to the potassium and trace minerals in apple cider vinegar, this tonic is especially helpful for pregnant mares and for older horses with arthritis or digestive trouble.

Forestall the stones. Mineral masses called enteroliths can cause some serious intestinal blockages in horses. They are becoming more common, especially in California and throughout the Southwest. But studies show that horses who ingest vinegar regularly, in either their food or water, are much less likely to develop stones. A great starting point is 1/4 cup a day, but if you live in the danger zone and/or have an Arabian or a Morgan horse (both high-risk breeds), ask your vet to recommend the optimum dose for your steed.

Q: I've always loved horses and longed to ride, but never had the time or the spare cash—until now. I'm almost 60, but in good health. Is it too late to start?

A: Not at all! In fact, all over the country, many stables offer classes for folks in their fifties, sixties, and beyond who have never ridden before, or who rode as youngsters but drifted away from it over the years. In fact, riding is one of the best forms of exercise for older adults because it strengthens your muscles and also improves your balance, thereby helping prevent falls. But it also has been proven to keep your mind sharp and help prevent memory loss. So go for it!

ANTI-AGING MATTERS

FLEE, FLIES! SPRAY

In equine circles, this ultra-simple blend has gained fame far and wide for its ability to repel horseflies from people and four-legged critters of all kinds. And it's perfectly safe to use even on foals.

1 part bath oil   **1 part white vinegar**
1 part water

Mix all the ingredients in a spray bottle. Spritz your vulnerable animal pals and yourself. For good measure, spray or wipe the mixture onto barn walls and other interior surfaces. Now for the "fine print": Do not use this, or any other spray, on animals' faces. Instead, gently dab it on, being very careful not to get any in their eyes. Avoid your own face, too. You can cover that area by treating your hat. Also, before you pull the trigger on your clothing, test a hidden area of the fabric to check for colorfastness or staining.

Get the blues. Correction: Buy some bluing if you have a white dog, or maybe a horse with a white mane and tail. To make that hair sparkle like new-fallen snow, simply wash and rinse your pal as usual, then add 2 or 3 drops of bluing to a quart of water, and comb the solution through his hair as a final rinse. **Note:** *You can find this old-time laundry aid in supermarkets and online.*

SAFE & SOUND

When using vinegar for topical purposes, the type to choose depends on the color of your pet's fur. Always apply white vinegar to a white or light-colored dog, cat, or horse because the apple cider variety could stain pale hair. Conversely, since white vinegar can bleach dark-colored fur, go with apple cider vinegar for black or other dark tones. If your pal sports large, individual patches of white and dark colors, simply use the appropriate type of vinegar to spot-treat problems like hot spots and insect bites. For whole-body rinses and baths, avoid vinegar altogether unless you have no other remedy at hand.

Give hairballs the heave-ho. These are natural by-products of a cat's self-grooming process, when loose hair is caught on the sharp, backward-facing barbs of the feline tongue, then swallowed. While there are a number of foods that target hairball prevention, the active ingredient in all of them is something you can easily add to your kitty's diet on your own—namely fiber. One of the best is canned pumpkin (not pumpkin pie filling!). A teaspoon or so each day should keep the hair moving smoothly.

After you've tossed Fido's plastic bowls, dab coconut oil onto his acne; if you don't see improvement within a few days, call your vet.

Keep your dog's nose on the job. When a canine schnoz becomes dry and cracked, it gets uncomfortable and ceases to function at its peak. Given the fact that dogs interpret the world mainly through their sense of smell, that can lead to stress and behavioral issues. Allergies, overexposure to the sun, and sleeping or lounging too close to a heater can all dry out that sniffer. While short-nosed breeds, like Boston terriers, bulldogs, and pugs, are most prone to the problem, it can befall any dog. To head off trouble, deliver rich moisture at the first hint of dryness. The best way to do that is to rub a drop or two of coconut oil onto the skin of the nose.

Nix the zits. Just like people of all ages, dogs and cats can get acne and it happens most often to those who eat out of plastic food bowls. That's because bacteria that build up in the scratches make the critters' skin break out. So switch to ceramic or stainless steel bowls. That just might solve the problem lickety-split.

Money Saver

If you live near a veterinary school, you can get excellent care at a much lower cost than you'd pay at one of the ultra-fancy clinic chains, and probably with a senior discount to boot. Plus, if your pet has a serious problem that new, high-tech surgery might cure, a vet school's docs will sometimes operate for next to nothing in the interest of research.

THE PET-CARE FINE PRINT

While it's true that vinegar is one of the most potent healers on the planet, for both people and pets, there are some important points you need to keep in mind. Here's the breakdown:

CHOOSE THE RIGHT STUFF. When you use apple cider vinegar for internal health-care purposes, always give your pets and livestock the same raw, organic, unfiltered apple cider vinegar that you'd use for human consumption.

PROCEED WITH CAUTION. If your cat, dog, or horse is getting along in years, has sensitive health, is taking medications of any kind, or is pregnant, check with your vet before using any vinegar treatments—even topically.

DIAL THE DOC. Any dosages recommended in this chapter are estimates based on average weights. Many other factors can influence the optimum dose for any individual critter. So, ask your vet how often you should give vinegar to your pal and in what amounts. (The same goes for herbs.)

DO NOT PUT VINEGAR IN WATERING TROUGHS. The acid will eat away at the metal and leach dangerous chemicals into the water. Use plastic tubs or buckets when adding vinegar to drinking water for horses or other livestock.

KNOW WHEN TO SAY WHEN. If your pet shows any adverse reactions to vinegar, go cold turkey *immediately* and ask your vet for alternate options.

BE CAREFUL WHAT YOU SPRAY INDOORS. If you use vinegar as an indoor critter repellent, either straight or mixed with water, always take these two precautions: Use *only* white vinegar for this purpose. Apple cider vinegar could stain the material you're trying to protect. So before you spray, test for colorfastness by spritzing a hidden spot, like the back side of a sofa skirt or drapery hem.

USE EXTREME CAUTION AROUND BIRDS. When vinegar is heated, it produces fumes that are toxic to birds and can even be fatal. So if you heat vinegar on the stove or nuke it in the microwave, add it to a dishwashing cycle, or use it to clean a coffeemaker, keep your winged wonder(s) out of the room, far away from the action.

CHAPTER 18

CRAFTS & GIFTS

In this final chapter, we focus on two topics that you may not think of as having a senior-centric connection: crafts and gifts. Well, think again, friends. Without exception, health and wellness gurus tell us that two factors are key to living longer and better: staying both mentally and physically active and maintaining strong social ties. Practicing an art or craft (or a number of them) benefits your mind and keeps your body moving. Dipping your toes into the creative waters can even lead to a new second-prime career. As for the gift angle, there are few better ways to say "You matter to me" than to present a friend or family member with something you've made with love and care.

As you know by now, vinegar plays a huge part in all the fun. In fact, it can help you make a fabulous, all-but-instant gift. I'm referring to fortified vinegar: a thickened blend of vinegar mixed with herbs, spices, fruits, and/or vegetables. You whip it up in a blender or food processor and use it as a dip, salad dressing, or topping for anything from meat and pasta to your favorite desserts. Fortified vinegar also gives you a sneaky way to ensure the picky eaters in your life (like young kids or elderly parents) are eating more essential fruits and vegetables.

Here's just one ultra-easy fortified vinegar: Mix 2 cups of fresh strawberries, 1 cup of sugar, and 1/2 cup of balsamic vinegar in a blender. Then pour the mixture into an attractive, sterilized bottle. By itself, it makes a welcome gift for any occasion. But if you go one step further and pair it with, let's say, a pound cake or a carton of ice cream, you'll be the hit!

SUPER-SAFE CRAFT GLUE

This great waterproof glue can be used on leather, paper, and fabrics. It's made from food-safe ingredients, so it's safe for grandchildren and pets to be around.

6 tbsp. of water

2 envelopes of unflavored gelatin (2 1/2 tsp. total)

2 tbsp. of white vinegar

2 tsp. of glycerin

Bring the water to a boil. Remove the pan from the heat, and stir in the gelatin until it's dissolved. Add the vinegar and glycerin, and mix thoroughly. Use a brush to apply the glue while it's still warm. When you're finished, store any remaining mixture in a tightly sealed jar at room temperature. It will gel after a few days, so before the next use, set the jar in a pan of hot water to warm it up.

Make the ultimate in safe paste. Flour and water glue (a.k.a. wheat paste) is not only perfectly edible, albeit not very tasty, but it's also harmless to furniture upholstery or any other surfaces. It's ideal for paper, cardboard, and light-weight fabric. To make it, just mix 1 part all-purpose flour with 2 parts water in a bowl, adding more of each as needed to reach a pancake-batter consistency. Store the paste in a covered container in the fridge, and use it within three to four days.

ANTI-AGING MATTERS

Q: I do a lot of hand sewing and cross-stitch embroidery, and now that my hands are less steady than they once were, I keep fraying the end of the thread as I try to get it through the needle's eye. Is there a simple way to solve the problem— short of getting a needle-threading device, which I've tried but keep losing?

A: Yep! This trick couldn't be simpler: All you need to do is stiffen the end of the thread or embroidery floss with a spritz of hair spray before you thread your needle. It should work like a charm every time.

Keep your embroidery colors in their place. Before you start a cross-stitch, crewelwork, or other embroidery project using cotton thread, soak the skeins in white vinegar for a few minutes. Then let them air-dry. This will set the dye and should prevent any fading or running when your creation is washed.

Snag the right ribbon—fast. If you use a lot of ribbon in craft work, or even to wrap presents, it's not always easy to find the color and width that you need at the moment you need it. For the simple and time-saving solution, store your collection on an upright paper towel holder. You'll be able to instantly spot the ribbon you want and pull out as much as your project requires without moving a single spool.

If you are a seamstress, delight a granddaughter by turning your fabric scraps into dollhouse curtains, slipcovers, tablecloths, and wall coverings.

Make a trash-to-treasure art medium. As strange as it may seem, you can cook up a fine modeling clay from dryer lint. Simply put 1 1/2 cups of the stuff in a saucepan, add 1 cup of water, and let it sit until the lint is saturated. Add 1/2 cup of all-purpose flour, and stir until the mixture is smooth. Add 2 to 3 drops of food coloring, if you like. Cook the mixture over low heat, stirring constantly until it holds together and you can form peaks with the spoon. Pour it out onto a cutting board and let it cool. Then it's time for the creative juices to flow. When the masterpiece is finished, let it dry for anywhere from three to five days.

Money Saver

Cooking up DIY modeling clay isn't the only way you can put dryer lint to work in the art-supply field. It also makes a fine—and absolutely free—filling for homemade toys or pillows (either full-size or doll-size, depending on how much lint you have on hand or care to save up).

TISSUE PAPER PAINT

In this case, the tissue paper is the paint with a little help from vinegar. It's a fun way for children or crafty grandparents to produce paintings, cards, wrapping paper, or even decorative coverings for storage boxes.

Brightly colored, non-colorfast tissue paper

White construction paper

White vinegar

Soft paintbrush

Cut out whatever shapes you desire from the tissue paper. Just make sure the images are simple enough to handle without falling apart. Next, brush vinegar all over the white paper, and immediately lay the tissue-paper shapes on top. As the vinegar dries, the tissue paper will fall off, leaving a colorful design behind.

Choose your "paint" with care. For best results, buy your tissue paper from an art- or craft-supply store, and be sure to tell the staff what you intend to do with the stuff. The type that's intended for gift wrapping (which is what you generally find in card shops and major retail stores) is colorfast, or close to it. To test it, run the paper between your fingers; if it has a light waxy feel, it's not worth beans for painting purposes.

Transfer the tools of your trade to a toolbox. It's perfect for corralling all the gear that can make a sewing box or craft-supply drawer look like an earthquake hit it. Just assign all the little odds and ends to separate compartments in the box. That way, it'll be a snap to find exactly what you need.

In this case, the help you want is a secure, locked cabinet where you can store your craft supplies. That's because many of the tools and materials that you use on a regular basis can be deadly for a small child or pet. The no-no list includes needles, pins, beads, buttons, scissors, bottles of paint or dye, and anything else that's small enough to swallow, sharp enough to cut, or enticing enough to drink.

Try another pizzazzy painting ploy. This is another technique that's fun for grandchildren, but works just as well for DIY grown-up greeting cards. In artistic circles, it's called wax-resist or wax-relief painting, but it's a lot simpler than that jargon makes it sound. All you do is draw a design with a white crayon, or even a white candle, on a sheet of white paper. Then paint over the paper with watercolors. When the paint dries, the wax outline will show through.

Bag this crafty idea. To make a one-of-a-kind wastebasket, grab a brown paper grocery bag, and paint designs on it, or cover it with pictures cut out from magazines or wrapping paper. Spray on a couple coats of clear acrylic enamel, both inside and out, and presto: It's a piece of functional art! These are terrific gifts for kids to make for their parents or teachers. But they're also showing up, more and more, in upscale craft galleries.

Give 'em fun and fancy soap. There's probably not a child or grown-up on your gift list who wouldn't get a kick out of receiving this colorful, festive soap. It's also a lot of fun to make. All you need

Time Saver

Even a white crayon can leave nasty marks on clothing or upholstered furniture. When that happens in the heat of the artistic action, simply brush the wayward streaks away with an old toothbrush dipped in white vinegar. The marks will simply vanish.

to do is grab a bowl, and mix 1 cup of grated floating soap (like Ivory); 4 to 6 drops of food coloring; 2 or 3 drops of flavored, scented extract; and 1/4 cup of warm water. Stir until the mixture starts to stiffen. Remove it from the bowl, and knead it until it reaches the consistency of very thick dough. Spoon the mixture into silicone molds or cookie cutters (the kind that are open on both sides). Press the dough firmly, smoothing the top with a knife to eliminate any air pockets. Set the filled molds in the freezer for 10 minutes. Then pop the soaps out of the molds, and let them dry until they're hard. Pack them in a decorative tin or glass storage jar. Or, to use large cookie-cutter versions in Christmas stockings or Easter baskets, simply tie colorful ribbon around each one. **Note:** *Good aromatic extract options abound, but you can't go wrong with vanilla, orange, cinnamon, or peppermint.*

STATE-OF-THE-ART EASTER EGGS

This method takes egg dyeing to a whole new level. But it's easy enough that toddlers can turn out masterpieces (with a little help from Grandma).

White vinegar

Hard-boiled eggs

Cool Whip® or shaving cream

Food coloring

Pour the vinegar into a bowl that's large enough to hold your eggs. When they're cool enough to handle, submerge them in the vinegar, and let them sit for 20 to 30 minutes. Spread the Cool Whip or shaving cream in a shallow baking dish, and dribble the food coloring over the surface. Use a blunt knife to swirl the colors. Set an egg into the mixture, and use a spoon to roll it once, completely covering it. Repeat with each egg, then let them all sit for 10 to 45 minutes to absorb the color. Rinse with cool water, and dry with paper towels.

Turn out the fanciest Easter eggs in town. This year, why not fill your family's baskets with hen fruit that'll knock their socks off? Start by collecting an assortment of tiny leaves and flowers. Then round up some old nylon stockings or panty hose, and make up some standard dye using vinegar and food coloring (see the Time Saver box, at right). Press a leaf or flower flat up against a hard-boiled egg, wrap a piece of panty hose around it, and tie it tight with string. Dip the egg into the dye, keep it there until it reaches the color intensity you want, then pull it out. Let the egg dry inside the panty hose, cut away the fabric, and presto: a one-of-a-kind egg designed by you!

If you intend to eat your Easter eggs, use Cool Whip when you dye them and they will be perfectly edible. Likewise, use Cool Whip if there is even a remote chance that one of your young helpers might take a taste of the dyeing medium or a lick of a drying egg. Otherwise, just go with the cheapest shaving cream you can find—any kind will work nicely.

The key to artistic success... Is to limit the palette to two or three colors. Otherwise, you'll end up with less vibrant, even muddy-looking, eggs. This approach also gives you a great opportunity to teach your grandchildren a lesson in basic color theory. Specifically, yellow and blue come together to make green. Blue and red become purple. Red and yellow will mix into a variety of lively orange tones.

To cushion the goodies in a grown-up's Easter basket, line the bottom with crumpled paper, and top it with sturdy blooms like roses or carnations.

Make the rubber meet the eggs.

Here's yet another way to turn out knock-their-socks-off Easter eggs. Just gather up some rubber bands of various widths, and wrap them around each egg before you dip it into the dye. The finished product will come out with stripes or diamond patterns. Best of all, it'll be a one-of-a-kind creation because no matter how hard or how many times you try, you will never be able to get the rubber bands in exactly the same spots each time.

Give your baskets air-cushioned linings. Instead of the same old plastic grass, cushion the grandkids' eggs and candy with little blown-up balloons. The 5-inch dart balloons sold at game-supply and toy stores are perfect. For good measure, tuck in a set of blunt-tipped safety darts. That way, after the baskets are empty, you can pin the balloons to a wall-hung board and the kids can use them for their "official" purpose.

Time Saver

When you have an Easter egg hunt planned for your grandchildren, color your hen fruit with food coloring and vinegar. The basic formula is 1 tablespoon of white vinegar and 1/4 teaspoon of food coloring per 3/4 cup of hot water. Then you simply dip a hard-boiled egg into the mixture, wait until it reaches the shade you want, and pull 'er out.

FOUND-FURNITURE GRIME REMOVER

"Upcycling" furniture is a rapidly growing hobby among older adults. The process often starts with a piece that's been sitting around so long it's covered in a thick layer of grimy dirt. This extra-strength formula will clean it up like new without harming the finish underneath.

1 cup of ammonia	**2 tbsp. of baking soda**
2/3 cup of white vinegar	**Warm water**

Dissolve the ammonia, vinegar, and baking soda in a bucket of warm water. Then pull on sturdy rubber gloves, grab a sponge or towel, and scrub-a-dub-dub. When your treasure is as clean as a whistle, rinse with clear water, and dry thoroughly with a soft, clean towel. **Note:** *This formula is also just the ticket for sprucing up any wood, indoors or out, that's gone too long between cleanings. Just as a warning, the mixture does have an unpleasant aroma. Thankfully, it'll vanish once you've rinsed the cleaner away.*

Get the joints jumping. To loosen old glue around joints of a table or chair that you're upcycling or simply repairing, apply some white vinegar with a plastic squirt bottle. Or if you need to get the vinegar into the joint itself, use a glue syringe (available online, at hardware stores, and in woodworking shops). These handy tools come with extension tips that are close to needle-thin, so they can reach into even the tightest spaces.

Labor Saver

Whether you're taking up the furniture-makeover game as a hobby or a second career, or you're simply sprucing up a few pieces for your new retirement quarters, one of the most work-saving tools you could ever ask for is the same one you use to clear ice and snow from your car's windows. That plastic blade is also just the ticket for removing dried paint splatters from wood or other easily scarred surfaces.

Liven up old leather. You say you'd like to stack some vintage leather suitcases to make an end table with storage space inside, but the valises you've found are looking worse for wear? No problem! Just mix 1 cup of vinegar with 2 cups of linseed oil in a jar with a tight-fitting lid, and shake it until the mixture reaches the consistency of cream. Rub it into the leather using a soft, clean cloth, and polish with a second cloth. Those old travelin' bags will be all set for their new career in the clutter-corralling business.

Create some class-act clay. It is safe enough for small children to use, but lasts long enough to please serious crafters. To make it, mix 4 cups of all-purpose flour and 1 cup of iodized salt in a large bowl. Stir in 1 3/4 cups of warm water. Then turn the mixture out on a bread board, and knead the lump until it's the consistency of bread dough. Add more flour, or more water if you need to. Store the clay in a sealed container, and use it to make sculptures, Christmas tree ornaments, or jewelry. Air-dry your creations (drying time will vary with the size of each piece), and decorate them with acrylic paint if you like. **Note:** *If you prefer to tint the clay itself, just mix food coloring into the dough before you knead it.*

Pack a present in a present.
The next time you send a fragile gift through the mail, like art you've made with your own homemade clay (see "Create some class-act clay," above), forget about filling the box with foam packing "peanuts." Use real peanuts instead. They'll cushion the contents as well as the fake type and the recipient can enjoy eating them afterwards.

Q: For a post-retirement career, a friend suggested turning my hobby of refinishing and decorating furniture into a business. Do you think this is a viable option?

A: Absolutely! In fact, "upcycling," as it's called in interior design circles, has become a popular second-prime venture for retired folks with a creative flair. In short, the process entails finding a down-at-the-heels piece of furniture and giving it either a decorative face-lift or a whole new purpose (like turning an old hutch into a stylish bar). There's a growing market for these pieces among young professionals who lack the time or inclination to do the work themselves.

ANTI-AGING MATTERS

WEATHERED-WOOD STAIN

Many commercial products can give a rustic, time-worn look to new wood, but they can't beat this DIY version. It's great for craft projects, planters, furniture, or even natural-wood floors or paneled walls.

6 fine-grade steel wool pads　　　**1 gal. of white or apple cider vinegar**
3–6 cups of coffee grounds (optional)　Large bucket with a lid

Put the steel wool pads in the bucket, and top them with the coffee grounds if desired. Pour in the vinegar, pop the lid on the bucket, and let it sit until the solution reaches the shade you want. The longer you wait, the darker the stain will be, so check it every day or so. When the color finally reaches the shade you want, give the concoction a quick stir and strain it to remove any solids. Then simply brush the stain onto your wood in the usual way.

Words to the wise about weathered-wood stain. Even for a small project, wear gloves and expendable clothes, and thoroughly cover your work surface because this stuff will stain anything it touches. For that reason, it's best to work outdoors if possible. Once the stain has dried, you can rinse it or not, as you prefer. Rinsing will remove any rusty residue from the steel wool, but it will also slightly lighten the color of the end product.

HELP WANTED? Some folks get major satisfaction from stripping a few coats of old paint or varnish from a piece of furniture, and there are nontoxic products on the market that make the process easier and safer than it once was. But if your mature system is sensitive even to new paint-removal formulas, don't try doing the project yourself. Instead, call a professional refinisher—preferably one recommended by a friend or an antique dealer. Whatever you do, avoid dip-stripping operations. They are extremely hard on furniture, and are especially notorious for causing joints to come unglued and veneer to loosen.

Age wood with no work. And no mess. If you lack the patience to fuss with mixing up stain to make your wood look weathered, don't do it. Instead, let Ol' Sol do the job for you. Just as your skin changes color when it's exposed to direct sunlight, so do many types of wood. For example, white pine left in intense sun for two or three days turns the orangey tone (a.k.a. pumpkin pine) that is so prized in antique furniture. Cherry will darken substantially in as little as just two hours of direct exposure. Other woods can become paler in response to the sun's UV rays. For instance, walnut lightens to a tan shade, and teak becomes silver.

Know when to say "when."

Woods vary in the time it takes them to lighten, but they all reach an end point. And leaving either lumber or a piece of unfinished furniture outdoors uncovered for too long causes what's called UV erosion, in which the surface can become rough. If you sand it, you'll remove the sunburned color. Your best bet: Set out a test scrap, and see how long it takes to reach the shade you want while still retaining its smooth texture.

One craft leads to another.

Attention, seamstresses! Don't toss all your empty thread spools into the trash. Instead, give them new "careers" in the decorative storage business. Paint them if you like. Then glue them to a board or the frame of a mirror, and use them to hang (and display) your collection of necklaces and bracelets, your scarves and sashes, or any of your small fabric purses and evening bags. This is also a great way to corral hats or dog leashes in an entry-way or mudroom.

Money Saver

If you do a lot of sewing, your empty-spool stash could give you the free makings of some clever costume jewelry. Just string them together to make necklaces. Unadorned, they make great play jewels for grandchildren. But creatively painted and trimmed with sequins, glitter, mini buttons, or what-have-you, they become wearable art and something you'd be proud to wear around town or even sell at the local craft fair. Of course, if you really take this idea to heart, you'll want to issue a request to all your seamstress pals to save all their denuded spools for you.

DIY DECORATIVE PAINT

This is perfect for adding colorful touches to anything that's made of wood. It's great on mirror or picture frames, furniture, or animals in a DIY mobile to hang over a grandbaby's crib.

1/2 cup of white vinegar	**Powdered poster paint**
1 tsp. of sugar	**Clear polyurethane**
Squeeze of dishwashing liquid	

Mix the vinegar, sugar, and dishwashing liquid in a jar. Then, put 2 tablespoons of the paint into a second jar, and stir in enough of the vinegar solution to make a mixture that's thick enough not to run when it's applied to a vertical surface. Brush the paint onto the wood if you like, using a texturizing tool to create whatever effect you desire. Erase any mistakes by wiping down the surface with a rag moistened with vinegar. When you're happy with the results, let the paint dry thoroughly, and then brush on several coats of polyurethane.

Pull off a squeeze play. Long-tipped plastic squeeze bottles (available on-line and in craft-supply stores) work great for storing homemade and store-bought paint. They're especially useful when you want to get an accent color into a tight space, like a design engraved into a wooden mirror frame or piece of furniture, where even your thinnest brush might not fit. At those times, you can just put the bottle's tip exactly where you want the paint to go, and give 'er a gentle squeeze for more precise painting.

SAFE & SOUND When a craft project leaves you with superglue all over your hands, it's only natural to pick at the stuff or try to peel it off. Well, don't even try it. If you do, it's likely that some of your aging skin will go with it. Instead, soak a cotton pad or cloth in nail polish remover, and hold it on your skin until the stubborn glue completely disappears on its own.

Roll it! Squeeze bottles aren't the only kind that make useful additions to your craft-supply arsenal. Roller bottles come in handy too. New versions are widely available online, especially from herb and essential oil suppliers. But this is also a good way to reuse bottles that formerly held roll-on deodorant. Just pry off the roller ball, wash the bottle thoroughly, and fill it with paint or fabric-painting ink before popping the ball back in.

Let's talk texture. Depending on the look you are after with a DIY decorative paint job (see DIY Decorative Paint, at left), there is almost no limit to the texturizing tools you can use. Good, easy-to-come-by choices include sponges, combs, or crumpled pieces of wax paper or aluminum foil. You can also try feathers or, for larger surfaces, a feather duster.

Cut some cookie-cutter capers. If you have more cookie cutters than you can use in your kitchen, don't toss them out or even give them away. Instead, add them to your (or your grandchildren's) craft-supply kit. They are perfect to use as stencils for wall decor, homemade wrapping paper, hand-painted fabric, or any other craft projects.

Repurpose another kitchen cast-off. Cookie cutters aren't the only kitchen utensils that can find new success in the craft game (see "Cut some cookie-cutter capers," above). A garlic press fits that mold too. It's just the ticket for making "hair" out of clay or play dough. Just put a lump of the material in the bowl of the press, squeeze the handles, and out comes the makings of, say, Santa's beard or a lion's mane.

Labor Saver

The chore at hand: removing the tempera paint that your grandson used to decorate your windows for Christmas or any other holiday. The quick and all-but-effortless solution: Dip a sponge in white vinegar, and wipe the designs away (after you have snapped pictures, of course!). Then follow up with damp paper towels to clear off any remaining traces of paint.

SAY IT WITH ROSES BATH VINEGAR

For centuries, herbalists and skin-care experts have touted the relaxing, skin-softening, antioxidant, and overall anti-aging effects of rose-infused bath vinegars. And that is what makes it the perfect gift for just about every occasion.

2 cups of fresh, fragrant rose petals

1 cup of distilled water

1 cup of white or white wine vinegar

Mix all the ingredients in a glass jar with a tight-fitting, non-metallic lid. Shake the jar, and store it in a cool, dark place for 30 days, shaking it every week or so. When the time's up, give the jar a final shake, strain out the petals, and pour the infused vinegar into a decorative glass bottle. Attach a card advising the recipient to use 1/2 cup or so in the bathwater of her preferred temperature, and to store the blend, tightly closed, at room temperature. It'll keep for two to six months.

Make a last-minute anti-aging gift. This DIY sugar scrub is a fabulous fix for mature skin, and you can put it together in five minutes flat. Just put 1/2 cup of coconut oil in a bowl, and nuke it on high in the microwave until it's softened (15 to 25 seconds). Pull it out, and mix in about 1 1/2 cups of sugar with 1 tablespoon of peppermint extract, and a drop or two of green food coloring. Finish it up by spooning the mixture into an airtight container, and trimming it with colorful twine or ribbon. Then step back to admire your handiwork, and you are good to go!

EARLY BIRD SPECIALS

The creative bug can bite at any age. And for that reason, all across the country, community colleges, senior centers, parks and recreation departments, and other organizations offer discounted or no-cost craft and art classes especially geared to seniors. Plus, in all 50 states, older adults (typically age 60 and up) qualify for free or low-cost tuition at public universities—which usually offer studio art classes. So go for it!

Tee up a bath-time tea bag. Or better yet, a whole festive gift box—maybe a Christmas stocking or an Easter basket full of them. Start by getting a supply of drawstring muslin bags from an herb shop or online herbal retailer. Fill each one with dried herbs of your choice, write their name(s) on a removable tag, and attach it to the sack. As for which herbs to use, that's strictly your call. If the intended recipient has particular favorites, those are obvious choices. Beyond that, two youth-enhancing superstars, either alone or in combination, are rosemary and yarrow. For the lowdown on those and other great options, see "Five-Star Skin-Care Allies" on page 120.

Talk about tea bags. When you package up your herbal pouches (see "Tee up a bath-time tea bag," above), be sure to include a card telling the future bather how to use it: Fasten the bag to the spigot so that very warm water flows right through the fabric. Once the tub is full, swish the bag around in the water, and leave it there to infuse its herbal magic for the duration. After that, the bag can be used for one or two more baths before the herbs run out of steam. Then, provided the material is 100 percent cotton, bury the whole thing in your yard to enrich the soil.

Money Saver

Instead of spending money on throwaway paper, make the wrappings part of the gift. For example, enclose a kitchen-appliance box in a tablecloth, or wrap a smaller present in a pretty scarf. Or for the young cowboy or cowgirl on your gift list, use a big bandanna.

Give guys a rummy good gift.

If you're looking for a homemade pleaser for the men in your life, this classic potion is the perfect answer for those guys who are old enough to recall the heyday of bay rum aftershave. In a bowl, mix 1/2 cup of vodka, 2 tablespoons of dark rum, 2 dried bay leaves, 1/4 teaspoon of allspice, 1 cinnamon stick, and the shredded rind from a small orange. Then pour the mixture into a clean jar with a tight-fitting lid, and set it in a cool, dark place for about two weeks. To make it gift ready, strain out the solids, and pour the liquid into an attractive bottle. That's all there is to it!

HAPPY HOLIDAYS CRANBERRY SHRUB

Shrubs (a.k.a. drinking vinegars) date back to Colonial days, but in the past decade, they've staged a big-time comeback in trendy cocktail bars from coast to coast. They make terrific gifts because they are versatile, long-lasting, easy to make, and filled with all the anti-aging goodness of vinegar and fruit.

2 cups of cranberries (fresh or frozen)	**1 cup of water**
1 cup of sugar	**1 cup of apple cider vinegar**

Combine the cranberries, sugar, and water in a saucepan and heat on medium-high, stirring until the sugar is dissolved. Simmer on low until the berries pop open and release their juices (about 10 minutes). Let the mixture cool, then strain it into a nonreactive bowl, pressing to release all the juice from the berries. Stir in the vinegar, and transfer the blend to an airtight glass container, and leave it to steep in the refrigerator for anywhere from 8 to 12 hours.

Don't forget the "operating instructions." Whenever you give a vinegar shrub to someone who may not be familiar with this everything-old-is-new-again treat, tuck in a card listing the various ways to use it. For example, add anywhere from 1 teaspoon to 2 tablespoons of it to sparkling wine or club soda. Use it as a glaze for meats or poultry, or mix 1 part shrub to 3 parts olive oil for a really delicious salad dressing. Add it to a cocktail and for good measure, include a few recipes, like A Calming Caregiver Cocktail on page 314.

SAFE & SOUND Some commercial culinary vinegars, particularly red wine and the inexpensive balsamic varieties, contain sulfites. So if you're making a shrub or an infused or fortified vinegar for someone who might be sensitive to those chemicals, read the labels carefully to make sure the brands you choose are all clear.

Get hip to this rosy gift idea. If you grow roses, or have access to wild rosebushes, you have the makings of a health- and longevity-enhancing superstar that also happens to make a delicious addition to sweet-and-sour sauces, salad dressings, and marinades. To make it, smash 1 cup of washed rose hips with a potato masher, or pulse them in a food processor. Put them in a sterilized glass jar, cover them with apple cider vinegar, and secure the lid. Set it in a cool, dark place for four to six weeks. Then strain the contents into a sterilized, decorative bottle. Tightly capped, it should last for up to six months.

> Many craft supplies are decorative in their own right, so instead of tucking them away, show them off in clear glass jars, bottles, and bowls.

Wake up and feel the coffee. The java lovers on your gift list will love these coffee soaps, and they couldn't be easier to make. Just mix 1/4 cup of coffee grounds, 1 teaspoon of pure vanilla extract, and 1 teaspoon of powdered milk with 8 ounces of liquid glycerin soap (available online and in health-food stores). Carefully spoon the mixture into four silicone muffin liners or similar-size silicone molds. Let them sit until they're solid (about four to six hours), then pop 'em out, wrap 'em up, and present 'em to your favorite coffee hound.

See what a candle can do. When you're wrapping a gift and run out of tape or you'd rather not spoil the pristine look with an outer layer of the sticky stuff, grab the closest candle. Light it, drip the melted wax between the layers of paper, and press down.

Labor Saver

Whether you make your shrub using the cooked method (see Happy Holidays Cranberry Shrub, at left) or the cold method (see "Cold-craft a shrub" on page 355), don't discard or try to compost the bits of fruit that you strain out. They are delicious when used as a relish with chicken, turkey, or even (depending on the type of fruit) grilled steak.

A POTENT PEPPERY PLEASER

This pungent vinegar is delicious whisked with extra virgin olive oil for a versatile vinaigrette dressing, or used in any recipe that calls for vinegar.

1 tsp. of whole black peppercorns	1 tsp. of whole Szechuan peppercorns
1 tsp. of whole green peppercorns	1 tsp. of whole white peppercorns
1 tsp. of whole pink peppercorns	2 cups of red wine vinegar

Crush the peppercorns slightly. Combine them with the vinegar in a pan and heat to 110°F. Remove from the heat, and let the vinegar cool slightly. Pour the contents into a sterilized glass jar, cover it tightly, and set it in a dark place at room temperature for seven days, shaking it every couple of days. Strain the vinegar into a gift-worthy, sterilized bottle, and seal it. Add a decorative label, and you're good to go.

Say "Cheers!" with a strawberry collins. This is one fine way to enjoy a shrub—and when served to friends of a certain age, it's bound to launch a flood of memories about the elegant cocktail parties of yore. To make it, combine 1 1/2 ounces each of lemon vodka and strawberry shrub in a collins glass. Fill the glass with ice, top it with club soda, and stir. Garnish with a strawberry if you like.

Whip up another berry fine cocktail. Fill a lowball glass with ice. Then add 1 ounce each of black raspberry shrub and vodka, and 1/2 ounce of Chambord® Black Raspberry Liqueur, and stir. Drop in a dash or two of bitters to taste. Top it off with club soda, and clink your glasses to good health and good times!

HELP WANTED? If you want to share the health-giving pleasure of shrubs with a lot of folks, but you lack the time or the inclination to make your own, don't fret. An Internet search will bring up specialty shops and online retailers offering a mind-boggling array of choices, ranging from individual fruit flavors like cranberry, strawberry, and cherry to unexpected blends like beet and carrot, honeydew-jalapeño, and pineapple-turmeric.

Cold-craft a shrub. To make a drinking vinegar without the cooking step, combine 2 cups of chopped fruit with 2 cups of vinegar in a large glass jar, and screw on the lid (if it's metallic, cover the jar opening with plastic wrap first). Shake the jar vigorously for 10 to 20 seconds, then let it sit for seven days at room temperature, shaking daily. Strain the infused vinegar into a fresh jar, add 1 1/2 cups of sugar (more or less, to taste), and shake again. Refrigerate for another seven days, shaking once a day. Then store the shrub in a decorative, sterilized bottle.

Tickle the tomato growers on your gift list. As they all know too well, tomatoes are prime targets for hordes of creeping, crawling, flittering, and flying pests. And basil repels every single one of them, while boosting the overall health of tomatoes to boot. Your easy gift-making mission: Pack 4 cups of fresh or 2 cups of dried basil into a 1-quart canning jar. Heat 1 quart of vinegar until it's warm, and pour it over the herbs. Cover the jar, put it in a dark place at room temperature, and let it sit for two to three weeks, or until the scent is good and strong. Strain out the solids, and pour the infused vinegar into a clean jar. Tie it up with colorful twine or ribbon and a nice card telling the recipient to spray the potion on and around his or her plants.

For your favorite salad fans. This dressing is perfect for mixed baby greens. To make it, put 2 cups of sliced fresh strawberries in a warm, sterilized glass jar. In a large pan, heat 2 cups of white wine vinegar, 2 tablespoons of sugar, and the rind of one orange (minus the pith) to just below the boiling point. Pour the mixture over the berries, cover, and set the jar in a cool, dark place for 10 days. Then strain it into a decorative, sterilized pint jar. Sealed tightly, the dressing will keep in the fridge for up to 6 months.

Time Saver

You can use any kind of fresh or frozen fruit to make a shrub, whether you opt for the cooked or cold-infused. But, especially when you're whipping up a number of batches for gift-giving purposes, you can save a lot of prep time by going with frozen berries or chopped fruit.

GIVE THE GIFT OF GOOD HEALTH

Whether you choose to infuse your vinegar, fortify it, or turn it into a shrub, these combos are sure to please all the folks on your gift list. In each case, there is virtually no limit to the herbs, fruits, and vegetables that will work perfectly well, either alone or together in clever combinations.

INFUSED VINEGARS. Follow the same basic guidelines on page 81 for making infused cosmetic vinegars, and these will turn out beautifully.

Basil-orange: White wine vinegar, basil, and the peel from one orange

Dill-peppercorn: Apple cider vinegar, black peppercorns, and dill

Garlic-chive: Rice vinegar; 2–3 peeled, chopped garlic cloves; and chives

Herbal quartet: Sherry vinegar, parsley, thyme, rosemary, and bay

Raspberry dream: Red wine vinegar and red or black raspberries

FORTIFIED VINEGARS. On page 337, you'll find a technique for whipping up any of these delicious, healthy combos.

Carrot: 1 cup of sliced carrots, 1/2 cup of apple cider vinegar, 1/2 cup of water, 3 to 4 tablespoons of honey (optional)

Cucumber, celery & onion: 1 large cucumber, 2 cups of chopped celery, 1 small chopped onion, 1 cup of champagne vinegar, 1 cup of water

Garlic: 8 garlic bulbs, peeled, and 1 cup of apple cider vinegar

Honeydew: 2 cups of chopped honeydew melon, 1/4 cup of champagne vinegar, 1/4 cup of water

Mint: 2 cups of fresh mint leaves, 1 cup of malt or red wine vinegar, 2 tablespoons of honey

SHRUBS. All of these combos work equally well whether you use the heated process on page 352 or the cold-infused version on page 355.

Blueberries + thinly sliced ginger + apple cider vinegar

Nectarine + peppercorn + brown sugar + white wine vinegar

Peach + cardamom pods + honey + apple cider vinegar

Pear + star anise + brown sugar + white wine vinegar

Plum + cardamom + brown sugar + white wine vinegar

A

AAA, 244
AARP alternatives, 6
accidents, 232
acne, in pets, 335
Acne 911 Response, 278
activated charcoal, 113
addictions, positive, 67
adult day care, 316
aftershave, 351
Age Spot Removal Remedy, 114
age spots, 114–115
aging in place
    bathrooms and, 144, 152
    kitchens and, 122, 123, 136, 137
    outdoor spaces and, 226, 230, 231, 240
    specialists in, 134
aging process, slowing, 40
air fresheners, 143, 144, 191. *See also* deodorizing treatments
air travel, 260, 261, 265
alarms, for personal safety, 270
alcohol. *See* rubbing alcohol uses
alcoholic beverages, 66, 314, 354. *See also specific types*
Alcoholics Anonymous, 66
Alka-Seltzer®, 157
allergies, 25, 26–27, 180
All-Purpose Cleaner, Tough, Gentle, 142
All-Purpose Cleaning Scrub, 128
all-purpose deodorizing cleaner, 123
All-Purpose Headache Reliever, 2
All-Purpose Poison-Plant Spray, 46
allspice, 351

almonds, almond oil uses
    Berry Nutty Health Blast, A, 94
    skin care, 104, 109, 111, 117
aloe vera uses
    cold sore treatment, 45
    hair care, 92
    poison plant rash relief, 46
    ringworm relief, 55
    skin care, 104
    sunburn relief, 48
    wound care, 53
aluminum foil, 239
Alzheimer's disease, 309
Amazing Aluminum Furniture Cleaner, 230
Amazing Anti-Aging Toner, 106
Amazing Auto Upholstery Cleaner, 242
American Sailing Association (ASA), 256
ammonia, 254, 344
animals. *See* pet care; wildlife watching
aniseed, 77
ankle sprains, 13
anti-fatigue mats, 123
antioxidants, 25, 105, 115
ants, 50, 139, 215, 266
ANTS (automatic negative thoughts), 315
anxiety, 70, 315. *See also* stress
aphids, 214, 220
Aphids-Away Spray, 214
appetite boosters, 298–299, 301
Appetite-Boosting Mocktail, 298
appetite suppressant, 73. *See also* weight control
apple cider vinegar. *See also specific health, beauty, cleaning, home, family, or pet issue*

in capsule form, 261
culinary or medicinal use, 20
homemade, 21
hot water and, 76
laundry use, 189
lawn and garden uses, 203, 221
pet care use, 336
apples, apple juice, 32, 36, 64
applesauce, 30
apple seeds, 280
appliance repair, 132, 182
    See also specific appliances
arborvitae essential oil, 233
arm pain, 15
arrowroot powder, 83
arthritis, 8, 10, 212
ASA (American Sailing Association), 256
aspirin uses, 50, 101, 179
asthma, 27
athlete's foot, 55
At-the-Ready Congestion Fighter, 22
At-the-Ready Wrinkle Releaser, 188
attic storage, 199
automatic negative thoughts (ANTS), 315
avocado leaves, 29
avocados, avocado oil uses
    callus removal, 43, 312
    skin care, 117
    vaginal dryness relief, 39
    wound care, 53

B

baby gates, 285
baby oil, 148
baby powder, 281
baby wipes, 104, 245
backaches, 12–13

Toodle-oo, Ticks Tonic, 270
toolboxes, for craft supplies, 340
tools
    for cleaning, 124, 147, 155, 174
    gardening, 203, 208
    storing in garage, 253
toothaches, 6–7
toothbrushes, as cleaning tool, 147, 247, 341
tooth loss, in grandchildren, 279
toothpaste
    as cleaning agent, 155, 328
    homemade, 7
topical remedy precautions, 15, 52, 259
Tough, Gentle All-Purpose Cleaner, 142
toys, cleaning, 282–285
trash cans, cleaning, 232
travel
    air travel, 260, 261, 265
    clothing and shoes for, 260, 262, 263
    general tips, 276
    with grandchildren, 275, 282
    group tours, 263
    health issues, 264–265
    Road Scholar trips, 272
    road trips, 261, 268
    safety precautions, 262, 263
    valuables and, 261
travel agents, 274
Travelin' Wrinkle-Release Spray, 262
trees and shrubs, 207, 217
Triple-Threat Shingles Relief Blend, 58
True Grit Multi-Surface Cleaner, 144
turmeric uses, 12, 44, 90

U

Ultra-Nourishing Shampoo, 82
Ultra-Strength Toy Cleaner, 284
Ultra-Strong, All-Over Stain Remover, 184
Ultra-Strong Mold & Mildew Remover, 252
Ultra-Strong Weed Killer, 210
upholstery cleaning, 168, 171, 242–243
Urine-Odor Eliminator, 306
ursolic acid, 64, 65

V

vaginal dryness, 39
vaginal yeast infections, 38–39
valerian root, 62
vanilla extract, 295, 307
varicose veins, 18, 19
vases, 175, 179
vegetable oil, 295, 318
vegetable shortening, 119
veterinary schools, 335
Village to Village Network®, 164
vinegar. See also specific health, beauty, cleaning, home, family, or pet issue
    buying, 20, 121
    containers for, 80
    infused (see infused vinegars)
    stains from, 189
    use precautions, 277, 297, 336
Vinegar-Lemon Cleaning Gel, 124
vinyl cleaning, 227, 234, 243
violets, 105
vitamin C, 8, 59, 105
vitamin D, 87

vitamin E uses
    hair care, 82, 84
    nail care, 98
    skin care, 109, 111, 112
    sunburn relief, 48
VOCs (volatile organic compounds), 241
vodka uses
    air freshener, 143
    cocktail, 314
    homemade aftershave, 351
    weed control, 210
    window cleaning, 228
volatile organic compounds (VOCs), 241
vomit, on floors, 327
Vomit-Stain Vanishing Spray, 294

W

wading pools, 285, 293
walker use, 312, 313
walking. See exercise, as remedy
walls, cleaning, 171
warts, 42–43
washing soda uses, 144, 182, 183, 260
wasps, 271
wastebasket project, 341
water. See also hydration benefits
    bottled versus tap, 19
    hard water, 153, 179, 204
    temperature precautions, 10, 57, 76
wax paper, 155
wax-resist painting, 341
Weathered-Wood Stain, 346
weather-related issues, 268, 303
weed control, 208–211, 224–225
weevils, 217, 220